Emerging Transformations in Tourism and Hospitality

This significant and timely book critically discusses the effects of emerging trends and shifting dynamics on the tourism and hospitality industry at local, regional, national, and international levels in a holistic manner.

This book offers a multi-disciplinary and inter-disciplinary approach and examines emerging topics such as technology and disruptive economies as well as the COVID-19 pandemic that are likely to change the future of the industry, either positively or negatively. The book thus advances the knowledge surrounding emergent controversies pertaining to tourism and hospitality including the growth of alternative business models (e.g., sharing economy business models), travel in light of climate change, and human resource ethics given the increasing adoption of artificial intelligence (AI), data, and algorithms.

Offering a platform for the critical discussion of pertinent transformations and, as such, providing theoretical and practical insights, this book will be of great value to destination planners, policymakers, industry practitioners, educators, and upper-level students of tourism and hospitality.

Anna Farmaki is Assistant Professor in Tourism Management at the Cyprus University of Technology, Cyprus. She holds a doctorate (PhD) in marketing. She has worked for several years in private institutions of tertiary education in Cyprus and was the course leader of the undergraduate hospitality and tourism management programme at the University of Central Lancashire (Cyprus). She has published extensively in reputable, peer-reviewed academic journals and has presented her work in various international conferences, seminars, and workshops. Anna is Fellow of the Higher Education Academy (UK) and a member of the Management Committee in several COST Actions. She has also been involved and/or led several nationally and internationally funded research projects. In addition, she is a member of the Editorial Board of the *International Journal of Contemporary Hospitality Management*, *Tourism Management Perspectives*, *Tourism Review*, and the *Journal of Service Theory and Practice*. Her research interests lie primarily in the areas of tourism planning and development with an emphasis on sustainable tourism and tourist behaviour.

Nikolaos Pappas is Associate Professor in Tourism, Hospitality, and Events, and Director of CERTE (Centre for Research in Tourism Excellence) at the University of Sunderland, United Kingdom. He holds a doctorate (PhD) in Tourism Planning and Development, and a post-doctorate (PDoc) in Risk and Crisis Management. He started his career in the tourism and hospitality industry in 1990, and for 10 years (2001–2010), he was also engaged in enterprising consultancy. Since 2001, he has been an academic in higher education, gaining experience from several institutions in Greece (Technological Education Institute of Crete, Hellenic Open University, EKDDA) and the UK (Derby, Northampton, Leeds Beckett, UWL). Nikolaos has participated in nationally and internationally funded research projects since 1998. He has numerous publications in international scientific refereed journals and conferences, and he is a reviewer in several academic journals including *Annals of Tourism Research*, *Journal of Sustainable Tourism*, *International Journal of Contemporary Hospitality Management*, *International Journal of Hospitality Management*, *Journal of Business Research*, and *Tourism Management*. His academic interests include crisis management communications, tourism and hospitality management, e-tourism and e-marketing, and destination planning and development.

New Directions in Tourism Analysis
Edited by Dimitri Ioannides, E-TOUR
Mid Sweden University, Sweden

Although tourism is becoming increasingly popular both as a taught subject and an area for empirical investigation, the theoretical underpinnings of many approaches have tended to be eclectic and somewhat underdeveloped. However, recent developments indicate that the field of tourism studies is beginning to develop in a more theoretically informed manner, but this has not yet been matched by current publications.

The aim of this series is to fill this gap with high quality monographs or edited collections that seek to develop tourism analysis at both theoretical and substantive levels using approaches which are broadly derived from allied social science disciplines such as Sociology, Social Anthropology, Human and Social Geography, and Cultural Studies. As tourism studies covers a wide range of activities and sub fields, certain areas such as Hospitality Management and Business, which are already well provided for, would be excluded. The series will therefore fill a gap in the current overall pattern of publication.

Suggested themes to be covered by the series, either singly or in combination, include: consumption; cultural change; development; gender; globalisation; political economy; social theory; and sustainability.

Resort Spatiality
Reimagining Sites of Mass Tourism
Zelmarie Cantillon

The Morphology of Tourism
Planning for Impact in Tourist Destinations
Philip Feifan Xie and Kai Gu

Public Memory, Race, and Heritage Tourism of Early America
Edited by Cathy Rex and Shevaun E. Watson

Emerging Transformations in Tourism and Hospitality
Edited by Anna Farmaki and Nikolaos Pappas

For more information about this series, please visit www.routledge.com/New-Directions-in-Tourism-Analysis/book-series/ASHSER1207

Emerging Transformations in Tourism and Hospitality

Edited by Anna Farmaki and
Nikolaos Pappas

LONDON AND NEW YORK

First published 2022
by Routledge
2 Park Square, Milton Park, Abingdon, Oxon OX14 4RN

and by Routledge
605 Third Avenue, New York, NY 10158

Routledge is an imprint of the Taylor & Francis Group, an informa business

© 2022 selection and editorial matter, Anna Farmaki and Nikolaos Pappas; individual chapters, the contributors

The right of Anna Farmaki and Nikolaos Pappas to be identified as the authors of the editorial material, and of the authors for their individual chapters, has been asserted in accordance with sections 77 and 78 of the Copyright, Designs and Patents Act 1988.

All rights reserved. No part of this book may be reprinted or reproduced or utilised in any form or by any electronic, mechanical, or other means, now known or hereafter invented, including photocopying and recording, or in any information storage or retrieval system, without permission in writing from the publishers.

Trademark notice: Product or corporate names may be trademarks or registered trademarks, and are used only for identification and explanation without intent to infringe.

British Library Cataloguing-in-Publication Data
A catalogue record for this book is available from the British Library

Library of Congress Cataloging-in-Publication Data
A catalog record for this book has been requested

ISBN: 978-0-367-61662-5 (hbk)
ISBN: 978-0-367-61668-7 (pbk)
ISBN: 978-1-003-10593-0 (ebk)

DOI: 10.4324/9781003105930

Typeset in Times New Roman
by Apex CoVantage, LLC

Contents

List of figures vii
List of tables viii
List of contributors ix

Introduction 1
ANNA FARMAKI AND NIKOLAOS PAPPAS

1 **Emerging transformations in the air transport sector in the post-COVID-19 era** 5
IOULIA POULAKI AND ANDREAS PAPATHEODOROU

2 **Climate change and tourism: emerging transformations** 18
C. MICHAEL HALL

3 **The sharing economy and its implications for inclusive tourism** 35
CHRISTOPH LUTZ AND JULIJANA ANGELOVSKA

4 **Digital transformation in tourism** 53
BILSEN BILGILI AND ERDOGAN KOC

5 **Attitudes towards robots as transformational agents in tourism and hospitality: robophobes versus robophiles** 66
CRAIG WEBSTER AND STANISLAV IVANOV

6 **Conceptualising system resilience in smart tourism destinations** 83
KYRIAKI GLYPTOU AND MIJU CHOI

7 **Big data analysis of social media sharing and destination image** 98
ZHAOYU CHEN (VICKY), XIAOLIN ZHOU (EVA), AND WENG SI (CLARA) LEI

Contents

8 **Digital transformation in tourism: archaeotourism and its digital potential** 115
HASAN ALI ERDOGAN

9 **The rise of meme tourism: tourism transformations towards 'fifteen minutes of fame'** 127
BENJAMIN OWEN AND ANITA ZATORI

10 **Accessible tourism as a transformational force for tourism and hospitality** 142
CHRISTINA KARADIMITRIOU, ANNA KYRIAKAKI, AND ELENI MICHOPOULOU

11 **Employee well-being in guest-oriented industries: evidence from food and beverage sector** 154
JAVANEH MEHRAN, OSCAR ESCALLADA AND HOSSEIN OLYA

12 **Climbing the virtual mountain: a netnography of the sharing and collecting behaviours of online Munro-bagging** 170
DAVID BROWN AND SHARON WILSON

13 **Sustainable Development Goals and tourism organisations: the enabling role of sustainable business models** 187
PIERFELICE ROSATO, SIMONE PIZZI, AND ANDREA CAPUTO

14 **Cannabis tourism: an emerging transformative tourism form** 201
YULIN LIU AND ADAM STRONCZAK

15 **The Tourism Lab: a place for change, participation, and future destination development** 216
DANIEL ZACHER, HANNES THEES, AND VALENTIN HERBOLD

Conclusion 232
Index 235

Figures

1.1	Emerging transformations in the air transport sector towards the post-COVID-19 era	13
2.1	Transformation and change within the tourism system panarchy	29
7.1	Map of the Greater Bay Area (GBA) of China	102
7.2	Example of Hong Kong's top 30 discussion topics	104
11.1	Santander map	159
11.2	Proposed conceptual models: symmetric model (i) and asymmetric model (ii)	161
15.1	Framing the local space in line with alternative development approaches	219

Tables

1.1	Actions taken by air carriers and respective governments to address the financial difficulties posed by COVID-19	8
2.1	International tourism arrivals and forecasts 1950–2030	21
2.2	Long-term forecast growth rates in tourism and associated transport of various organisations	23
3.1	Descriptive statistics and PCA results	44
3.2	Logistic regression	45
5.1	Sample's characteristics	70
5.2	General attitudes towards robots	71
5.3	Perceived appropriateness of service robots	73
5.4	Preferred human–robot ratio in the service process	77
5.5	Willingness to pay for fully robot-delivered services	78
6.1	Alignment of resilience principles to smart tourism destination applications	90
7.1	Example of selected data sets on RED	102
7.2	Sorted categories on discussion topics based on TextRank results	105
10.1	Main barriers/restrictions for the disabled people, recommendations, and prospects	148
11.1	Means, standard deviations, and correlations	162
11.2	Results of regression	162
11.3	Sufficient causal recipes to predict well-being	164
11.4	Sufficient causal recipes to predict engagement	164
11.5	Sufficient causal recipes to predict turnover intention	164
12.1	Criteria for achieving interpretive sufficiency and for evaluating ethnographic research	178
13.1	Triple-layered business model canvas	191
13.2	Proposed triple-layered business model canvas in cycling tourism	195
15.1	Overview of the Tourism Lab from an organisers' perspective	223

Contributors

Julijana Angelovska is a professor at the Faculty of Economics, University of Tourism and Management, Skopje, North Macedonia. The main scientific interest spheres are financial analyses, data analysis, and application of econometric models in different fields of economy including sharing economy and e-commerce. She has published in journals indexed in WoS.

Bilsen Bilgili is Associate Professor at the Faculty of Tourism, Kocaeli University, Turkey. She serves on the editorial boards of a number of journals. Her research primarily focuses on marketing and tourism (brand equity, brand management, consumer behaviour, tourism marketing, and marketing technology).

David Brown is Leader of the PhD Programme at Newcastle Business School, Northumbria University. His research interests include the interplay of landscape, exercise, mobility and self within serious leisure, and adventure tourism – especially within hillwalking and long-distance walking. He has also published research on qualitative methodology, pedagogy, and aspects of marketing and sustainability.

Andrea Caputo is Associate Professor in Management at the University of Trento (IT) and at the University of Lincoln (UK). His main research interests include entrepreneurial decision-making, negotiation, digitalisation and sustainability, internationalisation, and strategic management of SMEs. He is Editor of the book series 'Entrepreneurial Behaviour' (Emerald), and Associate Editor of the *Journal of Management & Organization*. His research was published in over 100 contributions, including articles in highly ranked journals.

Zhaoyu Chen (Vicky) is Lecturer at the Macao Institute for Tourism Studies, Macao, China. She received her PhD in School of Hotel and Tourism Management from The Hong Kong Polytechnic University, Hong Kong, China. Her research interests are cultural tourism, heritage conservation, and destination marketing.

Miju Choi serves as Senior Lecturer in Hospitality and Tourism at Leeds Beckett University. Dr. Choi's research interests include the adoption of digital technologies by hospitality and tourism businesses.

Hasan Ali Erdogan has a PhD from classical archaeology and tourism. His studies focus on tourism planning and tourism management in heritage sites. As a three-degree holder, his research focuses on multi-/inter-disciplinary approaches to archaeological tourism.

Oscar Escallada is International Hotel Manager/MBA with 15 years' experience in the 5* luxury and 4* Palace/Hotel/Cruise hospitality industry in various countries such as Spain, Mexico, Cuba, United Kingdom, Portugal, and Saudi Arabia and renowned companies like Iberostar hotels and resorts, Hilton Worldwide, Douro Azul, and River Advice.

Kyriaki Glyptou is Senior Lecturer in Tourism Management at Leeds Beckett University. Her current research explores strategic destinations' development and branding in light of sustainability, resilience, and uncertainty.

C. Michael Hall is Professor, Department of Management, Marketing and Entrepreneurship, University of Canterbury, New Zealand; Visiting Professor and Docent, Geography, University of Oulu, Finland; Guest Professor, Department of Service Management and Service Studies, Lund University, Helsingborg, Sweden; and Visiting Professor, Department of Organisation and Entrepreneurship, Linnaeus University, Kalmar, Sweden.

Valentin Herbold worked at the Chair of Tourism at the Catholic University of Eichstätt-Ingolstadt, conducting research on community development and sports tourism. As a project manager in the economic development department of the city of Ingolstadt, he is currently involved in citizen participation processes and the revitalisation of the city centre.

Stanislav Ivanov is Professor and Vice-Rector (Research) at Varna University of Management, Bulgaria (www.vum.bg), and Director of Zangador Research Institute (www.zangador.institute/en/). He is Founder and Editor-in-Chief of the *European Journal of Tourism Research* (http://ejtr.vumk.eu) and *ROBONOMICS: The Journal of the Automated Economy* (https://journal.robonomics.science).

Christina Karadimitriou is a PhD researcher at the University of Patras, Greece, and Public Relations Manager in ViRA (Virtual Reality Applications) in Athens. Her research interests include crisis management communications in tourism and hospitality, destination marketing, e-tourism and travel, and tourism for disabled people.

Erdoğan Koc is Professor of Consumer Behaviour and Marketing at the Faculty of Economics, Administrative and Social Sciences, Bahcesehir University, Turkey. He serves on the editorial boards of a number of journals. His research primarily focuses on the human element (both as consumer and as employee) in tourism.

Anna Kyriakaki is Academic Teaching Staff at the University of the Aegean. She holds a PhD in Sustainable Tourism Development and Locality, an MSc in Tourism, and a BSc in Business Administration from the University of the Aegean, Greece. Her research interests include sustainable tourism development, tourism and locality, and special and alternative forms of tourism.

Weng Si (Clara) Lei is Assistant Professor at the Macao Institute for Tourism Studies, China. She received her PhD in International Business from the University of Leeds in the United Kingdom. She also worked in the industries for some years and took part mostly in marketing and event management.

Yulin Liu teaches research methods and applied statistics. His research interests include travel behaviour, tourism marketing, methodological innovation, and statistics education.

Christoph Lutz is an associate professor at BI Norwegian Business School (Oslo, Norway). His research interests include online participation, privacy, the sharing economy, and social robots. Christoph has published extensively in top journals such as New Media & Society, Journal of Management Information Systems, and Information, Communication & Society.

Javaneh Mehran is Senior Researcher in Industrial Services and B2B Innovative Manufacturing Businesses in Karlstad University, Sweden. She is also Associate Professor of Service Management at the University of International Business in Almaty, Kazakhstan.

Eleni (Elina) Michopoulou is Associate Professor in Business Management at the University of Derby, UK. Her research interests include technology acceptance and online behaviours, and accessible and wellness tourism marketing and management. She has published over 60 academic journal articles, book chapters, and conference papers in these areas.

Hossein Olya is Associate Professor of Consumer Behaviour and Director of Research Development for Marketing and Cultural and Creative Industries at the Sheffield University Management School, Sheffield. He is Associate Editor of *International Journal of Consumer Studies*.

Benjamin Owen holds a Bachelor of Science from Radford University's Recreation, Parks, and Tourism program. He worked as a research assistant during his studies. He is currently working as a marketing assistant for the Halifax County Department of Tourism, USA. Research interests include pop-culture tourism and tourism experience.

Andreas Papatheodorou is a prolific academic researcher and advisor in air transport and tourism economics. He is currently Professor in Industrial and Spatial Economics with an emphasis on tourism at the University of the Aegean, Greece, and Adjunct Professor at the School of Aviation, University of New South Wales, Australia.

Simone Pizzi is Research fellow in Accounting at the University of Salento, Italy. He received his PhD from the University of Lecce, Italy. His main research interests include non-financial reporting, sustainable and digital business models. His research was published in highly ranked journals, for example, *Journal of Business Research*, *Journal of Cleaner Production*, and *Sustainability Accounting, Management and Policy Journal*.

Ioulia Poulaki is Assistant Professor in the Department of Tourism Management at the University of Patras and a member of the Laboratory of Information Systems and Forecasts in Tourism (TourISFlab). Her research interests focus on the fields of air transport demand forecasting and revenue management, distribution channels of tourism services, digital tourism, and tourism development.

Pierfelice Rosato is Senior Lecturer in Management at the University of Bari Aldo Moro, Italy. He received his PhD from the University of Bari Aldo Moro, Italy. His main research interests include destination management, tourism and hospitality, and corporate social responsibility. His research was published in highly ranked journals, for example, *Corporate Social Responsibility and Environmental Management*, *Ecological Indicators*, and *British Food Journal*.

Adam Stronczak has research interest in controversial tourism forms, which stems from his lifetime exposure to diverse cultures in Europe, America, and Australia. Adam's professional experience ranges from business consulting, hospitality, and tourism management to coaching extreme sports.

Hannes Thees is PhD Student and Research Associate at the Catholic University of Eichstätt-Ingolstadt, Chair of Tourism and Center for Entrepreneurship. His main fields of research are sharing economy, destination governance, technological development in tourism, and regional cooperation.

Craig Webster is Associate Professor in the Department of Applied Business Studies at Ball State University. His research interests include the political economy of tourism, events, and automation in tourism and hospitality. He is currently teaching courses in Hospitality Management in Ball State University's Miller College of Business.

Sharon Wilson is interested in tourism mobilities, social sciences, and the creative industries. Adopting inter-disciplinary and experimental research approaches to the study of social phenomena, she adopts experimental methodologies that seek to understand human mobility in an imaginative and embodied ways. She is also the founder of the MFRN (Mobilities Futures Research Network).

Daniel Zacher is a research fellow at Catholic University of Eichstätt-Ingolstadt (CU) and PhD candidate at the Chair of Tourism. He also works at the transfer office and is part of the structural development of regional cooperation. His research focuses on tourism in regional development and resilience in tourism destinations.

Anita Zatori is Assistant Professor at the Department of Recreation, Park, and Tourism at Radford University, USA. Her publications and research interest are focused on tourism experience phenomenology and design, consumer behaviour trends, cultural tourism, and well-being.

Xiaolin Zhou (Eva) is a PhD candidate in the Department of Land Surveying and Geo-informatics at The Hong Kong Polytechnic University, Hong Kong, China. Her research interests include GIScience, location-based social networks, and text mining.

Introduction

Anna Farmaki and Nikolaos Pappas

Arguably, tourism is one of the most vulnerable industries as it is highly susceptible to external and internal factors that impact structures, processes, and practices within the industry at the economic, social, and environment levels (Pappas, 2021). Even so, the tourism industry has been growing steadily at approximately 4% per annum indicating that the demand for travel and tourism is likely to continue increasing despite emerging adversities (e.g., pandemics; economic crises; and natural disasters) and transformations (WTO, 2020). In this context, tourism and hospitality businesses are called to adapt their strategies and practices to the continuous changes brought about by externalities and/or factors inherent to the industry and which, to a great extent, influence tourist demand and business operations (Farmaki et al., 2020; Ngin, Chhom, & Neef, 2020; Wang, Hung, & Huang, 2019). Indeed, as the industry continues to grow, successful adaptability is critical for business and destination competitiveness.

A foray into extant literature reveals that the tourism environment has been changing rapidly over the years as a result of a number of factors that have transformed the nature of the tourist activity and the structure of the tourist system. For example, the widespread use of the Internet and social media has significantly impacted destination marketing, travel behaviour, and business operations (Leung, Sun, & Bai, 2017; Li et al., 2021). Likewise, tourism and hospitality businesses are faced with increasing pressures to mitigate the negative impacts emanating from their operations on the local economy, society, and environment (Zopiatis, Savva, & Lambertides, 2020). For instance, concerns over the contribution of tourism to climate change have intensified lately with businesses called to respond accordingly (Ngin, Chhom, & Neef, 2020). In addition, changes to travel patterns have become noticeable over the years as new tourist markets are emerging (e.g., India and China), while tourists are showing increasing preference to new tourism forms (i.e., wellness tourism) that relate to experiential and ethical consumption (Aguilo, Rosello, & Vila, 2017). The industry has also recently been challenged by the changing dynamics brought about by the popularity of sharing economy models, which seem to exacerbate overtourism as they yield additional environmental pressures and problems on housing prices, labour exploitation, and residents' well-being among others (Stergiou & Farmaki, 2020; Yi, Yuan, & Yoo, 2020).

DOI: 10.4324/9781003105930-1

Whilst these transformations present several challenges to the tourism and hospitality industry, they also offer numerous opportunities. For example, the emergence of peer-to-peer platforms has offered individuals the opportunity to gain additional income and/or embark on micro-entrepreneurship by using their available assets to provide services to peers through platforms such as Airbnb and Uber (Delacroix, Parguel, & Benoit-Moreau, 2019). In this regard, tourists have also been presented with an alternative, cost-effective, and convenient accommodation or transport experience. Similarly, technological advances have increased the use of robots within the industry that, in turn, leads to simplified processes, maximum security, and cost-efficient operations (Hou, Zhang, & Li, 2021). Equally, tourism and hospitality practitioners and destination planners are confronted with immense opportunities as a result of the emergence of big data technology and analysis (Shamim et al., 2021). In this context, the adoption of innovative methodologies and analytical tools has contributed significantly to the advancement of knowledge and the improvement of decision-making processes and developmental approaches.

It is crucial for destinations and tourism and hospitality enterprises to fully encapsulate the importance of these transformations and, thus, gain a better understanding of the rapidly shifting business environment they are operating in. In so doing, destination planners, policymakers, and industry practitioners will be more sufficiently prepared for change and embrace pertinent opportunities whilst dealing with potential threats (Pappas, 2018; Pappas & Brown, 2020). On a similar note, tourism and hospitality researchers will need to acknowledge the collective effects of these transformations on the industry. Specifically, a reading of the emerging transformations in tourism and hospitality can assist scholars to better comprehend the ever-changing dynamics influencing the industry, thus allowing for a more holistic examination of tourism-related phenomena and for a greater appreciation of the shifting nature of the tourism industry as a whole. Such knowledge is also important for educational purposes as tourism and hospitality students need to be better prepared for their operational and managerial role in the industry by adopting critical thinking with regard to its changing dynamics. Accordingly, tourism and hospitality educators need to adapt their curriculum to reflect the influence of such transformation on the industry (Farmaki, 2018).

Notwithstanding, this is no single source that critically discusses the effects of emerging transformations on the tourism and hospitality industry in a holistic manner. The aim of this edited book is, therefore, to offer a platform allowing the critical discussion of pertinent transformations and, as such, provide theoretical and practical insights that may be of value to destination planners, policymakers, industry practitioners, educators, and students. The book, specifically, attempts to offer a multi-disciplinary and inter-disciplinary approach to the study of tourism and hospitality and examine emerging topics that are likely to change the future of the industry, either positively or negatively. Overall, this edited book contributes to the advancement of knowledge surrounding emergent controversies pertaining to tourism including the growth of alternative business models, travel in light of climate change, and human resource ethics given the increasing adoption of artificial intelligence (AI), data, and algorithms.

This edited book is a sum of 15 chapters written by 33 contributors across the world. These chapters provide an examination and evaluation of the transformations in the tourism and hospitality industry. More specifically, the first chapter is written by Ioulia Poulaki and Andreas Papatheodorou and focuses on the air transport transformation post-COVID-19 era. C. Michael Hall contributes the second chapter, conceptually focusing on the climate change and tourism nexus. Christoph Lutz and Julijana Angelovska discuss the implications brought about by the sharing economy transformations in terms of inclusive tourism in the third chapter. In the fourth chapter, Bilsen Bilgili and Erdoğan Koç evaluate the digital tourism transformation, whilst in the fifth chapter, Stanislav Ivanov and Craig Webster provide an interesting comparison between robophobes and robophiles in tourism. The sixth chapter highlights system resilience in smart destinations, a conceptual study contributed by Kyriaki Glyptou and Miju Choi. The seventh chapter is written by Zhaoyu Chen, Xiaolin Zhou, and Weng Si Lei and evaluates the impact of social media sharing upon destination image by using big data analysis. Hasan Ali Erdoğan discusses archaeotourism and its digital transformation potential in the eighth chapter. The ninth chapter is dedicated to the emerging phenomenon of meme tourism, a study carried out by Benjamin Owen and Anita Zatori. The tenth chapter is written by Christina Karadimitriou, Anna Kyriakaki, and Eleni Michopoulou and focuses on the transformative role of accessible tourism. The 11th chapter is dedicated to the hospitality employees' well-being and written by Hossein Olya, Javaneh Mehran, and Oscar Escallada, while David Brown and Sharon Wilson discuss a netnography on online munro-bagging in the 12th chapter. The 13th chapter is written by Pierfelice Rosato, Simone Pizzi, and Andrea Caputo and focuses on the contribution of sports business models (with special reference to cycle tourism) to the tourism sector. The 14th chapter concerns a study of Adam Stronczak and Yulin Liu and offers an overview of business and legal regulations concerning cannabis tourism. The final (15th) chapter of this edited book is written by Daniel Zacher, Hannes Thees, and Valentin Herbold and presents stakeholder participation aspects by linking city and destination development.

References

Aguilo, E., Rosello, J., & Vila, M. (2017). Length of stay and daily tourist expenditure: A joint analysis. *Tourism Management Perspectives*, *21*, 10–17.

Delacroix, E., Parguel, B., & Benoit-Moreau, F. (2019). Digital subsistence entrepreneurs on Facebook. *Technological Forecasting & Social Change*, *146*, 887–899.

Farmaki, A. (2018). Tourism and hospitality internships: A prologue to career intentions? *Journal of Hospitality, Leisure, Sport & Tourism Education*, *23*, 50–58.

Farmaki, A., Miguel, C., Drotarova, M. H., Aleksić, A., Časni, A. Č., & Efthymiadou, F. (2020). Impacts of Covid-19 on peer-to-peer accommodation platforms: Host perceptions and responses. *International Journal of Hospitality Management*, *91*, 102663.

Hou, Y., Zhang, K., & Li, G. (2021). Service robots or human staff: How social crowding shapes tourist preferences. *Tourism Management*, Article in press.

Leung, X. Y., Sun, J., & Bai, B. (2017). Bibliometrics of social media research: A co-citation and co-word analysis. *International Journal of Hospitality Management, 66*, 35–45.

Li, X., Law, R., Xie, G., & Wang, S. (2021). Review of tourism forecasting research with internet data. *Tourism Management, 83*, Article in press.

Ngin, C., Chhom, C., & Neef, A. (2020). Climate change impacts and disaster resilience among micro businesses in the tourism and hospitality sector: The case of Kratie, Cambodia. *Environmental Research*, Article in press.

Pappas, N. (2018). Hotel decision-making during multiple crises: A chaordic perspective. *Tourism Management, 68*, 450–464.

Pappas, N. (2021). COVID19: Holiday intentions during a pandemic. *Tourism Management*, Article in press.

Pappas, N., & Brown, A. E. (2020). Entrepreneurial decisions in tourism and hospitality during crisis. *Management Decision*, Article in press.

Shamim, S., Yang, Y., Zia, N. U., & Shah, M. H. (2021). Big data management capabilities in the hospitality sector: Service innovation and customer generated online quality ratings. *Computers in Human Behavior, 121*, Article in press.

Stergiou, D. P., & Farmaki, A. (2020). Resident perceptions of the impacts of P2P accommodation: Implications for neighbourhoods. *International Journal of Hospitality Management, 91*, 102411.

Wang, S., Hung, K., & Huang, W. J. (2019). Motivations for entrepreneurship in the tourism and hospitality sector: A social cognitive theory perspective. *International Journal of Hospitality Management, 78*, 78–88.

WTO (2020). *International tourism growth continues to outpace the global economy*. World Tourism Organisation. Retrieved April 12, 2021, from www.unwto.org/international-tourism-growth-continues-to-outpace-the-economy

Yi, J., Yuan, G., & Yoo, C. (2020). The effect of the perceived risk on the adoption of the sharing economy in the tourism industry: The case of Airbnb. *Information Processing and Management, 57*, Article in press.

Zopiatis, A., Savva, C. S., & Lambertides, N. (2020). The non-inclusive nature of "all inclusive" economics: Paradoxes and possibilities of the resort complex. *Tourism Management, 78*, Article in press.

1 Emerging transformations in the air transport sector in the post-COVID-19 era

Ioulia Poulaki and Andreas Papatheodorou

Introduction

The socio-economic impact of the COVID-19 pandemic crisis has proven very important if not cataclysmic at a world level. Given that tourism is a socio-economic phenomenon with explicit and wide geographical mobility connotations, its entire business ecosystem and related operations are profoundly affected, when it comes to health and hygiene, safety, and trust issues. Among others, aviation, a par excellence tourism sector, came to a standstill after the first outbreak of COVID-19, with demand falling sharply and the companies involved plunging into the battle for survival, using all possible means at their disposal (Papatheodorou, 2021). Some airlines have filed for bankruptcy, while the majority have turned to governments for funding to fill the gap between their high operating costs and remarkably low revenue as shown by the reports of the International Civil Aviation Organization (ICAO, 2020a) and the International Air Transport Association (IATA, 2020b). On the supply side, airlines experienced a significant reduction in terms of routes and capacity; fleet reshufflings had to take place to meet the new market environment.

Evidently, the aviation sector had to streamline operations and strictly comply with the protection measures against the spread of the pandemic, announced by the governments, while the international protocols were directly implemented by carriers and airports. Despite research showing that air transport is extremely safe in terms of hygiene and low transmission of the virus (IATA, 2020d), repeated travel instructions and the closure of borders, for both countries of origin and destination, have severely hit travel and transport in general. Furthermore, to boost demand, air carriers responded with offers and ticket discounts. Due to inelastic demand and the need for cash flow, yield drop was not enough to reverse the demand trend. Booking restrictions removal, such as rebooking fees, and marketing actions of health and safety appeared to be more effective than pricing strategies alone. At the end of 2020, the future of travel was still uncertain with companies planning their operations in the short term, keeping a close eye on daily facts and figures, in an unprecedented crisis that is rapidly evolving in the present, with no historical data for future predictions with a relative certainty. This chapter aims to assess the performance of the air transport industry in the context

DOI: 10.4324/9781003105930-2

of the pandemic and a 'travel unfriendly' global environment during the first three quarters (i.e., Q1, Q2, and Q3) of 2020. In parallel, market estimations and predictions are of high interest with emerging transformations of the air transport sector to become inevitable in the post-COVID-19 era.

The aim of this paper is to illustrate the emerging transformations in the air transport sector towards recovery from the pandemic crisis of COVID-19. Therefore, data collection from official air transport bodies and organisations, as well as market positions on the transformation of the industry during its anticipation for the next day should be collected and evaluated to draw the path towards the process of air transport's recovery. The theoretical contribution of the paper concerns the reasons why commercial (marketing and revenue management) and operational digital transformation of travel industry is more imperative than ever before, while practical implications refer to the ways that companies involved should digitalise their services to achieve an integrated system of travelling in the post-COVID-19 world. Undoubtedly, contactless travel and health certifications may consist of the driving force behind building passengers' trust and reengagement.

Implications of COVID-19 for aviation and tourism

As argued by the Air Transport Action Group (ATAG, 2020a), air transport is an essential component of the economy, accounting for 4.1% of gross domestic product (GDP), creating 87.7 million jobs with $3.5 trillion in global economic impact – including direct, indirect, induced, and catalytic effects on tourism. According to IATA (2019), more than 4.4 billion passengers used an airplane in 2018. 2020 started with very favourable forecasts regarding tourism and air transport demand. The companies involved were planning their commercial strategies in anticipation of a highly successful year in terms of occupancies and revenues. At the end of January 2020, the World Health Organization (WHO) declared the outbreak of a global health emergency; from then onwards and in a matter of weeks, Europe was shaken by the pandemic, with negative case records in Italy and Spain, among others, forcing governments to close borders and ban travel, trade, and education. By the end of March, most of EU countries had applied relevant measures and lockdowns against the virus spread. Immediately, the demand for travel collapsed and airlines stranded most of their fleet, while their operations were limited to necessary connections and transport of medical supplies. According to Maneenop and Kotcharin (2020) when it comes to the aviation industry, the number of flights and passengers has returned to numbers that existed decades ago. With respect to the demand elasticity, the level of fares is usually regarded as the most obvious determinant of air travel (Li, 2008); nonetheless, COVID-19 resulted in an inelastic demand, since reduced fares and offers did not trigger any relevant increase. In particular, the COVID-19 health crisis has led to new protective measures of hygiene and a corresponding change in the behaviour and expectations of tourists. Government interventions through restrictions and border closures have been a major factor in reducing the demand for air travel. According to the United Nations World Tourism Organization (UNWTO, 2020a, 2020b) in May 2020, 100% of destinations had travel restrictions, while in September 2020, the respective number was 50% but with significantly enhanced safety measures.

An International Civil Aviation Organization's (2020b) report on international passenger traffic indicated a decrease of 88.3% year-on-year in August 2020 (which is typically a month of high season in the Northern Hemisphere due to summer holidays), while an increase of +3.6% was recorded compared to the previous month. The same report indicates that international demand for long-haul air travel remained globally limited to less than 10% compared to 2019 levels, while in Europe, some increases were noted in intra-regional travel which recovered to around 20% of the previous year's demand. A similar trend of international passenger traffic is apparent in international tourist arrivals which have remained stagnant. In addition to health and safety issues, decreased demand has also been caused by the lack or decline in income, thus triggering a new wave of staycation as first experienced during the great economic recession in 2008–2009 (Papatheodorou, Rossello, & Xiao, 2010). Due to the lock down, many hours of work have been lost, resulting in high unemployment and loss of income according to the International Labour Organization (ILO, 2020). Many governments have provided benefits, but from a policymaking viewpoint, priorities relate to covering basic needs first before spending money on leisure and recreation. Passenger demand in September 2020 remained extremely low. Total demand (measured in revenue passenger kilometres) decreased by 72.8% compared to September 2019, capacity by 63%, while occupancy rate fell 21.8 percentage points to 60.1% (IATA, 2020c). The International Civil Aviation Organization (2020a) expects an overall reduction between 60% and 62% in air passenger traffic and a GDP contraction between 4.4% and 5.2% for the entire year 2020 compared to 2019. The Air Transport Action Group (2020b) reports a catastrophic impact in aviation employment prospects, with jobs potentially falling to 41.7 million (-52.5%).

As a result of the misfortunes mentioned earlier, several air transport companies have reached the brink of bankruptcy or have already gone bankrupt. According to the WTTC (2020a), as of 22 June 2020, 117 airlines had filed for bankruptcy since the beginning of the year, while forecasts indicate losses exceeding $84.3 billion for the full year 2020. Travel restrictions imposed by countries, low self-confidence of travellers and the increased spread of the pandemic (first and second wave), indicate the low prospects of the aviation industry for rapid recovery. According to the UNWTO (2020c), international travel exhibited a 70% reduction, resulting in 700 million fewer international tourist arrivals and a loss of $ 730 billion in tourism revenue for the first eight months of 2020, compared to 2019. COVID-19 tests the business resilience of airlines as uncertainty, low demand, and lack of liquidity prevail (Naftemporiki, 2020) with the challenges for airlines to be many. Admittedly, according to IATA (2020e), the main priority, in this time of very inadequate demand, is cost reduction. Unfortunately, cost reduction strategies will not be easy to introduce; to survive, airlines will have to adjust costs to revenue; this seems to be a challenge and a difficult task as this crisis is expected to last (even to a lesser extent) in 2021 and possibly also in 2022.

The cost structure of aviation is a major issue that air carriers need to address for the industry to recover faster.

More specifically, cost reduction strategies relate predominantly to fleet and infrastructure rationalisation and reduction of labour and fuel costs. The IATA (2020b) indicates oil as the highest cost, with its prices, in late 2020, to remain (fortunately for airlines) at low levels due to oversupply by oil companies. Reducing the airline fleet will also lead to a reduction in related costs. State aid is also expected to somewhat alleviate the pain of airlines. Labour costs are also likely to decrease as fewer people are needed and/or paid less. Airport charges due to reduced flights will also be reduced. Of course, all these are temporary measures until supply returns to 2019 levels and to do so demand would have to properly recover. Direct costs account for 45–60% of the total cost of Full-Service Network Carriers (i.e., traditional airlines such as Lufthansa in Europe and American Airlines in the USA) and 60–80% of Low Fare Airlines (e.g., Ryanair and easyJet in Europe and Southwest and JetBlue in the USA). These costs concern the flight operation of companies such as pilots' salaries and off-site expenses, aircraft fuel, airport charges, and aircraft rental (short term mainly) when needed (Profyllidis, 2010). Indirect operating costs such as ground staff fees, ground handling, cabin staff, and in-flight catering are proportionately higher for air carriers when operating routes. By reducing their schedules and/or staff, therefore, airlines are trying to minimise direct and some indirect costs, as demand for travel has dropped dramatically. Table 1.1 summarises indicative actions taken by air carriers and respective governments to address the financial difficulties posed by the COVID-19 pandemic.

The demand for winter 2020–2021 has also been significantly affected by the pandemic. Many cancellations are expected to take place until March 2021 (European Commission, 2020). Furthermore, it is essential to underline the target

Table 1.1 Actions taken by air carriers and respective governments to address the financial difficulties posed by COVID-19

Airline	Actions taken
Aegean Airlines (Greece)	Government support package of 120 million euros together with a 60 million euros injection of capital from existing shareholders
Air France – KLM (France and the Netherlands)	Government support package 10.4 billion euros (7 billion from France and 3.4 billion euros from the Netherlands)
British Airways (UK)	Withdrawal of Boeing 747 from the flight schedule
Cathay Pacific (Hong Kong SAR)	Compulsory staff furlough
Delta Airlines (USA)	Reduction of flight schedules by 75% compared to 2019
Emirates (UAE)	Personnel dismissal
Lufthansa (Germany)	Government approves 9 billion euros support package
Qantas (Australia)	Withdrawal of Boeing 747 from the flight schedule
USA Air Carriers	Government support conditional on no staff layoffs
Virgin Atlantic (UK)	Withdrawal of Boeing 747 from the flight schedule

Source: Delevengos (2020), Naftemporiki (2020) – processed by the authors

groups of passengers. Business travel is expected to remain at least 25% below pre-pandemic levels by 2021, as companies make travel cuts using teleconferencing, when it comes to meetings, conferences, and workshops. At this point, it is worth mentioning that many businesspeople travel by air. In addition, due to the rapid spread of COVID-19, leisure travel will remain at low levels until the rate of the virus transmission is reduced and the confidence of travellers is somehow restored (Wyman, 2020).

Air transport industry towards emerging transformations: the day after

Having the previous point in mind, air transport companies should reconsider their business models and operational standards to effectively deal with the economic impact of the pandemic crisis; meet the emerging needs of passengers; and gain back their trust. This may prove complicated, as unlike economic crises, the sole implementation of pricing strategies may now prove inadequate. Consequently, in addition to the urgent financial needs declared by airlines, the day after COVID-19 will require emerging transformations of commercial and operational strategies in air transport industry. On these grounds, the authors illustrate several issues that should be taken into consideration by the airlines, when building the new travel system after the pandemic crisis. Theoretical and practical implications related to emerging transformations in the post-COVID-19 air transport business environment are highlighted.

Operational tactics

Among others, it will prove essential to introduce hygiene, health, and safety protection measures in accordance with new international norms and to undertake operational changes such as network reshuffling and fleet management. The pandemic gave birth to a new form of collaboration, that is, cleaning-related partnerships such as those of Delta with Lysol and United with Clorox (Bogomolov, 2020). Nonetheless, these must now be readjusted to meet the new conditions prevailing in the changing environment. Among others, airlines need to improve their services by fully complying with the health protocols; target the highest possible load factors for their airplanes; Competition between Full-Service Network Carriers and Low Fare Airlines may become more intense especially on short-haul routes at both price and service quality levels, thus pushing forwards the pre COVID-19 trend regarding the emergence of a hybrid airline business model (Efthymiou & Papatheodorou, 2017; Power, 2020). Thus, three main issues emerge with respect to operational tactics:

Health certification

Both airlines and airports should insist on the adaptation of a solid, streamlined, and universally accepted procedure that includes health certification from the passenger's side and health and safety certifications from the side of the businesses involved in the travel process. Individual responsibility and international integration in measures and protocols, respectively, are required, certified by authorised bodies. In fact, integration is the key factor for the mobility restart since all countries will have to apply common measures without ad hoc border closures and travel bans.

Contactless travel

Contactless was one of the pandemic crisis' keywords. Contactless travel as a term started during the summer season of 2020, when tourism businesses (both transport and accommodation sectors) tried to eliminate the contact between customers as well as between customers and staff. Social distancing signs, scanners, and Plexiglas protectors were installed in airports and hotels, while the catering industry has made efforts to reduce this contact too. Food and beverage service has been totally transformed in all three sectors mentioned previously. Besides, effective service recovery requires the resolution of several customer issues and the ability of air transport staff to take swift decisions in this direction (Efthymiou et al., 2019).

Operational reshuffling

Travel bans, border closures, and thus limited demand have led air carriers to maintain their aircraft grounded for long periods of time. Consequently, network planning departments proceeded to fleet reshufflings, re-routings, and re-schedules to make airlines more efficient in terms of costs. The new pattern of air travel demand that is expected to dominate the post-COVID-19 era requires the maximum of such efficiency. Thus, new air travel maps are expected to be designed, emphasising on domestic and intra-regional networks that seem to recover those international and intercontinental routes faster. Having said that, operational reshuffling should also consider environmental issues: for example, the support provided by the French government to Air France – KLM was conditional upon the carrier accepting a drastic reduction of its domestic French network to make room for further development of the electrically-run high-speed trains. Additionally, ground handling services should become adjusted to the new standards and requirements with cleaning crews to be at the epicentre of the aircraft turnaround process. As mentioned earlier, airline and airport operators may cooperate with experienced cleaning services to deliver the best possible health and safety conditions for passengers; this may be promoted accordingly in the context of health and safety-related marketing.

Demand forecasting and revenue management

The duration and magnitude of the COVID-19 pandemic, as well as the restraining measures applied to address it, make pre-identified demand a key factor in effective revenue management (Stabler, Papatheodorou, & Sinclair, 2010). Carriers, considering the new price elasticity of demand for air travel, which varies from region to region, will have to move to lower fares to stimulate demand (Voneche, 2005), as the recovery process, according to the majority of CFOs in IATA's survey (2020a), is estimated to last until at least 2023. Nonetheless, pricing policy must also consider route, destination and stage stops, competitive pressures, and the long-term level of demand (Rodrigue, 2020). Revenue management requires pricing policy strategies and demand forecasting. Profyllidis (2010) discusses several pricing policy objectives implemented by airlines – to sell seats at the best possible price; use advanced methods in demand forecasting based on current data only as established historical trends are of limited use due to the emerging paradigm shift; to control the market efficiently based on current data only for similar reasons; to focus on advanced methods in demand forecasting; to invest in integrated digital transformation; and to focus on potentially new ancillary revenue sources. Consequently, another pillar emerges concerning the airlines' pricing approach, that is, the use of advanced methods in demand forecasting.

Use of advanced methods in demand forecasting

In particular, demand forecasting is derived from econometric models based on historical data. Due to this unprecedented crisis, there are no historical data to deliver a fairly accurate model. Therefore, the use of advanced demand forecasting methods that can use the current data and forecast the demand in the short term is an important tool for air carriers. Evidently, it is impossible for revenue managers to apply long-term pricing strategies since the footprint of the crisis is expected to remain apparent until at least 2023. Consequently, short-term revenue management, based on operational reshuffling, advanced methods in demand forecasting along with digital marketing tools, may achieve revenue maximisation which is particularly vital for the air transport recovery process.

Marketing strategy

Concerning the marketing of the lowest available fares, carriers may focus on direct and digital advertising by promoting bids and pushing for transactions that will allow them to expand their customer base. Additionally, airlines may strategically cooperate with other tourism stakeholders and institutions. Innovative marketing operations that respond to global events and crises are required by airlines to restore confidence in air travel, improve the psychology of customers, and rejuvenate customer base. Airlines, in addition to informing customers of policy changes and shifts, have changed the tone of their messages and want to reassure passengers that although the flight experience has changed, travel is safe with an emphasis on disinfection, cleanliness cabin air, protective equipment, etc., and raise customer satisfaction based on unique features and preferences. Therefore, the last pillar of recovery process relates to what airlines should adopt in terms of digital marketing strategy.

Digital marketing strategy

In particular, air carriers should be ready as soon as demand returns to entice the tourist public, using digital applications that include attractive personalised offers, for example, tourist packages and discounts for business travellers. They should also focus on keeping their passengers healthy and safe and providing them with comfort and convenience from booking to refunds. The use of Internet and social media in particular (especially Facebook, Twitter, and Instagram) is important as videos and images may be produced regarding aircraft and airport cleaning and disinfection procedures before, during, and after the flight. Finally, it has become essential for airlines to educate their employees on how to handle customers in health-related emergencies, such as the COVID-19 pandemic (Molenaar et al., 2020).

To sum up, all the previously mentioned considerations (pillars) may lead to cost reduction, revenue maximisation, and customer reengagement, thus helping the air transport sector in its turnaround process in the context of a new operational and commercial philosophy. When it comes to facts and figures as well to market perceptions and official estimations for the post-COVID-19 era, the previously discussed attributes should be adopted by air transport stakeholders targeting passengers' reengagement and air travel restart.

Discussion

The previous section highlighted the various pillars, upon which the involved air transport companies should focus to digitalise their services and achieve an integrated system of travelling in the day after COVID-19 pandemic. This system will be characterised by a new market configuration in terms of both operational and commercial features. Such emerging transformations will prove necessary for the recovery process in the air transport sector during the post-COVID-19 era. Figure 1.1 presents the interrelations that compose a proposed integrated travel system towards air transport recovery process in the post-COVID-19 era.

In particular and based on Figure 1.1, five emerging transformations are expected to take place:

1 **IHMP** which stands for Internationally Harmonised Measures and Protocols, reflecting the need of the air transport market for a single plan of measures for safe travel, adopted by all countries. This is because the so far fragmented approach followed by the various countries regarding the imposition of travel restrictions has created a thick cloud of uncertainty, thus damaging the air transport sector more than the pandemic crisis itself. In fact, integration in measures and protocols is referred by the businesses as the top priority upon recovery process.

2 **HSM** which stands for Health and Safety Marketing reflecting a strategic marketing approach to promote the application of IHMP in the businesses to reengage customers and regain their trust. Digital marketing channels highly contribute to direct marketing process and faster recovery. Customers need to

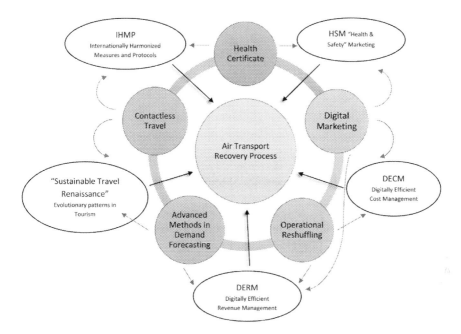

Figure 1.1 Emerging transformations in the air transport sector towards the post-COVID-19 era

feel safe to fly again and the faster they feel it, the faster they will return to air travel. Research data indicate that air travel is safe, when it comes to the virus spread and such findings should also be used in the airline and airport marketing campaigns.

3 **DECM** which stands for Digitally Efficient Cost Management reflecting the efficiently use of new technologies by the air transport businesses. Cost-efficient equipment, such as new aircraft with lower oil consumption, meeting the needs of each route in a carefully optimised network based on the current demand, may lead to significant cost reduction in terms of operations. From the commercial side, it is evident that air carriers' digital marketing and distribution channels, focusing on customised services and loyalty programs, along with offers and discounts may contribute into cost reduction by avoiding related travel distribution intermediaries.

4 **DERM** which stands for Digitally Efficient Revenue Management reflecting the new revenue management approach based on the advanced methods of demand forecasting, lower fare availability with the highest possible load factors, and the airlines' operational reshuffling, when it comes to capacity (network and equipment). Furthermore, digital marketing with Customer Relationship Management databases may contribute with profile-based dynamic pricing and new distribution capabilities. New ancillary revenue sources

should be explored capitalising on the emerging advancements in digital marketing.
5 **'Sustainable Travel Renaissance'** is a term that reflects the restart of tourism and air travel based on solid sustainability principles. It is the beginning of a new era based on a paradigm shift characterised by the emergence of new preferences, new determinant factors, new customer profiles and new routes. Tourism and air travel will have to be rebuilt based on solid economic, social, and certainly environmental foundations. Air transport businesses will focus on service quality, primarily in the context of advanced hygiene standards as this is of major concern among passengers: at the same time, however, the sector will have to build a new narrative regarding the importance of air travel in the presence of increasing environmental concerns about airline emissions and their negative impact on climate change (Efthymiou & Papatheodorou, 2020). Such evolutionary patterns in tourism include environmentally conscious customers in their activities. New travel preferences are emerging, with Generation Z customers being characterised as particularly demanding at all levels.

Conclusions and the way forward

This chapter provided an overview of the air transport market during the pandemic crisis of COVID-19, focusing on data covering the first three quarters of 2020. The crisis is expected to get under some sort of control by mid-2021, while its impact is expected to remain strong throughout the first years of the 2020s as the recovery of the aviation sector is estimated to last between two and nine years, depending on the type of the trip and the criteria set by the various organisations that publish related reports. The uncertain nature of the COVID-19 pandemic crisis has severely affected passenger confidence. Combined with the strict protection measures and adverse economic conditions prevailing in many countries, this is affecting the total number of passengers travelling. Still, airlines now have the opportunity to move onto a new business pathway characterised by better targeted customer acquisition, less reliance on travel agents, more efficient financial management, and the evolution of the digital toolkit for customer re-engagement. Winston Churchill's famous quote 'never let a good crisis go to waste' may be more relevant than ever before in conjunction with the Darwinian argument that 'it is not the strongest of the species that survive, nor the most intelligent, but the one more responsive to change'. Therefore, the aggregation of data and estimations in a strongly struggling market is necessary to come up with proposals for recovery strategies. Because of the prevailing uncertainty, it is necessary to combine the short-term planning of companies with modern and advanced tools that utilise current data with the integrated implementation of measures against the spread of the pandemic at an international level. This may ensure a restart for the travel in a safe environment, heading towards recovery. The proposed pillars (emerging transformations) for the air transport recovery process path should be continuously evaluated during the recovery period and fed with new data to expedite recovery in a sustainable manner. The chapter significantly contributes with theoretical and practical implications regarding operational tactics, demand forecasting, and revenue management and marketing strategy concerning the post-COVID-19 business and consumer environment that has been formed based on the needs of businesses and consumers, as they have emerged after the outbreak of the pandemic. Nonetheless, as this environment is dynamic and still evolving, further research and studies are required.

References

ATAG. (2020a). *Blueprint for a green recovery*. Retrieved from https://aviationbenefits.org/media/167142/bgr20_final.pdf

ATAG. (2020b). *Aviation: Benefit beyond borders*. Retrieved from https://aviationbenefits.org/media/167143/abbb20_full.pdf

Bogomolov, P. (2020, August 5). *How airline marketing has evolved due to COVID-19*. Retrieved from https://simpliflying.com/2020/airline-marketing-covid19/

Delevengos, D. (2020, November 23). *Liquidity vaccine provided to Aegean Airlines by the State and its shareholders (in Greek), Capital.gr (online financial newspaper)*. Retrieved from www.capital.gr/epixeiriseis/3497231/-embolio-reustotitas-apo-kratos-kai-metoxousgia-tin-aegean

Efthymiou, M., Njoya, E. T., Lo, P. L., Papatheodorou, A., & Randall, D. (2019). The impact of delays on customers' satisfaction: An empirical analysis of the British Airways on-time Performance at Heathrow airport. *Journal of Aerospace Technology and Management, 11*: e0219. https://doi.org/10.5028/jatm.v11.977

Efthymiou, M., & Papatheodorou, A. (2017). Evolving business models. In N. Halpern & A. Graham (Eds.), *The routledge companion to air transport management* (pp. 122–135). London: Routledge.

Efthymiou, M., & Papatheodorou, A. (2020). Environmental policies in European aviation: A stakeholder management perspective. In T. Walker, A. S. Bergantino, N. Sprung-Much, & L. Loiacono (Eds.), *Sustainable aviation: Greening the flight path* (pp. 101–125). Cham: Springer Nature/Palgrave Macmillan.

European Commission. (2020). Commission Delegated Regulation (EU) 2020/1477 of 14 October 2020 amending Council Regulation (EEC) No 95/93 as regards the temporary extension of exceptional measures to address the consequences caused by the COVID-19 pandemic. *Official Journal of the European Union*. Retrieved from https://eur-lex.europa.eu/legal-content/EN/TXT/PDF/?uri=CELEX:32020R1477&from=EN

IATA. (2019). *More connectivity and improved efficiency: 2018 airline industry statistics released*. Retrieved from www.iata.org/en/pressroom/pr/2019-07-31-01/

IATA. (2020a). *IATA economics: October 2020 survey airline business confidence index*. Retrieved from www.iata.org/en/iata-repository/publications/economic-reports/business-confidence-survey-october-2020/

IATA. (2020b). *COVID-19: Cost of air travel once restrictions start to lift*. Retrieved from www.iata.org/en/iata-repository/publications/economic-reports/covid-19-cost-of-air-travel-once-restrictions-start-to-lift/

IATA. (2020c). *September offers no relief to passenger downturn: Press release No. 88*. Retrieved from www.iata.org/en/pressroom/pr/2020-11-04-02/

IATA. (2020d). *Extremely low risk of viral transmission inflight*. Retrieved from https://airlines.iata.org/analysis/extremely-low-risk-of-viral-transmission-inflight?_ga=2.186911720.1909745786.1607253282-1767682786.1586762797

IATA. (2020e). *Remarks of Alexandre de Juniac at the IATA media briefing on 27 October 2020*. Retrieved from www.iata.org/en/pressroom/speeches/2020-10-27-01/

ICAO. (2020a). *Effects of novel coronavirus (COVID-19) on civil aviation: Economic impact analysis*. Retrieved from www.icao.int/sustainability/Documents/COVID-19/ICAO%20COVID%202020%2010%2028%20Economic%20Impact.pdf

ICAO. (2020b). *Air transport monthly monitor*. Retrieved from www.icao.int/sustainability/Documents/MonthlyMonitor-2020/Monthly%20Monitor_October_2020.pdf

ILO. (2020). *ILO monitor: COVID-19 and the world of work: Updated estimates and analysis* (6th ed.). Retrieved from www.ilo.org/wcmsp5/groups/public/-dgreports/-dcomm/documents/briefingnote/wcms_755910.pdf

Li, G. (2008). The nature of leisure travel demand. In A. Graham, A. Papatheodorou, & P. Forsyth (Eds.), *Aviation and tourism: Implications for leisure travel*. Aldershot: Ashgate Publishing Ltd.

Maneenop, S., & Kotcharin, S. (2020). The impacts of COVID-19 on the global airline industry: An event study approach. *Journal of Air Transport*, 89. https://doi.org/10.1016/j.jairtraman.2020.101920

Molenaar, D., Bosch, F., Guggenheim, J., Jhunjhunwala, P., Loh, H., & Wade, B. (2020). *The post-COVID-19 flight plan for airlines*. Retrieved from www.bcg.com/publications/2020/post-covid-airline-industry-strategy

Naftemporiki. (2020). *Can air carriers survive the pandemic? (in Greek)*. Retrieved from https://m.naftemporiki.gr/story/1624991/mporoun-na-epibiosoun-oi-aeroporikes-apo-tin-pandimia

Papatheodorou, A. (2021). A review of research into air transport and tourism: Launching the annals of tourism research curated collection on air transport and tourism. *Annals of Tourism Research*, 87, 103151.

Papatheodorou, A., Rossello, J., & Xiao, H. (2010). Global economic crisis and tourism: Consequences and perspectives. *Journal of Travel Research*, 49(1), 39–45.

Power, E. (2020). *Restart & re-acquire: How airlines can find opportunity post-crisis*. Retrieved from www.everymundo.com/how-airlines-can-find-opportunity-post-crisis/

Profyllidis, V. (2010). *Air transport: Airports*. Athens: Papasotiriou Publications. (in Greek).

Rodrigue, J.-P. (2020). *Tourism and transport*. Retrieved from https://transportgeography.org/?page_id=9622

Stabler, M., Papatheodorou, A., & Sinclair, T. (2010). *The economics of tourism* (2nd ed.). Oxon: Routledge.

UNWTO. (2020c). *International tourism down 70% as travel restrictions impact all regions*. Retrieved from www.unwto.org/news/international-tourism-down-70-as-travel-restrictions-impact-all-regions

UNWTO. (2020a). *World tourism remains at a standstill as 100% of countries impose restrictions on travel: Report: Travel restrictions* (7th ed.). Retrieved from www.unwto.org/more-than-50-of-global-destinations-are-easing-travel-restrictions-but-caution-remains

UNWTO. (2020b). *More than 50% of global destinations are easing travel restrictions-but caution remains: Report: travel restrictions* (3rd ed.). Retrieved from www.unwto.org/more-than-50-of-global-destinations-are-easing-travel-restrictions-but-caution-remains

Voneche, F. (2005). *Yield management in the airline industry*. Retrieved from https://docplayer.net/9804350-Yield-management-in-the-airline-industry.html

WTTC. (2020a). *To recovery & beyond: The future of travel & tourism in the wake of COVID-19*. Retrieved from https://wttc.org/Research/To-Recovery-Beyond

Wyman, O. (2020*). COVID-19 will challenge airlines for years*. Retrieved from www.oliverwyman.com/our-expertise/insights/2020/aug/covid-19-will-challenge-airlines-for-years.html

2 Climate change and tourism
Emerging transformations

C. Michael Hall

Introduction

Climate change is one of the defining international political, economic, and security concerns of the twenty-first century. Increased high magnitude weather events, such as drought, floods, and severe storms, have led national, regional, and local governments to place adaptation to climate change higher on to the political agenda, although implementation measures have tended to lag behind (European Environment Agency, 2014; Knowles & Scott, 2021). Responses to changing precipitation regimes; the effects of floods and drought on agricultural production, health, infrastructure, and regional economies; and the effects of extreme temperatures on health have also starting to bring into sharp focus the social and economic cost of climate change (Scott, Hall, & Gössling, 2016a, 2016b). The effects of climate had already begun to be felt in some developing countries, but in international political terms, the reality is that their experiences, while receiving some media coverage, arguably have lagged behind international climate change regime negotiations and concrete policy actions (Hoogendoorn & Fitchett, 2018), especially in light of the economic effects of other crises such as COVID-19 (Gössling, Scott, & Hall, 2021). However, as the realities of the climate crisis start to affect developed countries, the political problem ceases being something that exists elsewhere and is instead felt locally and experienced directly (Egan & Mullin, 2012), leading to demands for transformative action (Scott, Hall, & Gössling, 2016a, 2016b; Hall, Scott, & Gössling, 2020).

Tourism has long been recognised as a sector which contributes a significant share of emissions to global heating and the climate crisis (Gössling, 2013; UNWTO-UNEP-WMO, 2008). Yet, despite being identified more than a decade ago as being one of the six business sectors (along with aviation, transport, health care, the financial sector, and oil and gas) that lie in the 'danger zone' of the regulatory, physical, reputational, and litigation risks of climate change versus their level of preparedness (KPMG, 2008), the tourism industry continues to lag behind in adaptation and mitigation measures and is set on a course to double its emissions by 2040 (Gössling, Scott, & Hall, 2013; Scott, Hall, & Gössling, 2016a, 2016b, 2019).

This chapter examines the possibilities of transforming the BAU direction of tourism with respect to the climate crisis. However, while climate change-related

DOI: 10.4324/9781003105930-3

transformation is occurring without a doubt, the direction of such transformation remains open, particularly as to whether decarbonisation of the sector can actually be achieved given current strategies.

Tourism's contribution to the climate crisis

Tourism is a significant contributor to climate change. Tourism and travel contribute to climate change through emissions of greenhouse gases, including carbon dioxide (CO_2), methane (CH4), nitrous oxides (NOx), hydrofluorocarbons (HFCs), perfluorocarbons (PFCs), and sulphur hexafluoride (SF6). There are also various short-lived emissions that are important in the context of aviation and cruise ships, such as particulates (Scott, Hall, & Gössling, 2012). In addition, there is also a further, though unquantified, contribution to climate change as a result of tourism-related land-use changes, which may be significant in some areas of tourism-related urbanisation (Scott, Hall, & Gössling, 2012).

Without taking radiative forcing into account, tourism is estimated to have contributed approximately 5% to global anthropogenic emissions of CO_2 in the year 2005 (UNWTO-UNEP-WMO, 2008; World Economic Forum [WEF], 2009), a figure that remains widely referred to in the absence of a new UNWTO assessment of tourism's contribution. According to this study, the majority of CO_2 emissions are associated with transport, with aviation accounting for 40% of tourism's overall carbon footprint, followed by car transport (32%). Accommodation accounted for 21% of emissions in 2005 (UNWTO-UNEP-WMO, 2008). Cruise ships account for around 1.5% of global tourism emissions (Eijgelaar, Thaper, & Peeters, 2010; see also WEF, 2009). A more accurate assessment of tourism's contribution to climate change can be made on the basis of radiative forcing (RF). With RF considered, which is a particularly important uncertainty of aviation emissions, it has been estimated that tourism contributed 5.2–12.5% of all anthropogenic forcing in 2005, with a best estimate of approximately 8% (Gössling, Scott, & Hall, 2013). This estimate is in keeping with the more recent work by Lenzen et al. (2018) which examined tourism-related global carbon flows between 160 countries, and their carbon footprints under origin and destination accounting perspectives but which also did not include forcing. According to Lenzen et al. (2018) between 2009 and 2013, tourism's global carbon footprint increased from 3.9 to 4.5 GtCO$_2$e, accounting for about 8% of global greenhouse gas emissions. Significantly, given how often they are referred to, the assessments of the tourism sector's contribution to climate change conducted by the UNWTO-UNEP-WMO (2008) and WEF (2009) did also not include the impact of non-CO_2 greenhouse gases nor the effects of radiative forcing.

Anthropogenic climate change is not just about the future, it has already begun (IPCC, 2013a, 2014a). A key conclusion of the IPCC (2013b) is that 'Warming of the climate system is unequivocal, and since the 1950s, many of the observed changes are unprecedented over decades to millennia. The atmosphere and ocean have warmed, the amounts of snow and ice have diminished, sea level has risen, and the concentrations of greenhouse gases have increased' (IPCC, 2013b, p. 2). Although climate change is a natural phenomenon, it is extremely likely (>95%

level of certainty) 'that human influence has been the dominant cause of the observed warming since the mid-20th century' (IPCC, 2013b, p. 15). Furthermore, 'It is extremely likely that more than half of the observed increase in global average surface temperature from 1951 to 2010 was caused by the anthropogenic increase in greenhouse gas concentrations and other anthropogenic forcings together' (IPCC, 2013b, p. 15). Post the 2015 Paris Agreement and the challenge of limiting average global temperature increases to 1.5°C, the IPCC (2018, A.3.1) further reports that 'Impacts on natural and human systems from global warming have already been observed (*high confidence*). Many land and ocean ecosystems and some of the services they provide have already changed due to global warming (*high confidence*)'.

Although adaptation has developed as a focus of climate change response in the absence of an international agreement to reduce emissions, the reality is that without serious mitigation, adaptation efforts will also face significant limits, increasing the risk of major environmental, economic, and societal disruptions (IPCC, 2014a, 2018). The IPCC (2014b, 2018) has argued that in order to reduce the dangers of climate change, emissions will need to be reduced by all sectors with significant shares of emissions, noting that:

> Climate-related risks for natural and human systems are higher for global warming of 1.5°C than at present, but lower than at 2°C (*high confidence*). These risks depend on the magnitude and rate of warming, geographic location, levels of development and vulnerability, and on the choices and implementation of adaptation and mitigation options (*high confidence*).
> (IPCC, 2018, A.3)

The risks of climate change for tourism are extremely significant for many locations given the economic importance of tourism, an importance which has arguably only become even more pronounced following COVID-19 (Hall, Scott, & Gössling, 2020). For example, sometime between 2015 and 2017, total tourist arrivals (international and domestic tourist trips combined) became greater than the world's population for the first time (Hall, 2015). Growth projections for global tourism are also extremely significant for any consideration of climate change. Under the central projection of UNWTO (2012, 2014) forecasts, the number of international tourist arrivals is expected to increase an overage of 3.3% per year between 2010 and 2030 (representing an average increase of 43 million arrivals a year), reaching an estimated 1.8 billion international arrivals by 2030. Although these figures are clearly impacted by COVID-19, with the World Travel and Tourism Council (WTTC) estimating that the pandemic led to a 72% drop in international tourists in the first half of 2020 (BBC, 2020), it needs to be remembered that until 2020 international tourism growth was occurring at the very high end of the UNWTO forecasts. Similarly, the IATA expects air traffic in 2020 to be 66% below the level it was in 2019 and estimates that it will be at least 2024 before air traffic reaches pre-pandemic levels (BBC, 2020). Yet, in terms of the bigger picture of tourism growth, all this means is that international tourism will still likely achieve its original UNWTO forecast of the number of international arrivals at the global scale by 2030, although the relative growth arrivals in emerging economies by 2030, which were expected to be double the pace of arrivals in advanced economies, to 57% of international arrivals being in emerging economies are far more doubtful (Table 2.1).

Tourism ranks as one of the largest economic sectors together with fuels, chemicals, and food, generating an estimated 10.3% of world GDP in 2019 (WTTC, 2020). However, according to the WTTC (2020), more than 121 million global Travel and Tourism jobs and an estimated US$3.4 trillion in global GDP may be lost as a result of COVID-19. This is significant as, since the Global Financial Crisis, tourism is one of the top five export earners in over 150 countries and therefore a major source of foreign exchange, while in around two-fifths of these countries, it is the number one export sector (UNWTO & UNEP, 2011; UNCTAD, 2010; Hall, Scott, & Gössling, 2013). Reiterating the global economic significance of tourism is not necessarily to promote the supposed potential of tourism as a contributor to the UN Sustainable Development Goals (SDGs) (UNWTO & UNDP, 2017; Hall, 2019); rather, it is to highlight why international tourism is given such significance by national and regional governments in their policy positions for economy recovery from the COVID-19 pandemic (WTTC, 2020). However, doing so clearly raises some fundamental questions about the possible trade-offs that may exist between a focus on reviving destination economies and regenerating employment in tourism and hospitality and the potential effects that this will have on the future trajectory of emissions from the sector. In fact, rather

Table 2.1 International tourism arrivals and forecasts 1950–2030

Year	World	Africa	Americas	Asia and Pacific	Europe	Middle East
1950	25.3	0.5	7.5	0.2	16.8	0.2
1960	69.3	0.8	16.7	0.9	50.4	0.6
1965	112.9	1.4	23.2	2.1	83.7	2.4
1970	165.8	2.4	42.3	6.2	113.0	1.9
1975	222.3	4.7	50.0	10.2	153.9	3.5
1980	278.1	7.2	62.3	23.0	178.5	7.1
1985	320.1	9.7	65.1	32.9	204.3	8.1
1990	439.5	15.2	92.8	56.2	265.8	9.6
1995	540.6	20.4	109.0	82.4	315.0	13.7
2000	687.0	28.3	128.1	110.5	395.9	24.2
2005	806.8	37.3	133.5	155.4	441.5	39.0
2010	940	49.7	150.7	204.4	474.8	60.3
2019[b]	1 460	71.9	219.5	360.1	743.7	65.1
forecast						
2020[a]	1 360	85	199	355	620	101
2030	1 809	134	248	535	744	149

a Original UNWTO forecast
b UNWTO provisional data

Source: World Tourism Organisation (1997) and UN World Tourism Organization (2006, 2012, 2014, 2020)

than the COVID-19 experience leading to a transformative more environmentally friendly form of tourism, there is every possibility that the desperation to restart the tourism sector and the pent-up demand for leisure, VFR, and business travel may only serve to reinforce the globally unsustainable Business-as-Usual (BAU) direction of tourism (Hall, Scott, & Gössling, 2020).

Tourism and Business-as-Usual

Business-as-Usual is a somewhat misleading term with respect to tourism (Hall, Lundmark, & Zhang, 2021b). As while BAU conveys the notion that things stay the same, in the case of tourism, this means continuing growth, with the exception of the COVID-19 pandemic period, with tourist trips and the resultant emissions. The cut in greenhouse gas emissions of between 4.2% and 7.5% in 2020 due to the shutdown of travel and other activities is a 'tiny blip' in the continuous buildup of greenhouse gases in the atmosphere and less than the natural variation seen from year to year (World Meteorological Organization (WMO), 2020). The important thing in assessing such situations is to take a longer-term perspective because short term declines in growth, even if dramatic as in the case of COVID-19, do not necessarily affect the longer-term trajectories and trends. For example, in the case of travel, patterns and transport modes have been consistently shifting over the period 2010–2019, more than half of all international arrivals now travel by plane and this figure has been gradually increasing. With respect to transport modes, in 2013, just over half of international tourists arrived by air (53%), followed by road (40%), rail (2%), and over water (6%) (UNWTO, 2014). Over time, movement by air transport is growing faster than the use of surface and active transport modes, with subsequent global emissions impacts.

Even given the effects of COVID-19, growth in air transport is expected to continue through to the 2030s and 2040s (Gössling, Scott, & Hall, 2013; International Energy Agency (IEA), 2020) (Table 2.2). Over a longer time scale, the IEA (2009) in their evaluation of future transport trends, for example, developed a high baseline scenario in which air travel almost quadruples between 2005 and 2050 with an average worldwide growth rate of 3.5% per year but over 4% worldwide until 2025. The latter figure actually being an underestimate of growth until the COVID-19 pandemic, with the IEA (2020) noting that between 2000–2020, commercial passenger flight activity grew by about 5% per year and CO_2 emissions rose by 2% per year. As the IEA (2020) noted, forecasts suggest that aviation passenger growth rates are expected to be of the order of 4.3–4.6% per annum through to 2049 and 'While the COVID-19 crisis is likely to substantially curb near-term demand growth, aviation has been remarkably resilient to previous crises and, even with a structural reduction in demand, is likely to remain relatively strong in the coming decades'. Similarly, Transport & Environment (2020, p. 2) suggest,

> The Covid crisis has caused a severe, but temporary, fall in demand and therefore emissions. Directly, it does nothing to resolve the aviation's underlying

Table 2.2 Long-term forecast growth rates in tourism and associated transport of various organisations

Organization	Absolute growth rates expected
UNWTO-UNEP-WMO (2008)	Emissions of CO_2 will grow by 135% over 30 years, from 1,304 Mt CO_2 in 2005 to 3,059 Mt CO_2 in 2035
UNWTO (2012, 2014)	Growth in international tourist arrivals 2010–2030 of 3.3% per year (central projection)
World Economic Forum (2009)	Tourism-related CO_2 emissions (excluding aviation) will grow at 2.5% per year until 2035, and aviation emissions at 2.7%, with total estimated emissions of 3,164 Mt CO_2 by 2035 (plus 143%)
Airbus (2012)	Growth in revenue passenger kilometres by 150% between 2011 and 2031 (averaging 4.7% per year); with the global fleet of passenger aircraft growing from 15,560 to 32,550 in the same period
Boeing (2012)	Growth in global aircraft fleet from 19,890 in 2011 to 39,780 by 2031; airline traffic in revenue passenger kilometres: 5% per year
IEA (2009)	Air travel almost quadruples between 2005 and 2050 with an average worldwide growth rate of 3.5% per year, but over 4% worldwide until 2025
International Maritime Organization (2009)	Absolute emissions from shipping, including cruise ships, will grow by 1.9–2.7% per year up to 2050

climate which is its reliance on fossil fuels, and experience has shown that the sector can quickly bounce back from crisis to resume growth in demand and therefore emissions.

In taking a long-term perspective, this means that, according to the IEA (2009), the expected growth in aviation will represent a tripling of energy used, accounting for 19% of all transport energy used globally in 2050 as compared to 11% in 2006. Significantly, with respect to absolute emissions, even the IEA's (2009) more sustainable scenario developed to describe the impact of policies that dampen air travel growth, the development of high-speed rail, and the aggressive promotion of the use of telecommunications as a substitute for travel still predicted a tripling of air travel between 2005 and 2050.

The problem for transforming emissions from tourism transport, as well as other elements of the tourism system, is that efficiency gains that reduce emissions on a per passenger kilometre basis (known as emissions intensity) are not sufficient to keep pace with the absolute growth in the number of tourist trips, the distance travelled, and the speed at which they are taken. 'The rapid increase in tourism demand is effectively outstripping the decarbonisation of tourism-related technology' (Lenzen et al., 2018, p. 522). All major estimates for international tourism and travel to 2035 have growth occurring at a faster rate than predicted increases in per passenger/tourist energy efficiency by the sector which are optimistically estimated at around 1.5–2% per year (Hall, 2011; Gössling, Scott, &

Hall, 2013; IEA, 2020) and 'airline traffic repeatedly hits record highs after global crises' (Transport & Environment, 2020, p. 2). Even the UNEP's (2011, p. 438) green economy/green growth scenarios suggest that in a BAU scenario (2011–2050), tourism growth will mean increases in energy consumption (111%), greenhouse gas emissions (105%), water consumption (150%), and solid waste disposal (252%). Even under the highly optimistic greener investment scenario, tourism's negative affect on planetary health still increases:

> The tourism sector can grow steadily in the coming decades (exceeding the BAU scenario by 7 per cent in terms of the sector GDP) while saving significant amounts of resources and enhancing its sustainability. The green investment scenario is expected to undercut the corresponding BAU scenario by 18 per cent for water consumption, 44 per cent for energy supply and demand, 52 per cent for CO_2 emissions.
>
> (UNEP, 2011, p. 438)

Given the continuing focus on growth, even if supposedly green (Hall, Lundmark, & Zhang, 2021a), and the relationship between energy consumption and emissions production, it should therefore be no surprise that substantial concerns exist over the capacity of the tourism industry to make a positive contribution to minimising the effects of climate change.

The impacts of climate change on tourism: emerging transformations to the tourism landscape?

The UNWTO-UNEP-WMO (2008, p. 38) recognise climate change as 'the greatest challenge to the sustainability of tourism in the 21st century'. Scott, Hall, and Gössling (2012) identified four broad pathways by which climate change is affecting tourism and will also continue to do so in the foreseeable future – (1) direct climatic impacts (daily weather, seasonality, inter-annual variability, and extreme events) that alter the length and quality of climate-dependent tourism seasons, operating costs, location decisions and design, infrastructure damage and business interruptions, destination attractiveness, and tourist demand and destination choice; (2) indirect climate-induced environmental change that affects environmental, socio-economic, and tourism systems. This includes natural assets that define destination image and are critical attractions for tourists, environmental conditions that can deter tourists, operating costs, and the capacity of tourism firms to do business sustainably; (3) indirect climate-induced socio-economic change such as decreased economic growth and discretionary income that can be used for travel, increased political instability and security risks, and/or changing attitudes towards travel; and (4) the policy responses of other sectors, such as mitigation policy, that could alter transport cost structures and destination or modal choices as well as adaptation policies related to water rights or insurance costs, which have important implications for tourism development and operating costs.

The extent to which tourism is vulnerable to climate change is illustrated in the work of Mora et al. (2018) who, in a comprehensive review of how ten types of climate change impacts are affecting 89 attributes of human health, food, water, infrastructure, economy, and security, found that tourism was one of only five sectors that is being impacted by all ten types of climate impacts. Although there are a number of different ways in which climate change is transforming the landscape of tourism, several have received significant attention because of the scale and visibility of their impacts.

One of the most prominent impacts of climate change on tourism is that of the effects of sea level rise (SLR) on coastal tourism (Arabadzhyan et al., 2021). SLR affects infrastructure, attractions, services, and resources, such as beaches as a result of increased erosion and flooding (Wong et al., 2014). The impacts of SLR may be partly adapted to by coastal engineering and beach nourishment, but such measures are extremely expensive and even allowing the sea to reclaim low lying areas has substantial implications for the issue of who should pay for coastal withdrawal and the loss of what was once valuable beachfront real estate (Hall, 2017). Half of Florida's existing beaches, multiple airports, thousands of hotel rooms, and historic structures are deemed at risk to SLR. Similar threats to coastal tourism have been reported from locations as diverse as Australia (Climate Council, 2014) and the Caribbean (Scott, Simpson, & Sim, 2012). In the case of the latter, a geo-referenced database of 906 major coastal resort properties in 19 Caribbean Community (CARICOM) countries was created to assess their potential risk to a scenario of one-metre SLR. An estimated 266 (29%) resort properties would be partially or fully inundated by one-metre SLR; and between 440 (49%) and 546 (60%) of resort properties would be at risk of beach erosion damage associated with the same SLR scenario (Scott, Simpson, & Sim, 2012). Unlike developed coastal nations, many island and less developed country coastal destinations do not possess sufficient economic resources to protect many existing destinations from SLR. Yet for these countries, coastal tourism is often the mainstay of the destination economy (Scott, Hall, & Gössling, 2019). Ironically, the damage to many coastal tourism destinations from SLR and climate change is exacerbated by tourism developments in coastal ecosystems, such as the removal of wetlands and dune systems for resort developments and vacation homes (Spalding et al., 2014).

With its highly visible sensitivity to climate variability, the risks posed by climate change to the large international ski tourism industry have received considerable attention. Although snowmaking is an adaptation that can considerably lengthen the lifespan of many at-risk winter resorts from climate change, lower elevation ski areas and the early portion of the ski season (including the economically important Christmas – New year holiday period) remain increasingly vulnerable from climate change, especially in lower latitude regions (Demiroglu & Hall, 2020; Hall & Saarinen, 2020). Such vulnerabilities may be exacerbated by increased costs of access to water for artificial snowmaking in some regions (Pickering, 2011).

Importantly for many alpine areas, changed snow availability will potentially have significant flow-on effects for other parts of the tourism industry and for the regional economy. In some cases, visitors may switch from a destination of low snow security to one with higher likelihood of snow. Analysis of ski tourism demand during climate change analogue seasons in Canada, the United States, and Austria found that skier visits diminished between 7% and 15% compared to a climatically normal winter (Scott, Simpson, & Sim, 2012). In the case of Norway, the ski season is projected to be substantially shortened as early as the 2030s for the half of ski areas that currently do not have snowmaking infrastructure (Scott et al., 2020). Natural snow reliable ski areas decline from approximately half in the 2030s to a third in the 2050s. In a low emission scenario snowmaking, ski season losses may be substantially reduced and the majority of ski areas remain snow reliable until the end of the twenty-first century. However, in a high emission, future substantial shortening of the ski season (up to 40 days) nonetheless begins in the 2050s (Scott et al., 2020). Such transformation in the landscape has potentially dramatic implications for tourism. For example, a survey of Christmas tourists in Rovaniemi, Finland, found that less than a quarter of respondents would consider Rovaniemi as an appealing destination if there was no snow (Tervo-Kankare, Hall, & Saarinen, 2013).

The availability of seasonal tourism resources, such as snow, reflects some of the wider issues associated with the impacts of climate change on tourist seasons (Hoogendoorn et al., 2021). Climate is clearly important for the attractiveness of a number of destinations. However, sensationalist media reporting on the potential, for example, of the Mediterranean becoming too hot for tourism, does not reflect the realities of tourism in many locations and the capacities of tourists to change behaviours over time (Demiroglu et al., 2020). Indeed, studies of tourist visitation during the 2003 European heat wave indicate that many people seek relief from the heat of large cities by going to the coast and that higher summer temperatures may not dissuade tourism in the region to the extent that some have assumed (Martinez-Ibarra, 2011).

Changes in the geographic and seasonal distribution of climate resources, including with respect to biodiversity (Hall, 2010), will undoubtedly have significant consequences for tourism demand from the global to destination scale over the longer term. However, global- and regional-scale simulation models of tourism demand under climatic change are highly simplified and have major limitations as forecasting tools (Gössling & Hall, 2006; Scott, Hall, & Gössling, 2019). Nevertheless, if even remotely accurate (Hall, 2008), then existing and potential physical transformations to tourism landscapes and resources indicate that the implications of climatic change for the geographic redistribution of tourism demand are significant and will impose major adaptation challenges for destinations expected to experience shifts in tourist arrivals and expenditures over time and space. Such impacts will also flow through to the various dimensions of tourism development (e.g., property values, employment, supply chain, and foreign exchange earnings) as well as those expected to gain future tourism development (e.g., transport and water capacity and sustainability of environmental attractions) (Klint et al., 2012; Zeppel, 2012; Scott, Hall, & Gössling, 2019).

Responding to tourism and climate change

Tourism is both affected by climate change and is also a significant contributor of emissions. Climate change therefore influences the consumption and production of tourist products and has ramifications throughout the entire tourism system with respect to the relative attractiveness of destinations, market viability, and the health of tourism resources (Deutsche Bank Research, 2008; Scott, Hall, & Gössling, 2012, 2019). Although a global framework for emission reductions has been developed via the Paris Agreement, the majority of tourism specific policies are targeted at marketing and development programmes that increase arrivals and the growth of the sector, as opposed to substantive emissions reduction and climate change (Scott, Hall, & Gössling, 2016a, 2016b). This situation creates one of the first major barriers to the effective decarbonisation and sustainable transformation of tourism: how can the tourism specific policies of destinations that tend to focus on growth be reconciled with the broader environmental policy settings that seek to lower emissions within an economy? Government and industry initiatives to reduce emissions are usually focussed on increased efficiency at a per tourist/unit of consumption level rather than limiting or even reducing the number of tourists to a destination. Nevertheless, as the previous discussion of forecasting tourism and travel growth suggests, in order to achieve the emission reductions needed to avoid 'dangerous' climate change, absolute emission reductions will eventually be required of the aviation sector and of the tourism sector as a whole, especially as emissions reduction via efficiency measures faces diminishing returns over time. However, even limited aviation emission reduction measures, such as the EU Emission Trading System, which would not have affected arrival figures at all, have continued to face substantial opposition (Transport & Environment, 2020).

Arguably, the element of the tourism system that can most quickly change its behaviour to reduce emissions and favour more sustainable destinations and products is the consumers (Scott, Simpson, & Sim, 2012). Nevertheless, there is a very low inclination of tourists to *voluntarily* change their travel behaviour to reduce their environmental impacts (e.g., travel less by air and substitute transport modes and/or destinations). Although a significant proportion of travellers have stated a willingness to pay some additional charge or offset to reflect environmental costs, the proportion of travellers who actually purchased offsets is typically less than 5% (Gössling et al., 2009; Cohen & Higham, 2011; Gössling & Humpe, 2020). Furthermore, any assessment of tourism's 'significance' for climate change would also have to consider that tourism, and especially international travel, is only engaged in by a small proportion of the global population on a regular basis. In the US context, Ummel (2014) found that, on average, persons in the top 2% of income distribution have carbon footprints more than four times larger than those in the bottom quintile, with travel being a significant component of the consumption activities of the top 2%. This skewed distribution of hypermobility has been identified in a number of studies (Gössling et al., 2009; Gössling & Humpe, 2020). In the case of France, for example, half of the greenhouse gas emissions caused by the mobility of French citizens are caused by just 5% of the population, indicating the major importance of hypermobile travellers in addressing transport-related emissions (Gössling et al., 2009), while, more recently, Gössling and Humpe (2020) estimate that only 2–4% of the global population flew internationally in 2018 with 1% of world population emitting 50% of CO_2 from commercial aviation.

In the absence of enforceable regulatory intervention, reliance on improvements in technological improvements and voluntary behavioural change alone are not reducing tourism's contribution to climate change. The reality is that despite the optimism that surrounds advocacy for sustainable tourism, especially with respect to tourism's contribution to the SDGs, the application of behavioural economic and social marketing interventions with respect to tourism's contributions to the climate crisis has not had any significant impact on reductions in emissions and the long-term adoption of pro-environmental behaviour. The problem does not appear that there are not sustainable tourism initiatives that can reduce emissions rather that they are insufficient. One main reason for this is a failure to recognise the multi-scalar nature of transformation.

The tourism system is panarchical: 'the adaptive and evolutionary nature of adaptive cycles that are nested one within the other across space and time scales' (Holling, Gunderson, & Peterson, 2002, p. 74). From this perspective, different elements of the system are embedded inside each other from the level of the individual through to the global (Figure 2.1). Change can move up and down the different scales, although change at the macro level (institutional /socio-technical system level) occurs slower than at the micro-scale (individual). However, the critical thing for transformation is that for change to move up the scales, there need to be a sufficient number of actors at each level who modify their behaviours in a sustainable fashion in order to compensate for the actions of those actors who have not changed and whose emissions continue to grow. Isolated actions, whether by individuals, communities, businesses, or even destinations, while significant at that scale are not sufficient to lead to wider change, particularly at the global level, without changes to the way in the which the tourism system is structured and regulated so that the real cost of tourism is ameliorated and reduced.

Just having a minority of consumers or businesses engaged in sustainable behaviour does not lead to decarbonisation, especially as the evidence suggests that other businesses and individuals 'compensate' with their emissions (Gössling & Humpe, 2020). Shifting visitors around and away from areas of stress and unsustainability, as advocated as a response to overtourism (WTTC, 2017; UNWTO, 2018), does not solve the problem at the global scale as we have only one planet. Unless tourism growth in terms of distance and speed of travel is limited, greenhouse gas emissions cannot be reduced. The problem can only effectively be solved if managed from a global perspective. Local and individual responses need to become collective for decarbonisation to occur. The solution therefore lies in the structure and the development of new sustainable tourism practices and habits and not in the individual conscious decisions of consumers.

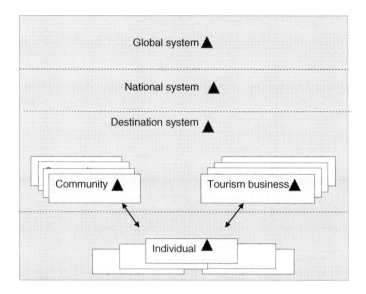

Figure 2.1 Transformation and change within the tourism system panarchy

Conclusions: transforming to what?

Given that growth in tourism is increasing at a higher rate than efficiency gains, the absolute contribution of tourism to climate change is therefore increasing. Even given the impacts of COVID-19, the emissions from tourism will continue to grow in the foreseeable future. Climate change is already affecting destinations and its impacts are only going to get more pronounced. Some destinations will benefit in the short term as the impacts of climate change on tourism destinations vary in space and time and cannot be treated in isolation. Instead, in the short- to mid-term, responses to climate change need to be seen in terms of the relative effects of global heating on all competitive destinations within the set of options that a potential tourist has (Tervo-Kankare, Hall, & Saarinen, 2013). However, in the longer term, all destinations and tourist generating regions will be affected.

There is a clear understanding of tourism's substantial contribution to climate change. Although research on the impacts of climate change on tourism and appropriate responses lags behind, arguably, this is because of a continuing commitment to short-term growth in the hope that a technical solution will be found that will allow BAU business and consumer behaviours to remain unchanged (Hall, Lundmark, & Zhang, 2021b). The fact that the UNWTO has not revisited its earlier support for research in this area speaks volumes as to the real global commitment to responding to a problem against which COVID-19 is relatively insignificant. Far more people will die from climate change than COVID-19. The reality is that existing research on tourism and global environmental change is only undertaken by a small number of scholars and is not a mainstream issue in tourism research or education (Hall, 2019). The desperate responses of governments and universities to the economic impacts of COVID-19 may only exacerbate this situation. There is also little analysis or understanding of implementation and change issues in tourism (Hall, 2011), at both a structural and an individual practice level. Transformation does not just occur; rather, it has to be worked for.

The impacts of the climate crisis on tourism therefore need to be understood in relation to all elements of the tourism system rather than destinations alone as the systemic effects of climate change will have significant consequences for tourism in all countries (Scott, Hall, & Gössling, 2012). Tourism has long been regarded as a means of generating employment and economic development in many countries, especially at times of economic crisis, such as COVID-19. Climate change and the inter-related issue of biodiversity loss are arguably the most severe threats to this economic capacity in the world today. Ironically, COVID-19 is only likely to make things worse rather than better, as governments are desperate to restart their economies and recreate jobs. Many people, businesses, and policy makers do want to be more sustainable. But it is not enough. There needs to be a critical mass of actors enacting change to reduce the effects of those who continue with BAU for their short-term competitive goals. In so doing, those actors trying to be sustainable have a major challenge. Do they continue to compete on the basis of quality and the polluter pays or do they compete, like the majority of the industry, on cost with the pollution becoming a public and planetary externality? Unfortunately, in seeking to transform tourism to meet the challenge of global heating, it is the latter option that is currently winning. An industry that for so long promotes itself on the basis of perceived freedom to 'escape' and 'experience' needs to recognise that the travel they promote comes with a substantial environmental impact that either sooner or later will cost the Earth. We cannot escape the experience of global heating and the climate crisis.

References

Airbus. (2012). *Global market forecast 2012–2031*. Airbus.
Arabadzhyan, A., Figini, P., García, C., González, M. M., Lam-González, Y. E., & León, C. J. (2021). Climate change, coastal tourism, and impact chains: A literature review. *Current Issues in Tourism*, 24(16), 2233–2268.
BBC. (2020, November 22). COVID-19: Hong Kong-Singapore travel corridor postponed. www.bbc.com/news/world-asia-55027305
Boeing. (2012). *Current market outlook 2012–2031*. Boeing.
Climate Council. (2014). *Counting the costs: Climate change and coastal flooding*. Climate Council.
Cohen, S. A., & Higham, J. E. (2011). Eyes wide shut? UK consumer perceptions on aviation climate impacts and travel decisions to New Zealand. *Current Issues in Tourism*, 14(4), 323–335.
Demiroglu, O. C., & Hall, C. M. (2020). Geobibliography and bibliometric networks of polar tourism and climate change research. *Atmosphere*, 11(5), 498.
Demiroglu, O. C., Saygili-Araci, F. S., Pacal, A., Hall, C. M., & Kurnaz, M. L. (2020). Future Holiday Climate Index (HCI) performance of urban and beach destinations in the Mediterranean. *Atmosphere*, 11(9), 911.

Deutsche Bank Research. (2008). *Climate change and tourism: Where will the journey take us?* Deutsche Bank Research.
Egan, P. J., & Mullin, M. (2012). Turning personal experience into political attitudes: The effect of local weather on Americans' perceptions about global warming. *Journal of Politics*, *74*(3), 796–809.
Eijgelaar, E., Thaper, C., & Peeters, P. (2010). Antarctic cruise tourism: The paradoxes of ambassadorship, "last chance tourism" and greenhouse gas emissions. *Journal of Sustainable Tourism*, *18*, 337–354.
European Environment Agency (EEA). (2014). *National adaptation policy processes in European countries: 2014*. EEA Report No 4/2014. EEA.
Gössling, S. (2013). National emissions from tourism: An overlooked policy challenge? *Energy Policy*, *59*, 433–442.
Gössling, S., Ceron, J.-P., Dubois, G., & Hall, C. M. (2009). Hypermobile travellers. In S. Gössling & P. Upham (Eds.), *Climate change and aviation*. Earthscan.
Gössling, S., & Hall, C. M. (2006). Uncertainties in predicting tourist travel flows based on models. *Climatic Change*, *79*, 163–173.
Gössling, S., Hultman, J., Haglund, L., Källgren, H., & Revahl, M. (2009). Voluntary carbon offsetting by Swedish air travellers: Towards the co-creation of environmental value? *Current Issues in Tourism*, *12*, 1–19.
Gössling, S., & Humpe, A. (2020). The global scale, distribution and growth of aviation: Implications for climate change. *Global Environmental Change*, *65*, 102194.
Gössling, S., Scott, D., & Hall, C. M. (2013). Challenges of tourism in a low-carbon economy. *WIRES Climate Change*, *4*(6), 525–538.
Gössling, S., Scott, D., & Hall, C. M. (2021). Pandemics, tourism and global change: A rapid assessment of COVID-19. *Journal of Sustainable Tourism*, *29*, 1–20.
Hall, C. M. (2008). Tourism and climate change: Knowledge gaps and issues. *Tourism Recreation Research*, *33*, 339–350.
Hall, C. M. (2010). Tourism and biodiversity: More significant than climate change? *Journal of Heritage Tourism*, *5*, 253–266.
Hall, C. M. (2011). Policy learning and policy failure in sustainable tourism governance: From first and second to third order change? *Journal of Sustainable Tourism*, *19*, 649–671.
Hall, C. M. (2015). On the mobility of tourism mobilities. *Current Issues in Tourism*, *18*(1), 7–10.
Hall, C. M. (2017). New Zealand: Planning responses to coastal climate change risks. In A. L. Jones & M. Phillips (Eds.), *Global climate change and coastal tourism: Recognizing problems, managing solutions and future expectations* (pp. 231–246). CABI.
Hall, C. M. (2019). Constructing sustainable tourism development: The 2030 agenda and the managerial ecology of sustainable tourism. *Journal of Sustainable Tourism*, *27*(7), 1044–1060.
Hall, C. M., Lundmark, L., & Zhang, J. (Eds.). (2021a). *Tourism and degrowth*. Routledge.
Hall, C. M., Lundmark, L., & Zhang, J. (2021b). Conclusions–degrowing tourism: Can tourism move beyond BAU (Brundtland-as-Usual)? In Hall, C. M., Lundmark, L., & Zhang, J. (Eds.), *Degrowth and tourism* (pp. 239–248). Routledge.
Hall, C. M., & Saarinen, J. (2020). 20 Years of Nordic climate change crisis and tourism research: A review and future research agenda. *Scandinavian Journal of Hospitality and Tourism*. https://doi.org/10.1080/15022250.2020.1823248
Hall, C. M., Scott, D., & Gössling, S. (2013). The primacy of climate change for sustainable international tourism. *Sustainable Development*, *21*(2), 112–121.

Hall, C. M., Scott, D., & Gössling, S. (2020). Pandemics, transformations and tourism: Be careful what you wish for. *Tourism Geographies*, *22*, 577–598.

Holling, C. S., Gunderson, L. H., & Peterson, G. D. (2002). Sustainability and panarchies. In L. H. Gundersson & C. S. Holling (Eds.), *Panarchy: Understanding transformations in human and natural systems* (pp. 63–102). Island Press.

Hoogendoorn, G., & Fitchett, J. M. (2018). Tourism and climate change: A review of threats and adaptation strategies for Africa. *Current Issues in Tourism*, *21*(7), 742–759.

Hoogendoorn, G., Stockigt, L., Saarinen, J., & Fitchett, J. M. (2021). Adapting to climate change: The case of snow-based tourism in Afriski, Lesotho. *African Geographical Review*, *40*(1), 92–104.

International Energy Agency (IEA). (2009). *Transport, energy and CO_2: Moving towards sustainability*. IEA.

IEA. (2020). *Aviation: More efforts needed: Tracking report June 2020*. IEA. www.iea.org/reports/aviation#acknowledgements

International Maritime Organization (IMO). (2009). *Climate change: A challenge for IMO too*! IMO.

IPCC. (2013a). *Climate change 2013: The physical science basis: Contribution of Working Group I to the fifth assessment report of the Intergovernmental Panel on Climate Change*. Cambridge University Press.

IPCC. (2013b). Summary for policymakers. In T. F. Stocker et al. (Eds.), *Climate change 2013: The physical science basis: Contribution of Working Group I to the fifth assessment report of the Intergovernmental Panel on Climate Change*. Cambridge University Press.

IPCC. (2014a). *Climate change 2014: Impacts, adaptation, and vulnerability*. Working Group II. IPCC. www.ipcc-wg2.gov/AR5/

IPCC. (2014b). Summary for policymakers. In *Climate change 2014: Mitigation of climate change*. Working Group III. IPCC. www.ipcc-wg2.gov/AR5/

IPCC. (2018). Summary for policymakers. In V. Masson-Delmotte et al. (Eds.), *Global Warming of 1.5°C: An IPCC Special Report on the impacts of global warming of 1.5°C above pre-industrial levels and related global greenhouse gas emission pathways, in the context of strengthening the global response to the threat of climate change, sustainable development, and efforts to eradicate poverty*. World Meteorological Organization.

Klint, L. M., Wong, E., Jiang, M., Delacy, T., Harrison, D., & Dominey-Howes, D. (2012). Climate change adaptation in the Pacific Island tourism sector: Analysing the policy environment in Vanuatu. *Current Issues in Tourism*, *15*(3), 247–274.

Knowles, N. L., & Scott, D. (2021). Media representations of climate change risk to ski tourism: A barrier to climate action? *Current Issues in Tourism*, *24*(2), 149–156.

KPMG. (2008). *Climate changes your business: KPMG's review of the business risks and economic impacts at sector level*. KPMG.

Lenzen, M., Sun, Y. Y., Faturay, F., Ting, Y. P., Geschke, A., & Malik, A. (2018). The carbon footprint of global tourism. *Nature Climate Change*, *8*(6), 522–528.

Martinez-Ibarra, E. (2011). The use of webcam images to determine tourist-climate aptitude: Favourable weather types for sun and beach tourism on the Alicante coast (Spain). *International Journal of Biometeorology*, *55*, 373–385.

Mora, C., Spirandelli, D., Franklin, E. C., Lynham, J., Kantar, M. B., Miles, W., & Barba, E. W. (2018). Broad threat to humanity from cumulative climate hazards intensified by greenhouse gas emissions. *Nature Climate Change*, *8*(12), 1062.

Pickering, C. (2011). Changes in demand for tourism with climate change: A case study of visitation patterns to six ski resorts in Australia. *Journal of Sustainable Tourism*, *19*, 767–781.

Scott, D., Hall, C. M., & Gössling, S. (2012). *Tourism and climate change: Impacts, adaptation and mitigation*. Routledge.
Scott, D., Hall, C. M., & Gössling, S. (2016a). A review of the IPCC fifth assessment and implications for tourism sector climate resilience and decarbonization. *Journal of Sustainable Tourism, 24*(1), 8–30.
Scott, D., Hall, C. M., & Gössling, S. (2016b). A report on the Paris climate change agreement and its implications for tourism: Why we will always have Paris. *Journal of Sustainable Tourism, 24*(7), 933–948.
Scott, D., Hall, C. M., & Gössling, S. (2019). Global tourism vulnerability to climate change. *Annals of Tourism Research, 77*, 49–61.
Scott, D., Simpson, M. C., & Sim, R. (2012). The vulnerability of Caribbean coastal tourism to scenarios of climate change related sea level rise. *Journal of Sustainable Tourism, 20*(6), 883–898.
Scott, D., Steiger, R., Dannevig, H., & Aall, C. (2020). Climate change and the future of the Norwegian Alpine ski industry. *Current Issues in Tourism, 23*, 2396–2409.
Spalding, M. D., Mcivor, A. L., Beck, M. W., Koch, E., Moller, I., Reed, D., et al. (2014). Coastal ecosystems: A critical element of risk reduction. *Conservation Letters, 7*, 293–301.
Tervo-Kankare, K., Hall, C. M., & Saarinen, J. (2013). Christmas tourists' perceptions of climate change in Rovaniemi, Finnish Lapland. *Tourism Geographies, 15*(2), 292–317.
Transport & Environment. (2020). *Aviation Covid recovery: Sustainability and resilience: A sustainable and secure future for aviation, June 2020*. Transport & Environment. www.transportenvironment.org/sites/te/files/publications/2020_06_Aviation_Covid_recovery_%20sustainability_resilience.pdf
Ummel, K. (2014). *Who pollutes? A household-level database of America's greenhouse gas footprint*. Center for Global Development Working Paper 381. Center for Global Development.
UNCTAD. (2010). *The contribution of tourism to trade and development*. 2010 Note by the UNCTAD Secretariat, TD /B/C.I/8. United Nations Conference on Trade and Development.
UNEP. (2011). *Towards a green economy: Pathways to sustainable development and poverty eradication*. Nairobi.
United Nations World Tourism Organization (UNWTO). (2006). *International tourist arrivals, tourism market trends, 2006 edition: Annex*. UNWTO.
United Nations World Tourism Organization, United Nations Environment Programme, and World Meterological Organization (UNWTO-UNEP-WMO). (2008). *Climate change and tourism: Responding to global challenges*. UNWTO.
United Nations World Tourism Organization (UNWTO) and United Nations Environment Program (UNEP). (2011). Tourism: Investing in the green economy. In UNEP, *Towards a green economy* (pp. 409–447). UNEP.
UNWTO. (2012). *UNWTO tourism highlights*. (2012 ed.). UNWTO.
UNWTO. (2014). *UNWTO tourism highlights*. (2014 ed.). UNWTO.
UNWTO. (2018). *Overtourism? Understanding and managing urban tourism growth beyond perceptions*. UNWTO.
UNWTO. (2020). *World Tourism Barometer, 18*(6).
UNWTO & UNDP. (2017). *Tourism and the sustainable development goals: Journey to 2030*. UNWTO.
Wong, P. P., Losada, I. J., Gattuso, J-P., Hinkel, J., Khattabi, A., McInnes, K. L., Saito, Y., & Sallenger, A. (2014). Coastal systems and low-lying areas. In C. B. Field et al. (Eds.), *Climate change 2014: Impacts, adaptation, and vulnerability: Part A: Global and*

sectoral aspects: Contribution of working group II to the fifth assessment report of the intergovernmental panel on climate change. Cambridge University Press.

World Economic Forum (WEF). (2009). *Towards a low carbon travel & tourism sector*. WEF.

World Meteorological Organization (WMO). (2020, November 23). *Carbon dioxide levels continue at record levels, despite COVID-19 lockdown*. WMO Press Release Number: 23112020. https://public.wmo.int/en/media/press-release/carbon-dioxide-levels-continue-record-levels-despoite-covid-19-lockdown

World Tourism Organisation (WTO). (1997). *Tourism 2020 vision*. WTO.

WTTC. (2017). *Coping with success*. McKinsey, www.wttc.org/-/media/files/reports/policy-research/coping-with-success–managing-overcrowding-in-tourism-destinations-2017.pdf

World Travel & Tourism Council (WTTC). (2020). *To recovery & beyond: The future of travel & tourism in the wake of COVID-19*. WTTC.

Zeppel, H. (2012). Climate change and tourism in the Great Barrier Reef Marine Park. *Current Issues in Tourism, 15*(3), 287–292.

3 The sharing economy and its implications for inclusive tourism

Christoph Lutz and Julijana Angelovska

Introduction

Sharing platforms allow individuals to share goods with each other in economic transactions mediated by the Internet (Gerwe & Silva, 2020). The sharing economy in this form is a modern phenomenon, affecting the global economy with exponential scale and attracting hundreds of millions in funding (Hamari, Sjöklint, & Ukkonen, 2016). In the European Union (EU), the size of the collaborative economy, which is the preferred term by the EU but largely synonymous with sharing economy, is estimated to be 26.5 billion Euro, providing jobs to 394,000 people (European Commission, 2018). A Eurobarometer study (2018), covering the EU 28 member states at the time, further found that 23% have used collaborative/sharing economy services, but only 4% are regular users. Moreover, the majority of the users are consumers and only 6% have used sharing economy platforms as providers.

At its core, the sharing economy promises a shift from an ownership-based economy to one that supports shared access, higher utilisation levels of existing but underutilised goods, and service exchanges that are otherwise hard to find on the market (Botsman & Rogers, 2010). Sharing initiatives include peer-to-peer accommodation (e.g., Airbnb), transportation services (e.g., BlaBlaCar), time banks, goods exchanges, and other forms of collaboration (Schor & Fitzmaurice, 2015). In this contribution, we will mostly focus on the sectors of the sharing economy that relate to tourism, especially peer-to-peer accommodation. Other areas of the sharing economy, such as goods exchanges and peer-to-peer lending, tend to occur in neighbourhoods or in local contexts but are not as tied to tourism – and potentially less dependent on it – as peer-to-peer accommodation. Tourism-oriented areas of the sharing economy come with partly different dynamics and issues, relating more strongly to emerging transformations. We will discuss some of these dynamics later. However, a clear distinction between tourism-oriented sharing economy and non-tourism-oriented sharing economy is sometimes difficult. For example, sharing economy platforms in the transportation sector, such as Uber and Lyft, cater to locals and tourists alike.

DOI: 10.4324/9781003105930-4

The sharing economy can promote factors central to the United Nations SDGs, such as economic growth, technological innovation, environmental sustainability, and social inclusion. Heinrichs (2013) discusses how the sharing economy can be a pathway for sustainability. In environmental terms, it promises increased resource efficiency and less environmentally harmful hyper-consumption. In social and cultural terms, the sharing economy reflects a more conscious and self-sufficient consumer habitus, characterised by access rather than ownership, and by citizen empowerment.

> The sharing economy is presented as necessary and desirable . . . on the grounds that it: offers a pathway to a 'new economy' built around concern for people and the environment; and, is driven by the values of liberty, democracy, social justice and environmental justice.
> (Martin, 2016, p. 154)

Thus, the sharing economy connects to and potentially helps address key emerging transformations such as climate change, mounting economic inequality, changed consumption patterns, and the digital transformation.

However, the sharing economy also comes with considerable challenges. Critical research has stressed that the sharing economy operates in a legal grey area and exploits regulatory loopholes (Calo & Rosenblat, 2017; Newlands & Lutz, 2020), disrupts neighbourhoods through the displacement of long-term tenants and gentrification (Wachsmuth & Weisler, 2018), and is an elite phenomenon that mostly benefits privileged groups (Schor et al., 2016). Thus, initial optimism towards the sharing economy has increasingly given way to more sobering accounts (Murillo, Buckland, & Val, 2017). Rather than promoting environmental and social sustainability, the sharing economy, especially in its commercial versions, might exacerbate the problematic effects of emerging transformations. For example, Al Balawi et al. (2020) found that the market entry of UberX in major US cities led to an increase, rather than a reduction, of gas emissions. In this contribution, we focus on the inclusivity of the sharing economy and discuss its openness and potential for inclusive tourism. Particularly, we approach the following questions: *How inclusive is the sharing economy in terms of its demographic and psychological composition? What implications does this have for inclusive tourism? What role should the sharing economy play in advancing inclusive tourism in the future?*

Existing research has shown that the adoption of sharing economy applications is unevenly spread throughout the population (Andreotti et al., 2017; Smith, 2016). Thus, the sharing economy might exacerbate existing inequalities in tourism rather than promoting inclusive tourism. We situate our contribution in the emerging literature on inclusive tourism, (Scheyvens & Biddulph, 2018), contributing to this novel strand of literature. We also embed the analysis in discourses on emerging transformations and sustainability.

Literature review

Inclusive tourism and its relation to the sharing economy

Inclusive tourism: overview

Inclusive tourism is defined as 'transformative tourism in which marginalized groups are engaged in ethical production or consumption of tourism and the sharing of its benefits' (Scheyvens & Biddulph, 2018, p. 592). From a normative standpoint, inclusiveness should be a core value of tourism and existing tourism often focuses on the middle and upper classes, framing tourism as something exclusive rather than inclusive (Biddulph & Scheyvens, 2018). Inclusive tourism goes beyond other prominent concepts in tourism such as accessible tourism (which is about reducing barriers for differently abled individuals), responsible tourism, community-oriented tourism, and pro-poor tourism (Scheyvens & Biddulph, 2018). The focus of inclusive tourism on marginalised groups implies a broad take on social inclusion that attempts to address SDG 10 Reduced Inequalities in particular. People can be excluded from social and economic life based on age, gender, ethnicity, socio-economic status, disability, area of residence, and other criteria, as well as combinations thereof. Inclusive tourism tries to foster the participation of marginalised groups from a holistic perspective. While including marginalised groups more in the consumption of tourism is an important part, other elements of inclusive tourism focus on the production (marginalised groups as tourism producers), the policies (more participatory tourism decision-making), and geographic diversity (new places and people).

Inclusive tourism touches on different emerging transformations in tourism more generally. For example, it relates to the ongoing digital transformation in tourism, specifically during the COVID-19 pandemic, where international travel has become severely restricted or impossible for many citizens. In this situation, tourism providers have shifted to digital experiences that can cater to broader audiences and are more accessible than normal travel. For example, national tourist bodies such as the German National Tourist Board and Tourism Ireland now offer immersive virtual reality tours (Debusmann Jr., 2020). Inclusive tourism also relates to environmental transitions, particularly climate change. Here, the policy aspects are particularly important, as a more diverse set of voices in decision-making processes around tourism could lead to novel ideas that promote environmental sustainability. In the following, however, our focus will be mostly on social inclusivity rather than environmental sustainability.

Inclusive tourism and the sharing economy

The sharing economy has potential to foster inclusive tourism on the consumption and production side. On the consumption side, lower prices and increased convenience are potentially attractive to less resourceful individuals. On the production side, the low thresholds of becoming a provider (e.g., on Airbnb) make participation for extra income attractive, something which might be particularly tempting for those who struggle to make ends meet. However, trust-related barriers such as privacy and security concerns (Lutz et al., 2018), the need to have a credit card for some of the platforms (Dillahunt & Malone, 2015), and the awareness and digital skills needed to use sharing platforms inhibit participation on the consumer side and make the sharing economy less inclusive. Similarly, on the provider side, owning assets in attractive tourist locations, having the necessary time to devote for self-branding, and having the cultural or social capital to accommodate consumers and their desires (and thus receive higher ratings) all favour privileged individuals, inhibiting inclusive tourism. These factors are likely to be exacerbated by the COVID-19 pandemic. While the pandemic affects all levels of society, emerging research shows that disadvantaged population groups (e.g., those with racial minority status, working class citizens, factory workers, and prisoners) suffer disproportionally from the pandemic (Mikolai, Keenan, & Kulu, 2020).

Factors explaining participation in the sharing economy

Research on digital inequalities is helpful to conceptualise how participation in online services is socially structured. Digital inequalities research includes the study of differences in access to digital technology (Robinson, 2009), skills or literacy (Hargittai, 2010), uses (Zillien & Hargittai, 2009), and outcomes in the form of benefits and harms from Internet use (Blank & Lutz, 2018). Such research has stressed the importance of socio-economic antecedents for participation, discussing the role of gender, education, and income, and how they reflect structural inequalities (Hargittai & Walejko, 2008; Hoffmann, Lutz, & Meckel, 2015; Lutz, 2016).

Demographic predictors

AGE

Age is inversely associated with sharing economy participation, so that younger individuals are most likely to engage in the sharing economy (Eurobarometer, 2016; Smith, 2016; Yang, Tan, & Li, 2019). In Europe, individuals aged 25–29 are most familiar with the sharing economy (PWC, 2016). Similarly, Smith (2016) found that a third of US-based respondents in the 18–45 age group had used a sharing economy platform in the past. Studies specifically on millennials underline the role of the sharing economy among younger individuals in particular (Amaro, Andreu, & Huang, 2019; Ranzini et al., 2017). Many sharing economy services seem to target millennials specifically with narratives of flexibility, ease of access, and authenticity (Bucher et al., 2018).

> *H1. Age negatively affects the likelihood of sharing economy participation.*

GENDER

Compared with age, the association between gender and sharing economy participation is less straightforward. In Europe, women are less familiar with the concept than men (Eurobarometer, 2016). While 48% of women had never heard of sharing platforms, only 43% of men had never heard of them. In the US, no significant gender differences in sharing economy participation exist (Smith, 2016). Looking beyond participation, gender roles seem to be perpetuated in the sharing economy. Schor et al. (2016), for instance, compared four sharing economy contexts (makerspaces, education/start-up initiative, food swap, and time bank) and found male overrepresentation in the makerspace and start-up case and female overrepresentation in the food swap and time bank case. Given our understanding of the sharing economy here that excludes makerspaces, time banks, and start-up initiatives, we refrain from stating a clear directionality in the hypothesis.

H2. Gender affects the likelihood of sharing economy participation.

EDUCATION

Education is an important predictor of sharing economy participation, as the sharing economy seems to cater strongly to educated people. Representative studies have found that individuals with higher levels of education are more likely to participate in the sharing economy (Eurobarometer, 2016; Smith, 2016) and education strongly influences both paid and unpaid uses. Beyond being a driver of participation, Cansoy and Schor (2016) suggest that success among sharing economy participants also depends on education. In their geographic analysis of Airbnb, areas with higher education levels correlated with more offers, more user reviews, and higher prices.

H3. Education positively affects the likelihood of sharing economy participation.

INCOME

In line with education, income is positively associated with sharing economy participation (Smith, 2016). In the US, individuals with a household income of more than 75,000 USD are most likely to rely on car-sharing and home-sharing platforms. In this income group, one-fourth have participated in the sharing economy, but in the lowest category (< 30,000 USD), only 4% had done so. Providers use sharing economy platforms such as Airbnb for extra income (Schor, 2017). While education seems to be a door opener for sharing economy participation in general, income and wealth – especially the availability of lettable capacities – favour providers on asset-oriented platforms such as Airbnb (Newlands, Lutz, & Fieseler, 2018). Consequently, those with less income and wealth migrate to labour-oriented areas of the sharing economy (e.g., crowdwork), where less economic capital is needed, but the economic gains are lower. In line with the findings about education, Cansoy and Schor (2016) show how higher income areas in the US come with higher prices.

> H4. Income positively affects the likelihood of sharing economy participation.

HOUSEHOLD SIZE

Little research has looked into aspects such as family composition and household size when studying the sharing economy. As an exception, Lutz and Newlands (2018) found no significant effect of living with children in the household for booking shared rooms. However, for entire homes, respondents with children in the household reported significantly lower participation. Guttentag et al. (2018) found one cluster of Airbnb users that is less likely to stay with children (money savers) and one that is more likely to stay with children (home seekers). Unfortunately, we did not find studies that control for household size. However, given the previous findings and the fact that booking sharing economy transactions seems tailored towards individual users – rather than users-by-proxy (Newlands, Lutz, & Hoffmann, 2018) – we hypothesise a negative association between household size and sharing economy participation.

> H5. Household size negatively affects the likelihood of sharing economy participation.

Psychological predictors

TRUST

The sharing economy involves transactions between strangers. Thus, it comes with reliability, security, safety, and privacy risks (Lutz et al., 2018). In the absence of personal bonds, trust becomes a key issue (Botsman & Rogers, 2010). In a widely used definition, trust has been conceptualised as the 'willingness of a party to be vulnerable to the actions of another party based on the expectation that the other will perform a particular action important to the trustor' (Mayer, Davis, & Schoorman, 1995, p. 715). Previous research has stressed how trust can address perceived vulnerabilities in the sharing economy (Dillahunt & Malone, 2015; Lampinen, Huotari, & Cheshire, 2015). A systematic literature review on trust and the sharing economy identified key antecedents such as reputation and interaction experience (Ter Huurne et al., 2017). The study also showed how most research has focused on trust in the provider, with less research interest in trust in the platform or consumer. Other work has explored how 'trust in strangers' affects participation in the sharing economy by low-income communities (Dillahunt & Malone, 2015).

> H6. Trust positively affects the likelihood of sharing economy participation.

INNOVATIVENESS

Sharing economy participation is characterised as innovative (Botsman & Rogers, 2010). Hence, participation in the sharing economy can be associated with personal innovativeness, which describes how willing individuals are to try out new things such as technologies, ideas, and products (Agarwal & Prasad, 1998). Indeed, the management and marketing literature stresses the importance of lead users as a valuable resource for the diffusion of new products and services (Von Hippel, 1986). Following diffusion of innovations theory (Rogers & Shoemaker, 1971), some consumers perceive the need for new products earlier than others and expect higher benefits, leading them to adopt earlier (Urban & Von Hippel, 1988). Similarly, participants in the sharing economy can be seen as early adopters and are expected to be more innovative. San-Martín and Herrero (2012) find that innovativeness in ICT influences travellers' intention to make a reservation for rural accommodations online.

H7. Innovativeness positively affects the likelihood of sharing economy participation.

MATERIALISM

Bucher, Fieseler, and Lutz (2016) studied the influence of materialism on sharing economy motivation. Based on previous research on materialism (Richins & Dawson, 1992), they found that materialism is positively associated with financial motivations for participating in the sharing economy. Financial motivations, in turn, are associated with positive attitudes towards the sharing economy and eventually sharing intention. Given that financial motivations have been identified as a key driver of sharing economy participation (Hawlitschek, Teubner, & Gimpel, 2018) and a positive connection between materialism and financial motivations has been established, we hypothesise a positive relationship between materialism and sharing economy participation. Davidson, Habibi, and Laroche (2018) corroborated this at first sight counterintuitive finding across two cultural contexts (US and India). Accordingly, we formulate our next hypothesis.

H8. Materialism positively affects the likelihood of sharing economy participation.

VOLUNTEERING

Volunteering, as a prosocial behaviour related to helpfulness and empathy (Penner & Finkelstein, 1998), positively affects moral motivations but not monetary and social motivations (Bucher, Fieseler, & Lutz, 2016). Thus, sharing economy participants who do volunteer work and get involved in the community are more likely to have moral motivations for sharing, which, in turn, results in more positive attitudes towards the sharing economy and intention. Given the community-oriented nature of the sharing economy, particularly in its early days, we hypothesise a positive association between volunteering and sharing economy participation.

> *H9. Volunteering positively affects the likelihood of sharing economy participation.*

Digital skills and frequency of online search

DIGITAL SKILLS

Digital inequalities research has stressed the importance of digital skills, finding that such skills are unevenly distributed in society (Litt, 2013). We are not aware of studies that have looked into skills specifically for sharing platforms, so that we draw on research about more general skills for online participation (e.g., Van Deursen, Helsper, & Eynon, 2015). Litt's (2013) review shows how previous research has been more interested in antecedents of digital skills than outcomes, but the studies on outcomes tend to find positive associations between skills and outcome variables such as privacy protection behaviour, Internet use, and academic performance. Given that the sharing economy is a relatively new phenomenon and participation requires overcoming some skills threshold, we postulate a positive association between skills and sharing economy participation.

> *H10. Digital skills positively affect the likelihood of sharing economy participation.*

ONLINE SEARCH FREQUENCY

In addition to access and digital skills, Internet use has been in the spotlight of digital inequalities research. Again, substantial differences between population groups exist in terms of the type and variety of online activities (Blank & Groselj, 2014). A key finding is that individuals who are privileged in socio-economic terms tend to use the Internet more for capital-enhancing and information-rich activities such as political news consumption (Zillien & Hargittai, 2009). Less privileged users, by contrast, tend to prefer recreational uses such as entertainment. The sharing economy reflects these patterns. In Europe, a Eurobarometer study (2016) shows how 'occasional use' is the predominant mode of engagement, with only 4% of users engaging at least monthly. Sharing economy participation is a capital-enhancing and information-rich type of Internet use, connected to e-commerce. Given the digitally mediated nature of the sharing economy, Internet use in general and online search in particular should positively predict participation.

> *H11. Frequency of online search positively affects the likelihood of sharing economy participation.*

Methods

Data and sample

The research uses a large survey in 12 European countries on the sharing economy (Andreotti et al., 2017). The survey was conducted in summer 2017 by a consortium of international researchers and explored the prevalence, antecedents, and outcomes of participation, privacy, and power in the European sharing economy. It involved more than 6,000 participants across the following 12 countries (Andreotti et al., 2017): Denmark, Germany, France, Ireland, Italy, the Netherlands, Norway, Poland, Portugal, Spain, Switzerland, and United Kingdom. While the researchers designed, programmed, and translated the questionnaire, a leading ESOMAR-certified market research company (Ipsos MORI UK) managed the participant recruitment. This collaboration ensured access to their panel and allowed for representative quotas on gender, age (18–65), area of residence, and working status. The respondents were divided into users, who were further categorised into providers and consumers, and non-users, who were further categorised into aware and non-aware non-users. In this study, the respondents are divided into users (providers and consumers) and non-users (aware and non-aware non-users) as the dichotomous dependent variable. Table A in Appendix 3.1 shows the demographic composition of the sample.

Measures

We used established measure for the independent constructs whenever possible. We included age in years, gender, household size, education based on the International Standard Classification of Education (ISCED) categories, and yearly gross household income in four categories as independent demographic variables. For income, we originally used between 13 and 17 relatively narrow categories in the respective local currencies in the survey, subsequently grouping the respondents based on the distribution and their distance from the mean in standard deviations for each country. This resulted in the four categories described earlier.

Trust, innovativeness, materialism, and volunteering were included as psychological variables. Trust was measured based on the general disposition to trust, as per the scale of McKnight, Choudhury, and Kacmar (2002). For technology innovativeness, we adopted the scale by Agarwal and Prasad (1998). To measure materialism and volunteering, we relied on the scales from Bucher, Fieseler, and Lutz (2016). All these scales showed high loadings and good measurement properties (Table 3.1).

To assess respondents' digital skills, we used the short version of the scale developed by Hargittai (2009). Table 3.1 shows summary statistics for each item. Finally, frequency of online search was measured with four items (frequency of looking for news, looking for travel information, looking for jobs, and getting product information).

Data analysis

We used two multivariate methods to analyse the data. First, principal component analysis (PCA) was conducted to reduce the number of variables. PCA was also used to determine the underlying structure of self-reported psychological variables and skills. To test convergent and discriminant validity, we relied on a PCA with Varimax rotation. All items had high loadings (above 0.50) on the intended factors, and all the constructs had a Cronbach's α value equal to or greater than 0.65, thus supporting convergent validity of the scales. Second, logistic regression was employed to find the predictive influence of the independent variables on sharing economy participation.

Results

Table 3.1 shows descriptive statistics in the form of arithmetic means and standard deviations of the independent variables that were extracted in the PCAs. The variables that had factor loadings below 0.5 were excluded.

Table 3.1 Descriptive statistics and PCA results

Factor/Cronbach's α	Variables	Mean	St Dev.	Loadings
Digital Skills/0.904	Advanced search	3.32	1.31	0.778
	PDF	3.75	1.24	0.723
	Spyware	2.83	1.38	0.854
	Wiki	2.94	1.48	0.773
	Cache	2.68	1.43	0.833
	Phishing	2.75	1.41	0.830
Innovativeness/0.902	Look for ways to experiment	3.21	1.16	0.845
	The first to try out	2.87	1.22	0.805
	Like to experiment	3.43	1.15	0.842
Trust/0.885	General trust in people	3.35	1.02	0.893
	General faith in humanity	3.34	1.01	0.868
	General reliability of people	3.29	1.00	0.899
Volunteering/0.826	Volunteering to help	2.57	1.32	0.813
	Getting involved in issues	2.68	1.22	0.823
	Working with a group to solve a problem	2.36	1.20	0.856
Online search/0.650	Look for news	4.73	1.30	0.635
	Look for travel information	2.92	1.27	0.715
	Look for jobs	2.45	1.55	0.575
	Get product information	3.79	1.24	0.704
Materialism/0.741	Happier if I could afford more	3.32	1.19	0.747
	Like a lot of luxury	2.70	1.17	0.795
	Admire people with expensive things	2.48	1.19	0.831

Note: $N = 6{,}111$, minimum 1, maximum 5

Table 3.2 shows the results of the logistic regression analysis. Except for gender, all demographic variables are statistically significant predictors ($p < 0.01$) of participation in the sharing economy. Hypotheses 1, 3, 4, and 5 are therefore supported. More specifically, respondents younger than 45 (H1) and in smaller households (H5) have a higher likelihood of using sharing economy platforms. The probability of being a sharing economy user increases with higher income, above the first quartile (H4), and higher levels of education, above primary school (H3). Gender is not a significant predictor for participation in the sharing economy (H2).

Psychological factors like trust, innovativeness, and materialism predict sharing economy participation in varied ways. Trust (H6) is not a statistically significant predictor of sharing economy participation and neither are innovativeness (H7) and materialism (H8). Only volunteering is a statistically significant predictor for participation (H9).

Digital skills and frequency of online search are important predictors for sharing economy participation. Respondents with self-reported higher digital skills and searching for information about news, jobs, products, and travel more frequently are more likely to be users in the sharing economy. Hypotheses 10 and 11 are supported.

Discussion

What do these findings tell us about inclusive tourism and the potential of the sharing economy for opening up tourism for broader groups in the future? We would argue that the unequal patterns in terms of participation in the sharing economy are not very surprising but a cause for concern. The study design did not allow for a clear demarcation of whether the use was primarily touristic or not, so that our interpretation has to be taken with caution. Nevertheless, our findings paint a picture of uneven participation. Individuals younger than 45, with education higher than primary school, with income higher than the first quartile, with

Table 3.2 Logistic regression

	B	S.E.	Sig.	Exp(B)
Age	−0.390	0.026	0.000	0.677
Gender	0.018	0.064	0.775	1.019
Income	0.155	0.032	0.000	1.168
Household size	−0.065	0.025	0.010	0.937
Education	0.273	0.031	0.000	1.314
Trust	0.000	0.034	0.995	1.000
Innovativeness	0.016	0.036	0.653	1.016
Materialism	0.003	0.034	0.939	1.003
Digital skills	0.254	0.035	0.000	1.289
Volunteering	0.237	0.031	0.000	1.267
Online search	0.299	0.038	0.000	1.349
Constant	−4.248	0.266	0.000	0.014

higher self-reported digital skills, who like to voluntarily help others, and who are searching for information frequently, are more likely to participate in the sharing economy. In turn, those less privileged in terms of their social position have lower chances to be sharing economy participants. The findings should be contrasted to general tourism participation. While general tourism seems most prevalent among privileged groups (Scheyvens & Biddulph, 2018), certain forms of tourism such as visiting friends and family have a more inclusive profile (Backer & King, 2017). We have brought up aspects of the sharing economy that could make the sharing economy particularly attractive for marginalised groups (convenience, flexibility, and lower prices) and some that might inhibit participation among such groups (trust, financial requirements such as a credit card ownership, digital skills, and online habitus). The absence of trust, innovativeness, and materialism as significant predictors can be interpreted as a good sign for inclusive tourism, but the significance of digital skills and online search indicates that the sharing economy caters strongly to digitally-savvy citizens. These findings show a mixed picture of the potential of the sharing economy for inclusive tourism. However, with the push for digitalisation in the wake of the COVID-19 pandemic, more individuals are likely to acquaint themselves with digital services, which might promote sharing economy participation in a post-COVID-19 world – granted that the commonly used sharing platforms survive, given their current struggles (Farmaki et al., 2020; Newlands & Lutz, 2020).

Our findings offer some insights for research on emerging transformations in tourism, especially when it comes to sustainability-related aspects. While environmental sustainability was not the focus of our study, certain implications about social sustainability become visible. Socially sustainable tourism needs to be able to positively transform the livelihoods of those involved, in the long run. Our analyses show that this promise might not hold – especially not for commercial services such as Airbnb, which were the most widely used ones. Despite marked growth in the years leading up to the pandemic, sharing economy platforms are still a minority phenomenon (Eurobarometer, 2018). Our analysis has shown that they cater especially to technologically savvy, young, and educated milieus. To reach beyond these circles, sharing economy platforms will need to come up with more inclusive and sustainable business models that offer value for broader audiences, including those marginalised in society. Initial observations indicate that sharing economy services are adapting to emerging transformations. Airbnb, for example, organised free or subsidised housing for healthcare workers in the wake of the COVID-19 pandemic (Ledsom, 2020).

Our research can help policy makers and platform managers support broader participation in the sharing economy, thus enabling inclusive tourism. Particularly, supporting digital skills and a culture of volunteering seem promising avenues for increasing the inclusivity of sharing economy services. The positive effect of online search shows that more information-driven Internet users are more likely to participate in the sharing economy. Thus, creating curiosity and an information-oriented habitus are promising strategies for fostering more widespread participation in the sharing economy. However, given the structural barriers (income and education both being significant predictors), sharing economy services should think about lowering prices and reducing access barriers through a more inclusive design.

Conclusion

In this chapter, we looked at the sharing economy in Europe as an emerging transformation that has important implications for tourism, for example, in the form of peer-to-peer accommodation (Airbnb). Building on the concept of inclusive tourism (Scheyvens & Biddulph, 2018), we investigated the inclusivity of the sharing economy in 12 European countries. We developed a model with 11 hypotheses that cover demographic and psychological predictors as well as information-habitus predictors (digital skills and frequency of online search). Using PCA and logistical regression, we found that lower age, higher education and income, more volunteering, more digital skills, and more frequent information search all predicted sharing economy participation significantly and in the expected direction. Thus, the sharing economy seems to leave out many segments of the broader population, especially under-privileged groups.

Our study comes with limitations that offer follow-up opportunities for future research on the sharing economy, inclusive tourism, and emerging transformations. First, our survey is cross-sectional and does not allow strong causal claims. Future research should use longitudinal data to study adoption over time. Second, despite featuring a multi-country survey, we could not do justice to cultural differences in sharing economy adoption. Future research should use a cross-cultural lens to compare adoption across countries and cities. Third, the survey data used here rely on a multitude of theories and frameworks to derive antecedents. This prevents the test of a specific social theory. Future research might want to specifically operationalise an existing model or theory and could connect the research more strongly to discourses on emerging transformations in tourism such as the digital transformation and environmental sustainability. In that sense, our study is exploratory but offers guidance for future research.

References

Agarwal, R., & Prasad, J. (1998). A conceptual and operational definition of personal innovativeness in the domain of information technology. *Information Systems Research*, 9(2), 204–215. https://doi.org/10.1287/isre.9.2.204

Al Balawi, R., Basak, E., Tafti, A., & Watson-Manheim, M. B. (2020). Ride-sharing services and environmental sustainability: An empirical investigation of UberX entry and gas emissions. In *Proceedings of the Americas Conference on Information Systems (AMCIS), Green IS and Sustainability (SIGGREEN) track (paper 11)*. Atlanta, GA: Association for Information Systems. Retrieved from https://aisel.aisnet.org/amcis2020/sig_green/sig_green/11

Amaro, S., Andreu, L., & Huang, S. (2019). Millenials' intentions to book on Airbnb. *Current Issues in Tourism*, 22(18), 2284–2298. https://doi.org/10.1080/13683500.2018.1448368

Andreotti, A., Anselmi, G., Eichhorn, T., Hoffmann, C. P., Jürss, S., & Micheli, M. (2017). European perspectives on participation in the sharing economy. *SSRN Electronic Journal*. Retrieved from https://papers.ssrn.com/sol3/papers.cfm?abstract_id=3046550

Backer, E., & King, B. (2017). VFR traveller demographics: The social tourism dimension. *Journal of Vacation Marketing, 23*(3), 191–204. https://doi.org/10.1177/1356766716665439

Biddulph, R., & Scheyvens, R. (2018). Introducing inclusive tourism. *Tourism Geographies, 20*(4), 583–588. https://doi.org/10.1080/14616688.2018.1486880

Blank, G., & Groselj, D. (2014). Dimensions of internet use: Amount, variety, and types. *Information, Communication & Society, 17*(4), 417–435. https://doi.org/10.1080/1369118X.2014.889189

Blank, G., & Lutz, C. (2018). Benefits and harms from internet use: A differentiated analysis of Great Britain. *New Media & Society, 20*(2), 618–640. https://doi.org/10.1177/1461444816667135

Botsman, R., & Rogers, R. (2010). *What's mine is yours: How collaborative consumption is changing the way we live*. New York, NY: HarperCollins.

Bucher, E., Fieseler, C., Fleck, M., & Lutz, C. (2018). Authenticity and the sharing economy. *Academy of Management Discoveries, 4*(3), 294–313. https://doi.org/10.5465/amd.2016.0161

Bucher, E., Fieseler, C., & Lutz, C. (2016). What's mine is yours (for a nominal fee): Exploring the spectrum of utilitarian to altruistic motives for Internet-mediated sharing. *Computers in Human Behavior, 62*, 316–326. https://doi.org/10.1016/j.chb.2016.04.002

Calo, R., & Rosenblat, A. (2017). The taking economy: Uber, information, and power. *Columbia Law Review, 117*(6), 1623–1690. Retrieved from https://live-columbia-law-review.pantheonsite.io/content/the-taking-economy-uber-information-and-power/

Cansoy, M., & Schor, J. (2016). *Who gets to share in the "sharing economy": Understanding the patterns of participation and exchange in Airbnb*. Boston College Working Paper. Retrieved from www.bc.edu/content/dam/files/schools/cas_sites/sociology/pdf/SharingEconomy.pdf

Davidson, A., Habibi, M. R., & Laroche, M. (2018). Materialism and the sharing economy: A cross-cultural study of American and Indian consumers. *Journal of Business Research, 82*, 364–372. https://doi.org/10.1016/j.jbusres.2015.07.045

Debusmann Jr., B. (2020, October 30). Coronavirus: Is virtual reality tourism about to take off? *BBC*. Retrieved from www.bbc.com/news/business-54658147

Dillahunt, T. R., & Malone, A. R. (2015). The promise of the sharing economy among disadvantaged communities. In *CHI'15: Proceedings of the 33rd Annual ACM Conference on Human Factors in Computing Systems* (pp. 2285–2294). New York, NY: ACM. https://doi.org/10.1145/2702123.2702189

Eurobarometer. (2016). *The use of collaborative platforms: Flash Eurobarometer: Vol. 438*. Retrieved from http://ec.europa.eu/COMMFrontOffice/publicopinion/index.cfm/Survey/getSurveyDetail/instruments/FLASH/surveyKy/2112

Eurobarometer. (2018). *The use of the collaborative economy: Flash Eurobarometer* (Vol. 467). Retrieved from https://ec.europa.eu/commfrontoffice/publicopinion/index.cfm/Survey/getSurveyDetail/instruments/FLASH/surveyKy/2184

European Commission. (2018). Study to monitor the economic development of the collaborative economy at sector level in the 28 EU member states. *Publications Office of the EU*. Retrieved from https://op.europa.eu/en/publication-detail/-/publication/0cc9aab6-7501-11e8-9483-01aa75ed71a1

Farmaki, A., Miguel, C., Drotarova, M. H., Aleksić, A., Časni, A. Č., & Efthymiadou, F. (2020). Impacts of Covid-19 on peer-to-peer accommodation platforms: Host perceptions and responses. *International Journal of Hospitality Management*, *91*, 102663. https://doi.org/10.1016/j.ijhm.2020.102663

Gerwe, O., & Silva, R. (2020). Clarifying the sharing economy: Conceptualization, typology, antecedents, and effects. *Academy of Management Perspectives*, *34*(1), 65–96. https://doi.org/10.5465/amp.2017.0010

Guttentag, D., Smith, S., Potwarka, L., & Havitz, M. (2018). Why tourists choose Airbnb: A motivation-based segmentation study. *Journal of Travel Research*, *57*(3), 342–359. https://doi.org/10.1177/0047287517696980

Hamari, J., Sjöklint, M., & Ukkonen, A. (2016). The sharing economy: Why people participate in collaborative consumption. *Journal of the Association for Information Science and Technology*, *67*(9), 2047–2059. https://doi.org/10.1002/asi.23552

Hargittai, E. (2009). An update on survey measures of web-oriented digital literacy. *Social Science Computer Review*, *27*(1), 130–137. https://doi.org/10.1177/0894439308318213

Hargittai, E. (2010). Digital na(t)ives? Variation in internet skills and uses among members of the "net generation". *Sociological Inquiry*, *80*(1), 92–113. https://doi.org/10.1111/j.1475-682X.2009.00317.x

Hargittai, E., & Walejko, G. (2008). The participation divide: Content creation and sharing in the digital age. *Information, Communication & Society*, *11*(2), 239–256. https://doi.org/10.1080/13691180801946150

Hawlitschek, F., Teubner, T., & Gimpel, H. (2018). Consumer motives for peer-to-peer sharing. *Journal of Cleaner Production*, *204*, 144–157. https://doi.org/10.1016/j.jclepro.2018.08.326

Heinrichs, H. (2013). Sharing economy: A potential new pathway to sustainability. *GAIA-Ecological Perspectives for Science and Society*, *22*(4), 228–231. https://doi.org/10.14512/gaia.22.4.5

Hoffmann, C. P., Lutz, C., & Meckel, M. (2015). Content creation on the internet: A social cognitive perspective on the participation divide. *Information, Communication & Society*, *18*(6), 696–716. https://doi.org/10.1080/1369118X.2014.991343

Lampinen, A., Huotari, K. J. E., & Cheshire, C. (2015). Challenges to participation in the sharing economy: The case of local online peer-to-peer exchange in a single parents' network. *Interaction Design and Architecture(s)*, *24*, 16–32. Retrieved from www.mifav.uniroma2.it/inevent/events/idea2010/doc/24_1.pdf

Ledsom, A. (2020, April 2). Airbnb offers a way to provide free housing to healthcare professionals and payouts to reimburse hosts. *Forbes*. Retrieved from www.forbes.com/sites/alexledsom/2020/04/02/airbnb-offers-a-way-to-provide-free-housing-to-healthcare-professionals-and-payouts-to-reimburse-hosts/

Litt, E. (2013). Measuring users' internet skills: A review of past assessments and a look toward the future. *New Media & Society*, *15*(4), 612–630. https://doi.org/10.1177/1461444813475424

Lutz, C. (2016). A social milieu approach to the online participation divides in Germany. *Social Media + Society*, *2*(1), 1–14. https://doi.org/10.1177/2056305115626749

Lutz, C., Hoffmann, C. P., Bucher, E., & Fieseler, C. (2018). The role of privacy concerns in the sharing economy. *Information, Communication & Society*, *21*(10), 1472–1492. https://doi.org/10.1080/1369118X.2017.1339726

Lutz, C., & Newlands, G. (2018). Consumer segmentation within the sharing economy: The case of Airbnb. *Journal of Business Research*, *88*, 187–196. https://doi.org/10.1016/j.jbusres.2018.03.019

Martin, C. J. (2016). The sharing economy: A pathway to sustainability or a nightmarish form of neoliberal capitalism? *Ecological Economics*, *121*, 149–159. https://doi.org/10.1016/j.ecolecon.2015.11.027

Mayer, R. C., Davis, J. H., & Schoorman, F. D. (1995). An integrative model of organizational trust. *Academy of Management Review*, *20*(3), 709–734. https://doi.org/10.5465/amr.1995.9508080335

McKnight, D. H., Choudhury, V., & Kacmar, C. (2002). Developing and validating trust measures for e-commerce: An integrative typology. *Information Systems Research*, *13*(3), 334–359. https://doi.org/10.1287/isre.13.3.334.81

Mikolai, J., Keenan, K., & Kulu, H. (2020). Intersecting household-level health and socioeconomic vulnerabilities and the COVID-19 crisis: An analysis from the UK. *SSM-Population Health*, *12*, 100628. https://doi.org/10.1016/j.ssmph.2020.100628

Murillo, D., Buckland, H., & Val, E. (2017). When the sharing economy becomes neoliberalism on steroids: Unravelling the controversies. *Technological Forecasting and Social Change*, *125*, 66–76. https://doi.org/10.1016/j.techfore.2017.05.024

Newlands, G., & Lutz, C. (2020). Fairness, legitimacy and the regulation of home-sharing platforms. *International Journal of Contemporary Hospitality Management*, *32*(10), 3177–3197. https://doi.org/10.1108/IJCHM-08-2019-0733

Newlands, G., Lutz, C., & Fieseler, C. (2018). Collective action and provider classification in the sharing economy. *New Technology, Work and Employment*, *33*(3), 250–267. https://doi.org/10.1111/ntwe.12119

Newlands, G., Lutz, C., & Hoffmann, C. P. (2018). Sharing by proxy: Invisible users in the sharing economy. *First Monday*, *23*(11). https://doi.org/10.5210/fm.v23i11.8159

Penner, L. A., & Finkelstein, M. A. (1998). Dispositional and structural determinants of volunteerism. *Journal of Personality and Social Psychology*, *74*(2), 525–537. https://doi.org/10.1037/0022-3514.74.2.525

PWC. (2016). *Assessing the size and presence of the collaborative economy in Europe*. Retrieved from www.pwc.co.uk/issues/megatrends/collisions/sharingeconomy/future-of-the-sharing-economy-in-europe-2016.html

Ranzini, G., Newlands, G., Anselmi, G., Andreotti, A., Eichhorn, T., Etter, M., . . . Lutz, C. (2017). Millennials and the sharing economy: European perspectives. *SSRN Electronic Journal*. Retrieved from https://papers.ssrn.com/sol3/papers.cfm?abstract_id=3061704

Richins, M. L., & Dawson, S. (1992). A consumer values orientation for materialism and its measurement: Scale development and validation. *Journal of Consumer Research*, *19*(3), 303–316. https://doi.org/10.1086/209304

Robinson, L. (2009). A taste for the necessary: A Bourdieuian approach to digital inequality. *Information, Communication & Society*, *12*(4), 488–507. https://doi.org/10.1080/13691180902857678

Rogers, E. M., & Shoemaker, F. F. (1971). *Communication of innovations: A cross-cultural approach*. New York, NY: Free Press.

San-Martín, H., & Herrero, A. (2012). Influence of the user's psychological factors on the online purchase intention in rural tourism: Integrating innovativeness to the UTAUT framework. *Tourism Management*, *33*(1), 341–350. https://doi.org/10.1016/j.tourman.2011.04.003

Scheyvens, R., & Biddulph, R. (2018). Inclusive tourism development. *Tourism Geographies*, *20*(4), 589–609. https://doi.org/10.1080/14616688.2017.1381985

Schor, J. B. (2017). Does the sharing economy increase inequality within the eighty percent? Findings from a qualitative study of platform providers. *Cambridge Journal of Regions, Economy and Society*, *10*(2), 263–279. https://doi.org/10.1093/cjres/rsw047

Schor, J. B., & Fitzmaurice, C. (2015). Collaborating and connecting: The emergence of the sharing economy. In L. A. Reisch & J. Thøgersen (Eds.), *Handbook of research on sustainable consumption* (pp. 410–425). Cheltenham, UK: Edward Elgar.

Schor, J. B., Fitzmaurice, C., Carfagna, L. B., Attwood-Charles, W., & Poteat, E. D. (2016). Paradoxes of openness and distinction in the sharing economy. *Poetics, 54*, 66–81. https://doi.org/10.1016/j.poetic.2015.11.001

Smith, A. (2016, May 19). Shared, collaborative and on demand: The new digital economy. *Pew Research Center: Internet & Technology*. Retrieved from www.pewinternet.org/2016/05/19/the-new-digital-economy/

Ter Huurne, M., Ronteltap, A., Corten, R., & Buskens, V. (2017). Antecedents of trust in the sharing economy: A systematic review. *Journal of Consumer Behaviour, 16*(6), 485–498. https://doi.org/10.1002/cb.1667

Urban, G. L., & Von Hippel, E. (1988). Lead user analyses for the development of new industrial products. *Management Science, 34*(5), 569–582. https://doi.org/10.1287/mnsc.34.5.569

Van Deursen, A. J., Helsper, E. J., & Eynon, R. (2015). Development and validation of the Internet Skills Scale (ISS). *Information, Communication & Society, 19*(6), 804–823. https://doi.org/10.1080/1369118X.2015.1078834

Von Hippel, E. (1986). Lead users: A source of novel product concepts. *Management Science, 32*(7), 791–805. https://doi.org/10.1287/mnsc.32.7.791

Wachsmuth, D., & Weisler, A. (2018). Airbnb and the rent gap: Gentrification through the sharing economy. *Environment and Planning A: Economy and Space, 50*(6), 1147–1170. https://doi.org/10.1177/0308518X18778038

Yang, Y., Tan, K., & Li, X. (2019). Antecedents and consequences of home-sharing stays: Evidence from a nationwide household tourism survey. *Tourism Management, 70*, 15–28. https://doi.org/10.1016/j.tourman.2018.06.004

Zillien, N., & Hargittai, E. (2009). Digital distinction: Status-specific types of internet usage. *Social Science Quarterly, 90*(2), 274–291. https://doi.org/10.1111/j.1540-6237.2009.00617.x

Appendix 3.1

Table A Demographic respondent profile

	Category	% N			Category	% N	
Age	18–24	13.0	793	**H-size**	One person	18.9	1155
	25–34	20.7	1268		Two persons	31.5	1924
	35–44	22.7	1390		Three persons	22.8	1394
	45–54	22.7	1389		Four persons	19.5	1193
	55–65	20.8	1270		Five persons	5.2	320
Gender	Male	50.0	3055		Six persons	1.5	92
	Female	50.0	3055		Seven persons	0.4	22
Working status	Not working	33.5	2047		Eight and more persons	0.2	11
	Working	66.5	4064	**Region**	Rural	27.0	1648
Education	No formal	0.4	22		Suburb	15.2	927
	Primary	3.5	211		Small to med city	37.8	2310
	Low. sec.	12.4	755		Big city	20.1	1226
	Higher sec.	42.4	2590	**Income**	First quartile	24.8	1519
	Bachelor	24.5	1498		Second quartile	38.8	2369
	Master	14.4	877		Third quartile	21.4	1305
	Doctorate or higher	2.6	158		Fourth quartile	15.0	918

4 Digital transformation in tourism

Bilsen Bilgili and Erdogan Koc

Introduction

Technological advances after the Industrial Revolution have led to significant increases in industrial productivity. Factories powered by steam engines in the nineteenth century and the electrification systems in the early twentieth century enabled the transition to mass production. The industries became automated with the increasing use of electronic systems and information technologies. The world met the digital age with the Industry 3.0 Revolution that took place with the transition from mechanical to electronic technology. With Industry 4.0, the use and applications of social networks, big data, virtual reality, augmented reality, robot, IoT, etc., new digital technologies have become prevalent. These developments have urged businesses, invariably almost in all industries, to take advantage of these technologies so as to continue to have or establish or maintain competitive advantage.

As the digital technologies mature and become widespread in several industries, the society as a whole faces rapid and radical changes (Guban & Kovacs, 2017). As a radical change, the digital transformation can be defined as the use of technology to radically improve the performance and business activities in a field of activity. The digital transformation is not a simple automation as it implies and involves information and communication technologies-oriented changes with implications for the creation of new talents in a wide variety of spheres such as business management, public administration, and individual life styles to societal changes (Martin, 2008).

As in several industries, advances in information communication technologies have resulted in significant changes in the tourism industry as well. Tourism which tends to play increasingly a more significant role in people's lives has gone through major changes over the past few decades (Dexeus, 2019). Technological developments have led to digital transformation in tourism, and this transformation, in turn, has added value to the customers in terms of speed of access and increased comfort in travel, accommodation, food and beverage-related aspects, and activities of tourism. The increased sophistication of tourists primarily accelerated by easier access to information has raised their expectations. Due to the extensive use of information technology (IT) in tourism, the industry has become

DOI: 10.4324/9781003105930-5

significantly dependent on information and communication technologies and digital transformation (Koo et al., 2015). The changes in the expectations of the tourists have urged tourism enterprises to develop new products and services, as well as establish new processes and carry out new activities geared towards harmonising existing products and services with the new technologies. The mobile technologies and developments in Internet technologies have increased the involvement of tourists in digital platforms. The concept of digital tourist has emerged to describe tourists who use tourism products or services with digitally enhanced marketing mix (Palumbo, Dominici, & Basile et al., 2014).

Business establishments and destinations have increasingly become smart tourism-oriented and transformed their operations to digitalise their offerings and started to adjust most of their activities from information collection about customers (Ozkul et al., 2019) to purchasing (e.g., reservation, ticket purchase, and check-in operations) and payment systems (Lee, Hunter, & Chung, 2020). At the same time, the demand for tourism has grown significantly due to various factors such as economic development, access to communication, technological advancements in transportation technology, increased leisure time, etc. Based on this background, the adaptation to technological transformation has become a necessity for businesses to survive and compete in the highly dynamic tourism market. Increasing numbers of tourists have considered and adopted technological advancements based on the 'ease of use and benefit of use'. The adoption of technology by customers has been investigated empirically from the perspectives of several theories and models such as technology acceptance model (TAM) theory (Davis, 1989), theory of reasoned action (Fishbein & Ajzen, 1975), and diffusion of innovation (Rogers, 1983), tourists tend to primarily evaluate technological advancements based on the 'ease of use and benefit of use'.

Based on the previous discussion, this chapter first aims to explain the digital transformation in tourism within the framework of the technological and socio-economic advances that occurred through Industry 3.0 and Industry 4.0 by extensively reviewing the literature. Second, the chapter evaluates and presents the main advantages and disadvantages of this transformation for both businesses and tourists. It is believed that the review, explanations, and the discussions presented in the chapter will not only guide customers, practitioners working in the industry, but also researchers carrying out research in this field.

Industry development and digitalisation in tourism

Industrial development process and tourism

The industrialisation process in the world is explained in four stages. The first Industrial Revolution, which began in the early 1760s, is Industry 1.0 based on division of labour and steam/hydro power. Then, the Industry 2.0 emerged, characterised by the widespread use of electricity. Later, based on Information and Communication Technology (ICT), the Industry 3.0 plays a critical role in shaping the scene in business and industry. Today, while there is an overwhelming influence of the Industry 3.0, the age of the Industry 4.0 has emerged, characterised by a decentralised control system that manages sensors, RFID (Radio Frequency Identification) chips, 'cyber-physical' systems and Internet of Things (IoT), production, and service processes along the entire value chain (Srivastava, 2015).

Industry 3.0 digital age and tourism

The use of the Internet, which started in the 1970s and started to become widespread rapidly in the 1990s, and the information age that started with the developments in technology have opened up new avenues on a global scale while significantly changing the world order. The importance of the concepts of innovation, change, and transformation is on the increase as individuals and businesses aim to produce, use, and spread as knowledge as possible. The Internet and technology are among the two main factors shaping the age and the society we live in. The digital transfer of information offers businesses significant advantages in delivering their products and services to their both domestic and global customers (Manyika et al., 2016). In order to reap advantages of this new system, many businesses are taking swift action to adapt to digital transformation by moving their activities to digital platforms. Likewise, tourism businesses are turning to new technologies with an effort to adapt to rapid changes in digitalisation. Additionally, customers in general are also adapting to these rapid changes to benefit more and avoid disappointment in the purchase, use, and consumption of tourism products and service (Pabel & Prideaux, 2016).

Information communication technologies have evolved and undergone various changes over the years. These changes are things like the Web 0.5, 1.0, 1.5, 2.0, 2.5, 3.0, 3.5, and 4.0. The Web 0.5, which is accepted as the infrastructure of ICT, is accepted as the beginning of the digital age as a web revolution since the 1980s. The interaction between the developers and the users tends to be low and low in Web1.0 (Patel, 2013). Applications where the lowest interaction is promoted through the websites of tourism enterprises are among the applications within the scope of this technology. After Web 1.0, 1.5 and 2.0 revolution took place in 2004. The Web 2.0 includes environments where video sharing such as Facebook and Twitter is made, facilitating the use of participatory, collaborative, and distributed applications that enable daily activities in formal and non-formal areas. For example, it was possible for the first time in the Web 2.0 era for tourists to share their experiences on the Internet as comments or information (Miguéns, Baggio, & Costa, 2008). The Web 2.5 has made it possible for mobile users to benefit from online platforms whenever they want. With the Web 3.0, 3.5, services such as software developments, data mining suggestions, personalised smart search, online shopping, and advertising activities have become possible. While the Web 4.0 refers to 'the relationship between humans and machines', the Web 5.0 refers to the enabling of the emotional interaction dimension of this relationship (Parvathia & Mariselvi, 2017). The recent developments allow the analysis of the data obtained from the interaction of customers with tourism businesses via the use of various software programs. Thus, these applications allow tourism businesses to define their target markets better, and develop segmentation and positioning strategies more effectively. At present, through B2B, B2C, and CRM software, the flow of information customer relationships can be managed more effectively with digital tools. Furthermore, the data can be analysed accurately by using methods such as artificial intelligence applications.

Industry 4.0 cyber-physical systems age and tourism

The Industry 4.0, which comprises several technologies, can be defined as the successful transition of in-house production systems and processes to 'Intelligent Manufacturing', 'Smart Industry', 'Integrated Industry', 'Connected Industry', or 'Industrial Internet', covering distributed and interconnected production equipment (Gökalp, Şener, & Eren, 2017). Cyber-physical production systems are defined as online equipment networks that connect IT technology and mechanical or electronic accessories that can communicate on a network. Machine-to-machine (M2M) communication is necessary in cyber-physical systems. In addition, the use of robots in production contributes to the productivity by reducing costs. The augmented reality is defined as the total of real and virtual objects created with virtual objects placed on the real-world environment for experiential purposes. Big data and analysis enable the collection and comprehensive evaluation of data from many different sources and customers to support real-time decision-making, optimise production quality, save energy, and improve equipment service (Bahrin et al., 2016). Therefore, this system uses digital technologies such as cloud computing. It refers to the IoT, all subsystems, processes, internal and external objects, and IT systems connected to supplier and customer networks. The systems communicate and cooperate with each other and with people. Cloud computing provides the opportunity to have access to a wider tourist network, to analyse the information obtained from this source through big data, to enable the personalised service design with the use of the IoT, and to establish strong communication with suppliers. The previously mentioned networks and relationships add value to the tourism industry, where costs are high and personalised service is very important (World Tourism Organization and World Tourism Cities Federation, 2018).

Activities such as kitchen and cleaning services, reservation systems in the tourism industry, as in transportation and transportation systems, are carried out through M2M using methods such as smart hotel applications, IoT, robot applications, and these systems are offered to tourists with mobile applications. Thus, the costs of the previously mentioned practices are reduced and productivity is increased. The use and application of technology in the tourism industry, referred to as smart tourism, is the 'provision of smarter, meaningful and sustainable connections between tourists and destinations through mobile digital connection' (Li et al., 2017). The smart investments in the tourism industry and smart hotel applications have become increasingly important with the emergence of smart building designs, comprising things such as lighting and heating systems, and energy- and time-saving-based applications (Boukhechba et al., 2017).

As labour-intensive industries, there are widespread influences and implications for tourism and hospitality. However, tourism and hospitality establishments, with its current workforce and other resource capabilities, are unable to create and adapt technological developments for use. They need specialist engineers and software designers to develop new ideas and create software that will put them into practice. Researchers put forward that although some of the aspects of digitalisation in the tourism industry may prove to be beneficial, the physical/social interaction with the service providers tends to offer advantages for customers as well (Bilgili & Özkul, 2019).

The digital transformation in tourism

The digital age and the ensuing development of information technologies and the innovations brought about by the Industry 4.0 have changed the marketing practices significantly. The digital marketing environment offers new products, new markets, new media, and new channels development opportunities. These technologies are used to improve customer service and increase success in the field, quality, and revenues. Dredge et al. (2018) put forward that as digitalisation reduces the number of transactions in tourism, it helps improve efficiency and effectiveness of businesses. Digitalisation may also increase the prestige of the business firm against the competitors, the establishment of competitive advantage, and the effective management of distribution channels (Zaidan, 2017). Digitalisation can also allow the design and organisation of holiday and tours, targeting specific age or interest groups through the use of online platforms. Hence, digital platforms and the Internet may enable the diversification of the marketing methods for a tourism business (Choi, Lehto, & Morrison, 2007).

Mobile applications in tourism

The first mobile application in tourism was used by Choice hotel chains in 2009. This application was downloaded 225 thousand times in 73 countries (Can et al., 2017). The application allowed guests to make a reservation and the purchase. With this mobile application, the 'RapidBook' application was developed by storing information about the preferences of the customers. As the application allows the remembering of details about a customer, it provides an opportunity to establish emotional bonds, and hence competitive advantage.

Mobile computing, which is represented by a smartphone called a mediator, and its applications for tourists, has a significant impact on travel and tourism planning (Wang, Li, & Li, 2013). With the increasing affordability of portable devices, the businesses have the opportunity to implement more tailor-made campaigns and marketing activities. Digital travel planning systems through the use of mobile applications via the Internet enable tourists to organise their holidays in terms of destinations, transportation, accommodations, and restaurants (Xiang, Magnini, & Fesenmaier, 2015).

The use of QR (Quick Response) code technology allows tourists to organise almost all aspects of their activities ranging from reserving a room to having access to participating in campaigns through the use of their mobile phones (Şanlıöz, Dilek, & Koçak, 2013). Also, the QR codes can be used for check in, security, marketing, and offers in tourism. The QR codes could allow tourists to have access to message boards in the lobby of a hotel, as well as to suggestions regarding what to eat during their stay. As tourists can provide feedback through the QR code technology, the application may provide an important database for quality improvement (Şanlıöz, Dilek, & Koçak, 2013).

The development and the wide spread use of mobile technologies have also enabled the use of virtual reality through mobile technologies. Along with virtual reality and augmented reality applications, tourists have the opportunity to have a virtual experience of the destination or the tourism and hospitality establishments. Rich content mobile applications can make destinations more attractive and provide consumers with interesting experiences, while reducing their risk perceptions (Safko, 2012). Tourism businesses can create more attractive mobile environments for tourists on their own by using their own rich content mobile software.

As the mobile applications customers enable the exchange of information for customers, they may be better equipped to compare and evaluate their experiences compared with the past (Neuhofer, Buhalis & Ladkin, 2015). Hence, tourism businesses are recommended to place greater importance on the design and use of mobile applications to develop a stronger brand image. Businesses are also recommended to make effective use of information gleaned from the customers through the mobile applications in the design and development of their processes.

Social media applications in tourism

Networks, which are called social media and allow mutual interaction with Web 2.0 technology, are a set of systems where media, marketing, and sociality take place together; 45% of the world's population currently uses social media, and the rate of use is increasing rapidly (Globe Digital Report, 2019). As customers tend to spend significant amount of time in social media, tourism businesses need to be present and effectively market their services through social media.

A tourist can share his/her experience with his/her surroundings, other social media users, and the business providing the service at the same time. As a result of this content, while businesses shape their services, individuals can determine their purchasing decisions according to the posts on social media (Xiang, Magnini, & Fesenmaier, 2015). In social media, content producers are consumers, not businesses.

Consumer groups that share their passion for a particular brand and develop society according to their norms, rituals, and traditions form groups called 'brand community'. In the tourism industry, there are destination brands, tourism business brands, or communities in social media for a field subject to tourism. For example, TripAdvisor is a social media platform where tourism content is shared or evaluated by individuals (Kotler, Kartajaya, & Setiawan, 2019). Social media platforms, in which word of mouth communication and viral marketing have an intense effect, are very important for the tourism industry.

Another critical opportunity offered by social media is social media influencers that share on certain topics. Social media influencers can be a reference to their followers and/or potential tourists seeking information on this subject by sharing their experiences with many tourism businesses and touristic activities such as destinations, accommodation businesses, food and beverage businesses, and entertainment venues. Reference groups, which have a significant impact on consumer behaviour (Koç, 2019), have evolved into influencers in the social media environment with the development of information technologies (Avcı & Bilgili, 2020). For example, the number of train tourism trips called 'Oriented Express' realised between the west and east of Turkey has increased five times with the effect of social media phenomenon (Ergun, Bayrak, & Doğan, 2019).

Smart applications in tourism

With the Industry 4.0 revolution, smart applications have started to spread in tourism. The concept of smart tourism was presented by Gordon Phillips for the first time in a presentation. It has been defined as a holistic, long-term, and sustainable approach to planning, developing, operating, and marketing tourism products and businesses (Li et al., 2017). Smart tourism includes touristic activities informed and supported by smart technology. In smart tourism, technology is seen as an infrastructure rather than individual information systems. It covers a range of intelligent computing technologies that combine hardware, software, and network technologies, providing real-time awareness of the real world to help people make smarter decisions about alternatives, as well as actions to optimise business processes and business performance.

Within the scope of smart tourism, the expressions of smart destination and smart hotel have become the most common ones. The smart destination concept is based on the smart city concept that emerged with digitalisation and Industry 4.0. Digital change, which started especially with smart tourism applications, has revealed the concept of smart tourism destinations with the development and change of smart cities (Boes, Buhalis, & Inversini, 2016). Smart tourism destination is a concept that ensures sustainable development of tourism areas and uses technology and is an innovative tourist destination that is accessible to everyone. It also facilitates the interaction and integration of the visitor with the environment and focuses on the quality of the experience in the destination and the quality of life of the local people. The concept of smart city and smart destination is interrelated, and it refers to the conservation of a city or a destination's resources and equipping it with technology that will create unique experiences for tourists visiting that destination.

The most common types of current smart hotel applications include integrated mobile data, facilitating room technologies, connections that are not affected by future changes, and technologies that strengthen security and save energy. The costs of secure payment and data privacy that hotels spend the most on are in the top three among the hotel expenditures in technological investments. Hotels using smart technologies such as Hilton Worldwide, aiming to reduce energy expenditures, control and monitor energy. When smart hotels are analysed in terms of revenues, for example, Fontainebleau Miami, which uses integrated mobile data, increases hotel revenue by providing its customers with the opportunity to check-in earlier or check-out later for a certain additional fee (Terry, 2016).

In smart hotels, guests are offered facilities such as lights, curtains, turning the TV on and off, and adjusting the temperature by giving voice commands (Balakrishnan, 2016). There are applications that allow the use of smart wristbands instead of keys or smartphones at the entrance to the rooms, associating these wristbands with credit cards for payments, recording the activities of tourists, and making analyses through big data.

RFID smart tag applications used in both travel businesses and accommodation businesses are also one of the smart applications. It is used in many areas such as luggage recognition, chip card keys, pass cards from sensor areas, tracking customer participation in events through wristbands, and tracking the stock in the mini bars in the rooms (Wang, Li, & Li, 2013). These smart applications are integrated into mobile applications via IoT, enabling advanced digitalisation in tourism. With the augmented reality and virtual reality applications integrated into these applications, it reveals the embodied form of the concept of Tourism 4.0.

Digital tourism and COVID-19

The COVID-19 pandemic process (Worldometers, 2020), which started on 11 March 2020, announced by the World Health Organization as an epidemic, has accelerated the digital transformation in tourism, and the use of digital technologies in this crisis period has revealed the importance of properties such as speed and reliability of these technologies.

Face recognition systems of digital technologies and smart applications, contactless door passes, online check-in operations, sensors that control distance between people in the service process, non-contact, remotely managed hardware in hotel rooms, smart wristbands that prevent crowded people gathering in service procurement, and digital tools such as the use of data matrix in services such as menu selection have gained importance. Smart digital applications have become strategic tools that positively affect customer satisfaction by making tourists feel safe, especially during the COVID-19 period. Thus, these applications have led 'benefit of use', which is one of the dimensions affecting the adoption of technology, to get ahead 'ease of use' and tourists have easily adapted to the use of technology. On the other hand, an important database has been created regarding especially the health sensitivities of the tourists interacted in this process, and it has been possible to develop personalised services for these audiences in the future (Hall, Scott, & Gössling, 2020).

During the COVID-19 period, tourists' interests in tour packages organised by large-scale hotels and travel agencies for large businesses have decreased, and their purchasing preferences have turned towards the services of villas, bungalows, caravans, and small boutique-scale hotels. During the COVID-19 process, the behaviour of consumers towards the types of tourism products has also changed, and most of their physical preferences have turned into online behaviours in digital environments. In the tourism market, C2C (consumer-to-consumer) applications such as 'virtual/online museum visits', 'online event attendance', 'intensive sharing about destinations and tourism brands in many platforms on social media and effective interpersonal communication', and 'interaction of individuals with each other without any businesses with regard to isolated tourism services' have emerged as digital tourism (Gretzel et al., 2020). This situation has revealed the need for small-scale tourism businesses to reach tourists who are online in digital environment more easily. It has also required businesses to invest in a way that meets the demands of these tourists to use digital technologies while purchasing accommodation and tourism services. Thus, the COVID-19 process has rapidly spread to small businesses in the tourism industry, resulting in an increasing use in the entire industry (Gössling, Scott, & Hall, 2020). This situation gives hints that the importance of digitalisation in tourism will increase in times of crisis such as pandemic.

Conclusion

The tourism industry has turned to digital transformation in the face of developments in digital and smart applications. Today, many tourism businesses use advanced technology mobile applications in order to present the information they publish on their websites with richer content to their customers through different platforms. With the increase of smartphone users, companies aim to use in-hotel, travel, and reservation mobile applications more efficiently to reduce marketing costs and reach potential customers (Kwon, Bae, & Blum, 2013).

The potential of tourist segments with different lifestyles has to be taken into account. Alternative strategies should be developed for market segments that do not use digital technology tools such as smartphones. On the other hand, customers who will receive service from smart hotels may complain about the low level of lighting applied to save energy in the hotel, and the hotel room is extremely hot/cold (Kim, Hlee, & Joun, 2016). Therefore, customers should be informed in detail about contents such as the smart hotel concept in advance. Discussions are still ongoing about how digital and smart applications such as augmented reality, virtual reality, and advanced software programs will affect tourism destinations in the future. On the one hand, it is generally accepted that the visualisation of information through technological applications will increase tourism experiences and contribute to the reconstruction of destroyed cultural heritage sites; on the other hand, there are concerns that a different tourist profile may emerge.

Some authors suggest that augmented reality and other technological applications will change the current tourist definition. Considering that they visit museums and historical places from their own homes thanks to a technological application, it is pointed out that individuals can no longer be considered tourists and this event can be seen as a structure that replaces tourism. It is also among the discussions that technology-supported travels of individuals at their homes or in different destinations will gradually isolate them and there will be a more passive touristic participation (Özgüneş & Bozok, 2017).

Studies on applications based on information technologies such as augmented reality and virtual reality generally focus on the positive effects of these applications on tourist satisfaction (Bilgili et al., 2019). However, another problem that arises is that these practices may reduce the need for human resources in the field of tourism. These applications are used in different sectors of the tourism industry, primarily tourist guiding, waitressing, reservation, etc. There are concerns that employment in different fields, especially professions, may decrease in the coming years. However, on the other hand, it is claimed that the need for employment will increase rather than reducing employment, especially Industry 4.0, and that this employment will be focused on qualified people (Bilgili & Özkul, 2019). This situation reveals the need to improve the scope of tourism education.

Despite all these concerns, of course, it is not possible for the tourism sector to be abstracted from technological developments. Although the technological development and adaptation process brings change in the first stage due to the supply and demand balance, it is generally accepted that those who cannot keep up with this will be eliminated from the competition. For this reason, measures should be taken to accelerate sectoral adaptation to the digital transformation experienced. It should be ensured that problems such as unemployment, migration, and exclusion that may arise due to the innovative changes experienced are foreseen and minimised by taking measures. Although some forms of business or occupations will disappear or decrease due to this change, it is a fact that new types of professions will emerge (Topsakal et al., 2018). In particular, developments regarding digital transformation in the COVID-19 pandemic process have shown that the power of digital infrastructure can provide a significant advantage in competition in times of crisis.

Along with digital transformation in tourism, the positive effects of using tools such as personalised experience, data-oriented approach, multi-channel customer experience, real-time marketing, mobile integration, messaging platforms and chatbots, artificial intelligence, IoT, and virtual reality in operations on efficiency and effectiveness cannot be denied. Digital transformation in tourism facilitates access to data not only for tourism companies but also for their customers. It is possible to say that it is necessary to evaluate the digital transformation in tourism as a whole, where strategies should be developed for multi-dimensional benefits and risks of the changing structure.

It will be useful for researchers who will work on digital transformation in tourism in the future to investigate technology compliance and technology acceptance in terms of demographic, psychographic, and social characteristics of tourists. Researchers will be able to make significant contributions to both theory and practice with studies that will determine the most appropriate product and marketing strategies for different market segments by examining the personality traits, lifestyles, personal values of tourists, and their attitudes towards different services that are digitalised in tourism. It is possible to recommend future researchers to conduct qualitative and quantitative studies in which they can produce reliable, generalisable, and highly valid scientific results by considering the developments regarding digital transformation in the tourism industry in terms of these theories.

References

Avcı, E., & Bilgili, B. (2020). Sosyal Medya Fenomen Özelliklerinin Takipçilerin Destinasyonu Ziyaret Etme Niyeti Üzerindeki Etkisi. *Tourism and Recreation*, Ek Sayı, 83–92.

Bahrin, M. A. K., Othman, M. F., Azli, N. H. N., & Talib, M. F. (2016). Industry 4.0: A review on industrial automation and robotic. *Jurnal Teknologi (Sciences&Engineering)*, 78(6–13), 137–143.

Balakrishnan, A. (2016, December 14). *Wynn Las Vegas to add Amazon Alexa to all hotel rooms*. Retrieved September 20, 2020, from www.cnbc.com/2016/12/14/wynn-las-vegas-to-add-amazon-alexa-to-all-hotel-rooms.html

Bilgili, B., & Özkul, E., (2019). Industry 4.0 tourism 4.0 and human factor: Re voice of customer. *The European Proceedings of Social Behavioural Sciences*, 1(1), 655–665.

Bilgili, B., Özkul, E., Koç, E., & Ademoğlu, M. O. (2019). An investigation of augmented reality applications from the perspectives of brand trust and purchase intentions of customer. In S. Grima, E. Özen, H. Boz, J. Spiteri, & E. Thalassions (Eds.), *Contemporary issues in behavioral finance*, Vol. 101 (pp. 53–64). Bingley, Bradford, UK: Emerald Published Ltd.

Boes, K., Buhalis, D., & Inversini, A. (2016). Smart tourism destinations: Ecosystems for tourism destination competitiveness. *International Journal of Tourism Cities*, 2(2), 108–124.

Boukhechba, M., Bouzouane, A., Gaboury, S., Gouin-Vallerand, C., Giroux, S., & ve Bruno, B. (2017). A novel bluetooth low energy based system for spatial exploration in smart cities. *Expert Systems with Applications*, 77, 71–82.

Can, B. K., Yeşilyurt, H., Sancaktar, C. L., & Koçak, N. (2017). Mobil Çağda Mobil Uygulamalar: Türkiye'deki Yerli Otel Zincirleri Üzerine Bir Durum Tespiti. *Journal of Yaşar University*, 12(45), 48–59.

Choi, S., Lehto, X. Y., & ve Morrison, A. M. (2007). Destination image representation on the web: Content analysis of Macau travel related websites. *Tourism Management*, 28(1), 118–129.

Davis, F. D. (1989). Perceived usefulness, perceived ease of use, and user acceptance of information technology. *MIS Quarterly*, 13(3), 319–340.

Dexeus, C. (2019). The deepening effects of the digital revolution. In E. Fayos-Solá & C. Cooper (Eds.), *The future of tourism: Innovation and sustainability* (pp. 43–69). Cham: Springer International Publishing.

Dredge, D., Phi, G., Renuka, M., Eóin, M., & Popescu, E. S. (2018). *Digitalisation in tourism, the European Commission's*. Denmark: EASME Final Report.

Ergun, N., Bayrak, R., & Doğan, S. (2019). Turizm Pazarlaması için Önemli Bir Pazarlama Kanalı Olan Instagram'da Nitel Bir Araştırma. *Güncel Turizm Araştırmaları Dergisi*, 3(1), 82–10.

Fishbein, M., & Ajzen, I. (1975). *Belief, attitude, intention, and behavior: An introduction to theory and research*. Reading, MA: Addison-Wesley.

Globe Digital Report. (2019). *Digital in 2019*. New York. Retrieved from https://wearesocial.com/global-digital-report-2019

Gökalp, E., Şener, U., & Eren, P. E. (2017). Development of an assesment model for industry 4.0: Industry 4.0-MM. In *International Conference on Software Process Improvement and Capability Determination* (pp. 128–142). Palma de Mallorka-Spain: Springer International Publishing AG.

Gössling, S., Scott, D., & Hall, C. M. (2020). Pandemics, tourism and global change: A rapid assessment of COVID-19. *Journal of Sustainable Tourism*. https://doi.org/10.1080/09669582.2020.1758708

Gretzel, U., Fuchs, M., Baggio, R., Hoepken, W., Law, R., Neidhart, J., Pesonen, J., Zanker, M., & Xiang, Z. (2020). e-Tourism beyond COVID19: a call for transformative research. *Information Technology & Tourism, 22*,187–203. https://doi.org/10.1007/s40558-020-00181-3

Guban, M., & Kovacs, G. (2017). *Industry 4.0 conception, acta technica corviniensis-bulletin of engineering, January–March*(1). Hunedoara: University POLITEHNICA Timisoara. ISSN:2067–3809.

Hall, C. M., Scott, D., & Gössling, S. (2020). Pandemics, transformations and tourism: Be careful what you wish for. *Tourism Geographies*. https://doi.org/10.1080/14616688.2020.1759131

Kim, J. Y., Hlee, S., & Joun, Y. (2016). Green practices of the hotel industry: Analysis through the windows of smart tourism system. *International Journal of Information Management, 36*(6), 1340–1349.

Koç, E. (2019). *Tüketici Davranışları ve Pazarlama Stratejileri: Global ve Yerel Yaklaşım* (8th ed.). Ankara: Seçkin Yayınları.

Koo, C., Gretzel, U., Hunter, W. C., & Chung, N. (2015). The role of IT in tourism. *Asia Pacific Journal of Information Systems, 25*(1), 99–104.

Kotler, P., Kartajaya, H., & Setiawan, I. (2019). *Pazarlama 4.0: Gelenekselden Dijitale Geçiş* (N. Özata, Çev.). İstanbul: Optimist Yayım Dağıtım.

Kwon, M., Bae, J., & Blum, S. C. (2013). Mobile applications in the hospitality industry. *Journal of Hospitality and Tourism Technology, 4*(1), 81–92.

Lee, P., Hunter, W. C., & Chung, N. (2020). Smart tourism city: Developments and transformations. *Sustainability, 12*(10), 3958.

Li, Y., Hu, C., Huang, C., & Duan, L. (2017). The concept of smart tourism in the context of tourism information services. *Tourism Management, 58*, 293–300.

Martin, A. (2008). Digital literacy and the "digital society. *Literacies Concepts Policies Practices, 30*, 151–176.

Manyika, J., Lund, S., Bughin, J., Woetzel, J., Stamenov, K., & Dhingra, D. (2016). *Digital globalization: The new era of global flows*. McKinsey Global Institue. Retrieved September 20, 2020, from https://www.mckinsey.com/business-functions/mckinsey-digital/our-insights/digital-globalization-the-new-era-of-global-flows.

Miguéns, J., Baggio, R., & Costa, C. (2008). Social media and tourism destinations: TripAdvisor case study. *Advances in Tourism Research, 26*(28), 1–6.

Neuhofer, B., Buhalis, D., & Ladkin, A. (2015). Smart technologies for personalized experiences: A case study in the hospitality domain. *Electronic Markets, 25*(3), 243–254.

Özgüneş, R. E., & Bozok, D. (2017). Turizm Sektörünün Sanal Rakibi (Mi?): Artırılmış Gerçeklik. *Uluslararası Türk Dünyası Turizm Araştırmaları Dergisi, 2*(2), 146–160.

Ozkul, E., Boz, H., Bilgili, B., & Koc, E. (2019). What colour and light do in service atmospherics: A neuro-marketing perspective. In D. Pfister & M. Volgger (Eds.), *Atmospheric turn in culture and tourism: Place, design and process impacts on customer behaviour, marketing and branding* (pp. 223–244). Bingley, Bradford, UK: Emerald Publishing Ltd.

Pabel, A., & Prideaux, B. (2016). Social media use İn pre-trip planning by tourists visiting a small regional leisure destination. *Journal of Vacation Marketing, 22*(4), 335–348.

Palumbo, F., Dominici, G., & Basile, G. (2014). The culture on the palm of your hand: How to design a user oriented mobile app for museums. In L. Aiello (Ed.), *Management of cultural products: E-relationship marketing and accessibility perspectives* (pp. 224–243). America: IGI Global.

Parvathia, M., & Mariselvi, R. (2017). A bird's eye on the evolution: Web 1.0 to Web 5.0: Lib 1.0 to Lib 5.0. *International Journal of Advanced Research Trends in Engineering and Technology (IJARTET), 4*(4), 167–176.

Patel, K. (2013). Incremental journey for world wide web: Introduced with web 1.0 to recent web 5.0: A survey paper. *International Journal of Advanced Research in Computer Science and Software Engineering, 3*(10).

Rogers, E. M. (1983). *Diffusion of innovations* (3rd ed.). New York: The Free Press.

Safko, L. (2012). *The social media bible tactics, tools & strategies.* New Jersey: John Wiley & Sons.

Şanlıöz, H. K., Dilek, S. E., & Koçak, N. (2013). Değişen Dünya, Dönüşen Pazarlama: Türkiye Turizm Sektöründen Öncü Bir Mobil Uygulama Örneği. *Anatolia: Turizm Araştırmaları Dergisi, 24,* 250–260.

Srivastava, S. K. (2015, November 15). Industry 4.0, invited paper for souvenir. *BHU Engineer's Alumni, Lucknoq,* 23–24.

Terry, L. (2016). *6 Mega-trends in hotel technology.* Retrieved September 9, 2020, from http://hospitalitytechnology.edgl.com/news/6-Mega-Trends-in-Hotel-Technology105033

Topsakal, Y., Yüzbaşıoğlu, N., Çelik, P., & Bahar, M. (2018). Turizm 4.0: Turist 5.0: İnsan Devriminin Neden Endüstri Devrimlerinden Bir Numara Önde Olduğuna İlişkin Bakış. *Journal of Tourism Intelligence and Smartness, 1*(2), 1–11.

Wang, D., Li, X., & Li, Y. (2013). China's "smart tourism destination" initiative: A taste of the service-dominant logic. *Journal of Destination Marketing & Management, 2,* 59–61.

Worldometers (2020). *Covid-19 coronavirus pandemic.* Retrieved September 20, 2020, from www.worldometers.info/coronavirus/

World Tourism Organization and World Tourism Cities Federation. (2018). *UNWTO/WTCF city tourism performance research.* Madrid: UNWTO. https://doi.org/10.18111/9789284419616

Xiang, Z., Magnini, V. P., & Fesenmaier, D. R. (2015). Information technology and consumer behavior in travel and tourism: Insights from travel planning using the internet. *Journal of Retailing and Consumer Services, 22,* 244–249.

Zaidan, E. (2017). Analysis of ICT usage patterns, benefits and barriers in tourism SMEs in the middle eastern countries: The case of Dubai in UAE. *Journal of Vacation Marketing, 23*(3), 248–263.

5 Attitudes towards robots as transformational agents in tourism and hospitality
Robophobes versus robophiles

Craig Webster and Stanislav Ivanov

Introduction

There would be no robotic transformation of modern industries without the invention of the robot. Karel Čapek introduced the word 'robot' in his 1920 play, R.U.R. (Rossum's Universal Robots) (NPR, 2011), so the concept of the robot is fairly new to humanity, in a historical sense. The word for the concept was derived from Slavonic to denote a forced labourer but seems to have taken on the implication that it is labour performed by a machine. The robot, now, is not just a concept and a part of science fiction but a vital part of the modern society and economy. However, although the robot is accepted as a concept, there are different segments, one that welcomes or accepts robots, the 'robophile', and one that rejects the robot, the 'robophobe'.

There are about two major aspects of the robot that are worthy of note since the word was coined about a hundred years ago. The first major aspect is how quickly the word took on usage and spread throughout the world in many different countries. So, while the robot remained largely a concept of science fiction, it was understood and appreciated across many different cultures, even when robots were originally merely a concept. The relative newness of the term and the broad acceptance of the robot as a concept have led to the word 'robot' being almost unchanged and recognisable from language to language. The concept and the language of the robot have been widely accepted by the collective consciousness of humanity quickly and universally. A second major consideration is that the robot has made massive strides in recent years in terms of capabilities and in many different industries. The first robot company was founded in 1954 (Unimate) to automate a great deal of production in the automotive industry. By the 1980s, many car plants began to use robots extensively. Since then, the capability of robots and the prominence of many robots have moved to many industries. As such, the robot is not simply a cute concept from literature, but it is increasingly a disruptor, revolutionising the way that businesses run in both manufacturing and service industries and transforming the workplace.

As of the time of writing, robots are used widely in many industries, but they have recently come into more significant usage in travel, tourism, and hospitality industries (Ivanov, Webster, & Berezina, 2017). With the rapid incursion of robots

DOI: 10.4324/9781003105930-6

and artificial intelligence into travel, tourism, and hospitality, there is a growing appreciation that robots are not something of science fiction or are hidden from the view of many employees or consumers but are increasingly prevalent and viewed by customers in commercial enterprises. As such, it is increasingly important to understand human attitudes towards robots and automation in travel, tourism, and hospitality. The robot will likely revolutionise the tourism and hospitality industry, changing the expectations of customers, managers, owners, and employees. Thus, the massive incorporation of robots will transform the industry for all the stakeholders in tourism and hospitality.

Here, we investigate the human acceptance of robots into the tourism ecosystem. This is a worthy thing to investigate because robots in manufacturing have been quite a disruptor, while the incorporation of the robot into the service economy has lagged quite a bit, likely because of the technical sophistication of the needs of the service sector relative to the manufacturing sector. What is necessary is to look more deeply into how employees, employers, and customers view these transformational agents in tourism. In the following, we look deeply into how robophobes and robophiles look upon the incursion of robots in the tourism industry. First, we look into the literature on attitudes towards robots in service industries. Then, we analyse the data to identify how robophiles and others view using robots for the delivery of specific services. Finally, we conclude, illustrating what has been learned in the analysis, the implications of the findings, and suggestions for future research with regard to how robots, as a major transformational agent, will face resistance or acceptance from customers.

Literature review

There is a tradition in the academic literature of exploring attitudes of consumers and managers towards new technologies (see, for example, Bruner & Kumar, 2005; Cui, Bao, & Chan, 2009; Denis-Rémis, 2011; Lin & Hsieh, 2006; Morosan & DeFranco, 2014). While this general literature on new technologies exists, there is also a tourism and hospitality literature that exists and delves into attitudes towards new technologies as well as practical issues with regard to incorporating new technologies into hospitality and tourism enterprises (see, for example, Berezina, Ciftici, & Cobanoglu, 2019; Ivanov, Webster, & Berezina, 2017, 2020; Ivanov et al., 2019, Ivanova, 2019; Morosan & DeFranco, 2019; Wang & Qualls, 2007). The literature, both the general one and the hospitality/tourism-specific ones, illustrates that there are different groups of people who are either attracted to the novelty of these new automation technologies and those who reject them, condensing into two different distinct groups (Lin & Hsieh, 2006).

There is a segment of the population that seems to outright reject robots and service automation (Singh, 2014) and there is a large and growing academic literature that explores segments of the population that are likely to reject or accept robots as co-workers, employees, and service providers in many different businesses and business environments (see, for example, De Graaf, Allouch, & Klamer, 2015;

Dinet & Vivian, 2014; Frennert & Östlund, 2014; Hudson, Orviska, & Hunady, 2017; Katz & Halpern, 2014; Malchus et al., 2013; Piçarra, 2016; Pino et al., 2015; Pochwatko et al., 2015; Reich-Stieber & Eyssel, 2015; Yan, Ang Jr., M. H., & Poo, 2014). The literature that deals with perceptions of robots and artificial intelligence used many different approaches, including large-scale public opinion surveys (Hudson, Orviska, & Hunady, 2017), psychometric tests (Pochwatko et al., 2015; Katz & Halpern, 2014), small-scale guided interviews (De Graaf, Allouch, & Klamer, 2015), and various other methods/mixed methods (Yan, Ang Jr., M. H., & Poo, 2014; Pino et al., 2015). The findings illustrate that there are identifiable segments of the population that are more likely to be receptive to robots in the workplace and the economy.

Apart from a general delineation of the population into robophiles and robophobes, there are demographics that seem to shape the way that people look at robots in the economy. Almost all studies, with few exceptions (Dinet & Vivian, 2014; Ivanov, Webster, & Seyyedi, 2018), show that females are less accepting of robots than males. While there is no indication of the reason that females are more suspicious of robots, there seems to be a general notion that females have an innate distrust of robots. However, there is also indication that urbanites (Hudson, Orviska, & Hunady, 2017) are more accepting of robots that people from less dense populations. There are other demographics that have been and can be explored, although none seems to be particularly predictive across samples. The best indicator of whether a person will accept using a robot or another automated system for services is whether the individual is generally receptive to robots (Malchus et al., 2013; Ivanov, Webster, & Garenko, 2018; Ivanov, Webster, & Seyyedi, 2018).

So it is clear that there seem to be noteworthy and identifiable segments of the population 'robophiles' and 'robophobes'. However, while previous literature has identified these two segments, there has not been specific and in-depth investigation as to how these two clusters can be identified from a population and how they view various different types of tasks being done by robots in the travel, tourism, and hospitality sectors. Here, we use a large-scale global survey to investigate how robophobic and robophillic segments can be identified using available demographic data and look into how robophobes and robophiles look upon robotic delivery of specific services in hospitality and tourism. Since there is a significant growing academic literature illustrating the growth in the academic literature (Ivanov et al., 2019) and a strong indication that robots and artificial intelligence may impact upon ways to make a noteworthy transformation in the way that tourism is experienced (Samala et al., 2020), further knowledge of those who may oppose or support the use of robots for the provision of tourism and hospitality services is needed.

Methodology

This book chapter presents part of the findings of the first global survey on robots in tourism, implemented by the authors (Webster & Ivanov, 2020). Data were collected during the period March 2018 to October 2019 through an online questionnaire available in English and 11 other languages, translated by native speakers. The questionnaire had several blocks of questions. This chapter focuses on the blocks dealing with the general attitudes towards robots, perceived appropriateness of robot use for various tasks in tourism and hospitality, preferred 'humans-robots' ratio, and the willingness to pay for robot-delivered services. The link to the questionnaire was distributed by email and through social media. The authors posted it in various social media groups in order to obtain a sample with diverse demographic characteristics. No personally identifying information was collected. To stimulate participation and increase the response rate, the authors distributed five $100-e-vouchers. Table 5.1 presents the characteristics of respondents who have answered to all questions analyses in this chapter.

Cluster analysis was used to identify the existence of groups of respondents based on their attitudes towards robots. The number of respondents in the cluster analysis (1,273) exceeded 91 times the number of variables in the segmentation base (14), hence it was much higher than the minimum ratio of 70 recommended by Dolnicar et al. (2014). Independent samples t-test was used to identify the differences in respondents' answer based on their cluster membership.

Findings

The cluster analysis revealed the existence of two clusters of respondents based on their general attitudes towards robots, namely: robophobes and robophiles. Their characteristics are presented in Table 5.1. While there were no statistically significant differences between the two clusters based on age, education, and travel experience, that was not the case regarding biological sex. Men were approximately equally distributed between the two clusters, while most of the women were in the robophobes cluster ($\chi^2 = 24.465$, $p < 0.001$). This is in line with previous studies who have found that women were more sceptical towards service robots compared to men (Hudson, Orviska, & Hunady, 2017; Katz & Halpern, 2014; Piçarra, 2016; Pino et al., 2015; Pochwatko et al., 2015; Reich-Stieber & Eyssel, 2015; Yan, Ang Jr., & Poo, 2014). Thus, the general pattern in the research findings supports what most previous research has shown that females have a tendency to be more sceptical of robots, although some research finds that this is not necessarily true in some samples (see, e.g., Dinet & Vivian, 2014; Ivanov, Webster, & Seyyedi, 2018).

Table 5.2 presents the general attitudes of both clusters towards robots. As a whole, the respondents were quite optimistic about the perceived social benefits of robots and they evaluated the benefits higher than the dehumanisation effects of robots. However, the robophiles were systematically more positive towards the social benefits of robots and less concerned about their dehumanisation effect than the robophobes. All differences were statistically significant at $p < 0.001$. An interesting point is that the differences in the answers of the two clusters were larger for the statements related to the dehumanisation effects of robots (between 1.58 and 2.47) than for the statements related to the social benefits of robots (between

Table 5.1 Sample's characteristics

Characteristic		Total	Cluster 1 Robophiles	Cluster 2 Robophobes	χ2
Gender	Female	708	270	433	24.465***
	Male	565	295	269	
Age	18–30	623	260	361	7.033
	31–40	308	149	156	
	41–50	199	85	113	
	51–60	89	41	48	
	61+	54	30	24	
Education	Secondary or lower	189	75	113	2.824
	2 year/Associate degree	86	37	49	
	Bachelor	395	174	220	
	Postgraduate	603	279	319	
Economic well-being	Much less wealthy than average for the country	42	14	27	13.830*
	Less wealthy than average for the country	78	27	51	
	Slightly less wealthy than average for the country	131	52	78	
	About the average for the country	420	192	228	
	Slightly more wealthy than average for the country	377	166	208	
	More wealthy than average for the country	191	102	88	
	Much more wealthy than average for the country	34	12	22	
Times stayed in hotels during the last 12 months	None	123	46	77	5.143
	One to three times	588	257	329	
	Four to six times	321	143	175	
	Seven times or more	241	119	121	
Total		1,273	565	702	

Note: Six respondents not classified in clusters due to missing answers to questions.

***Significant at $p < 0.001$
*Significant at $p < 0.05$

0.9 and 1.62). Therefore, it seems that the robophobes put greater emphasis on the dehumanisation effects of robots than the robophiles, who acknowledged these concerns, but they were more focused on the benefits that robots would bring to society. This indicated about deeper differences in the *Weltanschauung* of the two clusters – the robophiles focus on the benefits that robots bring, while the

Table 5.2 General attitudes towards robots

	Total Mean	Standard deviation	Cluster 1 Robophiles Mean	Standard deviation	Cluster 2 Robophobes Mean	Standard deviation	t-Test
Perceived benefits of robots							
Robots will be responsible for many of the good things we will enjoy in life	4.38	1.631	5.19	1.296	3.74	1.580	17.936***
Robots will improve our standard of living	4.90	1.513	5.76	1.011	4.20	1.492	22.098***
Robots will bring us a bright future	4.39	1.556	5.29	1.153	3.67	1.457	22.138***
Life will be easier with robots	5.02	1.461	5.79	0.954	4.39	1.494	20.246***
Robots will make our lives more convenient	5.25	1.390	5.95	0.911	4.69	1.449	18.873***
Robots will eliminate a lot of tedious work for people	5.49	1.343	5.99	1.019	5.09	1.431	12.995***
Robots will make people happier	3.96	1.609	4.75	1.350	3.32	1.506	17.836***
Dehumanisation effects of robots							
Robots will hurt our human relationships in society (r)	3.55	1.812	4.92	1.436	2.45	1.232	32.395***
In the future, robots will dominate society (r)	4.51	1.733	5.38	1.436	3.80	1.623	18.143***
The overuse of robots may be damaging and harmful to human beings (r)	3.18	1.719	4.39	1.558	2.20	1.100	28.295***
The overuse of robots may be damaging and harmful to the society as a whole (r)	3.21	1.820	4.53	1.607	2.15	1.164	29.548***
People will become slaves to robots (r)	4.80	1.772	5.91	1.196	3.90	1.645	25.137***
Robots will dehumanise the workplace (r)	3.40	1.786	4.68	1.532	2.37	1.207	29.320***
Robots will lead to deskilling of jobs (r)	3.49	1.723	4.48	1.595	2.69	1.374	21.069***

Note: 1. Coding of statements: 1 – completely agree, 7 – completely disagree; 2. (r) Reverse coding

***Significant at $p < 0.001$

robophobes – on the negative impacts of robots. So while both groups shared concerns, the two groups are largely differentiated by their focus upon either benefits or dehumanisation that robots bring to services.

Table 5.3 presents respondents' opinions about what robots should do in a tourism context. The respondents generally agreed that robots should be used for tasks related to provision of information and for dealing with dirty, dull, dangerous, and repetitive tasks such as housekeeping and cleaning or carrying items. More interactive tasks that require significant social skills and emotional intelligence or would require the human to be physically or psychologically subordinate to the robots (e.g., babysitting, hairdressing, massages, and dancing) were considered as inappropriate for robotisation. The differences between the two clusters were all significant at $p < 0.001$, but the overall patterns in their responses were similar. The data show a general consensus by respondents that humans have the judgement and spirit for many positions, but those tasks that are dirty, dull, or dangerous can be given to robots to do.

Table 5.4 shows respondents' preferences towards the 'human employees-robots' ratio in the service delivery process in various tourism and hospitality services. As a whole, respondents preferred to be served by slightly more humans than robots (all total means m > 4), but for some services, the robophiles preferred to be served by slightly more robots than humans. These include the services that are currently well automated through self-service technologies as kiosks (e.g., selling tickets at stations) that have short interaction between customers and service employees compared to the whole period of the service usage (e.g., rent-a-car), which are related to provision of information only (e.g., tourist information centres) or to carrying items (e.g., room service). At the same time, both groups of respondents preferred mostly humans in restaurants and bars, recognising the social function of the F&B outlets.

Finally, Table 5.5 presents respondents' willingness to pay for fully robot-delivered services. As a whole, customers perceive robots as cost-saving devices and request that these savings be transferred to them through price discounts. The expected discount for robot-delivered services compared to fully human-delivered service ranged from −8.53% (entrance fee for a museum/gallery) to −10.55% (restaurants). It is important to emphasise that both clusters were expecting lower prices for robot-delivered services not only the robophobes, although the discounts that the robophiles were smaller (between −6.47% and −8.20%) compared to the robophobes (between −9.97% and −12.62%) (all t-statistics were significant at $p < 0.001$). Thus, there is a strong indication from the data analysed that consumers expect that automation of services should result in savings for the consumer.

Discussion

The findings confirm the results of previous studies (Malchus et al., 2013; Ivanov, Webster, & Garenko, 2018; Ivanov, Webster, & Seyyedi, 2018) that the people are not uniform in their perceptions of robots – some have a more optimistic and positive view of the social benefits robots would bring, while others are more

Table 5.3 Perceived appropriateness of service robots

Activity	Total Mean	Total St. dev.	Cluster 1 Robophiles Mean	Cluster 1 Robophiles St. dev.	Cluster 2 Robophobes Mean	Cluster 2 Robophobes St. dev.	t-Test
Travel, tourism, and hospitality industries in general							
Welcoming/greeting a tourist/guest/passenger	4.39	2.060	5.14	1.781	3.79	2.075	12.440***
Accompanying the guest when leaving the hotel/restaurant/theme park	4.16	1.936	4.89	1.665	3.57	1.937	13.045***
Providing information about facilities of the hotel/restaurant/theme park/airport/bus station/train station, etc.	5.64	1.565	6.24	1.046	5.17	1.373	13.492***
Providing information about the destination	5.65	1.561	6.19	1.088	5.21	1.732	12.309***
Booking tourist services (e.g., flight tickets, hotel accommodation, transfers, rent-a-car, travel insurance, etc.)	5.29	1.702	5.90	1.298	4.81	1.823	12.396***
Concierge services (e.g., ordering tickets for shows and taxis)	5.18	1.752	5.84	1.331	4.65	1.864	13.263***
Issuing travel documents (e.g., voucher and tickets)	5.45	1.650	5.98	1.276	5.04	1.789	10.885***
Issuing payment documents (e.g., invoice and receipt)	5.52	1.620	6.05	1.235	5.10	1.751	11.304***
Processing cash payments	5.26	1.715	5.80	1.404	4.83	1.814	10.716***
Processing credit card and debit card payments	5.47	1.690	6.01	1.327	5.03	1.810	11.079***
Luggage carrying in hotels/airports, etc.	5.73	1.571	6.22	1.140	5.33	1.734	10.929***
Luggage storage in hotels/airports, etc.	5.65	1.578	6.19	1.116	5.21	1.743	12.051***
Garbage collection	5.88	1.444	6.27	1.111	5.58	1.591	8.996***
Cleaning the common areas of the hotel/theme park/airport/restaurant	5.77	1.503	6.31	1.001	5.35	1.675	12.672***
Providing gardening services	5.14	1.672	5.68	1.344	4.72	1.775	10.943***
Providing repair and maintenance in a facility	5.04	1.758	5.53	1.513	4.65	1.837	9.353***
Serve as guards/security	3.87	2.005	4.47	1.826	3.38	2.010	10.089***
Helping tourists/guests/passengers in case of emergency	3.97	2.044	4.52	1.908	3.52	2.036	9.032***

(Continued)

Table 5.3 (Continued)

Activity	Total Mean	Total St. dev.	Cluster 1 Robophiles Mean	Cluster 1 Robophiles St. dev.	Cluster 2 Robophobes Mean	Cluster 2 Robophobes St. dev.	t-Test
Hotel > reception							
Check-in	4.89	1.895	5.69	1.443	4.25	1.967	15.031***
Guiding to the room	4.91	1.883	5.65	1.494	4.31	1.950	13.782***
Check-out	5.11	1.814	5.85	1.327	4.52	1.931	14.394***
Hotel > housekeeping							
Cleaning the room	5.23	1.749	5.81	1.394	4.76	1.860	11.499***
Taking customer orders for laundry	5.51	1.601	6.08	1.180	5.06	1.730	12.355***
Laundry service	5.61	1.569	6.12	1.171	5.20	1.714	11.322***
Ironing service	5.29	1.701	5.78	1.370	4.90	1.826	9.818***
Delivering ready laundry	5.72	1.546	6.28	1.042	5.27	1.723	12.864***
Taking customer orders for new towels, linen, etc.	5.62	1.566	6.16	1.187	5.19	1.692	11.928***
Delivering new towels, linen, etc.	5.63	1.597	6.19	1.139	5.18	1.757	12.329***
Hotel > food and beverages/restaurants							
Taking orders for room service	5.45	1.641	6.10	1.130	4.93	1.790	14.153***
Delivering food and drinks in room service	5.20	1.835	5.96	1.355	4.58	1.938	14.790***
Guiding guests to tables in the restaurant	4.86	1.933	5.59	1.543	4.28	2.012	13.130***
Providing information about the menu	5.15	1.848	5.83	1.431	4.61	1.962	12.772***
Taking orders in the restaurant	4.99	1.865	5.77	1.385	4.36	1.959	14.933***
Cooking food	3.71	1.971	4.33	1.893	3.20	1.881	10.618***
Serving food in the restaurant	4.53	1.973	5.38	1.592	3.84	1.978	15.370***
Making drinks (coffee, tea, and cocktails) in the restaurant/bar	4.51	1.967	5.25	1.688	3.92	1.973	12.911***
Serving drinks in the restaurant/bar	4.51	2.000	5.36	1.621	3.82	2.010	15.044***
Cleaning the table	5.27	1.751	5.75	1.461	4.88	1.866	9.232***
Hotel > additional services							
Massages	3.68	2.023	4.35	1.909	3.14	1.955	11.033***
Playing games with the guests	4.36	1.956	5.03	1.703	3.82	1.978	11.646***

Entertaining the guests	4.36	1.947	5.01	1.702	3.84	1.977	11.210***
Dancing with guests	3.29	1.976	3.85	1.976	2.84	1.862	9.331***
Babysitting	2.47	1.814	2.86	1.895	2.15	1.674	6.928***
Provision of very short 1–2 hour workshops to guests (e.g., on gardening, cooking, painting, astronomy, etc.)	4.03	1.896	4.73	1.707	3.47	1.853	12.548***
Hairdressing	3.05	1.834	3.60	1.926	2.61	1.629	9.692***
Travel agency/tourist information centre							
Provision of information about the offers (in the office of the agency/TIC)	5.29	1.674	5.99	1.205	4.74	1.778	14.866***
Robot tour guide in the destination (outside the office of the agency/TIC)	4.58	1.935	5.32	1.605	3.99	1.973	13.169***
Theme park							
Automation of rides	4.83	1.812	5.46	1.457	4.32	1.903	12.084***
Robotic control of the rides	4.55	1.898	5.19	1.612	4.03	1.951	11.561***
Serve as robot-entertainers/show participants	4.46	1.950	5.07	1.716	3.96	1.983	10.705***
Events							
Providing information about the event	5.59	1.560	6.19	1.057	5.12	1.721	13.574***
Guiding the participants to their seats	5.08	1.819	5.78	1.371	4.52	1.934	13.614***
Serving food during the event	4.71	1.900	5.52	1.455	4.05	1.958	15.310***
Serving drinks during the event	4.76	1.903	5.59	1.423	4.10	1.976	15.585***
Serve as robot-entertainers/show participants	4.48	1.940	5.07	1.698	4.00	1.991	10.269***
Museums and galleries							
Providing information about the exhibits	5.64	1.584	6.23	1.124	5.19	1.732	12.843***
Robot tour guide in the museum/gallery	5.11	1.838	5.86	1.381	4.52	1.936	14.264***
Rent-a-car							
Self-driving cars	4.67	1.906	5.36	1.591	4.10	1.953	12.609***
Cleaning the vehicles	5.74	1.457	6.21	1.051	5.36	1.613	11.145***
Robotic car key delivery	5.36	1.690	6.03	1.260	4.82	1.762	13.992***
The car is opened and started by access code received with the booking (no physical key)	5.30	1.667	5.85	1.346	4.85	1.762	11.411***
The car is electric	5.72	1.511	6.21	1.144	5.33	1.642	11.162***

(*Continued*)

Table 5.3 (Continued)

Activity	Total Mean	Total St. dev.	Cluster 1 Robophiles Mean	Cluster 1 Robophiles St. dev.	Cluster 2 Robophobes Mean	Cluster 2 Robophobes St. dev.	t-Test
The car goes to a gas station/charging station automatically when the fuel tank/battery is below a specific limit	4.89	1.831	5.36	1.695	4.51	1.846	8.488***
Airplanes/buses/trains							
Self-driving planes	3.67	2.118	4.36	2.035	3.10	2.008	11.007***
Self-driving buses	4.11	2.096	4.91	1.875	3.46	2.039	13.100***
Self-driving trains	4.41	2.078	5.13	1.822	3.84	2.090	11.726***
Self-driving vessels (e.g., ships and cruise ships)	3.96	2.080	4.73	1.933	3.35	1.988	12.423***
Check-in (e.g., at airports)	5.43	1.705	6.11	1.228	4.88	1.831	14.191***
Guiding the passenger to the seat	5.15	1.799	5.82	1.421	4.60	1.884	13.072***
Providing information about the vehicle	5.81	1.443	6.33	1.019	5.40	1.587	12.611***
Providing information about the trip/flight/route	5.83	1.448	6.35	0.995	5.42	1.602	12.607***
Providing information about the safety and security procedures and regulations on board	5.76	1.500	6.30	1.064	5.33	1.650	12.514***
Serving food on board	4.85	1.894	5.65	1.447	4.20	1.964	15.100***
Serving drinks on board	4.85	1.905	5.64	1.483	4.21	1.967	14.629***
Cleaning the vehicle/vessel/aircraft	5.64	1.544	6.13	1.178	5.25	1.682	10.880***
Airports and other transportation stations							
Provision of information about departures/arrivals	5.97	1.361	6.46	0.908	5.59	1.525	12.516***
Provision of information about seat/berth availability	5.93	1.352	6.44	0.887	5.53	1.505	13.277***
Provision of information about ticket prices/fees	5.92	1.405	6.43	0.939	5.53	1.568	12.675***
Provision of information about special legal regulations, visa formalities, etc.	5.56	1.631	6.11	1.240	5.14	1.761	11.532***

Note: Coding of statements: 1 – extremely inappropriate, 7 – extremely appropriate

***Significant at $p < 0.001$

Table 5.4 Preferred human–robot ratio in the service process

Indicate your preferences towards the human employees–robots ratio in the following industries	Total Mean	Total Standard deviation	Cluster 1 Robophiles Mean	Cluster 1 Robophiles Standard deviation	Cluster 2 Robophobes Mean	Cluster 2 Robophobes Standard deviation	t-Test
Hotel	4.68	1.608	3.95	1.516	5.27	1.424	−15.931***
Room service	4.31	1.795	3.52	1.669	4.93	1.637	−15.080***
Restaurant	5.07	1.560	4.43	1.573	5.60	1.336	−14.006***
Bar	5.16	1.555	4.54	1.575	5.66	1.342	−13.414***
Travel agency	4.72	1.649	4.02	1.634	5.27	1.430	−14.359***
Tourist information centre	4.29	1.719	3.60	1.596	4.85	1.604	−13.866***
Rent-a-car	4.26	1.695	3.58	1.591	4.80	1.575	−13.579***
Airplane	4.90	1.636	4.27	1.673	5.40	1.411	−12.801***
Bus	4.46	1.692	3.76	1.588	5.02	1.555	−14.191***
Train	4.51	1.653	3.80	1.581	5.08	1.474	−14.944***
Ship/cruise ship	4.83	1.562	4.13	1.520	5.39	1.351	−15.460***
Airport	4.44	1.698	3.67	1.591	5.06	1.518	−15.853***
Bus station	4.21	1.685	3.51	1.570	4.77	1.557	−14.312***
Train station	4.20	1.688	3.44	1.523	4.82	1.554	−15.831***
Port	4.49	1.620	3.83	1.528	5.02	1.489	−13.955***
During an event (e.g., concert, congress, and exhibition)	4.73	1.589	4.12	1.529	5.21	1.462	−12.918***
Museum/gallery	4.42	1.701	3.80	1.626	4.92	1.588	−12.407***

Note: Coding of statements: 1 – I prefer to be served only by robots, 4 – I prefer to be served by an approximately equal number of human employees and robots, 7 – I prefer to be served only by human employees

***Significant at $p < 0.001$

pessimistic and frightened about the dehumanisation effects of robots. From a theoretical perspective, the results of the study indicate that these overall perceptions of robots shape how people think about the use of robots in specific contexts such as tourism and hospitality – the tasks that robots are accepted to perform, the human employees–robots ratio in the service delivery process, and the willingness to pay for robot-delivered services. More specifically, people with more positive attitudes towards robots ('robophiles') report higher perceived appropriateness of robots use for implementing various tasks in tourism and hospitality, prefer slightly more robots in the delivery process for some services, and expect lower discount for robot-delivered services compared to people with negative attitudes ('robophobes'). Another noteworthy finding is that robophobes tend to be female, supporting, what previous research has shown with regard to gender differences and interests, that females tend to be interested in people and males tend to be interested in things (Su, Rounds, & Armstrong, 2009). Apart from robophobes

Table 5.5 Willingness to pay for fully robot-delivered services

If you were to be served entirely by robots in the following industries, instead of human employees, how much would you be willing to pay for a fully robotised service compared to a service fully delivered by human employees?	Total Mean	Total Standard deviation	Cluster 1 Robophiles Mean	Cluster 1 Robophiles Standard deviation	Cluster 2 Robophobes Mean	Cluster 2 Robophobes Standard deviation	t-Test
Hotel accommodation	−9.56	12.519	−7.27	11.657	−11.43	12.889	6.019***
Room service	−9.39	12.444	−7.18	11.782	−11.21	12.683	5.827***
Restaurant	−10.55	12.711	−8.01	12.151	−12.62	12.769	6.550***
Bar drinks	−10.42	12.497	−8.20	11.942	−12.23	12.654	5.801***
Travel agency services	−9.96	12.282	−7.96	11.444	−11.64	12.661	5.423***
Tourist information centre services	−9.36	12.462	−7.45	11.655	−10.99	12.822	5.141***
Rent-a-car	−8.66	12.517	−6.47	11.684	−10.45	12.836	5.765***
Flight ticket	−9.01	12.390	−6.95	11.652	−10.73	12.694	5.498***
Bus ticket	−8.70	12.024	−6.67	11.196	−10.35	12.429	5.522***
Train ticket	−8.84	12.074	−7.02	11.294	−10.29	12.448	4.896***
Ship ticket	−9.15	12.261	−7.07	11.453	−10.90	12.578	5.654***
Cruise package	−9.57	12.620	−7.30	11.760	−11.46	12.963	5.978***
Event ticket (e.g., concert, congress, and exhibition)	−8.74	12.192	−6.79	11.372	−10.35	12.592	5.278***
Entrance fee for a museum/gallery	−8.53	12.098	−6.74	11.324	−9.97	12.527	4.801***

Note: Percentage difference compared to the price of a fully human-delivered service

***Significant at $p < 0.001$

and robophiles being delineated by gender, the other demographic characteristics do not really show much predictive capability, although there is some indication of a class bias in attitudes towards robots.

The data also show that the clusters (robophiles vs. robophobes) seem to have predictive value in just about anything asked about. With no exception, when asked about a particular service that a robot could provide, those respondents that could be classified as robophiles showed a greater willingness to have robots provide them services, to accept a higher ratio of robots to human employees, and to pay for services provided to robots. In short, the data analysis supports the notion that a general acceptance of robots leads to specific attitudes towards robots in the tourism ecosystem. So, those who are robophilic have less of an issue having robots provide them with services, are willing to see more robots than humans in the service environment, and do not seem to mind paying for robot-provided services. For a full transformation into a more robotised tourism ecosystem, the resistance of the robophobes will have to be addressed.

Conclusion

The findings show that there is an empirical basis to the robophobe and robophile archetype and that these two archetypes have a very different mindset with regard to the transformation into a robotised service economy in the tourism ecosystem. The robophiles seem to be receptive to just about any task being done by a robot. The robophiles are generally willing to see more robots than humans in the service environment and are willing to pay for robot-delivered services. While the two different archetypes differ in their attitudes towards robots, there seems to be no way to demographically differentiate them, apart from the fact that females are much more likely to be robophobes.

From a practical and managerial perspective, the findings reveal that companies cannot apply a 'one size fits all' approach to robotisation of services, since not all customers have the same view of robots in the service environment. When deciding on the implementation of service robots, tourism and hospitality managers need to consider not only on which tasks customers consider as suitable for robotisation, how much they would be willing to pay for robot-delivered services, or how many robots they would use in the service delivery system, but they also have to consider the different attitudes towards robots as well. From a marketing standpoint, within the context of diffusion of innovations theory (Rogers, 1983), the robophiles would be the most open to innovations and would be the first to adopt the robot-delivered services in tourism and hospitality. Hence, attracting them would help the tourism and hospitality companies that implement robots create a sufficient customer base for their innovative services and recover their investments. However, companies need to offer price discounts if they introduce a fully robotised service delivery system because customers expect the cost savings robots are perceived to provide to companies be shared with them as well. From an operations view point, the findings reveal that it may be too early for fully robotised tourism and hospitality services. Although the robophiles preferred slightly more robots than humans in the delivery process, it would be wise companies to deploy only one or a few robots initially and gradually expand the number of robots in the service delivery if necessary and economically justified. In that way, the robots will not dominate in the service delivery; they would not be perceived as a threat but as innovation and might even contribute to changing the attitudes of the robophobes when they actually use the robots. Focusing on the tasks perceived as most appropriate for robotisation (information provision, housekeeping, cleaning, and delivery of various items) and avoiding those that face resistance would stimulate robot acceptance by customers and might mitigate their negative attitudes towards them.

The research is not without a limitation, since the data are only quantitative in nature. The lack of qualitative data limits the interpretation of findings because one cannot delve deeper into the actual reasons and motives behind respondents' answers. Future research may try to overcome this limitation by adopting a qualitative (or mixed methods) approach to evaluating the attitudes towards service robots in travel, tourism, and hospitality to gain deeper insights on the topic. Future research may also shed light on the drivers of the willingness to pay for robot-delivered services. In addition, future research should explore the patterns of robophobia and robophilia in different national markets, since it seems that there may be a very deep positive regard that the Japanese and other nationals have with regard to robots that may not be as universal and that the patterns for what composes the robophilic and robophobic segments within countries may vary by country. In addition, future research may look into the very different predispositions of males and females towards robots in tourism and hospitality context.

Acknowledgements

The authors would like to thank Ulrike Gretzel, Katerina Berezina, Iis Tussyadiah, Jamie Murphy, Dimitrios Buhalis, and Cihan Cobanoglu for their valuable comments on the initial drafts of the questionnaire. The authors also thank Sofya Yanko, Katerina Berezina, Nadia Malenkina, Raul Hernandez Martin, Antoaneta Topalova, Florian Aubke, Nedra Bahri, Frederic Dimanche, Rosanna Leung, Kwang-Ho Lee, Minako Okada, Isa Vieira, Jean Max Tavares, Seden Dogan, and Isabella Ye for devoting their time and effort into the translation of the questionnaire. Financial support for electronic vouchers was provided by Zangador Ltd. (www.zangador.eu). Ethics approval for the research was granted by Ball State University, Muncie, Indiana, USA. The authors would like to thank Hosco (www.hosco.com) and Industrial Engineering & Design (www.facebook.com/Ind.eng.design) for their support in the distribution of the link to the online questionnaire. Finally, the authors are grateful to all those anonymous respondents who participated in the survey and made their opinion heard.

References

Berezina, K., Ciftici, O., & Cobanoglu, C. (2019). Robots, artificial intelligence and service automation in restaurants. In S. Ivanov & C. Webster (Eds.), *Robots, artificial intelligence*

and service automation in travel, tourism and hospitality (pp. 185–220). Bingley: Emerald.
Bruner, G. C., & Kumar, A. (2005). Explaining consumer acceptance of handheld internet devices. *Journal of Business Research, 58*(5), 553–558.
Cui, G., Bao, W., & Chan, T. S. (2009). Consumers' adoption of new technology products: The role of coping strategies. *Journal of Consumer Marketing, 26*(2), 110–120.
De Graaf, M. M. A., Allouch, S. B., & Klamer, T. (2015). Sharing a life with Harvey: Exploring the acceptance of and relationship-building with a social robot. *Computers in Human Behavior, 43*, 1–14.
Denis-Rémis, C. (2011). Relation of green IT and affective attitude within the technology acceptance model: The cases of France and China. *Management & Avenir, 9*, 371–385.
Dinet, J., & Vivian, R. (2014). Exploratory investigation of attitudes towards assistive robots for future users. *Le travail humain, 77*(2), 105–125.
Dolnicar, S., Grün, B., Leisch, F., & Schmidt, K. (2014). Required sample sizes for data-driven market segmentation analyses in tourism. *Journal of Travel Research, 53*(3), 296–306. https://doi.org/10.1177/0047287513496475
Frennert, S., & Östlund, B. (2014). Review: Seven matters of concern of social robots and older people. *International Journal of Social Robotics, 6*(2), 299–310.
Hudson, J., Orviska, M., & Hunady, J. (2017). People's attitudes to robots in caring for the elderly. *International Journal of Social Robotics, 9*(2), 199–210.
Ivanov, S., Gretzel, U., Berezina, K., Sigala, M.& Webster, C. (2019). Progress on robotics in hospitality and tourism: A review of the literature. *Journal of Hospitality and Tourism Technology, 10*(4), 489–521. https://doi.org/10.1108/JHTT-08-2018-0087
Ivanov, S., Webster, C., & Berezina, K. (2017). Adoption of robots and service automation by tourism and hospitality companies. *Revista Turismo & Desenvolvimento, 27/28*, 1501–1517.
Ivanov, S., Webster, C., & Berezina, K. (2020). Robotics in tourism and hospitality. In Z. Xiang, M. Fuchs, U. Gretzel, & W. Höpken (Eds.), *Handbook of e-tourism*. Springer, (in press). Retrieved from https://link.springer.com/referenceworkentry/10.1007/978-3-030-05324-6_112-1
Ivanov, S., Webster, C., & Garenko, A. (2018). Young Russian adults' attitudes towards the potential use of robots in hotels. *Technology in Society, 55*, 24–32. https://doi.org/10.1016/j.techsoc.2018.06.004
Ivanov, S., Webster, C., & Seyyedi, P. (2018). Consumers' attitudes towards the introduction of robots in accommodation establishments. *Tourism, 63*(3), 302–317.
Ivanova, M. (2019). Robots, artificial intelligence, and service automation in travel agencies and tourist information centers. In S. Ivanov & C. Webster (Eds.), *Robots, artificial intelligence and service automation in travel, tourism and hospitality* (pp. 221–238). Bingley: Emerald.
Katz, J. E., & Halpern, D. (2014). Attitudes towards robots suitability for various jobs as affected robot appearance. *Behaviour and Information Technology, 33*(9), 941–953.
Lin, J.-S. C., & Hsieh, P. (2006). The role of technology readiness in customers' perception and adoption of self-service technologies. *International Journal of Service Industry Management, 17*, 497–517.
Malchus, K., Jaecks, P., Wrede, B., & Stenneken, P. (2013). Application of social robots in speech and language therapy?! An investigation into speech and language pathologists' attitudes towards embodied agents [Einsatz sozialer Roboter in der Sprachtherapie?! Erhebung eines Stimmungsbildes von SprachtherapeutInnen]. *L.O.G.O.S. Interdisziplinair, 21*(2), 106–116.

Morosan, C., & DeFranco, A. (2014). Understanding the actual use of mobile devices in private clubs in the US. *Journal of Hospitality and Tourism Technology*, 5(3), 278–298.

Morosan, C., & DeFranco, A. (2019). Using interactive technologies to influence guests' unplanned dollar spending in hotels. *International Journal of Hospitality Management*, 82, 242–251.

NPR. (2011). *Science diction: The origin of the word "robot"*. Retrieved from www.npr.org/2011/04/22/135634400/science-diction-the-origin-of-the-word-robot

Piçarra, N., Giger, J.-C., Pochwatko, G., & Gonçalves, G. (2016). Making sense of social robots: A structural analysis of the layperson's social representation of robots [Donner un sens aux robots sociaux: une analyse structurelle de la représentation sociale des robots]. *Revue Europeenne de Psychologie Appliquee*, 66(6), 277–289.

Pino, M., Boulay, M., Jouen, F., & Rigaud, A.-S. (2015). "Are we ready for robots that care for us?" Attitudes and opinions of older adults toward socially assistive robots. *Frontiers in Aging Neuroscience*, 7, article 141.

Pochwatko, G., Giger, J.-C., Różańska-Walczuk, M., Świdrak, J., Kukiełka, K., Możaryn, J., & Piçarra, N. (2015). Polish version of the negative attitude toward robots scale (NARS-PL). *Journal of Automation, Mobile Robotics and Intelligent Systems*, 9(3), 65–72.

Reich-Stiebert, N., & Eyssel, F. (2015). Learning with educational companion robots? Toward attitudes on education robots, predictors of attitudes, and application potentials for education robots. *International Journal of Social Robotics*, 7(5), 875–888.

Rogers, E. M. (1983). *Diffusion of innovations* (3rd ed.). London: The Free Press.

Samala, N., Katkam, B. S., Bellamkonda, R. S., & Rodriguez, R. V. (2020). Impact of AI and robotics in the tourism sector: A critical insight. *Journal of Tourism Futures* (in press). https://doi.org/10.1108/JTF-07-2019-0065

Singh, V. (2014). "We are not phobic but selective": The older generation's attitude towards using technology in workplace communications. *Development and Learning in Organizations: An International Journal*, 28(4), 18–20.

Su, R., Rounds, J., & Armstrong, P. I. (2009). Men and things, women and people: A meta-analysis of sex differences in interests. *Psychological Bulletin*, 135(6), 859–884.

Wang, Y., & Qualls, W. (2007). Towards a theoretical model of technology adoption in hospitality organizations. *International Journal of Hospitality Management*, 26(3), 560–573.

Webster, C., & Ivanov, S. (2020). *Robots in travel, tourism and hospitality: Key findings from a global study*. Varna: Zangador.

Yan, H., Ang Jr., M. H., & Poo, A. N. (2014). A survey on perception methods for human-robot interaction in social robots. *International Journal of Social Robotics*, 6(1), 85–119.

6 Conceptualising system resilience in smart tourism destinations

Kyriaki Glyptou and Miju Choi

Introduction

Tourism is considered amongst the leading sectors to adopt early transformational processes throughout its supply chain (Song, 2011). Whether it is digital transformation or product differentiation, the tourism industry has manifested over the years strong reflexes to ensure continuous growth and innovative business solutions that safeguard both the competitiveness and the sustainability of the industry. Even if such advancements are predominant at the micro business level, their implementation at tourism destinations at the macro level remains fraud with challenges. With tourism destinations being continuously exposed to external disturbance and change, there comes an imperative need to establish strong grounds for their systemic resilience, to ensure their competitive market edge and maximise value for all stakeholders (Hall, Prayag, & Amore, 2018).

The recognition of tourism destinations as social-ecological systems (SES) that operate over spatial and temporal scales calls for practices to cope with system disturbance in the short and longer term (Folke, 2006). This approach gains particular importance amidst times of natural and anthropogenic crises, shifts in market trends, and political or socio-economic instability. Tourism destination management should thus focus on building destination resilience to secure societal development and avoid destination vulnerability. Resilience refers to the ability of a SES and a tourism destination to respond to and deal with change through adaptation and self-organisation (Folke et al., 2005, 2010).

At the same time, new age destinations and cities bare increasingly elements of 'smartness' aiming to respond more efficiently to the emerging needs of urban residents and visitors. A smart destination not only has a smart infrastructure but also connects elements of the urban ecosystem, such as smart government, smart citizens, smart economy, smart environment, and smart life. The ultimate goals of smart destinations are to improve the quality of human life and to achieve sustainable economic development (Bifulco et al., 2016). Harrison et al. (2010) summarised the main characteristics of smart destinations in three key categories. First, a smart destination should continuously collect, analyse, and distribute destination-related data that optimise efficiency and effectiveness so that networks within the destination are interconnected. Technology and data can then be

DOI: 10.4324/9781003105930-7

used to improve the destination's competitiveness and ensure its growth. Second, common definitions and standards should be established so that data and information on destinations can be shared so that they can be easily reused. Third, a smart destination must work multifunctionally to provide solutions to various problems from a holistic destination perspective.

To ensure a dynamic destination management system that drives transition towards resilience, destinations should rather embrace uncertainty and unpredictability and better benefit from management approaches that shape adaptability rather than approaches that aspire to control change (Berkes, Colding, & Folke, 2003). For Folke et al. (2005), adaptive governance and management should consider four crucial interactive aspects: (1) building knowledge and understanding of system dynamics; (2) feeding knowledge into adaptive management practices; (3) supporting flexible institutions and multilevel governance systems; and (4) dealing with external perturbations, uncertainty, and surprise. The management of CAS is thus effectuated through the development of continuous monitoring mechanisms that capture the inherent complexity of a destination system and translate knowledge into capacity for the attainment of systems' resilience baring the information of feedback loops, as well as the variations of the local context.

Over the last years, the international literature has addressed more profoundly the concept of resilience in tourism destinations with an emphasis on their function as SES (Butler, 2017; Cheer & Lew, 2018; Hall, Prayag, & Amore, 2018). Despite the extensive analytical and synthetic approaches, there is still no consensus on the underlying principles for resilience enhancement in tourism destinations and only little empirical evidence to support its operationalisation. To explore this research area with an emphasis on the features and structure of 'smartness', this book chapter adopts the recognition of tourism destinations as complex adaptive socio-ecological systems and explores the relevance and application of the seven generic principles approach introduced by Biggs et al. (2012) on ecosystem services. This context offers the grounds to explore the multi-component diversity expressed though the participation and engagement of various stakeholders and information sources (action groups or institutions) that could provide multiple alternative pathways when dealing with uncertainty and responding to change (Hall, Prayag, & Amore, 2018).

Within a continuously changing socio-economic, political, health and safety, and technological environment, tourism destinations are prompted by circumstances to develop strong self-adaptation and self-organisation structures to ensure timely, acute, and effective responses to external disturbances and speed up their recovery process. Building on the theories of SES and CAS, this conceptual study aims to explore the structural and operational advantages of the emerging transformations inherent in smart tourism destinations and their contribution for ensuring system resilience. Its theoretical contribution lies in the novel exploration of the conceptual interface between the defining principles of destination resilience and smartness, thus highlighting the contribution of emerging tourism transformations in ensuring tourism destinations adaptability and self-organisation ability. Although the study doesn't make any prominent methodological contribution, it builds on the three key components of Future City Glasgow to demonstrate applicability and relevance.

Tourism destination resilience

The recognition of tourism destinations as complex adaptive SES acknowledges the plethora of underlying interactions along their dimensions and scales, their ability for self-organisation, and the unexpected changes as a response to both external and internal triggers. Emphasising on ecosystem services, Biggs et al. (2012) conceptualised the enhancement of resilience in SES through the achievement of these seven principles: maintain diversity and redundancy [P1]; manage connectivity [P2]; manage slow variables and feedbacks [P3]; foster CAS thinking [P4]; encourage learning and experimentation [P5]; broaden participation [P6]; and promote polycentric governance systems [P7].

The principle of *Maintaining System Diversity and Redundancy* [P1], more specifically, allows for complementarity and the assurance that certain components could potentially cover or compensate for the inadequacy and failure of others (Walker & Salt, 2012) and hence support a faster system recovery in the face of adversity. In fact, the higher the diversity and distinctiveness of system components, the stronger its redundancy due to the variant timing and type of response to disturbance. In the case of tourism destinations, the response diversity encompasses the pluralism of the tourism destination facets considered, the size and strength of stakeholders involved, as well as the scale of their influence and power which is usually subject to their financial and human capital (Folke et al., 2005; Westley et al., 2013). In that regard, destination stakeholders and information agents may provide complementary and even overlapping functions through divergent trajectories and different strengths and contribution. Enhanced destination redundancy thus allows for the necessary response diversification that reduces the risk of complete system failure by minimising the possibility of a particular disturbance to horizontally and homogeneously impact all system components within the same period of time (Kotschy et al, 2015).

The *Principle of Systems Connectivity* [P2] encompasses the structure and strength of resources' and actors' interactions across the SES domains (Bodin & Prell, 2011). System connectivity is thus associated with both the speed and the spread of effects across a system.

Well-connected systems can overcome and recover from disturbances more quickly, but overly connected systems may lead to the rapid spread of disturbances across the entire system so that all components/actors are impacted (Dakos et al., 2015). To build resilience in SES, the principle of connectivity needs to be embedded within destinations governance. Pluralism and diversity remain paramount, as the homogenisation of knowledge, information, resources, and target increases the risk of simultaneous exposure to disturbance, and hence compromise the systems' resilience (Hall, Prayag, & Amore, 2018). To enhance a SES resilience through the mitigation of the negative implications of enhanced connectivity in tourism destination systems, it is important to identify vulnerable nodes and their triggers (Schoon et al., 2014). This would potentially invoke alternative connection trajectories that could either eliminate certain system nodes or provide more modular structures.

SES are characterised by a certain sense of structure and order that ensures their ability to provide ecosystem supporting, provisioning, regulating, and cultural services. In that regard, Principle 3 of *Managing Slow Variables and Feedbacks* [P3] of systems' configuration and functioning is achieved through the management of fundamental slow variables of ecosystem services' components and their feedback loops. In the case of tourism destination systems, examples of slow variables may include the legal frameworks, values, and traditions (Berbés-Blázquez & Scott, 2017). System resilience further revolves around the management challenge of identifying and monitoring the critical system thresholds after which the system will require reconfiguration. In the case of tourism destinations, this could involve the unexpected increase in tourism arrivals due to safety concerns in a neighbouring competitor or the promotion of low fares from the main air or tour operator. The challenge in terms of managing revolves around the strengthening of feedbacks that maintain the desirable core functions and regimes (Biggs et al., 2012), while at the same time impose stricter controls on any activities and subsidies that might obscure the feedbacks by translocating the problem or coming up with opportunistic alternatives, such as illegal accommodation provision.

Principle 4 of *Fostering Complex Adaptive Systems Thinking* [P4] recognises the inherent complexity of the multidimensional dynamic connections amongst the components and actors of a SES, which goes beyond any reductionist thinking (Levin et al., 2013). To foster complex adaptive thinking in SES and more specifically in tourism destinations, it is necessary to de-code the behaviour and cognitive decision-making process of social actors. The process recognises that there is no defined or set solution to a problem, but it is more the process of setting acceptable thresholds and boundaries within which multiple interventions can be piloted (Bodin & Prell, 2011). In the context of tourism destinations, this could deter destinations from over-dependency on a single tourism product (e.g., mass coastal tourism) or a tour operator and instead develop a more flexible and adaptive approach to their supply (e.g., multiple complementary sea-based activities). Upon identifying the inter-dependencies of SES components, a structured process like scenario planning may facilitate the evaluation and feasibility of alternative trajectories based on the intended and unintended chain effect of decision-making.

Principle 5 on *Encouraging Learning* [P5] reflects the need for continuous information flow through monitoring and experimentation to enable system adaptation and appropriate management interventions. SES are dynamically changing and adapting systems, hence knowledge is always partial and incomplete and exact system behaviour cannot be fully predicted (Westley et al., 2013). Other than the continuous re-iteration and data collection of learning by doing, the multidimensional and cross-scale learning is paramount for the development of new system norms and the enhancement of communication and building of trust on system values and the promotion of cooperation (Olsson, Folke, & Berkes, 2004). Within a tourism destination system, learning can be encouraged and achieved through the development of a continuous monitoring system that enables the assessment of both tourism supply and demand elements but primarily through the monitoring of the interface and interactions between the two (Glyptou et al., 2014). Management and governance structures should promote and facilitate the interaction between system components, and they should engage with participants in a variety of social contexts to share and advance knowledge and to create communities of practice.

Broadening Participation [P6] and active engagement of all system actors are fundamental for the resilience of a SES. Broad and harmonious participation among participants builds trust and consensus and reveals multiple facets and perspectives of a parameter through the expansion of depth and diversity of information (Biggs et al., 2012). It could further help set management priorities and needs and identify system perturbations. It also strengthens awareness and raises support through representing the greater well-being of the system. Participatory monitoring improves the transparency of decisions which in turn ensures enhanced relationships between project stakeholders and ensures the comprehension and validity of information (Hall, Prayag, & Amore, 2018). Participation, if not supported by balanced power relations, might result into competition and conflict. Co-management where participation includes little authority but much responsibility may degrade both the ecosystem resilience and the ability of the system to deliver ecosystem services (Cheer & Lew, 2018). Enabling participation entails setting clear goals, expectations, and objectives, providing capacity building and secure sufficient resources for effective participation, and dealing on time with power issues and potential conflicts.

Finally, Principle 7 of *Promoting Polycentric Governance* [P7] fosters collective action among multiple governing bodies with the aim to make and enforce policy rules. Collaboration across institutions, system dimensions, and scales with an emphasis on connectivity, learning, and information exchange is the prerequisite for almost all other principles of resilience, particularly in the context of tourism destinations. Polycentricity abides by the contribution of nested institutions to promote social engagement and participatory processes that addresses SES challenges through collective action (Levin et al., 2013). Polycentric governance enhances tourism destinations' resilience through the enhancement of pluralism and response diversity, as well as the effectuation of system redundancy that can minimise governance mechanism shortcomings. The latter is particularly relevant when moving away from national scales and policies into the specifics of local and regional destinations, where the local knowledge can be better capitalised through the encouragement of an industry culture of learning and experimentation.

Smart tourism destinations

In smart destinations, physical, information and communication, social, and business infrastructures are combined to build their collective intelligence. A smart destination improves urban life and increases the efficiency of destination management by integrating the physical and virtual urban infrastructures (Gretzel et al., 2015). Smart destinations optimise the operation of destination services using destination operation data on traffic congestion, electricity consumption, and public safety events. According to Koo et al. (2016), smart destinations are marked by instrumentation, interconnection, and intelligence. 'Instrumentation' refers to the collection of data from the real world in real time using a physical and virtual data acquisition system (Koo et al., 2016). For example, physical devices such as sensors, kiosks, meters, and smartphones are used in addition to social networks to collect real-world data. 'Interconnection' involves integrating the collected data into a comprehensive computing platform and communicating the information generated there between various destination services. 'Intelligence' improves decision-making on urban management by analysing, modelling, optimising, and visualising the urban management business process (Koo et al., 2016).

The initial concept of smart tourism was to provide effective customised tourism services based on real-time tourism information and location information tailored to tourists' current situation (tourist location, time, budget, etc.) centred on smartphones (Gretzel et al., 2016). However, it is necessary to expand the Fourth Industrial Revolution to the cooperation target of the tourism industry with robots and IT that can replace human services and to the IoT with sensor-based and network connections. Therefore, the definition of smart tourism should be extended to include renewing existing tourism methods and providing sufficient intelligent tourism services to form shared values among tourism participants and achieve mutual benefits (Gretzel et al., 2016; Jovicic, 2019). Thus, smart tourism includes not only the creation and sharing of content via smartphones, various user-customised services, and social network services using ICT but also the experiences of smart destination-based citizens and tourist users in smart destinations, and this concept is expanding and developing globally. Smart tourism destinations should be understood from a macro perspective that considers the impact of the tourism industry on local residents, tourism factors (tourist destinations, lodging, and transportation), related industries (shopping and medical), and the national economy (Bifulco et al., 2016).

In visualising smart destinations as a system platform, a smart destination consists of three distinctive layers of information and dynamics: an infrastructure layer, a data layer, and an institutional and service layer. Undoubtedly, not all ICT can be applied to the tourism field.

From the perspective of tourists who are users of lodging, transportation apps, and platform services, tourism experiences and products that have become more intelligent, user-friendly, and efficient can be defined as smart tourism (Wang et al., 2020). The smart tourism destination is the basis and the location for such smart tourism. The smart tourism destination creates synergy by combining the technologies necessary for smart tourism into a single system and ecosystem and by the convergence of various industries, thus enhancing the quality of tourist experience and providing efficient and effective tourism services (Gretzel et al., 2016).

IoT technology has emerged rapidly with the development of ICT. Elements of the IoT can interact in real time as a connected network to recognise, manage, and monitor things at anytime and anywhere. Smart devices can be used to search information related to tourism destinations and tourism experiences, leading to the creation of vast multidimensional data, commonly known as big data (Wang et al., 2020). Tourism-related organisations can gain valuable insights that can enhance the tourist destination experience based on big data from past tourists. The IoT can also create a platform for exchanging vast amounts of data, so IoT technology can also be applied in the tourism field. Smart hotels using IoT devices may also appear, and areas where ICT can be used can provide customised/real-time services to customers by analysing big data or making payment systems more convenient through the use of fintech.

Pillars of resilience in smart tourism destinations

Adaptive tourism destination management and governance place continuous learning and information flow at the core of decision-making to mitigate any effect associated with uncertainty and external disturbance to the system (Hall, Prayag, & Amore, 2018). To nurture the process of complex adaptive systems thinking, tourism destinations should move away from the fragmented management approach towards a more integrative SES management culture that embraces openness and flexibility through the recognition of the cognitive barriers of change (Westley et al., 2013). Smart tourism destinations have inherently the structure to perform as continuous monitoring mechanisms. This allows the detection and recording of slow changes that challenge the system thresholds and hence could result into a reconfiguration into a different regime (Folke et al, 2010). Table 6.1 presents key literature on the applications of smart tourism destinations along the seven principles of resilience to delineate the inherent 'goodness of fit' between the two concepts. The literature review highlights that through the multiple agent channels of dynamic information flow and exchange, smart destinations ensure the systematic and collaborate thinking and promote connectivity and all participatory processes that foster systems' resilience. Moreover, the acute interpretation of system information into action responses further establishes system resilience through the timely adaptive management interventions over changes that threaten the credibility and quality of the system or support its controlled transition into an upgraded system regime (Walker & Salt, 2012).

Case study: future city Glasgow

In 2013, Glasgow received £24 million in funding from the Technology Strategy Board (now Innovate UK) under the Department for Business, Innovation and Skills to use the latest science and technology to conduct a project to make urban life smarter, safer, and more sustainable (Leleux & Webster, 2018). The Technology Strategy Board provided 30 British cities with £50,000 each to study ways to use new technologies to improve urban life in the areas of transport, housing, health, energy, and the environment. Glasgow was selected as the first demonstration smart city in the UK, overtaking the 29 other cities with an application

Table 6.1 Alignment of resilience principles to smart tourism destination applications

Principles of Resilience	Relevance to Smart Tourism Destination Applications
P1. Maintain diversity and redundancy	• IT: value, pleasure, and experiences co-creation (Boes, Buhalis, & Inversini, 2015) • Enhance visitor experience though product/service personalisation and awareness of available tourism services (Lamsfus et al., 2015) • Infrastructure and accessibility (Lopez de Avila, 2015; Coca-Stefaniak, 2019) • Market ties (Coca-Stefaniak, 2019)
P2. Manage connectivity	• Smart-tailored services and applications for co-creation (Cavalheiro, Joia, & Cavalheiro, 2020) • ICT: dynamic interconnection of multiple stakeholders to support prompt information exchange (Buhalis & Amaranggana, 2013) • ICT: visitor's interaction with and integration into surroundings and increases the quality of the experience at the destination (Lopez de Avila, 2015) • ICT: knowledge-based destination, as a technological platform for instant exchange of tourism information and knowledge (Jovicic, 2019)
P3. Manage slow variables and feedbacks	• Tourism integrated information platform (Cavalheiro, Joia, & Cavalheiro, 2020) • Tourism product diversification resulting into wealth, profit, and benefits for the organisations and the destination (Boes, Buhalis, & Inversini, 2015)
P4. Foster complex adaptive systems thinking	• Enhanced economic, socio-cultural, political, and ecological value (Cavalheiro, Joia, & Cavalheiro, 2020) • Dynamic machine-to-machine learning algorithm (Buhalis & Amaranggana, 2013) • ICT: self-operation and automation: cloud services, Internet of things (IoT), and end-user Internet service system are typically recognised for their indispensable roles in realising smart tourism destinations (Koo et al., 2016) • AI Technology (Wang et al., 2016) • Destination Intelligence (Ivars-Baidal et al., 2019) • Smart Innovation (Coca-Stefaniak, 2019)
P5. Encourage learning	• ICT: knowledge-based destination, as a technological platform for instant exchange of tourism information and knowledge (Jovicic, 2019) • AI Technology (Wang et al., 2016)
P6. Broaden participation	• Full smart experience: smart tourists-smart destinations (Femenia-Serra, Neuhofer, & Ivars-Baidal, 2019) • Full smart experience: smart tourists-smart destinations (Femenia-Serra, Neuhofer, & Ivars-Baidal, 2019) • Smart experience co-creation: interaction, sharing, and active participation (Cimbaljević, Stankov, & Pavluković, 2019) • Integration, coordination, and cooperation among stakeholders (Cavalheiro, Joia, & Cavalheiro, 2020)
P7. Promote polycentric governance systems	• Interconnection of multiple stakeholders to support prompt information exchange and hence enhance their decision-making process (Buhalis & Amaranggana, 2013) • Empowering destination management organisations and local stakeholders to make decisions and take actions based upon the data produced in within the destination, gathered, managed, and processed by means of the technology infrastructure (Lamsfus et al., 2015)

Conceptualising system resilience 91

focusing on urban mobility, cycling and walking, energy, public mobility support services, and public safety (Innovate UK, 2017). Since receiving funding from the UK government in 2013, the City of Glasgow has implemented many of its proposals, including updating the central transport and public safety control centre with the latest science and technology, achieving big and open data, developing an app that allows easy and simple communication between citizens and local governments, and improving urban mobility and urban energy consumption (Leleux & Webster, 2018). Glasgow's smart city project, entitled Future City Glasgow, includes three major components – the Glasgow Operations Centre, Open Glasgow, and Four Demonstrators – and features energy efficiency, integrated social transport, intelligent street lighting, and active travel, which promote directly or indirectly resilience at the tourism destination level.

Glasgow Operations Centre

The Glasgow Operations Centre established an up-to-date central traffic and public safety control system. The centre is equipped with central operation and access to over 500 public CCTVs that have been upgraded to full HD to share video information with the police. It provides real-time central traffic management and features a central control system using 800 traffic signals and a real-time notification system in case of emergency using the latest video analysis technology. In addition, the centre provides central security management for municipal museums and art galleries. Other than ensuring the *Management of Connectivity* [P2] through the dynamic interconnection of information agents and sources, the central Glasgow Operations Centre serves a continuous monitoring system that fosters *Complex Adaptive Systems Thinking* [P4] which contributes to the *Management of Slow Variables and Feedbacks* [P3] and the nurturing of Polycentric Governance Systems [P7].

Open Glasgow

The Open Glasgow project aims to strengthen innovation and capacity in all areas of the community by increasing the accessibility of data to citizens, academia, companies, and the *public through the Internet*. In an era in which a large amount of information is rapidly produced by research institutions, the Open Glasgow initiative greatly aligns with the resilience principle on *Broadening Participation* [P6] and *Encouraging Learning* [P5]. Data collected by 60 different research organisations on Glasgow's population, economy, education, environment, geography, energy, health, life, public safety, travel, and transport can be easily accessed by anyone regardless of location, which then ensures both the *Management of Connectivity* [P2] and *Slow Variables and Feedbacks* [P3].

In fact, the city of Glasgow is carefully evaluating the impact and ripple effects of making big data widely available in the following areas:

- Partnership development through increased understanding of cities and communities

- Promotion of communication and cooperation between the community and its service providers
- Urban planning and urban regeneration development
- Improvement of the services provided in the city
- Participation in the policy-making process
- Increasing innovation that promotes urban economic growth
- Increased information transparency

Four Demonstrators

The Four Demonstrators project is designed to increase the energy efficiency of buildings in Glasgow and expand the use of low-carbon energy. In collaboration with Integrated Environmental Solutions (a firm located in Glasgow), a 2D/3D map was developed of the energy consumption of residential and commercial buildings throughout the city based on the information provided by Glasgow citizens. Through the different facets of the four demonstrators (building efficiency, integrated social transport, intelligent street lightning, and active travel), the initiative allows the personalisation and co-creation of experiences between service providers and consumers which aligns with the *Maintaining of Diversity and Redundancy* principle [P1] with clear and direct applications for the tourism system. Additionally, the energy efficiency project may effectuate the measurement of pollutant emissions and the indirect costs of fuel shortage through accurate information collection, which supports the *Management of Slow System Variables and Feedbacks* [P3] and *Foster Complex Adaptive Systems Thinking* [P4] through the continuous monitoring and automation of processes.

> **Building efficiency:** When a user enters information about the building in which he or she lives or works through the website or app, the building's actual energy consumption and the results of a simulation that calculates the expected energy consumption can be compared (Innovate UK, 2017). This information can be used by tourism service providers to offer services at a lower cost and by users themselves to increase the energy efficiency during their chosen operations. The figures provided by users contribute to the development of a 3D energy model that allows to geographically determine actual energy consumption and consumption patterns in Glasgow and the effects of each action taken to increase energy efficiency.
>
> **Integrated social transport:** The MyGlasgow app was initially developed to allow Glasgow citizens to report problems related to roads, traffic signals, street cleanliness, and garbage collection and to check on the problem-solving process and receive feedback. The app has been then used my Glasgow visitors and tourists as well. The Social Transport app enables those who are vulnerable due to physical difficulty to receive free transport services provided by the city. Integrated Social Transport has helped Glasgow's most vulnerable citizens access social and educational services. The smart wayfinding scheduling software reduces

operating costs while improving the flexibility and responsiveness of service provision.

Intelligent street lighting: Real-time motion/noise recognition sensors are equipped with a notification function for police and emergency rescue teams, and in the case of an emergency, the accident location is indicated by a blinking signal. The system improves understanding of the city and city planning by collecting data on air pollution and the movement of the population through its measurement system.

Active travel: Apps created through Active Travel were able to create a more friendly environment for travellers by helping pedestrians and cyclists plan their travel routes, monitor traffic congestion, and record their travel. Community participation in the development process played an important role in data collection and city mapping. Through this programme, Glasgow was able to explore the possibility of creating an environment in which 10% of travel is by bicycle, a target set by the Scottish government.

Smart tourism transformations and destination resilience

While new age destinations and cities aim to increasingly adopt emerging transformations of 'smartness' and respond more efficiently to the needs of urban residents and visitors, their adaptive governance and management approach in the context of SESs establishes consideration of human activity within the broader destination system. Traditional destination governance and management approaches that fail to capture the chain dynamics of a tourism destination system as a whole often result in transposing rather than solving problems. A system thinking approach that extends to all the facets of the tourism destination product is thus essential to capture the whole spectrum of system dynamics and to strengthen its capacity to respond to unexpected events and disturbances.

Whether it is digital transformation, product differentiation, or service enhancement, tourism destinations engage in the race of adopting smart innovative transformations to safeguard their competitive edge and to ensure high-quality tourist experience. As demonstrated by the Glasgow case study, behind each transformation in smart tourism lay elements of polycentricity, multi-layering, network structure learning, and collaborative innovation. Smartness extends beyond just infrastructure to connect elements of the urban ecosystem such as smart government, smart citizens, smart economy, smart environment, and smart life. Emerging transformations in destinations infused with elements of smartness appear to contribute to the three key categories identified by previous works (e.g., Boes, Buhalis, & Inversini, 2015; Harrison et al., 2010; Ivars-Baidal et al., 2019; Shafiee et al., 2019) namely: (1) contribute and support the continuous collection, analysis, and distribution of destination-related data that optimise network effectiveness and hence support a destination's competitiveness and ensure its growth; (2) enhance consistency among definitions and standards so that data and information on destinations can be shared so that they can be easily reused; and (3) ensure multifunctionality to provide solutions to various problems from a holistic destination perspective.

By adopting such robust tourism structures that lay the basis for their resilience, tourism destinations will be able to adapt, self-reorganise, and hence effectively respond to external shocks and drivers of change that prevail the continuously changing environment that we are experiencing. Tourism destinations are inherently subject to socio-economic, technological, political, and health and safety externalities and crises that could dramatically change their performance within a very short period of time. Building destinations' resilience through smart emerging transformations sets the grounds for effective and timely responses to crises with a stronger system ability for self-regulation and hence spill over disturbance control throughout all system elements. A controlled and evidence supported response is key for an effective and swift recovery of the system, to either its initial state or a new adapted equilibrium of full functionality that is based on all seven principles and core values of system resilience.

Conclusion

This conceptual study explores the structural and operational advantages of digital transformations related to smart tourism destinations in their pursuit of tourism system resilience. It contributes to smart tourism destination literature by aligning destination resilience and smart tourism destinations. The discussion shows that seven aspects of resilience are relevant to smart tourism destination applications for delineating the inherent goodness of fit of the two concepts. For example, 'maintaining diversity and redundancy' is aligned with the infrastructure and accessibility of smart tourism destinations and with smart-tailored services and applications for co-creation. 'Managing connectivity' is aligned with visitors' interactions with and integration into the surroundings, and it increases the quality of the experience at the destination through ICT. Building on the case study of Future City Glasgow, this study delineates smart tourism interventions and applications that contribute directly and indirectly to the continuous improvement of tourism performance and tourists' experiences, as well as to the optimisation of a destination's resources to benefit its competitiveness and resilience. The seven principles of resilience are discussed in terms of their application to three major components of Future City Glasgow.

Despite its academic contributions, this study has some limitations. Caution is required in generalising the findings of a limited case study. Governments worldwide strive to enhance citizens' lives by making urban life smarter, safer, and more sustainable. Tourists and visitors enjoy the benefits of such interventions during the stay and destination interactions as well. Findings from the Glasgow case study reveal that currently smart applications are embedded at destination level structures without necessarily a deliberate consideration of the tourism sector nor tourism experience. System resilience is thus primarily operationalised along the attributes of the whole destination system and not only its tourism ecosystem. The nesting of smart tourism ecosystem within the overall destination smartness operationalisation is inherently aligned with the concept of resilience. It is, however, important for tourism practitioners and researchers to explore the specifics of tailor-made smart applications in the tourism and hospitality industry in order to better understand the benefits and challenges of their implementation and adoption within the tourism industry and tourism destination ecosystem. Future research should thus consider a number of tourism destinations of varying tourism products and life cycle stages, to explore the alignment of resilience principles with designated smart tourism applications at destination level.

References

Berbés-Blázquez, M., & Scott, D. (2017). The development of resilience thinking. In R. W. Butler (Ed.), *Tourism and resilience* (pp. 9–22). Wallingford, UK: CABI.

Berkes, F., Colding, J., & Folke, C. (Eds). (2003). *Navigating social-ecological systems: Building resilience for complexity and change*. Cambridge, UK: Cambridge University Press.

Bifulco, F., Tregua, M., Amitrano, C. C., & D'Auria, A. (2016). ICT and sustainability in smart cities management. *International Journal of Public Sector Management*, 29(2), 132–147.

Biggs, R., Schlüter, M., Biggs, D., et al. (2012). Towards principles for enhancing the resilience of ecosystem services. *Annual Review of Environment and Resources*, 37, 421–448.

Bodin, O., & Prell, C. (Eds). (2011). *Social networks and natural resource management: Uncovering the social fabric of environmental governance*. Cambridge, UK: Cambridge University Press.

Boes, K., Buhalis, D., & Inversini, A. (2015). Conceptualising smart tourism destination dimensions. In *Information and communication technologies in tourism 2015* (pp. 391–403). Cham: Springer.

Buhalis, D., & Amaranggana, A. (2013). Smart tourism destinations. In *Information and communication technologies in tourism 2014* (pp. 553–564). Cham: Springer.

Butler, R. W. (Ed.). (2017). *Tourism and resilience*. Wallingford, UK: CABI.

Cavalheiro, M. B., Joia, L. A., & Cavalheiro, G. M. D. C. (2020). Towards a smart tourism destination development model: Promoting environmental, economic, socio-cultural and political values. *Tourism Planning & Development*, 17(3), 237–259.

Cheer, J. M., & Lew, A. A. (Eds.). (2018). *Tourism, resilience and sustainability: Adapting to social, political and economic change*. London and New York: Routledge.

Cimbaljević, M., Stankov, U., & Pavluković, V. (2019). Going beyond the traditional destination competitiveness: Reflections on a smart destination in the current research. *Current Issues in Tourism*, 22(20), 2472–2477.

Coca-Stefaniak, J. A. (2019). Marketing smart tourism cities: A strategic dilemma. *International Journal of Tourism Cities*, 5(4), 513–518.

Dakos, V., Quinlan, A., Baggio, J. A., Bennett, E., Bodin, O., & BurnSilver, S. (2015). Principle 2-manage connectivity. In R. Biggs, M. Schluter, & M. L. Schoon (Eds.), *Principles for building resilience: Sustaining ecosystem services in social-ecological systems* (pp. 80–104). Cambridge, UK: Cambridge University Press.

Femenia-Serra, F., Neuhofer, B., & Ivars-Baidal, J. A. (2019). Towards a conceptualisation of smart tourists and their role within the smart destination scenario. *The Service Industries Journal*, 39(2), 109–133.

Folke, C. (2006). Resilience: The emergence of a perspective for social-ecological systems analyses. *Global Environmental Change*, 16, 253–267.

Folke, C., Carpenter, S. R., Walker, B. H., Scheffer, M., Chapin, T., & Rockstrom, J. (2010). Resilience thinking: Integrating resilience, adaptability and transformability. *Ecology and Society, 15*(4), 20. Retrieved November 10, 2020, from www.ecologyandsociety.org/vol15/iss4/art20/

Folke, C., Hahn, T., Olsson, P., & Norberg, J. (2005). Adaptive governance of social-ecological systems. *Annual Review of Environment and Resources, 30*, 441–473.

Glyptou, K., Paravantis, J. A., Papatheodorou, A., & Spilanis, I. (2014). Tourism sustainability methodologies: A critical assessment. In IEEE (Ed.), *IISA 2014: The Fifth International Conference on Information, Intelligence, Systems and Applications* (pp. 182–187). Los Alamitos, CA: IEEE Computer Society.

Gretzel, U., Sigala, M., Xiang, Z., & Koo, C. (2015). Smart tourism: Foundations and developments. *Electronic Markets, 25*(3), 179–188.

Gretzel, U., Zhong, L., Koo, C., Boes, K., Buhalis, D., & Inversini, A. (2016). Smart tourism destinations: Ecosystems for tourism destination competitiveness. *International Journal of Tourism Cities, 2*(2), 108–124.

Hall, M. C., Prayag, G., & Amore, A. (2018). *Tourism and resilience: Individual, organisational and destination perspectives*. Bristol, UK: Channel View Publications.

Harrison, C., Eckman, B., Hamilton, R., Hartswick, P., Kalagnanam, J., Paraszczak, J., & Williams, P. (2010). Foundations for smarter cities. *IBM Journal of Research and Development, 54*(4), 1–16.

Innovate UK. (2017). *Innovate UK: About us*. Retrieved November 11, 2020, from www.gov.uk/government/organisations/innovate-uk

Ivars-Baidal, J. A., Celdrán-Bernabeu, M. A., Mazón, J. N., & Perles-Ivars, Á. F. (2019). Smart destinations and the evolution of ICTs: A new scenario for destination management? *Current Issues in Tourism, 22*(13), 1581–1600.

Jovicic, D. Z. (2019). From the traditional understanding of tourism destination to the smart tourism destination. *Current Issues in Tourism, 22*(3), 276–282.

Koo, C., Shin, S., Gretzel, U., Hunter, W. C., & Chung, N. (2016). Conceptualization of smart tourism destination competitiveness. *Asia Pacific Journal of Information Systems, 26*(4), 561–576.

Kotschy, K., Biggs, R., Daw, T., Folke, C., & West, P. (2015). Principle 1-maintain diversity and redundancy. In R. Biggs, M. Schluter, & M. L. Schoon (Eds.), *Principles for building resilience: Sustaining ecosystem services in social-ecological systems* (pp. 50–79). Cambridge, UK: Cambridge University Press.

Lamsfus, C., Wang, D., Alzua-Sorzabal, A., & Xiang, Z. (2015). Going mobile: Defining context for on-the-go travelers. *Journal of Travel Research, 54*(6), 691–701.

Leleux, C., & Webster, W. (2018). Delivering smart governance in a future city: The case of Glasgow. *Media and Communication, 6*(4), 163–174.

Levin, S., Xepapadeas, T., Crépin, A. S., et al. (2013). Social: Ecological systems as complex adaptive systems: Modeling and policy implications. *Environment and Development Economics, 18*, 111–132.

Lopez de Avila, A. (2015, February). Smart destinations: XXI century tourism. In L. Tussyadiah & A. Inversini (Eds.), *ENTER2015: Information and communication technologies in tourism 2015* (pp. 4–6). Switzerland: Springer International Publishing.

Olsson, P., Folke, C., & Berkes, F. (2004). Adaptive co-management for building resilience in social: Ecological systems. *Environmental Management, 34*, 75–90.

Schoon, M. L., Baggio, J. A., Salau, K., & Janssen, M. (2014). Insights for managers from modeling species interactions across multiple scales in an idealized landscape. *Environmental Modelling and Software, 55*, 53–59.

Shafiee, S., Ghatari, A. R., Hasanzadeh, A., & Jahanyan, S. (2019). Developing a model for sustainable smart tourism destinations: A systematic review. *Tourism Management Perspectives, 31,* 287–300.

Song, H. (2011) (Ed). Information Communication Technologies and TSCM. In *Tourism Supply Chain Management* (1st ed). London, UK: Routledge.

Walker, B. H., & Salt, D. (2012). *Resilience practice: Building capacity to absorb disturbance and maintain function.* Washington, DC: Island Press.

Wang, J., Xie, C., Huang, Q., & Morrison, A. M. (2020). Smart tourism destination experiences: The mediating impact of arousal levels. *Tourism Management Perspectives, 35,* 100707.

Wang, X., Li, X. R., Zhen, F., & Zhang, J. (2016). How smart is your tourist attraction?: Measuring tourist preferences of smart tourism attractions via a FCEM-AHP and IPA approach. *Tourism Management, 54,* 309–320.

Westley, F., Tjornbo, O., Schultz, L., Olsson, P., Folke, C., Crona, B., & Bodin, O. (2013). A theory of transformative agency in linked social: Ecological systems. *Ecology and Society, 18*(3), 27. Retrieved November 10, 2020, from http://dx.doi.org/10.5751/ES-05072-180327

7 Big data analysis of social media sharing and destination image

Zhaoyu Chen (Vicky), Xiaolin Zhou (Eva), and Weng Si (Clara) Lei

Introduction

Social media is based on computer-mediated interaction in an internet environment and pervasively manifested in visualised platforms such as Facebook and Twitter (Lin, 2010). It has significantly shaped the tourism industry into an intense informational platform (Narangajavana et al., 2017). Tourism transformation has required advanced support technically and strategically (Smith, 2017). Social media acts as an effective tool to facilitate smart connections between people and the surrounding environment (Lam, Ismail, & Lee, 2020). People constantly adapt to the transformation process in their daily lives and travelling time. The tourism industry has to respond promptly to the emerging trend (e.g., crisis) with timely feedback and reactions through their continuous marketing effects ahead of time (Adeola, Hinson, & Evans, 2019). Given that social media is considered a critical source of destination image formation (Garay, 2019), a growing number of tourism studies have paid attention to the examination of the effects of social media on destination image and the effectiveness of different social media platforms in destination marketing (Molinillo, Liébana-Cabanillas, & Anaya-Sánchez, 2017; Tamajón & Valiente, 2017). However, the social media platforms used in past studies, such as Facebook, Twitter, and Instagram, are mostly based in western contexts (Iglesias-Sánchez et al., 2020; Karna, Qiang, & Karn, 2017; Martinez-Camara et al., 2012). Limited studies have covered Asian-based platforms like RED, which is a fast-growing social media application in China.

Relevant tourism studies have relied mostly on the survey research method (Lam, Ismail, & Lee, 2020; Molinillo, Liébana-Cabanillas, & Anaya-Sánchez, 2017) which has its limitations in terms of generalisation. Big data analytics is a scientific algorithm that a large pool of raw information can be processed. It allows for a systematic analysis of user-generated content (UGC) on social media platforms. This study will respond to existing research gaps by using big data analytics in processing and analysing the post contents on the RED platform. In so doing, the study focuses on the examination of the regional destination image of the Guangdong–Hong Kong–Macao Greater Bay Area (hereafter called GBA), which was included in a national development strategy initiated by the Chinese central government in 2017. Therefore, this study contributes to extant literature

DOI: 10.4324/9781003105930-8

that has primarily focused on the influential factors, meanings, and measurements of destination image (Beerli & Martin, 2004; Tasci & Gartner, 2007) in a single destination context (Yu & Sun, 2019). In the GBA area, tourism is considered one of the pillar industries that can further stimulate regional development and collaboration. Hence, knowledge of how social media users perceive the area's destination image is important in understanding regional development outcomes. The findings of this study can supplement current tourism literature with regard to regional destination image and demonstrate an innovative and feasible method of analysis in exploring destination image on social media platforms in tourism transformation. Managerial implications also emerge because findings may facilitate both the individual destination marketing efforts and the regional collaboration on joint marketing strategies.

Social media in tourism

Social media sites or platforms started to operate in the late 1990s. For example, sixdegrees.com was the first social media site (Ray, 2020) that offered functions that were similar to but less comprehensive than those offered by contemporary social media platforms (e.g., Facebook). The introduction of social media has revolutionised society in many ways as they facilitated connection and communication among people and businesses (Adeola, Hinson, & Evans, 2019). With the introduction of Web 2.0, social media has become an essential platform for individual travellers in dispersing travel information and allow information searching and identification of information sources (Chung & Han, 2017). Tourists start to rely on electronic Word-of-Mouth as credible information sources and further involve these shared components in their travel itinerary (Bronner & de Hoog, 2013; Duffy, 2015). In addition, the information richness of social media has successfully formed a social network enabling virtual communities (users) in information searching, organisation, and decision-making (Amaro, Duarte, & Henriques, 2016; Lin, 2010). Thus, the tourist gaze is expanding as a consequence of rapid social media dissemination (Campbell, 2018). As such, social media has also become a promotional channel for destination management organisations (DMOs) to approach tourists through information dissemination (Tamajón & Valiente, 2017).

Previous studies concentrated on social media usage in western contexts covering various topics, such as its influence on consumer purchase decision (Hudson & Hudson, 2013), community interests on social media (Williams et al., 2015), the value of participants who join social networks (Hoksbergen & Insch, 2016), and effects in promoting events (Rothschild, 2011). Martinez-Camara et al. (2012) conducted a sentiment analysis on Twitter and identified challenges in dealing with comment issues in Twitter messages from the linguistic perspective. Barry (2014) used an analysis of personal photography in social media (Flickr) to gain insights on the US public's perceptions and concerns about natural resource management and argued that social media is an effective platform to discover public values, interests, and perceptions.

Nikjoo and Bakhshi (2019) compared the photo-sharing manner of residents and tourists on Facebook and found that portrait photos are the biggest share. The analysis is restricted to photo titles and all comments for each data set but not on the post contents themselves. Barry (2014) calls for future study to integrate text and visual social media information to amplify specific viewpoints, interests, or values and how such information can inform public decision-making. Social media platforms of Asian destinations are largely neglected. This neglect is surprising considering the importance of certain Asian destinations including China.

Among Chinese social media platforms, Sina Weibo is the most popular. Operated by 'Sina.com', Weibo is the first microblog in China, and it is similar to Twitter. It had 523 million active users in the second quarter of 2020 (Lin, 2020). Studies investigating this platform covered topics of tourism information quality (Kim et al., 2017), the spatiotemporal relationship among places (Zhang, 2017), information diffusion (Wang et al., 2020), and tourist movement patterns (Xue & Zhang, 2020). However, studies related to destination image and Chinese social media platforms are rarely seen except for those examining the comments of short food videos on TikTok (Li et al., 2020), geotagged information of Hangzhou (Jia, 2020), and users' experience in following official pages of tourism organisations (Kim, et al., 2017).

Founded in 2013, RED is an emerging social media platform in China with monthly active users in 2020 reaching 30 million, an increase of 300% compared with 2017 data. Approximately 70% of its users are millennials (Xiaohongshu, 2020). RED covers various lifestyle-oriented themes like food, travel, entertainment, cosmetics, and fitness. RED allows users to share their daily life or travelling experiences using diverse ways of sharing, including photos, texts, and short videos. RED is even favoured by businesses as an emerging marketing tool because they foresee the potential market share on this platform (Xiaohongshu, 2020). With its increasing popularity, RED offers researchers considerable opportunities to explore the role of this platform in constructing and promoting the destination image.

Interest is growing in using social media platforms in promoting Asian destination image. Currently, not many studies have explicitly examined the textual sharing information on social media from users' perspectives. Rather, past studies concentrate on the users' sharing manners and not the post contents (Liu et al., 2017). Karna, Qiang, and Karn (2017) discussed how Facebook is used for crisis propagation and destination image restoration using the case of Nepal. Similarly, Shao et al. (2016) evaluated the social media marketing of a Chinese destination by using netnography. Kim et al. (2017) examined the design of a particular DMO official account on Sina Weibo in affecting the destination image of South Korea. Previous studies on destination image concentrated mostly on a single destination context (Tamajón & Valiente, 2017; Wang, Chan, & Pan, 2015; Yu & Sun, 2019). Even the examination of online consumer reviews focused on the effects at the personal level such as changing consumers' attitudes or purchase intentions towards a tourism product (Almohaimmeed, 2019; Park, Kim, & Ryu,

2019) but not at a macro level in a cross-regional context. Therefore, this study is the first of its kind to examine the destination image within a large territory in China, namely, the GBA. In so doing, it uses big data analysis, thereby contributing to existing literature that relies on traditional research approaches, namely, content analysis (Lin, 2010) and questionnaire survey (Almohaimmeed, 2019; Duffy, 2015) that pose concerns as regards the generalisability of results (Molinillo, Liébana-Cabanillas, & Anaya-Sánchez, 2017). A few innovative approaches have used application programming interfaces (API) as obtained from social media platforms, but API information is limited to tag information or simple data collection such as number of likes, views, or re-posts (Chua et al., 2016; Zhang, 2017).

Methodology

Study context

In 2019, the Chinese Central Government announced a national strategy of 'Development of a city cluster in the Guangdong–Hong Kong–Macao Greater Bay Area', which covers 56,500 square kilometres across 11 cities (Figure 7.1). This plan is promulgated to leverage the composite advantages of the two special administrative regions (Hong Kong and Macao) and nine cities in Guangdong province. Hong Kong, Macao, Guangzhou, and Shenzhen are four core engines in this regional development with their different comparative advantages as economic, commercial, technology, and entertainment centres. With their leading roles, the neighbouring cities Zhuhai, Foshan, Huizhou, Dongguan, Zhongshan, Jiangmen, and Zhaoqing are seven key partners with distinct characteristics and potentials to enlarge the accumulative effects for regional development. Ultimately, the national development agenda of GBA is to strengthen the cooperation among them and further boost regional economic development while realising the vision of GBA to be a world-class bay area (Constitutional and Mainland Affairs Bureau, 2018).

Data collection and analysis

As a promising social sharing app, RED was used in this study. We crawled posts by searching the keyword 'tourism' for each city from RED in May 2020. Each city's top 1,000 posts were downloaded and sorted according to the number of 'likes', 'stars', and comments. Table 7.1 shows the examples of downloaded information. 'Title' and 'Content' were combined into a 'full-script' for subsequent text mining. HTML tags and special symbols in 'full-script' were then eliminated. To improve the validity of the data set and avoid data availability bias (Ruths & Pfeffer, 2014), some irrelevant posts were removed mainly because (1) contents were for advertising and (2) city name mentioned in the post is not the subject of discussion. We ultimately obtained 8,295 notes.

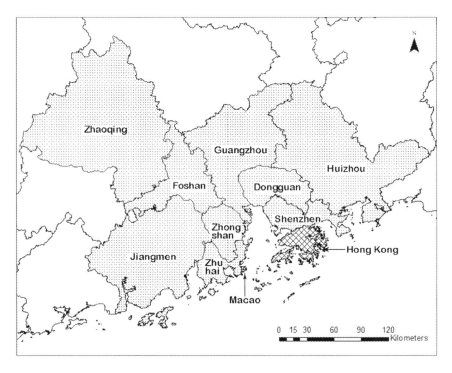

Figure 7.1 Map of the Greater Bay Area (GBA) of China
Source: Authors' compilation

Table 7.1 Example of selected data sets on RED

Post ID	User ID	Keyword	Title	Content
5a17ae***	595657***	Dongguan Tourism	Authentic delicacy in Dongguan	I went to Dongguan for friends in this National Day ...
59aa46***	58c429***	Foshan Tourism	A full day tour in Foshan	My boyfriend is in Foshan. I visited him secretly on Chinese Valentine's Day ...
5562e7***	54872a***	Macao Tourism	Koi Kei Bakery in Macao	Nine out of ten people would buy Koi Kei Bakery as long as he went to Macao ...
...	...	...	...	...

Given that all content on RED is in Chinese, an open-source Python package, namely, jieba, was used (GitHub, 2020). It is commonly used for Chinese word segmentation in big data analysis (Liu et al., 2020; Xiao, Li, & Gong, 2018). The following sequential steps show the details of data processing before analysis.

1 Custom dictionary construction: to improve the accuracy of segmentation result, proper nouns for tourism in the study area were collected to supplement the jieba lexicon. The dictionary included the names of the top 50 tourism hotspots, central business districts, popular restaurants, and those local cuisines related by taking the references from Meituan.com (Meituan, 2020).
2 Stop word corpus customisation: stop words (such as 'a', 'the', 'on', and 'in' in English) are common in any context but have little lexical content. For this study, three general Chinese stop word lists provided by Baidu.com, Sichuan University, and Harbin Institute of Technology were combined to filter the posts.
3 Chinese word segmentation: following the accurate model provided by jieba, sentences in a post were cut off into the most accurate segmentations for text mining. As a result, each city would have its own term pool C for text mining.

TextRank, a graph-based ranking model for unsupervised keyword extraction (Mihalcea & Taray, 2004), was used on each city's term pool C. TextRank has been recently used in tourism analytics and other fields (Chen et al., 2020; Spruit & Ferati, 2020; Wang et al., 2019). The significance of each node is represented by its weight and it is defined as

$$WS(t_i) = (1-d) + d * \sum_{t_j \in In(t_i)} \frac{w_{ij}}{\sum_{t_k \in Out(t_j)} w_{jk}} WS(t_j)$$

$WS(t_i)$ is the weight of a term t_i, assigned as 1 initially. d is the damping coefficient. $In(t_i)$ and $Out(t_i)$ are the terms that co-occur with term t_i, and w_{ij} is the weight of the edge between t_i and t_j in the graph (co-occurrence frequency in this case). The final weight was obtained after the iteration until convergence. The higher the weights, the greater the importance indicated by the terms. Eventually, the top 30 terms were extracted that demonstrate the highest weights (Figure 7.2 shows the top 30 terms and their co-occurrence relationship). These results indicated the hotly discussed topics among users.

Results

On the basis of the TextRank results of the most referred words in each city separately (Appendix 7.1), these discussed topics were further sorted into the categories that summarise the tourist activities people mentioned. Instead of using the top 30 terms at this stage, the top 10 terms are applied to conclude the most significant and visible results. The more relevant wordings mentioned, the more interest people revealed, helping to consolidate destination images as indicated from their sharing contents. For instance, in cities like Macao, Guangzhou, and Zhaoqing, people talked about 'gastronomy', 'delicious', or 'taste' to further emphasise the perception of the dining experience. Table 7.2 summarises the nature of the discussion topics based on the wordings and rankings.

104 *Zhaoyu Chen, Xiaolin Zhou, and Weng Si Lei*

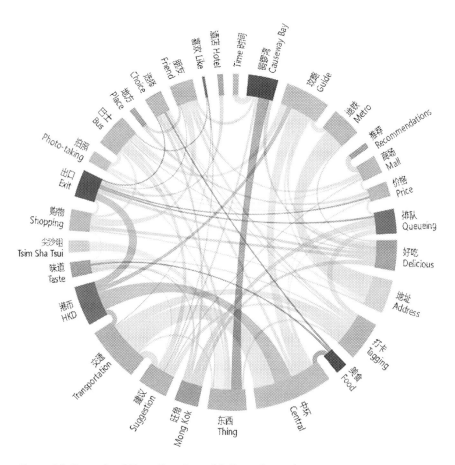

Figure 7.2 Example of Hong Kong's top 30 discussion topics

Seven categories indicate the direct reflections on tourism-related activities in terms of dining, accommodation, transportation, sightseeing, and photo-taking, as well as indirect reflections on the sentiments which demonstrate the users' efforts in recommending the relevant information to the viewers by using the persuading words such as 'like', 'suitable', and 'recommendation'. Another topic provides practical information in general, including the opening times of sites, address details, currency exchange, and entrance fees. A hierarchy of discussed content is displayed on the basis of the weights and correlations on the terms. The more weights and number of relevant terms discussed, the stronger the image revealed. For instance, in Guangzhou, a distinctive feature was found that did not exist in other cities: users talked about 'metro' service (ranked fourth) and '(metro service) line' (ranked ninth). This finding indicates a strong necessity to provide metro network information to tourists. By contrast, if only one term is mentioned

Big data analysis of social media 105

Table 7.2 Sorted categories on discussion topics based on TextRank results

City	Dining	Accommodation	Transportation	Sightseeing	Photo Taking	Sentiments (e.g., like, suitable, recommendation, and place)	Information Practicality (e.g., time and address)
Macao	+++	++			++	++	+
Hong Kong	+++	++		++	++	++	+++
Guangzhou	+++	+	+++		+++	+	+++
Zhuhai		+++			+++	++	++
Shenzhen			+	++	++	+	+
Huizhou	+	+++			++	+++	
Foshan	+	++			++	+	+
Zhongshan	+			++	+++	++	
Zhaoqing	++	+		++	++	++	
Dongguan	+	+			+++	+++	+
Jiangmen	+	++		+	+++	+++	

Note: Empty column indicates no discussion on the topic.

+++ indicates the highest weight in discussing the topic
++ indicates a medium weight in the topic
+ indicates a low weight in the topic

in any tourism activity (e.g., dining, accommodation, and transportation) and the ranking of the term is not high, it indicates low interest in the topic and a weak image as such. For instance, in Dongguan, only one gastronomy-related term is included in the list and ranked eighth. It is relatively weak compared with the performance of other cities (e.g., Macao and Hong Kong). Following such a rationale, the following regional destination image of GBA is consolidated.

Regional destination for photo-taking

There are no strong findings on the entertainment activities based on UGC, but users mentioned the most photo-taking activities on site. 'Photo-taking' is included in the top three rankings among all cities, within which six cities (Guangzhou, Zhuhai, Shenzhen, Zhongshan, Dongguan, and Jiangmen) are ranked the top. Photo-taking thus becomes the strongest regional destination image of GBA. This finding also indicates that on social media platforms like RED, which has a rich functionality of sharing visual images and texts, a regional destination image was successfully transformed into visual forms and stimulated tourist interest in the destination. Such a result can provide implications to DMOs in using digital social platforms for destination marketing.

City clusters and distinctive feature

The findings suggest that several cities shared similar destination images such as gastronomy. Macao, Hong Kong, and Guangzhou demonstrated a strong perception of dining experience. This finding is understandable because Macao and Hong Kong are two special administrative regions and Guangzhou, as the capital city of Guangdong province, receives a considerable number of international and domestic tourist arrivals. Thus, they offer diverse cuisine that can effectively satisfy the needs of diverse tourism markets. Zhuhai and Huizhou are favoured for their accommodation service because users on RED shared their concerns about hotels and homestay service. In Shenzhen and Zhongshan, users shared the destination images as sightseeing places while mentioning the scenic areas, sacred places, parks, and film studios.

Although several cities shared similar destination images, they are distinctive from each other with different tourist resources. Notably, Guangzhou is the only city that offers a comprehensive destination image on RED with practical information covering aspects such as dining, accommodation, and transportation. Hong Kong is a shopping paradise. Apart from the shared images on dining, accommodation, and sightseeing, users on RED shared useful tips (including currency exchange, commodity price information, and the time of site/shop opening) in a practical sense for potential tourists who come to Hong Kong for shopping.

RED: an effective social media for destination image building

In addition to the terms (e.g., hotel and gastronomy) that directly express tourist-related information, many other sentiments are seen in the post contents. For instance, 'like', 'suitable', and 'recommendation' guide texts that attempt to lead tourist behaviours in certain activities. Expressions are used in situational contexts like 'Zhongshan is worth visiting. The buildings are painted in pink, which is quite *suitable* for girls who *like* photo-taking and tagging on social platforms. It is really beautiful' (excerpt of a post on Zhongshan). 'Foshan Lingnan World is *suitable* for couples to have fun and take photos. There are also a lot of bars and shops selling handicrafts' (excerpt of a post on Foshan).

The contents of the majority of the cities like Hong Kong, Guangzhou, Zhuhai, Macao, Shenzhen, Foshan, and Dongguan also cover the practical tourism information that provides tourists with useful tips such as opening times, free shuttle buses, addresses, and ticket information. This finding indicates that RED is becoming an information source for tourists to obtain practical travel tips while exploring the recommended sites and activities. The exploration of the RED platform further reveals the trend of social media platforms as tools for interactive information searching.

Social media and tourism transformation

With the uncertainty of the COVID-19 pandemic, social media has become a communication tool to compensate tourists' willingness to travel and seek and share information in this 'critical turn'. People enter a stage to rethink an advanced and transformative normal in post-pandemic tourism. They have to adapt to the new norm by using other alternative tools like social media for social connections in work, leisure, and daily life. To cope with such a transformation, various new forms of travelling, such as smart tourism, are proposed. Such forms are equipped with high technology like virtual reality and augmented reality to enable an immersive experience. Tourism transformation is also closely related with sustainable development goals (SDGs) because it stimulates people by inventing new tools to facilitate tourist activities in a long-standing sustainable way from economic, socio-cultural, and environmental aspects (Smith, 2017). Social media enables tourism transformation with an even more vivid and interactive channel towards a positive and forward-thinking change rather than a traditional way of promoting destinations, especially during crises. Therefore, reviewing how destination image is evolving through the social media platform is timely. Such findings of which can effectively provide insights for DMOs and tourists themselves with useful marketing and travelling information and help them adapt to the tourism transformation process. RED is one effective social media platform for destination image building.

The prosperous process of tourism transformation requires not only the efforts from tourism organisations or practitioners but also the correspondingly supports at various levels equipped with appropriate facilities and tools keeping pace with time. At the operational level, the availability of big data enables information to be retrieved from online platforms, facilitating the possibility of in-depth understandings of tourist preferences and behaviours. Compared with traditional analytical tools (e.g., surveys and interviews), big data analysis allows tourism suppliers, users, and even researchers to use data mining resources and information. DMOs can improve marketing strategy formulation by using big data analysis. Especially in regional destination marketing, a collaborative effort is needed to use regional resources effectively to better serve tourists' needs and lighten up the destination image in the emerging tourism transformation.

Conclusion

Using big data analysis, this study explored the regional destination image of the GBA on an emerging Asian-based social media platform, namely, RED, and demonstrated the possibility of building a regional destination image by using the information shared by tourists themselves in this tourism transformation era. The findings suggested that the GBA is suitable for photo-taking activities. This new insight contributes to the previous literature on destination image. The cities of GBA collectively form a diversified regional destination image with various components including gastronomy, accommodation, transportation, and sightseeing. At the same time, they retain their distinctive features to attract particular tourists in need.

In the digital era, that is, an information-intensive world, destination marketing should be sufficiently innovative to cope with the challenges in the process of tourism transformation, such as by using social media in digital marketing and user feedback for marketing improvements. To meet the emerging trend of technology-based tourism development, digital information can be used for tourism purposes, ranging from information searching to information sharing. The UGCs on social media platforms are valuable resources in offering insights for DMOs to plan and strengthen their online marketing strategies while satisfying tourists' ever-changing needs.

Theoretically, this study contributes to the current literature on social media platform effects on destination image by considering multiple destinations in a regional context, specifically the GBA. It demonstrates the applicability of big data analysis in tourism. Practically, the DMOs in the GBA can use social media platforms in creating destination images and to customise physical promotional materials dynamically while embedding photo opportunities to stimulate potential visitation. As indicated from the current post contents, not all cities cover a full range of tourism resource information. For those cities that have not yet provided information on transportation or sightseeing (e.g., Jiangmen, Dongguan, and Zhaoqing) or for cities without a strong impression of these characteristics (e.g., Shenzhen), a balanced effort into the destination image formation is necessary.

As a limitation, this study covers only one social media platform. Diverse social media platforms in the Asian tourism market are an emerging trend. Such diversity is expected to attract a prosperous market of users on platforms such as Sina Weibo or WeChat Moments. These platforms are also the ones that people of different age ranges use. Future research may consider comparing regional destination images of GBA among these platforms in China to explore the particular preferences and behavioural patterns of tourist groups in their respective platforms.

References

Adeola, O., Hinson, R. E., & Evans, O. (2019). Social media in marketing communications: A synthesis of successful strategies for the digital generation. In B. George & J. Paul (Eds.), *Digital transformation in business and society: Theory and cases* (pp. 61–81). Cham, Switzerland: Palgrave Macmillan. https://doi.org/10.1007/978-3-030-08277-2_4

Almohaimmeed, B. M. A. (2019). The effects of social media marketing antecedents on social media marketing, brand loyalty and purchase intention: A customer perspective. *Journal of Business and Retail Management Research, 13*(4), 146–157. https://doi.org/10.24052/JBRMR/V13IS04/ART-13

Amaro, S., Duarte, P., & Henriques, C. (2016). Travelers' use of social media: A clustering approach. *Annals of Tourism Research, 59*, 1–15. https://doi.org/10.1016/j.annals.2016.03.007

Barry, S. J. (2014). Using social media to discover public values, interests, and perceptions about cattle grazing on park lands. *Environmental Management, 53*, 454–464. https://doi.org/10.1007/s00267-013-0216-4

Beerli, A., & Martin, J. D. (2004). Factors influencing destination image. *Annals of Tourism Research, 31*(3), 657–681. https://doi.org/10.1016/j.annals.2004.01.010

Bronner, F., & de Hoog, R. (2013). Economizing on vacations: The role of information searching. *International Journal of Culture, Tourism and Hospitality Research, 7*(1), 28–41. https://doi.org/10.1108/17506181311301336

Campbell, B. J. (2018). *Image based social media and the tourist gaze: A phenomenological approach.* (Master's dissertation), Arizona State University, Arizona.

Chen, W., Xu, Z., Zheng, X., Yu, Q., & Luo, Y. (2020). Research on sentiment classification of online travel review text. *Applied Sciences, 10*(15). https://doi.org/10.3390/app10155275

Chua, A., Servillo, L., Marcheggiani, E., & Moere, A. V. (2016). Mapping Cilento: Using geotagged social media data to characterize tourist flows in southern Italy. *Tourism Management, 57*, 295–310. https://doi.org/10.1016/j.tourman.2016.06.013

Chung, N., & Han, H. (2017). The relationship among tourists' persuasion, attachment and behavioral changes in social media. *Technological Forecasting & Social Change, 123*, 370–380. https://doi.org/10.1016/j.techfore.2016.09.005

Constitutional and Mainland Affairs Bureau. (2018). *Overview.* Retrieved November 16, 2020, from www.bayarea.gov.hk/en/about/overview.html

Duffy, A. (2015). Friends and fellow travelers: Comparative influence of review sites and friends on hotel choice. *Journal of Hospitality and Tourism Technology, 6*(2), 127–144. https://doi.org/10.1108/jhtt-05-2014-0015

Garay, L. (2019). Visitspain: Breaking down affective and cognitive attributes in the social media construction of the tourist destination image. *Tourism Management Perspectives, 32*. https://doi.org/10.1016/j.tmp.2019.100560

GitHub. (2020). *Jieba.* Retrieved November 16, 2020, from https://github.com/fxsjy/jieba

Hoksbergen, E., & Insch, A. (2016). Facebook as a platform for co-creating music festival experiences. *International Journal of Event and Festival Management, 7*(2), 84–99. https://doi.org/10.1108/IJEFM-02-2016-0012

Hudson, S., & Hudson, R. (2013). Engaging with consumers using social media: A case study of music festivals. *International Journal of Event and Festival Management, 4*(3), 206–223. https://doi.org/10.1108/ijefm-06-2013-0012

Iglesias-Sánchez, P. P., Correia, M. B., Jambrino-Maldonado, C., & de las Heras-Pedrosa, C. (2020). Instagram as a co-creation space for tourist destination image-building: Algarve and Costa del Sol case studies. *Sustainability.* https://doi.org/10.3390/su12072793

Jia, F. (2020). A study on the image perception of tourist destinations in coastal cities based on big data analysis. *Journal of Coastal Research*, *115*, 106–109. https://doi.org/10.2112/JCR-SI115-032.1

Karna, R. K., Qiang, Y., & Karn, A. L. (2017). Facebook as destination image formation tool after Nepal earthquake: The collective essence of events in social media dialogue by travel marketers. *Transformations in Business & Economics*, *16*(3C(42C)), 397–412. https://doi.org/10.1080/13683500.2019.1646225

Kim, S., Lee, K. Y., Shin, S. I., & Yang, S. (2017). Effects of tourism information quality in social media on destination image formation: The case of Sina Weibo. *Information & Management*, *54*, 687–702. https://doi.org/10.1016/j.im.2017.02.009

Lam, J. M. S., Ismail, H., & Lee, S. (2020). From desktop to destination: User-generated content platforms, co-created online experiences, destination image and satisfaction. *Journal of Destination Marketing & Management*, *18*. https://doi.org/10.1016/j.jdmm.2020.100490

Li, Y., Xu, X., Song, B., & He, H. (2020). Impact of short food videos on the tourist destination image: Take Chengdu as an example. *Sustainability*, *12*. https://doi.org/10.3390/su12176739

Lin, L. (2020). *Number of monthly active users of Sina Weibo from 4th quarter 2017 to 2nd quarter 2020*. Retrieved November 16, 2020, from www.statista.com/statistics/795303/china-mau-of-sina-weibo/

Lin, Y. R. (2010). *Community discovery in dynamic, rich-context social networks*. (PhD thesis), Arizona State University, Arizona, US.

Liu, Q., Zheng, Z., Zheng, J., Chen, Q., Liu, G., Chen, S., Chu, B., Zhu, H., Akinwunmi, B., Huang, J., Zhang, C. J. P., & Ming, W. K. (2020). Health communication through news media during the early stage of the COVID-19 outbreak in China: Digital topic modeling approach. *Journal of Medical Internet Research*, *22*(4). https://doi.org/10.2196/19118

Liu, Z., Shan, J., Balet, N. G., & Fang, G. (2017). Semantic social media analysis of Chinese tourists in Switzerland. *Information Technology & Tourism*, *17*, 183–202. https://doi.org/10.1007/s40558-016-0066-z

Martinez-Camara, E., Martin-Valdivia, M. T., Urena-Lopez, L. A., & Montejo-Raez, A. (2012). Sentiment analysis in Twitter. *Natural Language Engineering*, *20*(1), 1–28. https://doi.org/10.1017/S1351324912000332

Meituan. (2020). About Meituan. Retrieved November 16, 2020, from https://about.meituan.com/about/desc

Mihalcea, R., & Taray, P. (2004, July 25–26). TextRank: Bringing Order into Texts. *Proceedings of the 2004 Conference on Empirical Methods in Natural Language Processing, Barcelona, Spain* (pp. 404–411). Association for Computational Linguistics. https://aclanthology.org/W04-3252

Molinillo, S., Liébana-Cabanillas, F., & Anaya-Sánchez, R. (2017). Destination image on the DMO's platforms: Official website and social media. *Tourism & Management Studies*, *13*(3), 5–14. https://doi.org/10.18089/tms.2017.13301

Narangajavana, Y., Fiol, L. J. C., Tena, M. A. M., Artola, R. M. R., & Garcia, J. S. (2017). The influence of social media in creating expectations: An empirical study for a tourist destination. *Annals of Tourism Research*, *65*, 60–70. https://doi.org/10.1016/j.annals.2017.05.002

Nikjoo, A., & Bakhshi, H. (2019). The presence of tourists and residents in shared travel photos. *Tourism Management*, *70*, 89–98. https://doi.org/10.1016/j.tourman.2018.08.005

Park, O.-J., Kim, M. G., & Ryu, J.-h. (2019). Interface effects of online media on tourists' attitude changes. *Tourism Management Perspectives*, *30*, 262–274. https://doi.org/10.1016/j.tmp.2019.03.005

Ray, M. (2020). Social network. Retrieved November 16, 2020, from www.britannica.com/technology/social-network#ref1073275

Rothschild, P. C. (2011). Social media use in sports and entertainment venues. *International Journal of Event and Festival Management*, 2(2), 139–150. https://doi.org/10.1108/17582951111136568

Ruths, D., & Pfeffer, J. (2014). Social media for large studies of behavior. *Science*, 346(6213), 1063–1064. https://doi.org/10.1126/science.346.6213.1063

Shao, J., Li, X., Morrison, A. M., & Wu, B. (2016). Social media micro-film marketing by Chinese destinations: The case of Shaoxing. *Tourism Management*, 54, 439–451. https://doi.org/10.1016/j.tourman.2015.12.013

Smith, J. (2017). *Transforming travel: Realising the potential of sustainable tourism*. Wallingford, United Kingdom: CABI.

Spruit, M., & Ferati, D. (2020). Text mining business policy documents: Applied data science in Finance. *International Journal of Business Intelligence Research*, 11(2), 28–46. https://doi.org/10.4018/IJBIR.20200701.oa1

Tamajón, L. G., & Valiente, G. C. (2017). Barcelona seen through the eyes of TripAdvisor: Actors, typologies and components of destination image in social media platforms. *Current Issues in Tourism*, 20(1), 33–37. https://doi.org/10.1080/13683500.2015.1073229

Tasci, A. D. A., & Gartner, W. C. (2007). Destination image and its functional relationships. *Journal of Travel Research*, 45(4), 413–425. https://doi.org/10.1177/0047287507299569

Wang, D., Chan, H., & Pan, S. (2015). The impacts of mass media on organic destination image: A case study of Singapore. *Asia Pacific Journal of Tourism Research*, 20(8), 860–874. https://doi.org/10.1080/10941665.2014.948464

Wang, P., Luo, Y., Chen, Z., He, L., & Zhang, Z. (2019). Orientation analysis for Chinese news based on word embedding and syntax rules. *IEEE Access*, 7, 159888–159898. https://doi.org/10.1109/access.2019.2950900

Wang, Z., Liu, H., Liu, W., & Wang, S. (2020). Understanding the power of opinion leaders' influence on the diffusion process of popular mobile games: Travel Frog on Sina Weibo. *Computers in Human Behavior*, 109. https://doi.org/10.1016/j.chb.2020.106354

Williams, N. L., Inversini, A., Buhalis, D., & Ferdinand, N. (2015). Community crosstalk: An exploratory analysis of destination and festival eWOM on Twitter. *Journal of Marketing Management*, 31(9–10), 1113–1140. https://doi.org/10.1080/0267257x.2015.1035308

Xiao, Y., Li, B., & Gong, Z. (2018). Real-time identification of urban rainstorm waterlogging disasters based on Weibo big data. *Natural Hazards*, 94(2), 833–842. https://doi.org/10.1007/s11069-018-3427-4

Xiaohongshu. (2020). *About Xiaohongshu*. Retrieved November 16, 2020, from www.xiaohongshu.com/protocols/about

Xue, L., & Zhang, Y. (2020). The effect of distance on tourist behavior: A study based on social media data. *Annals of Tourism Research*, 82. https://doi.org/10.1016/j.annals.2020.102916

Yu, C.-E., & Sun, R. (2019). The role of Instagram in the UNESCO's creative city of gastronomy: A case study of Macau. *Tourism Management*, 75, 257–268. https://doi.org/10.1016/j.tourman.2019.05.011

Zhang, Q. (2017). *Building dynamic ontological models for place names using social media data from Twitter and Sina Weibo*. (Master's dissertation), San Diego State University, San Diego.

Appendix 7.1
Top 10 TextRank information of each city in GBA

Macao	English Translation	Chinese Wordings	Ranking Based on Weights
1	Hotel	酒店	0.01216
2	Travel	旅游	0.00705
3	Photo-taking	拍照	0.00703
4	Gastronomy	美食	0.00552
5	Recommendation	推荐	0.00543
6	Tagging	打卡	0.00521
7	Free	免费	0.00446
8	Place	地方	0.00438
9	Delicious	好吃	0.00372
10	Guide	攻略	0.00364

Hong Kong	English Translation	Chinese Wordings	Ranking Based on Weights
1	Recommendation	推荐	0.00535
2	Photo-taking	拍照	0.00535
3	Hotel	酒店	0.00535
4	HKD	港币	0.00523
5	Tsim Sha Tsui	尖沙咀	0.00463
6	Time	时间	0.00426
7	Gastronomy	美食	0.00420
8	Place	地方	0.00407
9	Tagging	打卡	0.00394
10	Delicious	好吃	0.00390

Zhaoqing	English Translation	Chinese Wordings	Ranking Based on Weights
1	Travel	旅游	0.00782
2	Recommendation	推荐	0.00607
3	Photo-taking	拍照	0.00487
4	Like	喜欢	0.00470
5	Scenic area	景区	0.00446
6	Dinghu Mountain	鼎湖山	0.00434
7	Place	地方	0.00434
8	Taste	味道	0.00429
9	Hotel	酒店	0.00403
10	Gastronomy	美食	0.00392

Dongguan	English Translation	Chinese Wordings	Ranking Based on Weights
1	Photo-taking	拍照	0.00904
2	Travel	旅游	0.00813
3	Place	地方	0.00604
4	Like	喜欢	0.00453
5	Recommendation	推荐	0.00445
6	Suitable	适合	0.00438
7	Hotel	酒店	0.00425
8	Gastronomy	美食	0.00412
9	Tagging	打卡	0.00402
10	Ticket	门票	0.00360

Jiangmen	English Translation	Chinese Wordings	Ranking Based on Weights
1	Photo-taking	拍照	0.00943
2	Travel	旅游	0.00887
3	Hotel	酒店	0.00763
4	Shops exploration	探店	0.00582
5	Recommendation	推荐	0.00500
6	Place	地方	0.00496
7	Food	美食	0.00489
8	Like	喜欢	0.00460
9	Tagging	打卡	0.00418
10	Suggestion	建议	0.00363

Guangzhou	English Translation	Chinese Wordings	Ranking Based on Weights
1	Photo-taking	拍照	0.01016
2	Recommendation	推荐	0.00761
3	Travel	旅游	0.00718
4	Metro	地铁	0.00663
5	Gastronomy	美食	0.00526
6	Address	地址	0.00496
7	Tagging	打卡	0.00489
8	Homestay	民宿	0.00442
9	Line	号线	0.00421
10	Delicious	好吃	0.00391

Zhuhai	English Translation	Chinese Wordings	Ranking Based on Weights
1	Photo-taking	拍照	0.00965
2	Travel	旅游	0.00847
3	Hotel	酒店	0.00751
4	Recommendation	推荐	0.00599
5	Tagging	打卡	0.00521
6	Place	地方	0.00472
7	Time	时间	0.00426
8	Like	喜欢	0.00387
9	Suitable	适合	0.00367
10	Homestay	民宿	0.00351

Huizhou	English Translation	Chinese Wordings	Ranking Based on Weights
1	Hotel	酒店	0.01109
2	Travel	旅游	0.00927
3	Photo-taking	拍照	0.00852
4	Recommendation	推荐	0.00581
5	Homestay	民宿	0.00438
6	Suitable	适合	0.00426
7	Like	喜欢	0.00424
8	Gastronomy	美食	0.00424
9	Shops exploration	探店	0.00414
10	Place	地方	0.00400

Shenzhen	English Translation	Chinese Wordings	Ranking Based on Weights
1	Photo-taking	拍照	0.01998
2	Scenic area	景点	0.00716
3	Tagging	打卡	0.00679
4	Travel	旅游	0.00673
5	Sacred place	圣地	0.00508
6	Address	地址	0.00506
7	Park	公园	0.00467
8	Metro	地铁	0.00466
9	Suitable	适合	0.00435
10	Free	免费	0.00435

Foshan	English Translation	Chinese Wordings	Ranking Based on Weights
1	Travel	旅游	0.01090
2	Photo-taking	拍照	0.00999
3	Hotel	酒店	0.00725
4	Guangzhou	广州	0.00646
5	Gastronomy	美食	0.00541
6	Place	地方	0.00516
7	Tagging	打卡	0.00508
8	Recommendation	推荐	0.00504
9	Address	地址	0.00499
10	Suitable	适合	0.00462

Zhongshan	English Translation	Chinese Wordings	Ranking Based on Weights
1	Photo-taking	拍照	0.01047
2	Travel	旅游	0.00979
3	Japan	日本	0.00763
4	Scenic area	景区	0.00754
5	Zhongshan city	中山市	0.00512
6	Recommendation	推荐	0.00490
7	Suitable	适合	0.00462
8	Delicious	好吃	0.00454
9	Like	喜欢	0.00451
10	Place	地方	0.00447

8 Digital transformation in tourism
Archaeotourism and its digital potential

Hasan Ali Erdogan

Introduction

The coronavirus (COVID-19) pandemic has produced great challenges for global tourism and has seriously impacted the industry. Heritage tourism, especially archaeological tourism also known as archaeotourism (AT), has been particularly affected by bans on domestic and foreign travel, restrictions on community gatherings, and lockdown orders. Most well-known global AT destinations (ATDs) have been negatively affected by the pandemic, which has had a devastating effect on the world's largest tourism economies. AT-based businesses were closed, and there have been virtually no tourists at archaeological sites including Machu Picchu, Angkor Wat, Petra, Pompeii, and Ephesus since the third month of the pandemic (Erdogan, 2020b, pp. 717–722).

Culture and heritage differ from archaeology and should not be used as substitutes for AT (Walker & Carr, 2013). AT, while related to other components pertinent to cultural and heritage tourism (Timoty & Nyaupane, 2009), is limited mostly to archaeological materials and their interpretations. AT focuses specifically on edutainment (McKercher & Cros, 2002) or, in other words, on education and dissemination of knowledge (Dore & Aitchison, 2018). Therefore, digital technology can serve this purpose as AT methods require the active participation of various scientists from discrete fields, such as archaeologists, historians, architectures, litterateurs, and other actors like managers, government officers, service providers, and tourists. AT classified as a distinct form of digital tourism with its own methods, principles, and manifestations can reformulate and convey the importance of archaeological assets to the wider public as another component that can be represented in digital AT. Moreover, AT tourist types deserve to be classified distinctly from other cultural and heritage tourist types. They make the conscious decision to visit archaeological sites, interpretive centres, and museums to feel nostalgia for the past, to experience the thrill of exploring and understanding material culture and the unique quests therein, and to have authentic encounters with past civilisations (Giraudo & Porter, 2010). In terms of tourist typology, the World Tourism Organization (WTO) defines AT as the 'movements of persons essentially for cultural motivations such as a visit to [archaeological] sites and monuments' (WTO, 1985, p. 6). These tourists, who are keen on learning, are

DOI: 10.4324/9781003105930-9

potential customers and can ensure that digital archaeological tourism (DAT) can survive, even during circumstances like a pandemic. After all, DAT, in the simplest sense, is a form where potential customers reach archaeological sites digitally through platforms on their computers. It includes all means of technology to be used in maintaining AT digitally in a sustainable way. Given this potential customer base, in addition to its edutainment potential to be presented via DAT, AT is unique and worth being cited as a digital form of the tourism industry with regard to its tourist typology.

AT experiences have great potential to improve with DAT, which has recently prevailed in the industry as the most effective means for communication with potential tourists. DAT accounts for all ICT powered by the Internet and other telecommunication technologies. The use of technology has already introduced smartness for communities, organisations, and individuals and has added value to the overall tourist experience (Buhalis & Amaranggana, 2014; Buhalis & Law, 2008). DAT in the form of social media applications has had a significant influence on the decision-making processes of tourists (Kim et al., 2016), informing activities such as trip planning (Cai, Feng, & Breiter, 2004). Another potential form of AT would be to use DAT to broadcast archaeological activities, such as surface surveys and scientific or rescue excavations of areas of interest in the common history of humanity, online from start to finish. In this way, almost every aspect of such a process is digitally kept confidential and open to the interpretation of other scientists, creating a platform for worldwide discussions and global consensus. Such collaboration will no doubt contribute to the sustainability of AT for future generations.

This chapter aims to examine the digitalisation of AT and discusses how this form of tourism is a good candidate to undergo transformation as a result of emerging technologies. Specifically, by looking at DAT, this chapter analyses AT's potential to transform its characteristics and ultimately the tourist experience – a transformation that will yield numerous opportunities for AT-oriented destinations. Likewise, as a result of physical sites' visits facilitated by digital technology, culture-based interactions, mutual understanding, and tolerance can be promoted across destinations.

Archaeotourism as a tourism product

Archaeological tourism is a purposeful tourist activity for visiting and experiencing ancient and historical destinations with the passion for the past (Erdogan, 2021). As part of cultural and heritage tourism, AT is of a significant proportion among the cultural tourists that account for 40% of all international tourists (Richards & Munsters, 2010). Archaeological assumptions and actions are affective for non-archaeological communities (Hodder, 1997). It is this effect that makes up the core paradigm of archaeological tourism, referring to almost anything from the past that can be visited (Erdogan, 2022). Accordingly, archaeological sites are not for archaeologists only, and they need to be developed to appeal to much broader interest groups (Holtorf, 2007; Young, 2006; Malcolm-Davies, 2004).

Through international interpretations, worldwide discussions, and global consensus, DAT can facilitate mutual understanding among archaeologists, scholars, and thus tourism professionals and tourists. Museums and other AT attractions can improve their narratives to enable tourists to 'link between what is visible and what it represents' (Hughes, Little, & Ballantyne, 2013, p. 81). An effective DAT allows the narratives to reach each customer who is curious about archaeological materials, ranging from minuscule soil particles at specific strata to a town of thousands of settlers. By turning these sites into precious tourist destinations, digitalisation plays a crucial role in facilitating collaboration between various discrete disciplines and conceptualising the intangible from the tangible by working backwards from material clues (Comer, 2012, p. 10).

Archaeologists have already played a critical role in initiating the work of digitalisation to turn fragile and unique archaeological heritage assets into noteworthy ATDs (Erdogan, 2020a; Girard & Nijkamp, 2009). The challenges of following documentation protocols, completing surface surveys and excavations, and introducing new materials and interpreting them have been simplified as digital technology is used instead of having to persistently complete these activities manually. All the assemblage, gathering, hybridisation, restitution, restoration, and reconfiguration of identity in every step require time-consuming, arduous work without the ease and pace that digitalisation provides. Archaeological studies have already provided the infrastructural digital data required for tourism.

AT involves the commodification of archaeological assets through which past cultures become a product that is packaged and sold to tourists (Medina, 2003; Timothy & Boyd, 2003; Hughes-Freeland, 1993; Cohen, 1988). This does not need to happen at the site of the archaeological asset. In DAT, it is possible to create promotions, plan media, and conduct public relations strategies in harmony with other sophisticated tasks of capturing, digitalising, storytelling, organising, marketing, and managing. DAT necessitates working in cohesive groups to complete projects (Walker & Carr, 2013), with mutual agreement among all stakeholders, including the technical staff. This allows tourism and archaeological heritage to become powerful allies to deliver positive experiences for tourists (McKercher & Cros, 2002). All these distinct disciplines, the pedagogical education programmes for the local community, and the interactions between different cultures can be brought together in DAT, which provides education for both local people and scholars. After all, archaeologists are not trained in tourism issues, and tourism scholars are not trained in the sensitivities of archaeological heritage (Giraudo & Porter, 2010; Ouf, 2001; Hawas, 1998), and thus collaboration is essential for sustainable AT through DAT.

The digital potential of archaeotourism

Digitalisation in archaeology has its roots in a long tradition of creative, analytical, and methodological techniques for illustration and visualisation. Today, digital transformation in archaeology has expanded in scope and significance with contributions from digital technologies and methods such as the use of Global

Positioning System (GIS), 3D Global Information System (GIS), visualisation, 3D reconstruction, and ICT. Their introduction has accelerated the archaeological process and made archaeological destinations informative, accessible, and more attractive to the general public (Lercari, 2017). Although the use of technology in the tourism industry is not a new phenomenon, it was almost non-existent in AT prior to the COVID-19 pandemic and remains less widespread than in other areas of tourism. The outbreak highlighted the need for digital technology to be incorporated into AT. All the data available in archaeology laboratories can be made accessible to the public through an online repository (Lercari et al., 2017). DAT can also be facilitated by ICT, which has profoundly shaped archaeological studies (Stevanovic & Tringham, 2012; Zubrow, 2006). Alternative prospects for technological use of archaeological resources, such as digital archaeology (Daly & Evans, 2006), archaeological computing (Eiteljorg, 2008), virtual archaeology (Forte & Beltrami, 2000), videography, ethnography, and blogging (Cakmak & Isaac, 2012; Parsons & Maclaran, 2009), have emerged in the field and can be utilised in AT. Experimental systems including 3D GIS, visualisation, 3D reconstruction, digital documentation (Dell'Unto et al., 2016), online streaming, and their integration with ICT play significant roles in transforming the AT industry. Through technology, archaeologists are already gathering more accurate data on landscapes, artefacts, monuments, and sites that can be clearly interpreted and turned into tourist attractions by tourism professionals.

Today, education systems from primary school to university make use of digital technology, and the same processes can be applied in DAT as well. As Apaydin (2016, p. 838) says, 'Ineffective community education programs do not help to improve people's perceptions of heritage awareness in a positive way'. Therefore, AT requires specialists for pedagogical education programmes that can be homogenised through DAT. Indigenous people living in or around ATDs play crucial roles (Ashworth & Kavaratzis, 2014) in the sustainability and surveillance of archaeological assets, which are prone to looting with irreversible damage (Merhav & Killebrew, 1998) and natural devastation (Matero, 2008). They lose their authenticity and uniqueness as a result of ignorant actions on the part of the local community. With the introduction of online education programmes through DAT, awareness of the sensitivity of ATDs is promoted in the local population. Scientists should be key actors in communications with the local community instead of secluding themselves in study areas (Radziwiłko, 2019; Lipe, 2002). During the pandemic, this was not physically possible, but even in such extreme situations, DAT enables this communication. Cultural interaction through digital means can have positive effects (Chang, 2002; Ashley, Boyd, & Goodwin, 2000), such as reviving lost or disappearing elements of past cultures (Kolas, 2004; Smith, 2003; Rogers, 2002), depending on how well it is conducted (Chen & Rahman, 2018; Zhang et al., 2018).

Unlike traditional AT, DAT has two main goals: (1) to use data gathered from digital archaeological studies to benefit the tourism industry and (2) to digitalise AT entities to create tourism products for tourists. DAT signifies a potential paradigm shift from traditional to unconventional tourism through a fourth technological revolution. Digital and physical destinations are developed by DAT through *data gathering*, *data processing*, and *data representation*, which are the main steps in the digitalisation of archaeological areas.

The digitalisation of archaeological areas begins with data gathering either by archaeologists or tourism scholars. The use of technology in ATDs for different purposes helps researchers gather and generate work that would otherwise be physically impossible or extremely demanding. For example, the laser scanning technique (Balletti, Guerra, & Gerbaudi, 2003) overcomes reduced visibility and allows researchers to accurately determine the size of heritage assets in AT areas. This accuracy and visual precision obtained by technology are critical to increase tourist satisfaction both onsite and online AT. Traditional methods, such as direct or photogrammetric surveys, do not offer such precision. The integration of digital cameras in laser scanners that utilise an encoded light, which is almost indifferent to the light conditions of the environment (Guidi, Russo, & Beraldin, 2010), makes it possible to get an accurate depiction of the geometry of the structures without any damage to the assets. The use of technology like this makes the acquisition of data simple, reliable, precise, and less time consuming. Thus, DAT promotes reflexivity, multivocality, and heritage awareness in local communities and youth. It makes it feasible to explore alternative means for establishing meaning in archaeology based on non-linear narratives, three-dimensional perspectives, and virtual reconstruction. Such studies contribute to producing new knowledge regarding archaeological heritage, as well as constituting fundamental frameworks for digital tourism in that these data compose the core information communicated to tourists through DAT.

Data gathered from ATDs can be processed according to archaeotourist types, depending on which data are presented for which tourist type and whether it is presented to audiences onsite or online. Accordingly, data can be processed in fictional, realistic, and untouched manners. When the data are processed, the automatic or semi-automatic recognition of targeted assets is transformed into very dense and detailed high-quality data that can be used to craft narratives and experiences that are satisfying to tourists. Keeping this in mind, a purposeful data alignment is initially required for each method. Various software programmes, such as FARO Scene (Balletti et al., 2014), can help with this alignment. They are used to analyse accounts from earlier studies. Archaeologists reinterpret and bring them to the attention of tourism scholars. The data are then processed again and either recorded and registered or left untouched based on whether it will be delivered remotely to audiences online.

When a fictional approach is taken, the data are edited to remove anything unnecessary that will be uninteresting to tourists, and the rest are manipulated using editing techniques to ensure that they have the maximum impact on tourists. Various software programmes, such as Pointools and 3D Studio Max (Balletti et al., 2014), can assist with effective data management and modelling. This is a breakthrough, since the traditional drawings allow for only partial comprehension of spatial complexity and analyse the process from only a couple of perspectives. These programs can provide tourists with 3D visualisations, such as animations, which allows them to feel the antiquity of the assets either at the physical cites or the Internet sites. Integrating all the data gathered from archaeological studies using means of DAT to reach prospective tourists through media has stimulating results. For example, as Lercari (2017) showed in Çatalhöyük, a Neolithic city in Turkey, the data can be made accessible to the public online with 3D visualisation, diachronic reconstruction, and simulation of ATD's landscape to increase tourists' attraction.

When a realistic approach is taken, the data are edited, and unnecessary parts are deleted. The rest are organised deliberately using editing techniques to serve the purpose of the presentation without any manipulation. For example, this form of editing tends to be used for documentary or publicity films about an ATD that are created as part of the media strategy for the site.

An untouched approach is used for live broadcasts from ATDs. The development of wearable cameras combined with their ubiquitous high quality has made live video streaming available at ATDs with the support of a large number of live streaming platforms, such as YouTube Live and Ustream. DAT provides the opportunity to digitalise AT attractions by allowing for live broadcasts from archaeological sites (Buhalis & Law, 2008). These live streams are likely to become more popular as visitors discover that they can have a realistic experience that makes them feel as if they are physically present at the sites, and they can experience a sense of personal participation that is not obtainable from books, videos, or television programmes (Rosenzweig & Thelen, 1998). This also offers potential tourists the opportunity to be part of academic surveys, excavations, or interpretation processes. Furthermore, the ability of DAT to capture, edit, and save all the data that are gathered facilitates the preservation and sustainability of the site. Also, powerful digital online learning tools, such as Zoom and Adobe Connect, enable visual-interactive explorations that allow tourists to contact archaeologists in real time to learn about their analytical online interpretations. Such combinations bring radical new options for interactive experiences (Reeves et al., 2015) for tourists, local residents, and university students in the archaeology, history, anthropology, and tourism departments at different universities.

AT can take place through physical visits to sites, museums, or exhibitions with assembled artefacts (Mulaj, 2015), but less travelled in situ destinations in remote locations have also increasingly become preferred destinations for tourists (Pinter, 2005). DAT provides a better digital option for situations like the pandemic when there are significant restrictions. It also presents a solution for distance decay (McKercher & Lew, 2003), market access (Pearce, 1989; McKercher, 1998), and time availability (Johnson, McKean & Walsh, 1995), which are among the determinants of demand for AT products in physical destinations. Moreover, the difficulties faced in physical ATDs, such as material types, volumes of data, variety of capture conditions, accuracy, and environmental challenges (White et al., 2004), are overcome through DAT online. The most recent innovations have, to some extent, contributed to AT by creating destination images online (Choi, Lehto, & Morrison, 2007) or by providing virtual museum tours. Traditionally, it is primarily knowledge/information-based products that are provided at

ATDs (Qu & Lee, 2011), and these technologies have the capacity to provide AT consumers across the world with an abundance of data on AT attractions through online visualisation (Ashley, Tringham, & Perlingieri, 2011) and virtual reality tours. Today, a few ATDs also offer access to their attractions through video sharing, image uploading, and promoting the positive sides of word-of-mouth (WOM) (Takamitsu, 2019). Basic archaeotourists can therefore become knowledgeable after a few hours of site inspection. After all, attitudes manipulated by consumer-generated information have become the main source of information in travellers' decision-making processes (Gretzel & Yoo, 2008) and in developing smart tourism destinations (Koo et al., 2016; Xiang, Tussyadiah, & Buhalis, 2015; Buhalis & Amaranggana, 2014).

Discussion

Physical ATDs need to maintain authenticity and have a sustainable form of tourist visits, whereas DAT is ideal for these purposes. Archaeotourists are usually discerning visitors, and it is necessary to meet their high expectations; DAT presents very first-hand information and satisfaction. Visitations can be directed according to tourist type or the level of guidance: basic, intermediate, or advanced. Exceeding the carrying capacity can cause irreversible damage to physical heritage assets, but not digital substitutes. Managers of delicate ATDs must be on high alert and take careful precautions to protect and maintain the actual site. However, this is not the same in DAT as the system saves all the digital data. Therefore, the transformation is in the preservation procedures of these fragile areas. DAT does not pose any of the risks that traditional physical tourist visitations pose to ATDs. Moreover, DAT provides a substitute for those who are unable to travel to these sites physically, such as people with disabilities (PwD) or illness or who are too elderly to manage a trip, enabling them to reach ATDs digitally through platforms on their computers. Hence, online DAT is a better option in the post-COVID era.

Local communities' primary involvement with physical ATDs is to protect the area, make tourism sustainable, and provide services. Similar services can also survive in DAT through e-publicity and e-shopping so that tourists can take part in indigenous cultures. Local representatives on DAT sites can promote their AT-based goods and send them anywhere in the world. Therefore, DAT can provide economic gain and improve the standard of life for local people.

Conclusion

The COVID-19 pandemic caught the AT industry unprepared, although digital technology has been available for approximately three decades. Consequently, the industry should make use of the great potential in digital technology, such as embracing the DAT approach discussed in this chapter. Cohesive, unified, and effective planning and management is necessary to include all the components of DAT in all means, such as texts, images, audio, and video recordings, including those created on the web by non-professional users, those created on social media, and those uploaded to video-sharing platforms. In this way, DAT brings different cultures together through the common interest in experiencing human heritage either physically or digitally and builds bridges between them by fostering mutual appreciation, respect, and friendship. ATDs should be embraced and promoted locally (by individuals from any part of the world), nationally (by any nation from any part of the world besides the host states), and transnationally (by UNESCO, the European Commission, and states of Africa and Central Europe). DAT has the capacity to revolutionise traditional AT through technology and serve many individuals around the globe, including scholars in related fields and tourists. Digital AT has the potential to create a paradigm shift in the AT industry through the transformational capacity of technology. DAT will make it easier for local and national governments to manage these common, critical areas of humanity and protect them from looters and the destructive effects of nature by digitalising them on a regular basis.

Despite the aforementioned benefits, DAT is still in its infancy. Archaeologists do not yet care much about tourism, and tourism professionals do not yet know much about archaeology, and the lack of collaborative studies between the fields is preventing DAT from being developed further. Moreover, AT is less common and too specific for many of the tourism professionals concerned, so they fail to appreciate the benefits of cooperating to promote AT. A wide range of issues must be resolved before the industry can fully develop credible digital AT destinations in the value chain.

This chapter, like all studies, is not without limitations. The insights herein need to be supported by empirical studies to confirm the applicability of DAT. Further studies provide natural extensions to the chapter by focusing on the effects of technological developments on AT and including a wider body of publications. Questions can be raised concerning how DAT responds to tourists' demands for intangible archaeological heritage, safeguarding sensitive data, and data ownership. Despite these limitations, this chapter contributes valuably to the literature and provides insights regarding the digitalisation process for AT planning and management.

References

Apaydin, V. (2016). Effective or not? Success or failure? Assessing heritage and archaeological education programmes-the case of Çatalhöyük. *International Journal of Heritage Studies*, *22*(10), 828–843. http://dx.doi.org/10.1080/13527258.2016.1218912

Ashley, C., Boyd, C., & Goodwin, H. (2000). Pro-poor tourism: Putting poverty at the heart of the tourism agenda. *Overseas Development Institute Natural Resource Perspectives*, *51*, 1–6.

Ashley, M., Tringham, R., & Perlingieri, C. (2011). Last house on the hill: Digitally remediating data and media for preservation and access. *Journal on Computing and Cultural Heritage*, *4*(4), 1–26. http://dx.doi.org/10.1145/2050096.2050098

Ashworth, G. J., & Kavaratzis, M. (2014). Cities of culture and culture in cities: The emergent uses of culture in city branding. In T. Haas & K. Olsson (Eds.), *Emergent Urbanism: Urban planning and design in times of systemic and structural change*. Aldershot, UK: Ashgate.

Balletti, C., Berto, M., Gottardi, C., & Guerra, F. (2014). 3D technologies for the digital documentation of an ancient wooden structure. *International Journal of Heritage in the Digital Era, 3*(1), 19–32. https:// http://dx.doi.org/10.1260/2047-4970.3.1.19

Balletti, C., Guerra, F., & Gerbaudi, F. (2003). The survey of the wooden structure of the roof of Palazzo Ducale in Venice. *The International Archives of Photogrammetry, Remote Sensing, and Spatial Information Sciences, 34*, 5/W12, 49–53.

Buhalis, D., & Amaranggana, A. (2014). Smart tourism destinations. In Z. Xiang & I. Tussyadiah (Eds.), *Information and communication technologies in tourism* (pp. 553–564). Springer, Cham. http://dx.doi.org/10.1007/978-3-319-03973-2

Buhalis, D., & Law, R. (2008). Progress in information technology and tourism management: 20 years on and 10 years after the Internet-the state of e-tourism research. *Tourism Management, 29*(4), 609–623. http://dx.doi.org/10.1016/j.tourman.2008.01.005

Cai, L. A., Feng, R., & Breiter, D. (2004). Tourist purchase decision involvement and information preferences. *Journal of Vacation Marketing, 10*(2), 138–148. http://dx.doi.org/10.1177/135676670401000204

Cakmak, E., & Isaac, R. K. (2012). What destination marketers can learn from their visitors' blogs: An image analysis of Bethlehem, Palestine. *Journal of Destination Marketing & Management, 1*(1–2), 124–133. https://doi.org/10.1016/j.jdmm.2012.09.004

Chang, T. C. (2002). Heritage as a tourism commodity: Traversing the tourist local divide. *Singapore Journal of Tropical Geography, 18*(1), 46–68. https://doi.org/10.1111/1467-9493.00004

Chen, H., & Rahman, I. (2018). Cultural tourism: An analysis of engagement, cultural contact, memorable tourism experience and destination loyalty. *Tourism Management Perspectives, 26*, 153–163. https://doi.org/10.1016/j.tmp.2017.10.006

Choi, S., Lehto, X. Y., & Morrison, A. M. (2007). Destination image representation on the web: Content analysis of Macau travel related websites. *Tourism Management, 28*(1), 118–129. https://doi.org/10.1016/j.tourman.2006.03.002

Cohen, E. (1988). Authenticity and commoditization in tourism. *Annals of Tourism Research, 15*, 371–386. https://doi.org/10.1016/0160-7383(88)90028-X

Comer, D. C. (2012). *Tourism and archaeological heritage management at Petra; driver to development or destruction?* New York: Springer.

Daly, P., & Evans, T. L., (2006). Archaeological theory and digital pasts. In T. L. Evans & P. Daly (Eds.), *Digital archaeology: Bridging method and theory*. London: Routledge.

Dell'Unto, N., Landeschi, G., Touati, A.-M. L., Dellepiane, M., Callieri, M., & Ferdani, D. (2016). Experiencing ancient buildings from a 3D GIS perspective: A case drawn from the swedish pompeii project. *Journal of Archaeological Method and Theory, 23*(1), 73–94. https://doi.org/10.1007/s10816-014-9226-7

Dore, C. D., & Aitchison, K. (2018). Heritage business and marketing. *The Encyclopedia of Archaeological Sciences*, 1–6. https://doi.org/10.1002/9781119188230.saseas0292

Eiteljorg, H. (2008). *Archaeological Computing* (2nd ed.). Bryn Mawr: Center for the Study of Architecture.

Erdogan, H. A. (2020a). Archaeologist effect on archaeological heritage tourism (archaeotourism) planning. *Selçuk University, Journal of Social Science Institute, 43*, 343–351.

Erdogan, H. A. (2020b). COVID-19 Sürecinin Arkeoturizme Küresel Etkileri ve Arkeoturizm Planlamasında Yeni Normal. In F. Kaleci & E. Başaran (Eds.), *Pandemi Sürecinde Sosyoekonomik Değişim ve Dönüşümler "Fırsatlar, Tehditler, Yeni Normaller"* (pp. 709–738). Konya: NEU Basımevi.

Erdogan, H. A. (2021). A key to various opportunities for the development in culture, economy and integration in Asia minor: A successful archaeotourism planning. *Journal of Yasar University, 16*(Special Issue), 30–39. https://doi.org/10.19168/jyasar.807404

Erdogan, H. A. (2022). Archaeotourism (archaeological tourism). In D. Buhalis (Ed.), *Encyclopedia of tourism management and marketing*. Cheltenham: Edward Elgar Publishing.

Forte, M., & Beltrami, R. (2000). A proposito di virtual archaeology: Disordini, interazioni cognitive e virtualit'a. *Archeologia e Calcolatori, 11*, 273–300.

Girard, L. G., & Nijkamp, P. (2009). *Cultural tourism and sustainable local development*. Aldershot: Ashgate.

Giraudo, R. F., & Porter, B. W. (2010). Archaeotourism and the crux of development. *Anthropology News, 51*(8), 7–8. https://doi.org/10.1111/j.1556-3502.2010.51807.x

Gretzel, U., & Yoo, K. H. (2008). Use and impact of online travel reviews. In P. O'Connor, W. Höpken, & U. Gretzel (Eds.), *Information and communication technologies in tourism* (pp. 35–46). New York: Wien Springer.

Guidi, G., Russo, M., & Beraldin, J. A. (2010). *Acquisizione 3D e modellazione poligonale*. Milano: McGraw-Hill Companies.

Hawas, Z. (1998). Site management: The response to tourism. *Museum International, 50*(4), 31–37. https://doi.org/10.1111/1468-0033.00174

Hodder, I. (1997). Always momentary, fluid and flexible: Towards a reflexive excavation methodology. *Antiquity, 71*, 691–700.

Holtorf, C. (2007). *Archaeology is a brand: The meaning of archaeology in contemporary popular culture*. Walnut Creek, CA: Left Coast Press.

Hughes, K., Little, B., & Ballantyne, R. (2013). Integrating education and entertainment in archaeological tourism: Complementary concepts or opposite ends of the spectrum? In C. Walker & N. Carr (Eds.), *Tourism and archaeology: Sustainable meeting grounds*, pp. 65–90. Walnut Creek, CA: Left Coast Press, Inc.

Hughes-Freeland, F. (1993). Packaging dreams: Javanese perceptions of tourism and performance. In M. Hitchcock, V. T. King, & M. J. G. Parnwell (Eds.), *Tourism in Southeast Asia* (pp. 138–154). London: Routledge.

Johnson, D., McKean, J., & Walsh, R. (1995). Valuing time in travel cost demand analysis: An empirical investigation. *Land Economics, 71*(1), 96–105. https://doi.org/10.2307/3146761

Kim, M. J., Kim, W. G., Kim, M., & Kim, C. (2016). Does knowledge matter to seniors' usage of mobile devices? Focusing on motivation and attachment. *International Journal of Contemporary Hospitality Management, 28*(8), 1702–1727. https://doi.org/10.1108/IJCHM-01-2015-0031

Kolas, A. (2004). Tourism and the making of place in Shangri-La. *Tourism Geographies, 6*(3), 262–278. https://doi.org/10.1080/1461668042000249610

Koo, C., Shin, S., Gretzel, U., Cannon, W., & Chung, N. (2016). Conceptualization of smart tourism destination competitiveness. *Asia Pacific Journal of Information Systems, 26*(4), 61–576. http://dx.doi.org/10.14329/apjis.2016.26.4.561

Lercari, N. (2017). 3D visualization and reflexive archaeology: A virtual reconstruction of Çatalhöyük history houses. *Digital Applications in Archaeology and Cultural Heritage*. http://dx.doi.org/10.1016/j.daach.2017.03.001

Lercari, N., Shiferaw, E., Forte, M., & Kopper, R. (2017). Immersive visualization and curation of archaeological heritage data: Çatalhöyük and the Dig@IT app. *Journal of Archaeological Method and Theory, 25*(2), 368–392. https://doi.org/10.1007/s10816-017-9340-4

Lipe, W. D. (2002). Public benefits of archaeological research. In B. J. Little (Ed.), *Public benefits of archaeology* (pp. 20–28). Gainesville: University Press of Florida.

Malcolm-Davies, J. (2004). Borrow robes: The educational value of costumed interpretation at historic sites. *International Journal of Heritage Studies*, *10*(3), 277–293.
Matero, F. (2008). *Heritage, conservation, and archaeology: An introduction.* Retrieved November 11, 2020, from www.archaeological.org/news/hca/89
Mckercher, B. (1998, August). The effect of market access on destination choice. *Journal of Travel Research*, *37*, 39–47. https://doi.org/10.1177/004728759803700105
McKercher, B., & Cros, du, H. (2002). *Cultural tourism; the partnership between tourism and cultural heritage management.* New York, NY: Routledge.
Mckercher, B., & Lew, A. A. (2003). Distance decay and the impact of effective tourism exclusion zones on international travel flows. *Journal of Travel Research*, *42*(2), 159–165. DOI:10.1177/0047287503254812
Medina, L. K. (2003). Commoditizing culture: Tourism and Maya identity. *Annals of Tourism Research*, *30*, 353–368. https://doi.org/10.1016/S0160-7383(02)00099-3
Merhav, R., & Killebrew, A. (1998). Public exposure: For better and for use. *Museum International*, *50*(4), 15–20.
Mulaj, I. (2015, October 11). What marketing strategy for sacred geometry discoveries to make archaeotourism work? *Institute for Economic Policy Research and Analyses (INEPRA)*, Pristina, Republic of Kosovo. https://mpra.ub.uni-muenchen.de/67176/
Ouf, A. M. S. (2001). Authenticity and the sense of place in urban design. *Journal of Urban Design*, *6*(1), 73–86. https://doi.org/10.1080/13574800120032914
Parsons, E., & Maclaran, P. (2009). *Contemporary issues in marketing and consumer behavior.* San Francisco: Butterworth Heinemann.
Pearce, D. (1989). *Tourism development* (2nd ed.). London: Longman.
Pinter, T. (2005). Heritage tourism and archaeology: Critical issues. *SAArchaeological Record*, *5*(3), 9–11.
Qu, H., & Lee, H. (2011). Travelers' social identification and membership behaviors in online travel community. *Tourism Management*, *32*, 1262–1270. https://doi.org/10.1016/j.tourman.2010.12.002
Radziwiłko, K. (2019). Archaeological tourism: A chance or a threat to southern Jordanian community: Case study of HLC project. In P. Kołodziejczyk (Ed.), *Discovering Edom: Polish archaeological activity in Southern Jordan* (pp. 99–120). Kraków. https://doi.org/10.33547/Discedom2019.06
Reeves, S., Greiffenhagen, C., Flintham, M., Benford, S., Adams, M., Row Farr, J., & Tandavantij, N. (2015). I'd hide you. *Proceedings of the 33rd Annual ACM Conference on Human Factors in Computing Systems-CHI'15*. https://doi.org/10.1145/2702123.2702257
Richards, G., & Munsters, W. (2010). Developments and perspectives in cultural tourism research. In G. Richards & W. Munsters (Eds.), *Cultural tourism research methods* (pp. 1–12). Wallingford: CABI.
Rogers, S. C. (2002). Which heritage? Nature, culture, and identity in French rural tourism. *French Historical Studies*, *25*(3), 475–503. https://doi.org/10.1215/00161071-25-3-475
Rosenzweig, R., & Thelen, D. (1998). *The presence of the past: Popular uses of history in American life.* New York, NY: Columbia University Press.
Smith, M. (2003). *Issues in cultural tourism studies.* London: Routledge.
Stevanovic, M., & Tringham, R. (2012). Last house on the hill: BACH area reports from Çatalhöyük, Turkey. *Çatalhöyük vol.11.* Los Angeles, CA: Cotsen Institute of Archaeology Publications, UCLA.
Takamitsu, J. (2019). *World heritage sites tourism; local communities and conservation activities.* London: CABI.

Timothy, D. J., & Boyd, S. W. (2003). *Heritage tourism*. England: Pearson Education Limited.

Timoty, D. J., & Nyaupane, G. P. (2009). *Cultural heritage and tourism in the developing world: A regional perspective*. New York: Routledge.

Walker, C., & Carr, N. (2013). *Tourism and archaeology: Sustainable meeting grounds*. Walnut Creek, CA: Left Coast.

White, M., Mourkoussis, N., Darcy, J., Petridis, P., Liarokapis, F., Lister, P., Walczak, K., Wojciechowski, R., Cellary, W., Chmielewski, J., Stawniak, M., Wiza, W., Patel, M., Stevenson, J., Manley, J., Giorgini, F., Sayd, P., & Gaspard, F. (2004). ARCO: An architecture for digitization, management and presentation of virtual exhibitions. *Computer Graphics International Conference* (pp. 622–625). CGI.

WTO. (1985). *The states' role in protecting and promoting culture as a factor in tourism development and the proper use and exploitation of the national cultural heritage of sites and monuments for tourists*. Madrid: World Tourism Organization.

Xiang, Z., Tussyadiah, I., & Buhalis, D. (2015). Smart destinations: Foundations, analytics, and applications. *Journal of Destination Marketing & Management*, *4*(3), 143–144. https://doi.org/10.1016/j.jdmm.2015.07.001

Young, C. (2006). Hadrian's wall: Conservation and archaeology through two centuries. In J. Wilson (Ed.), *Romanitas: Essays on roman archaeology in honor of Sheppard Frere on the occasion of his nintieth birthday* (pp. 203–210). England: Oxbow Books.

Zhang, H., Cho, T., Wang, H., & Ge, Q. (2018). The influence of cross-cultural awareness and tourist experience on authenticity, tourist satisfaction and acculturation in world cultural heritage sites of Korea. *Sustainability*, *10*(4), 927–941. https://doi.org/10.3390/su10040927

Zubrow, E. B. W. (2006). Digital archaeology: A historical context. In T. L. Evans & P. Daly (Eds.), *Digital archaeology: Bridging method and theory*. London: Routledge.

9 The rise of meme tourism

Tourism transformations towards 'fifteen minutes of fame'

Benjamin Owen and Anita Zatori

Introduction

The influence of Internet memes on consumer behaviour has been discussed in other disciplines; however, memes have received little attention in the field of tourism so far. An Internet meme (referred simply as a meme in this chapter) is defined as '*units of popular culture that are circulated, imitated, and transformed by Internet users, creating a shared cultural experience*' (Shifman, 2013, p. 367).

Memes have been with us for over a decade as a popular content type of social media, and they are also widely used in travel-related settings. They play an emerging role as a tourist motivation and affect how a destination is consumed. Surprisingly enough, despite the popularity of the phenomenon, 'meme tourism' is a rather new term in the tourism literature as there is an almost non-existent academic discussion on the topic. The theoretical gap is rather prevalent creating numerous opportunities for research in this novel field. The relevancy of generating theoretical discussion on this topic is undoubtedly strong. Several real-life cases indicate the emerging but already significant impact of memes on the tourism industry and tourist behaviour. Some less-known destinations have gained popularity thanks to meme tourism, while tourist attractions are popping up from one day to another solely generated by user-generated memes. Furthermore, the phenomenon described as 'meme tourism' has also been causing some unique sustainability issues and social tension between hosts and guests.

The chapter argues that in 'meme tourism', people are primarily or secondarily motivated to visit a destination or tourist attraction by viral Internet memes, while once on location, visitors recreate and reenact elements of the meme before sharing the results on social media. Roots of meme tourism originate in pop-culture tourism. However, meme tourism can be viewed as a next generation niche tourism product of cultural tourism (more specifically: pop-culture tourism). Nevertheless, it represents an unrevealed and underutilised resource for tourism marketing and destination management.

The aim of the chapter is to conceptualise 'meme tourism' through theoretical discussion and to extend the understanding of the phenomenon based on real-life case studies. Four detailed case studies have been carried out to gain a valuable insight into the phenomenon. While seeking to analyse and define meme tourism,

DOI: 10.4324/9781003105930-10

the chapter also aims to identify and discuss sustainability and visitor management issues induced by meme tourism.

Four cases are examined, each faced with different sustainability issues and varying degrees of community acceptance. However, they are united by a common issue: it is assumed that like the memes that spawned them, attendance at these locations will be somewhat short-lived, as the next meme captivates Internet users. Despite their typical short-lived popularity, the evolving popularity and importance of memes as generators of tourist attractions is relevant as a new trend in the age of social media and peer-to-peer content.

Nevertheless, the increasing popularity of memes points out important transformations taking place in the tourism industry due to the growing importance of peer-to-peer content, experience co-creation, and changed cultural consumption. Along with the meme and the visitor recreating and sharing the meme to earn 'likes' (i.e., popularity/fame), tourism destinations and tourist attractions are also earning their 'fifteen minutes of fame'. No wonder destinations impacted by meme tourism are often showcasing visitor management and sustainability issues.

Due to its peer-to-peer character, meme tourism may represent a rather big challenge for destination stakeholders; thus, a detailed exploration and understanding of real-life cases is crucial. The study does not aim to discuss ready-to-be-used solutions for destination stakeholders; it rather aims to uncover and analyse the phenomenon of meme tourism and to identify its critical aspects and momentums.

Literature review

Memes

Evolutionary biologist Richard Dawkins first used the term meme in his book 'The Selfish Gene' (1976). The concept describes the human spreading, replication, and modification of ideas and culture (Dawkins, 1976). Conceived before the digital era, it should be noted that Dawkins' concept was not connected to the Internet. With the emergence of the Internet and digital technology, Shifman (2013) notes that the spread and diffusion of memes is much more visible, and the term 'Internet Meme' became popular (Kulkarni, 2017).

Several researchers have identified qualities of the Internet meme. Knobel and Lankshear (2007) suggest that an Internet meme is the circulation of a '*particular idea presented as a written text, image, language "move", or some other unit of cultural "stuff"*' (p. 202). Davison (2012) posits that an Internet meme '*is a piece of culture, typically a joke, which gains influence through online transmission*' (p. 122). According to Shifman (2013), Internet users attribute memes to specific phenomenon, referencing 'Leave Britney Alone' and 'Star Wars Kid'. Chen (2012) notes that the Internet memes are often humorous and very contagious. Internet memes are a participatory medium of communication in which consumers aren't simply passive recipients, they may actively participate, as well (Kulkarni, 2017).

As Internet memes have increased in popularity, they have been embraced by marketing organisations to influence public opinion. Several companies, including

Nike and Delta Airlines, have used memes to advertise their brands and services (Bury, 2016). Similarly, memes have been used to promote tourist destinations, such as the campaign 'It's more fun in The Philippines', which sought to promote the country as a vacation destination through content and memes created by locals (Valdez, Tupas, & Tan, 2017). Memes have also been a source of political discourse. In the 2016 United States presidential election, the meme #ZodiacTed went viral, falsely suggesting that candidate Ted Cruz was the infamous Zodiac killer. A survey determined that around 40% of Florida voters believed Cruz to be the killer, which influenced their decision when voting (Kulkarni, 2017). Bury (2016) notes that memes have become an important part of the online environment, and they are now capable of influencing consumers in the offline world of advertising.

In tourism settings, 'meme tourism' can be defined as trips motivated by memes and/or tourists recreating memes during their travel.

Pop-culture tourism

Lundberg and Lexhagen (2014) define popular culture as being accessible, commercial, favoured by many, produced for the people by the people, positioned in the context of mass production and mass consumption. In the field of tourism, various facets of pop-culture have appeared in the form of niche tourism studies, including music tourism (Gibson & Connell, 2007), film tourism (O'Connor & Kim, 2014), video game tourism (Dubois & Gibbs, 2018), and literary tourism (O'Connor & Kim, 2014). These special interests motivate people to visit locations portrayed in pop-culture. Thus, pop-culture tourism refers to tourism caused by popular culture. It is suggested that meme tourism is also a niche product of pop-culture tourism along film tourism, music or video game tourism.

There are several proposed motivations for pop-culture tourism. In the context of music tourism, tourists were motivated by emotions induced by the music, such as nostalgia, sorrow, euphoria, and desire for journey (Lundberg & Lexhagen, 2014). Beeton (2016) notes that film tourists may visit film locations to view scenery and relive experiences portrayed in the film, adding that the power of celebrity and fame may serve as inspiration. Gyimóthy et al. (2015) highlight the importance of socialisation and fan communities within pop-culture tourism, in which tourists may meet other like-minded fans on site or share their experience with other fans online. Drawing similarities between pop-culture tourists and serious leisure sports fans, Gyimóthy et al. (2015) suggest that pop-culture tourists may use their experiences to signal social status and belonging.

Media is viewed as having a progressively large impact on society altogether, along with tourism (Jensen & Waade, 2009). Furthermore, studies have shown that locations depicted in pop-culture media may increase awareness of these places, subsequently affecting tourist flows to the area (Gyimóthy et al., 2015). Urry (1990) notes that tourist thoughts of locations are frequently '*constructed and sustained through a variety of non-tourist practices, such as TV, literature, magazines, records, and videos*' (p. 3).

Gyimóthy et al. (2015) propose that media convergence is a significant driver in pop-culture tourism, as it increases the probability and frequency a pop-culture phenomenon will arise in a consumer's thoughts. Media convergence is a phenomenon brought about by the digitisation of media and the popularity of the Internet, in which communication technologies, media content, and computer networks are interconnected (Jenkins, 2006). The role of the media consumer has changed as well, instead of passively consuming media they may actively participate in the creation of media (Jenkins, 2006). Fans create their own content such as art or fanfiction (Brown, 2007). Consequently, Månsson (2011) would argue that the study of a single media product's influence on tourism is limiting, because contents in books, movies, and other forms of media are often interconnected.

Methodology

Case studies as a research methodology serve to critically analyse industry practices and theorise and construct new knowledge. The methodology is typically used to examine the interplay of all factors in order to analyse and understand a real-life event or phenomenon.

Case study methodology is preferred 'when', 'how', or 'why' questions are asked or when the researcher has no or little control over the events (George, 2019). In addition, case studies are focusing at a problem that seeks a holistic understanding of the event or situation in question using inductive logic and reasoning from specific to more general terms. The goal of a case study is to offer new variables and questions for further research. The reliability and validity of case studies can be ensured if several different sources of information are used, if more than one side to the story is revealed, if it revolves around at least one major issue that is easy to identify but not necessarily easy to resolve, and if it uses quotations from interviewees or stakeholders of the case (Riege, 2003).

Case studies

'Storm Area 51'

Background

Area 51, a classified U.S. military base located in Nevada, has been rumoured to house extraterrestrial secrets and aircraft among conspiracy theorists and in pop-culture. The state's official website, Travel Nevada, notes that Area 51 is among the most heavily guarded military bases in the world, stressing that the location is not a tourist destination. It further urges visitors to obey all signs and discourages trespassing (Travel Nevada, 2020).

'Storm Area 51, They Can't Stop All of Us' was created on 27 June 2019 (Roberts, 2019) hosted by the meme page '$hitposting because im in shambles' and 'SmyleeKun'. Having created the event, Matty Roberts became the unofficial spokesperson for Storm Area 51. The event was decided to take place at 3:00AM on 20 September 2019 (Sheets, 2019). The description for the event stated:

> We will all meet up at the Area 51 Alien Center tourist attraction and coordinate our entry. If we naruto run, we can move faster than their bullets. Let's see them aliens.
>
> (Tingley, 2019)

The meme would go on to spawn three events in Nevada that weekend: Alienstock in Las Vegas, Alien-Stock in Rachel, and Storm Area 51 Basecamp in Hiko.

The 'Naruto run' or 'ninja running' is a reference to the Japanese anime 'Naruto' (Milan, 2019). Performed by characters of the series, Naruto running is characterised by the user leaning forwards while running with arms stretched out behind them (Brice-Saddler, 2019). Milan (2019) reports that this style of running was already a widely-spread meme and had become popular to perform in real life within fanbases of the show and anime in general.

Timeline: going viral

According to Roberts, the event gained little attention the first 72 hours the event was live before quickly gaining traction (Roberts, 2019). By 5 July 2019, over 53,000 had pledged to storm Area 51 first reported by Tingley in an article for the website Mysterious Universe (Tingley, 2019). The number of users marked as going had tripled to 165,000 by 9 July (Sheets, 2019). The event began to gain media attention; being covered by The Washington Post (Brice-Saddler, 2019) and The Daily Mail (Sheets, 2019). Several brands, including Kool-Aid, Funyuns, and Burger King tried to capitalise on the popularity of the meme by sharing Area 51 and alien themed content to their social media pages (Anderson, 2019). At over 540,000 RSVP's on 12 July, US Air Force spokeswoman Laura McAndrews acknowledged that the Air Force was aware of the event and discouraged attendees from trespassing on the base (Brice-Saddler, 2019).

As the meme continued to reach a greater audience, businesses near Area 51 began to plan ways to capitalise on the influx of visitors. The Alien Research Center, a gift shop, planned on hosting Storm Area 51 Basecamp on 20 September to entertain tourists. Similarly, the Little A'Le'Inn, a motel in nearby Rachel, Nevada, planned on hosting events and offering camping to visitors (Knapp, 2019).

Sustainability concerns

On 18 July, Roberts appeared in his first public interview with George Knapp of KLAS, a CBS News affiliate out of Las Vegas, Nevada. At the time of recording, over a million had RSVP'd as attending the event, with an additional million labelled interested. In the interview, Roberts confirmed that the event started as a joke, but the movement had since taken on a life of its own. He acknowledged that he was worried some attendees may take the event seriously and try to trespass at the government facility. To prevent people from storming the base, he considered planning an actual event to serve as an alternative for attendees (Roberts, 2019).

The following day, Knapp reported about the geography surrounding Area 51. He pointed out several inconsistencies in the raid plan, stating that the meeting location was nowhere near Area 51. Turning his attention to the nearest settlement, Rachel, Nevada, he noted that the town had only around 50 residents, no gas station, and limited resources. An article accompanying the video asserted that the vast, unforgiving, and secluded environment had been a factor in the government's decision to put a military base in that location (Knapp, 2019).

On 12 August, Roberts tried to seize control of the movement, rebranding the event 'Alienstock' and launching a new website (Hopkins & Underwood, 2019). Partnering with Connie West, owner of The Little A'Le'Inn, the two promised a weekend-long festival of art installations, music, and performances. Though the event itself was free, they asked for donations to cover costs of medical services, security, food, water, event staff, portable toilets, and performers (Lawrence, 2019).

As RSVPs continued to rise, the citizens of Lincoln County and Rachel began to grow concerned. Fears included congestion of highways, trashing the desert, depleting the local water table (Healy, 2019), lack of infrastructure, and overwhelming local law enforcement (Nevett, 2019). In a Vice Specials interview, resident Joerg Arnu confirmed that the town lacked the resources and infrastructure to host a festival. Concerned that attendees would turn hostile towards residents and raid their homes for supplies, citizens vowed to protect each other and their property (Vice Specials, 2019). According to Lincoln County Commissioner Kevin Phillips, fears of an unsustainable crowd were not unwarranted. Phillips reported that, based on parking permits that had been acquired, the town should prepare for at least 10,000 visitors (Vice Specials, 2019).

On 19 August, with Facebook attendance listed at 2 million, Lincoln County pre-signed an emergency declaration (Hopkins & Underwood, 2019), expecting anywhere between 5,000 and 50,000 visitors (Nevett, 2019). Lincoln County Sheriff Kerry Lee stated that even if only 1% of attendees arrived, it would overwhelm his department; adding an additional 150 officers and 300 paramedics would be brought in from across the state to aid his staff of 26 (Nevett, 2019).

On 9 September, amid concerns of a humanitarian crisis, Roberts cut ties with West and the Little A'Le'Inn (Hopkins & Underwood, 2019). The Alienstock event spawned by the meme was being compared to the infamous Fyre Festival, with Rachel's webpage urging tourists to stay home (Vice Specials, 2019). An official statement from Alienstock read:

> *Due to the lack of infrastructure, poor planning, risk management and blatant disregard for the safety of the expected 10,000+ Alienstock attendees, we decided to pull the plug on the festival.*
>
> (Nevett, 2019)

In the following days, Roberts announced a new partnership with Budweiser and plans for a free concert in Las Vegas using the Alienstock name (Vice Specials,

2019). He sent a cease and desist notice to West, demanding Alienstock be shut down (Hopkins & Underwood, 2019). Hopkins and Underwood (2019) report West refused, assuring people that Rachel and the Little A'Le'Inn were prepared to meet the demands of festival attendees.

The events

On 19 September, the night before the scheduled raid, Roberts and Bud Light hosted Alienstock in Las Vegas. Many attendees wore alien and anime themed clothing (Conroy, 2019). The one-night event featured electronic dance music, with a line-up of bands that remained 'classified' proceeding without incident. Once concluded, promoters revealed that Alienstock had drawn over 10,000 attendees (Yopko, 2019).

Much to the relief of Lincoln County and Rachel citizens, the events spawned by the Storm Area 51 meme fell short of projected attendance. Roughly 150 people attended the Storm Area 51 event in the early hours of September 20 at the gates of Area 51. Most followed security's warnings, with only minor incidents being reported (The Guardian, 2019).

Attendees who visited Alien-Stock in Rachel dressed as aliens, anime characters, or donned tin-foil hats (Vice Specials, 2019). Throughout the weekend, groups visited the Area 51 gates to livestream, pose for selfies, and pretend to raid Area 51, often Naruto running. Attendees entertained themselves, often socialising or playing games. Vice reported that most attendees were members of media, including professionals, streamers, and influencers (Vice Specials, 2019). Frank (2019) reported that non-media attendees were mostly alien enthusiasts, anime fans, and meme lovers, some having travelled from as far as Peru and Germany. She noted that many didn't expect to breach the gates and were satisfied in meeting like-minded enthusiasts. After the event, a spokesman for the Lincoln County sheriff's department reported that around 6,000 people had visited the county over the course of the weekend (Frank, 2019).

Meanwhile, Storm Area 51 Basecamp held in Hiko attracted a more serious crowd. Attendees were reported to predominately consist of dedicated UFO enthusiasts, conspirators, and souvenir salesmen, though people who had seen the memes were in attendance too (Conroy, 2019). Conroy (2019) added that attractions included art instalments, music, and mock raids of Area 51. According to Fox News, after a low turn-out of around 200, the second day's events were cancelled (Fox 5, 2019b).

Aftermath

Though a humanitarian crisis was averted, Lincoln County was left facing the aftermath. Though a boon for the local economy (Conroy, 2019), the county amassed a bill of over $200,000 to pay for emergency staff from across the state, including labour, meals, lodging, and travel costs, in addition to portable toilets and hand-washing stations (Fox 5, 2019a). The Lincoln County District Attorney has considered suing Facebook or Roberts (Fox 5, 2019a), though at the time of writing, no charges have been filed.

In total, the meme drew around 16,000 attendees to three separate events (Yopko, 2019; Frank, 2019). A 19 September news report on location at Area 51 in which an attendee Naruto ran behind the reporter would go viral after the event.

The joker stairs

Background

On 3 April 2019, ahead of its theatrical release, a trailer was released for the upcoming 'Joker' movie. One scene in the trailer depicted the Joker, portrayed by Joaquin Phoenix, dancing down a set of stairs in clown makeup (Outlaw, 2019). An image of Phoenix's descent later appeared in promotional material with another shot of Phoenix on the stairs being used as the theatrical poster (Ellis, 2019). The stairs, located in The Bronx, a borough of New York City, were unremarkable. Linking Shakespeare and Anderson Avenues, the staircase is one of many 'step streets' found throughout the Bronx (Jacobs, 2019).

The Joker dancing down the stairs went on to spawn various memes, including: 'Dancing Joker', using the original image as a template; the dance itself became a meme; and 'Joker and Peter Parker Dancing', with a previous meme, 'Emo Peter Parker', photoshopped alongside the Joker (Ellis, 2019). Variations of the meme were shared on other platforms throughout September.

On 4 October 2019, the film was released. Prior to 8 October, an unknown user had named the steps 'The Joker Stairs' on Google Maps and labelled them a religious site (Outlaw, 2019). An iFunny user posted a screenshot from Google street view including an image of the stairs and their address (Ellis, 2019). The story was first reported by Kofi Outlaw on the website ComicBook.com, noting that it appeared Google was altering search results for the Joker Stairs. Outlaw (2019) suggested that the notoriety of the stairs may benefit the neighbourhood.

The stairs as an attraction

Over the following week, the image continued to be shared and Instagrammers began seeking out the location, drawing dozens to hundreds of tourists a day (Jacobs, 2019). The first article documenting the phenomenon was published on 22 October. By that time, #JokerStairs had over 700 results on Instagram (Vad, 2019), with the number having doubled to over 2,000 on 30 October (Jacobs,2019). Reports indicate that many tourists recreated the dance, some wearing face paint, or even dressing as the Joker (Ellis, 2019; Jones, 2019; Jacobs, 2019). These visitors were not limited to residents of New York City, attracting even international tourists (Jones, 2019). Recreations were often shared on social media. It is worth noting that not all tourists were fans of 'The Joker'. Jones reported that several tourists he spoke with had not seen the movie, one stating the meme had made the stairs popular (Jones, 2019).

Some locals did not appreciate tourists descending upon their neighbourhood to visit The Joker Stairs. Vad (2019) noted that some residents complained they had trouble using the stairs getting to school or work, some avoiding the stairs altogether because they didn't want to appear in pictures. It was reported that a shop owner threw eggs at tourists because they were not spending money, rather only visiting to take pictures (Mahdawi, 2019). Signs posted around the staircase read:

> *It is disrespectful to treat our community and residents as a photo opportunity.*
> (Vad, 2019)

However, Jacobs (2019) suggested that such reports of hostility were exaggerated. Some residents welcomed the attention and increased visitation the stairs were receiving. The Bronx Borough President, Ruben Diaz Jr., hoped that visitors would spend money in local businesses (Vad, 2019). One resident was happy to see tourists, hoping that The Bronx was shedding its previously bad reputation (Jibilian, 2019). Because it was drawing in so many visitors, the city began cleaning the staircase more often which some residents had hoped would happen (Jones, 2019).

The West Maple Omaha Rock

In an Omaha, Nebraska parking lot median, a small boulder was placed to prevent cars from jumping the curb. The rock gained attention after drivers kept getting their cars stuck on top of it, often in a similar position. Arrow Towing responded to six calls over the course of six weeks to remove vehicles (Alfonso, 2019).

Because of the continued accidents, which residents often found comical, a Facebook page 'The W Maple Omaha Rock' was created on 21 October 2019. By 9 November, the group had over 20,000 members (Alfonso, 2019). Group members dubbed the boulder 'Rocko', with staff at a nearby UPS store serving as moderators and providing updates. Similarly, a subreddit was created honouring the boulder. Members of both groups created memes and posted selfies with Rocko.

At some point, an unknown user submitted it as a tourist attraction on Google Maps. The boulder received a five-star rating based on the reviews of 215 users (Wray, 2019). Having garnered so much attention online, news outlets, including CNN and NBC, reported stories on the rock.

Most locals have embraced the rock, finding humour in the accidents. Local businesses have welcomed Rocko's fame, including the previously mentioned UPS employees. Another, Mars Bar and Grill, offered diners a discount on their meal or drinks by showing servers a photo of themselves with the rock (Stewart, 2019). Other businesses have offered similar discounts and promotions.

The tourism group, Visit Omaha, unveiled a bronze sculpture under a pedestrian bridge. Named 'Omar the Troll', the sculpture was created to maintain visitor excitement about the riverfront bridge. Ironically, a Google Trends search reveals that 'West Maple Rock' received almost double the searches of 'Omar the Troll', when both were at the height of their popularity.

The Pink Wall

Located in Los Angeles, California, the Pink Wall has become a popular destination for people to have their photos taken (Mau, 2017). Mau (2017), Muller (2018), and Barker (2019) attribute its popularity to Instagram, with Mau (2017) noting that most visitors she spoke to had heard about the wall on social media. The storefront wall of Paul Smith's is painted bright pink, frequently topping lists of LA's most Instagrammable walls. Mau (2017) notes though the wall has been pink since the store opened in 2005, it was not until 2014 or 2015 that the wall began to gain attention. Barker (2019) reports that more than 100,000 people upload pictures of the wall yearly. Because the Pink Wall has more than 55,000 visitors a year, it is officially classified as a Los Angeles landmark. Assistant store manager Jose Lemus estimates that around 75% of visitors are international tourists (Barker, 2019).

The Pink Wall has guidelines visitors must follow, which are enforced by a security guard, including: no professional photography, no putting shoes on the wall, no costumes, and no props (Barker, 2019). Additionally, a sign notifies visitors of the location's geotag, Instagram handle, and preferred hashtag (Mau, 2017). Barker (2019) reported that Paul Smith spends $60,000 annually on the upkeep of the wall, which is repainted every three months and hand-cleaned by an employee. Despite its popularity, Barker (2019) reports that only around 3% of visitors make a purchase from the store.

In September 2018, The Pink Wall was vandalised (Muller, 2018). A graffiti artist sprayed the message 'go fuck your selfie' across the wall. Muller (2018) reports that ironically, this made the location more instagrammable, calling it a 'special edition Instagram'.

Discussion

Evolving transformations: towards 'fifteen minutes of fame'

Several case studies point out that meme tourism can easily create sustainability issues. At Storm Area 51, residents worried about a humanitarian crisis in which large numbers of tourists would arrive unprepared for the scant resources available in the town. Though the crisis was avoided, the county was left $200,000 in debt, having tried to prepare for an overwhelming number of tourists. At the Joker Stairs, Bronx, some residents felt disrespected when tourists used their neighbourhood as the backdrop for Instagram photos, failing to realise that the Bronx is not a movie set.

In all cases, locals responded to an influx in visitors in different ways. In Rachel, Nevada, most locals worried that their small town would be overwhelmed by tourists. Though the events would only last a weekend, most feared a humanitarian crisis, using their town webpage to discourage people from attending. In the case of The Joker Stairs, tourist reception was both accepted and rejected by locals. Though some were reportedly openly antagonistic against tourists, others welcomed the idea of visitors in their neighbourhood, happy to see that The Bronx was shedding its bad reputation. The Pink Wall has implemented rules to protect the wall, in addition to a set of guidelines that continue to grow the wall's online presence and the Paul Smith brand.

Meme tourism is fuelled by social media; thus, it might become overly challenging to oversee its visitor management. This might be highly concerning for the destination stakeholders. As the Area 51 meme demonstrated, regardless of intention, popular memes may gain a life of their own, with users interpreting the information differently. Though Roberts ultimately tried to divert people to a safe event in Las Vegas, more than 6,000 visited Rachel. Despite warnings of the townspeople and Roberts himself, they were unable to deter people from visiting and participating in the joke. Though not a humanitarian crisis, aggravated locals could not dissuade influencers from visiting The Joker Stairs.

On the other hand, West Maple Omaha Rock managed to handle a tourist attraction created by a meme – even though their visitor numbers have never peaked similar to the Joker-stairs or Area 51 event. In their case, a Facebook page was created and moderated by staff of a local business. A tourist attraction was created unintentionally, only for fun. Moderators documented and created posts on the group page as accidents continued to happen on a near weekly basis. The increased attention and absurdity of the accidents led to the story being picked up by national news outlets. Furthermore, with Mars Bar and Grill offering promotions for pictures with the rock, they added incentive to visit and photograph the rock. In theory, this promotion increases visits to both the boulder and the restaurant, and the photos can easily be shared online, further spreading knowledge about the rock. Despite all the challenges associated with meme tourism's visitor management, the Omaha rock proves that it can be done in a sustainable manner. The case of Omaha rock illustrates how a tourist attraction can be formed, promoted, and managed by a meme on social media outlets.

The impactful role of social media on meme tourism attractions' manifests itself in the unique characteristics of the tourism product, as well. The popularity of meme tourism attractions can be peak-like or rather balanced. The case of Area 51 is related to an event, while the case of the Joker-stairs in The Bronx started off with a movie release, both of which had a peak-like but short-term increase in visitors. However, the visitor numbers have been more balanced over time in case of the Omaha rock and the Pink Wall, and the hype related to the meme tourism attraction proved to be longer lasting.

Evolving transformations: from pop-culture tourism to meme tourism

There are certainly parallels between pop-culture tourism and meme tourism. Gyimóthy et al. (2015) note that pop-culture tourists may visit filming locations and re-enact scenes, imitate fictional characters, or follow in the footsteps of lead actors. Similarly, meme tourists recreate the dance of the Joker or match his pose from the meme. They may imitate animated characters, such as the running style of Naruto outside the gates of Area 51 as the meme suggested. Finally, they may follow in the footsteps of their favourite Instagram influencer, as opposed to lead actor, and recreate a photo where their favourite Influencer once stood. Pop-culture tourism has been shown to grow rapidly and proved difficult to predict (Lundberg & Lexhagen, 2014), as can be said of the Joker Stairs, Pink Wall, and the Raid Area 51 event.

Supporting Gyimóthy et al.'s (2015) proposal that media convergence drives pop-culture tourism, elements of the Area 51 meme were recreated and repurposed across various forms of media, including text, images, and a music video. The same can be said about the Joker Stairs. Because the image of Phoenix dancing down the stairs was used as promotional material prior to the film's release, there was little context behind the scene. As depicted in the movie, the scene is rather powerful and said to be symbolic of the Joker's descent into madness. However, many memes using the template focus on the seemingly celebratory pose of the Joker, with examples including a dog expecting pizza rolls or a wife celebrating her husband's pay cheque on payday.

How is meme tourism different from pop-culture tourism? Unlike pop-culture tourism where fans are inspired by visit a destination tied to an established form of media, often with an existing mythology, a meme tourist may be inspired by a combination of existing ideas in a new format. For example, Raid Area 51 began as a joke, with no preexisting identity. As seen in memes and pop-culture, several unrelated pop-culture elements were combined and repurposed to create the meme, notably Area 51's alleged status of harbouring alien secrets, and anime culture in the form of Naruto running; two concepts that had not previously overlapped. Therefore, there was no underlying story or motive for fans to be nostalgic for or choose to relive. This is supported by Jones (2019) report that not all visitors to the Joker Stairs had seen the movie; instead, they were there to recreate images they had seen online.

However, other motivations of pop-culture tourism may explain motives for meme tourism, notably social aspects. It is theorised that social aspects, such as showcasing one's dedication to a fandom or being trend-savvy, may serve as motivations of the meme tourist. This lines up Shifman's view (2013) according to the era of networked individualism, one may create memetic contents to simultaneously express both their uniqueness of themselves and their connectivity to the community.

Andy Warhol famously said in the 1960s that in the era of pop-culture, everyone can be famous for 15 minutes. While this still holds true, it seems to become even more prevalent. A half century later, the chance of earning a short-lived fame has become even higher. It could be argued that social media sites, due to their peer-to-peer character, help to 'democratize' fame. User-generated and peer-to-peer content in the form of Internet memes is gaining in popularity. Given the fact that memes are recreated, they can be viewed as products of the online community's co-creation process. In fact, the social media platform Tik Tok is basically built around providing an online community seeking fame and creating self-made content with an aim of turning into a meme. Creating a meme is an act of self-expression and creativity despite the fact that memes are often replicas of the same content – see the case of the Pink Wall.

Conclusion

Meme tourism is a consumption pattern. Memes are products of the evolving transformation taking place in the communication, media, and cultural consumption of the individual with clear implications not only on tourist motivation but also on their tourist behaviour. Co-created, user-generated, and peer-to-peer content has an increased significance in the era of participatory culture. As participants of meme tourism frequently recreate moves, poses, and images, it may be a more participatory form of tourism than pop-culture tourism. When visiting a pop-culture attraction, the tourist is not the artist and is passively observing the location. Meme tourism is a manifestation of changed cultural consumption. Individuals consume and experience differently even when they travel.

Meme tourism serves as a tourist motivation. By the increasing prevalence of virtual communication and peer-to-peer content, trips motivated by memes are gaining in popularity. Media convergence is also a driving force of meme tourism. Memes appear across different forms of media, and they also frequently arise in a consumer's thoughts. People's attention spans are becoming shorter. How many memes will one see while scrolling through social media today, versus how many books will they read, or movies will they watch in the same amount of time?

According to the case study findings, meme tourism has several managerial implications. As noted in the case of the Omaha Rock, local businesses embraced the meme by offering patrons a discount for taking pictures with the rock. While the popularity of a meme cannot be guaranteed, savvy business owners may capitalise on the meme. Some destinations such as the Philippines have already experimented with memes as a form of tourism marketing (Valdez, Tupas, & Tan, 2017). In the future, destination marketers may create memes to promote their destination or capitalise on the popularity of a user-created meme featuring the destination.

Although the study faced a major limitation given the fact of a very limited number of literature sources, it is suggested that the findings have a major contribution to the theoretical discussion of the concept of meme tourism. The findings provide a detailed insight from four different distinct case studies and uncover new perspectives and novel issues related to the phenomenon. The applied methodological approach, case study research, has proven to be successful in providing rich and valuable data.

The recent study is one of the first to examine the phenomenon while it relies heavily on case studies. Further research is needed to better understand meme tourism. Given the novelty of the topic, there are numerous research opportunities within the subject. It would be useful to collect data at specific locations depicted in memes or that are experiencing an increase in visitation after appearing in a meme. Memes as a destination marketing tool may also be an area of interest for future research. Other than destination focused studies, big data analysis might be a suitable approach studying Internet memes and the related consumer behaviour.

References

Alfonso, F. (2019, November 9). *A rock in Omaha became an overnight attraction thanks to the cars that can't seem to avoid it*. Retrieved from https://cnn.com

Anderson, S. (2019, July 16). *We regret to inform you that brands are storming area 51 memes*. Retrieved from https://mashable.com

Barker, T. (2019, March 7). *It costs $60,000 a year to upkeep this Instagram landmark*. Retrieved from https://losangeleno.com

Beeton, S. (2016). *Film-induced tourism*. Bristol: Channel View Publications.
Brice-Saddler, M. (2019, July 12). *Half a million people signed up to Storm Area 51: What happens if they actually show?* Retrieved from www.washingtonpost.com
Brown, S. (2007). Harry Potter and the phantom menace. In B. Cova, R. Kozinets, & A. Shankar (Eds.), *Consumer tribes* (pp. 177–192). Abingdon, UK: Routledge.
Bury, B. (2016). Creative use of internet memes in advertising. *World Scientific News*, 57, 33–41.
Chen, C. (2012). The creation and meaning of Internet memes in 4chan: Popular internet culture in the age of online digital reproduction. *Habitus*, 3(1) 6–19.
Conroy, J. O. (2019, September 24). *I 'stormed' Area 51 and it was even weirder than I imagined*. Retrieved from www.theguardian.com.
Davison, P. (2012). The language of internet memes. In M. Mandiberg (Ed.), *The social media reader*. New York: New York University Press.
Dawkins, R. (1976). *The selfish gene*. Oxford: Oxford University Press.
Dubois, L. E., & Gibbs, C. (2018). Video game–induced tourism: A new frontier for destination marketers. *Tourism Review*.
Ellis, E. G. (2019, October 24). *"Joker Stairs" and the problem with meme tourism*. Retrieved from www.wired.com
Fox 5. (2019a, September 16). *Lincoln County considering legal action against Facebook, "Storm Area 51" creators*. Retrieved from www.fox5vegas.com
Fox 5. (2019b, September 21). *Storm Area 51 Basecamp cancelled, Alienstock going on as planned*. Retrieved from fox5vegas.com
Frank, A. (2019, September 27). *"Storm Area 51" weekend had neither raids nor aliens: But it wasn't a bust*. Retrieved from www.vox.com
George, A. L. (2019). Case studies and theory development: The method of structured, focused comparison. In A. L. George (Ed.), *A pioneer in political and social sciences* (pp. 191–214). Cham: Springer.
Gibson, C., & Connell, J. (2007). Music, tourism and the transformation of Memphis. *Tourism Geographies*, 9(2), 160–190.
The Guardian. (2019, September 20). *Area 51 raid: People gather near US military base to "see them aliens"*. Retrieved from www.theguardian.com
Gyimóthy, S., Lundberg, C., Lindström, K. N., Lexhagen, M., & Larson, M. (2015). Popculture tourism: A research manifesto. In D. Chambers & T. Rakic (Eds.), *Tourism research frontiers: Beyond the boundaries of knowledge* (pp. 13–26). Bingley: Emerald.
Healy, J. (2019, September 21). *Area 51 raid: How a town of 40 coped with an invasion*. Retrieved from www.nytimes.com
Hopkins, J., & Underwood, X. (2019, September 20). *Storm Area 51 is no joke, a timeline of how it began*. Retrieved from www.8newsnow.com
Jacobs, J. (2019, October 31). *"Joker" Stairs become a Bronx tourist draw: Hope you're in shape*. Retrieved from www.nytimes.com
Jenkins, H. (2006). *Convergence culture*. New York: New York University Press.
Jensen, J., & Waade, A. M. (2009). *Medier og turisme*. Århus: Academica.
Jibilian, I. (2019, October 19). *No "Joker": Bronx 'step street' becomes New York hot spot thanks to hit movie*. Retrieved from www.reuters.com
Jones, N. (2019, October 23). *An afternoon at the Joker Stairs, New York's newest tourist attraction*. Retrieved from www.vulture.com
Knapp, G. (2019, July 19). *George Knapp maps out Area 51*. Retrieved from www.8newsnow.com
Knobel, M., & Lankshear, C. (Eds.). (2007). *A new literacies sampler* (Vol. 29). New York: Peter Lang.

Kulkarni, A. (2017). Internet meme and political discourse: A study on the impact of internet meme as a tool in communicating political satire. *Journal of Content, Community & Communication Amity School of Communication, 6*.

Lawrence, C. (2019, August 12). *"Storm Area 51" Facebook event rebrands as "Alienstock"*. Retrieved from www.reviewjournal.com

Lundberg, C., & Lexhagen, M. (2014). Pop culture tourism: A research model. *Fan studies: Researching Popular Audiences*, 13–34.

Mahdawi, A. (2019, October 30). *Meme tourism has turned the world into the seventh circle of selfie hell*. Retrieved from www.theguardian.com

Månsson, M. (2011). Mediatized tourism. *Annals of Tourism Research, 38*(4), 1634–1652.

Mau, D. (2017, April 6). *Paul Smith's Pink Wall is an LA Instagram phenomenon*. Retrieved from https://fashionista.com

Milan, A. (2019, July 19). *What is a Naruto run and how is it linked to Area 51?* Retrieved from https://metro.co.uk

Muller, M. (2018, September 12). *The Paul Smith Pink Wall was defaced, making it all the more Instagrammable*. Retrieved from www.wmagazine.com

Nevett, J. (2019, September 13). *Storm Area 51: The joke that became a "possible humanitarian disaster"*. Retrieved from www.bbc.com

O'Connor, N., & Kim, S. (2014). Pictures and prose: Exploring the impact of literary and film tourism. *Journal of Tourism and Cultural Change, 12*(1), 1–17.

Outlaw, K. (2019, October 11). *Joker Stairs named religious destination on Google Maps*. Retrieved from https://comicbook.com

Riege, A. M. (2003). Validity and reliability tests in case study research: a literature review with "hands-on" applications for each research phase. *Qualitative Market Research, 6*(2), 75–86. https://doi.org/10.1108/13522750310470055

Roberts, M. (2019, July 18). *Man behind "Storm Area 51" talks about joke gone awry* (G. Knapp, Interviewer).

Sheets, M. (2019, July 9). *More than 165,000 "alien hunters" say they will storm Area 51 in September*. Retrieved from www.dailymail.co.uk

Shifman, L. (2013). Memes in a digital world: Reconciling with a conceptual troublemaker. *Journal of Computer-Mediated Communication*, 362–377.

Stewart, K. (2019, November 5). *Omaha bar offers discount to people who take selfies with famous West Maple rock*. Retrieved from www.omaha.com

Tingley, B. (2019, July 5). *53,000 People have pledged to raid Area 51 this fall*. Retrieved from https://mysteriousuniverse.org

Travel Nevada. (2020, February 19). *Area 51*. Retrieved from https://travelnevada.com

Urry, J. (1990). The tourist gaze. In *Leisure and travel in contemporary societies*. London: Sage Publications.

Vad, J. (2019, October 22). *Tourists flood the "Joker Stairs," frustrating Bronx residents*. Retrieved from https://gothamist.com

Valdez, P. N. M., Tupas, R., & Tan, N. C. (2017). "It's more fun in the Philippines": Resemiotizing and commodifying the local in tourism discourse. *Discourse, Context & Media, 20*, 132–145.

Vice Specials. (2019, November 1). *How a viral meme almost destroyed a town*. Retrieved from https://video.vice.com

Wray, M. (2019, November 12). *"World famous": Omaha boulder gets 5-star Google review after cars keep driving over it*. Retrieved from https://globalnews.ca

Yopko, N. (2019, September 23). *Alienstock 2019 drew over 10,000 attendees*. Retrieved from https://edm.com

10 Accessible tourism as a transformational force for tourism and hospitality

Christina Karadimitriou, Anna Kyriakaki, and Eleni Michopoulou

Introduction

Academic interest in accessible tourism and travellers with disabilities emerged in the 1990s, when it was recognised that disabled people could represent a new niche tourism market (Lee, Agarwal, & Kim, 2012). Since then, different aspects of accessible tourism have been investigated, such as the travel decision-making processes of disabled people (Burnett & Baker, 2001; Israeli, 2002; Ray & Ryder, 2003), the meaning of holidays (Shaw & Coles, 2004), and the experiences and satisfaction of PwD in relation to travel agents (McKercher et al., 2003) and tourism products and services (Daniels, Rodgers, & Wiggins, 2005; Darcy, 2002; Yau, McKercher, & Packer, 2004). The wider benefits of tourism for PwD have also been well documented (Kim & Lehto, 2012; McKercher et al., 2003; Ray & Ryder, 2003). Exclusion of PwD from tourism activities results in them experiencing social marginalisation and discrimination which has negative impacts on disabled people and their caregivers' lives (McCabe & Johnson 2013). Horner and Swarbrooke (2004) note that the tourism industry has often discouraged disabled tourists to travel. However, there have been developments that show how the tourism industry has recently become more disability friendly by comprehending the needs of PwD (Yau, McKercher, & Packer, 2004).

To this end, various public sector bodies of different scale and scope have also pushed for making tourism more accessible. For example, the special issue of the United Nations (2006) Convention on the Rights of Persons with Disabilities (by 160 countries) has focused on the rights of persons with disabilities to access transport, structured environment, and tourism goods, services, and experiences. This issue provides the opportunity for researchers and stakeholders to participate in current discussions about accessible tourism and its prospects. Furthermore, in 2010, the EU created a new European Disability Strategy 2010–2020, which focuses on removing barriers, emphasising eight key areas of action: accessibility, participation and integration, equality, employment, education and training, social protection, health, and external action. This strategy recognises the weaknesses that exist in the society of all EU member states regarding the accessibility and integration of citizens with disabilities in social becoming. It proposes legislation by states and optimisation of the accessibility of the built environment, transport,

DOI: 10.4324/9781003105930-11

and efficient ICT (European Union, 2010). In 2015, the UNWTO also published 'The Handbook on Accessible Tourism for All: Principles, Tools and Good Practices' which devotes a part of its strategy to the promotion of responsible, sustainable, and accessible tourism on a global level. It proposes guidelines for planners and encourages stakeholders to implement measures in order to achieve a greater participation of different population groups in tourism activities. It also supports the implementation of accessibility practices at destinations. This publication discusses four main issues related to the implementation of accessibility in tourism: (1) the chain of accessibility and recommendations; (2) the main areas of action; (3) the indicators for studying accessibility in tourism; and (4) good practices (UNWTO, 2015). It is therefore important to understand the different aspects of accessible tourism, its management, and implementation in order to ensure social, economic, and environmental benefits for both host and guest communities (Michopoulou et al., 2015).

This chapter first provides an overview of accessible tourism, continues with insights into the PwD needs, and concludes with envisioning the transformations that will occur in the tourism industry. The theoretical contribution of this study lies within the unpacking of the complexities inherent in accessible tourism as well as exploring the dynamics surrounding it, so as to highlight accessible tourism as a force of transformation for the tourism industry and its sustainable development.

The accessible tourism industry: a brief presentation

According to the World Bank (2016) and the World Health Organization (2016), at least 80 million people in Europe face a disability and about 15% of the total world population has at least one. It is predicted that these figures will increase due to the increase in life expectancy and the ageing population (WHO, 2013). Despite the sensitisation campaigns that were implemented throughout the years from several governments, there is still a gap in accessible tourism provision even though considerable progress has been made (Shaw & Coles, 2004).

Buhalis and Michopoulou (2011) suggest that there are three primary requirements for accessible tourism: (1) accessibility of physical/build environment; (2) information regarding accessibility; and (3) accessible information online. The quality and accuracy of information (and even more so online) is a particularly important requirement (Michopoulou & Buhalis, 2013) for PwDs to engage in travel. Eichhorn et al. (2008) and Shi, Cole, & Chancellor (2012) also note that even if a destination is fairly accessible in terms of the physical infrastructure, the unreliability of information regarding the destination's accessibility deters PwD and their caregivers from making a travel decision.

Since the work of Smith (1987) which identifies three types of barriers to tourism participation (intrinsic barriers, environmental barriers, and interactive barriers), the situation in tourism industry for the disabled people seems to be marginally improving. According to Agovino et al. (2017), there are still three types of obstacles in the accessible tourism industry: informational obstacles, economic obstacles, and environmental obstacles, while Gladwell and Bedini (2004) identify physical, social, and emotional obstacles, which European Network for Accessible Tourism (ENAT) (2007) suggests eventually destroy the tourism experience. Financial restrictions make the travel decision for the individual with disabilities and their caregivers even harder. Most of them usually travel via programs that social tourism provides due to the lack of income, which is a result of limited access to the labour market (Shaw & Coles, 2004). Social tourism's aim is to encourage tourism participation for disadvantaged people in order to benefit from the tourism experience (Minnaert, Maitland, & Miller, 2009; Pagán, 2012; Shaw & Coles, 2004). However, some destinations now tend to focus more on adopting accessibility guidelines and design for all principles in their strategies as a means of competitive advantage (Dominguez Vila, Darcy, & Gonzalez Alen, 2015; Kastenholz et al., 2012).

Disabled people and caregivers

Many studies view PwD as a single group with the same constraints and the same needs (Figueiredo, Eusebio, & Kastenholz, 2012). Yet, other researchers propose that there are different types of disabilities according to different types of impairments and these are placed on a spectrum in accordance to the required level of support they need as well as the extent of disability (Buhalis & Michopoulou, 2011). These views are closely related to the medical and the social models of disability. Within the medical model, disability is treated as illness, while within the social model, disability arises from environmental inadequacies (Oliver, 2013; Oliver & Barnes, 2012). Whilst the conceptualisations of disability can be varied and complex, often lacking clear distinctions (Davis, 2002; Landsman, 2005; Shakespeare, 2004), it is acknowledged that tourism and leisure have the propensity to offer a transformative experience for PwDs.

As Páez and Whalen (2010) note, travel remains a necessity for travellers with disabilities as it offers a different daily routine and also the opportunity to feel more autonomy (Pritchard, Morgan, & Ateljevic, 2011). According to Pritchard, Morgan, and Ateljevic (2011), tourism promotes not only social capital but also social inclusion. That is very important because PwD often experience isolation and suffer from sadness (Bergstad et al., 2011; Currie & Delbosc, 2010). In this context, scholars concur that tourism offers PwD the prospect of self-recovery, psychological and physical renewal and it constitutes a main vehicle through which PwDs can further bond with their families and the wider society (Hunter-Jones, 2003; Hyde & Olesen, 2011; Minnaert, Maitland, & Miller, 2009). The benefits of tourism are not just applicable to PwD, but they also extend to their wider social networks and families, and perhaps even more so to their caregivers.

According to Pearlin et al. (1990), caregivers are those who provide assistance to anyone who doesn't have the ability to be fully independent in their everyday life, including not only formal but also informal caregivers which are usually friends or family members (Pearlin et al., 1990). Specifically, informal caregivers hold the most neural points due to their involvement in political, economic, and social issues (Van Durme et al., 2012). Investigating the impact of caregiving, a considerable number of studies focus on the positive impact concerning the physical and psychological health of PwDs (Carbonneau, Caron, & Desrosiers, 2010; Farfan-Portet et al., 2007) but highlight the negative impacts especially for the health of caregivers. Many caregivers suffer from health problems (Goldstein et al., 2004; Powers, Gallagher-Thompson, & Kraemer, 2002; Schneider et al., 2002; Visser-Meily et al., 2004) such as stress and depressive symptoms (Joling et al., 2008; Sherwood et al., 2005), social isolation (Sherwood et al., 2005), and even according to Schulz et al. (2009) and van Exel et al. (2004) premature death.

Hence, tourism and leisure not only provide PwDs and their caregivers opportunities for socialisation but also give them the prospect of psychological and physical renewal (Hunter-Jones, 2003; Hyde & Olesen, 2011; Minnaert, Maitland, & Miller, 2009). As Mactavish et al. (2007) suggest, leisure and tourism improve the quality of life of caregivers and contribute positively to their psychological well-being. By engaging in tourism activities and changing their routine, PwD can improve their skillset and autonomy, concurrently reducing caregivers' stress levels and increasing their productivity. However, according to Morris (2001) and O'Grady et al. (2004), PwD and their caregivers are often excluded from tourism activities due to the lack of proper tourist planning. The lack of research about the formal and informal tourism experiences of caregivers (Gladwell & Bedini, 2004) leaves a significant knowledge gap that further research should address in order to customise their travel experience and improve their living standards. Pernecky (2012) very aptly notes that the examination of disabled travellers and their caregivers within tourism may offer a fresh perspective for a more sustainable world.

Transformation of the tourism industry

Transformation of travel transportation

We can almost foresee the future of accessible transport becoming reality as the modernisation of industry transportation is impending and inevitable in all transporting areas. Today, relatively few places present low accessibility to the public but that does not include PwD who still have limited access. Despite the calls for accessible transportation systems (Wang et al.,2017; Wasfi, Steinmetz-Wood, & Levinson, 2017), many problems still exist and unfortunately some of the most important obstacles that disabled people face during travel are related to in the transportation process. Problems that still remain in the transportation sector include barriers on platforms, limited ramps, priority services, and accessibility at specific arrival points.

On the other hand, transportation constitutes the cornerstone of the tourism industry (Page, 2009; Palhares, 2003). Gradually, the transportation sector will be accommodating the needs of PwD and will develop a more disability-friendly policy as a result of the increased demand for equal access to all destinations (Michopoulou et al., 2015). Airports, ports, and train stations could be fully accessible to PwD and have special areas for people in the autistic spectrum for resting and relaxing in case of delay. They are likely to offer programs especially for people in the autistic spectrum, which will prepare the autistic person and their caregivers for the trip (Michopoulou et al., 2015). There are already some good practice examples in Europe as for example Vienna, which has one of the most integrated and accessible public transport networks in Europe (European Parliament, 2018). Milan also won the first prize in the European Competition 'Accessible City' in 2016 (ENAT, 2016). Considering the importance of accurate and timely information as well as customer service, individual transport companies should be staffed by knowledgeable and well-trained staff that will be sensitive to customers' needs, solve problems quickly and efficiently which will result in a more efficient service. Consequently, individual transport companies will have to update their services in order to be compatible with the needs of PwD; as yet there is limited information (if any) available to people with cognitive impairments (Smith, Amorim, & Umbelino, 2013). Destinations are also expected to exercise pressure due to the need to be more competitive than other destinations.

Destination transformation

When someone expresses the desire to make a trip, information gathering becomes the most important step to organise one. To enable PwD to engage in travel, destinations and DMOs will need to address their informational needs and provide relevant, accurate, and trustworthy accessibility information. Considering the significant market segment that PwDs will represent in the near future, destinations may include them in strategic planning, marketing, and promotion activities in order to capitalise on this market (Buhalis & Michopoulou, 2011). Reliable information should be available through multiple communication channels. Information on accessible tourism is likely to be more comprehensive and organised through certifications, which will guarantee the level of accessibility and safety of the destination.

Tourism and leisure are therefore expected to be transformed in a considerable manner. Many tourist activities today aren't yet focused on disabled individuals; environmental barriers and reduced number of attendees make designing experiences with accessibility in mind an afterthought. However, the increasing demand for more extensive and inclusive experiences will eventually trigger perhaps a renewed interest in the tourism industry to develop products and services that are guided by universal design principles and are usable to the greatest extent possible by everyone.

Intermediaries such as travel agents and tour operators may perhaps include accessible products and services into their mainstream provision. Whilst the seamless promotion of products and services (with accessibility embedded within all provision) would be the ideal scenario in the distant future, it may be that first (in the near future) we may witness the establishment of sizable 'accessibility dedicated' departments. These departments could be focused on accessible tourism destinations and leisure activities (e.g., accessible cruises). They could exist alongside departments that look after other established segments (i.e., romance and honeymoons) and would be mainstream rather than niche. It is important to clarify here that whilst it is only the individual that can judge whether a product/service is accessible, comfortable, and acceptable for him/her, the provision of objective information and description of the bundle of products/services on offer would firmly sit within these 'accessibility dedicated' departments. Hence, the availability of accessible tourism products and services would not be the unique privilege and unique selling point (USP) of smaller specialised intermediaries (perhaps only for the high end of access needs); rather, it would be incorporated into the mainstream tourism market.

Due to the increased number of disabled consumers and the continuous demand for accessible tourism, hospitality providers may be forced to redesign interior spaces and surrounding areas in order to be functional, comfortable, and safe for travellers with disabilities (of any type and perhaps extend). This redesign includes not just architectural accessibility, but it extends to the appropriateness and reliability of information about the venue, which is essential, for example, to people in the autism spectrum as a training tool before and during their journey (Grady & Ohlin, 2009). Darcy and Pegg (2011) point out that it is not enough for a hotel to have appropriate infrastructure and facilities to accommodate tourists with disabilities but should also have properly trained staff.

Food and beverage enterprises may be also transformed into disabled friendly environments. Changes could include, for instance, independent access from the main entrance to all areas and until the emergency exit through portable, removable, or retractable ramps and the availability of Braille code in signage and menus as a default. It is also worth mentioning that the number of people with allergies and/or food intolerances is constantly increasing and is often associated with other diseases or disabilities (comorbidity) (Buchalis & Michopoulou, 2011). Therefore, the food and beverage sector should also take into account the special needs and dietary habits of these groups.

Many attractions and museums are designed to be accessible for impaired people, and a small niche of them have programs for people in the autism spectrum. In order to be more competitive, museums should redesign their outdoor and indoor space so that to be fully accessible, and they should adjust their programs as a way to offer a better experience to all individuals equally (Black, 2005; Dodd & Sandell, 2001; Hooper-Greenhill et al., 2000; Newman, McLean, & Urquhart, 2005). Similarly, cultural monuments may gradually be more inclusive and accessible by making adaptations where it is feasible, or by using new technology systems, for example, using virtual augmented and mixed reality technology when the access is limited in order to be more 'visitable' from PwDs and offer the most possible integrated experience.

Transformations in the transportation, leisure, and hospitality sectors will invariably prompt a new version of tourism, which will include more sustainable ways to increase profitability and not exceed the carrying capacity of the destination. By actively making an effort to attract travellers with disabilities at a destination, destinations will actively be partially addressing seasonality since PwD (and wheelchair users in particular) would enjoy spaces of leisure when they are not 'packed' and have higher flexibility of movement around the place. What is perhaps most critical in terms of pending transformations is the change in attitude that many professionals and entrepreneurs have to undergo in order to be more inclusive, responsive, effective, and successful in the new marketplace. This attitudinal and behavioural change, together with the better understanding of the needs and requirements of travellers with disabilities, should contribute at the very least to the familiarisation with the image of disability.

However, before this reality becomes commonplace, there is still a multitude of barriers to be overcome; a summary of those barriers as well as the proposed solutions and expected results are presented in Table 10.1.

Table 10.1 Main barriers/restrictions for the disabled people, recommendations, and prospects

Researchers	*Barriers/Limits/ Restrictions*	*Solutions/ Recommendations*	*Results/Prospects*
Smith (1987)	(a) Intrinsic (b) Environmental (c) Interactive	• Social embodiment and representation disabled people • Law and legislation • Policy-making for accessible tourism • Markets and needs analysis • Accessible destinations • Education/training • Accessible transport and accommodation • Accessible services and events • Accessible physical and cultural attraction • Technology and applications	Transformation of tourism industry ↓ Social, economic, and environmental positive impacts ↓ Sustainable development
Gladwell and Bedini (2004)	(a) Physical (b) Social (c) Emotional		
Buhalis and Michopoulou (2011)	(a) Physical/build environment (b) Information regarding accessibility (c) Accessible information online		
Agovino et al. (2017)	(a) Informational (b) Economic (c) Environmental		

Conclusion

Accessible tourism constitutes a dynamic field in the tourism industry (Darcy & Buhalis, 2011) and has positive impacts on PwD. The importance of accessibility is intensified considering the fact that it also applies to other sectors (i.e., hospitality, events, spa, and wellness) that interface with tourism and support leisure activities. PwDs as a customer base is also promising due to the increasing number of people with access needs (often with considerable disposable income) and the multiplier effect created by the companions/caregivers.

In the next few years, the number of PwDs globally is expected to increase due to the ageing demographic which will incite prevalence of injury and permanent disability of many people (Schneider et al., 2006). This sizable new segment of PwDs will actively claim the right to be equal in every social, economic, and political aspect, including the right to have equal access to tourism activities and leisure. Increasing familiarisation with disability and the growth of the accessibility market are likely to gradually contribute to the transformation of the tourism industry (i.e., higher accommodation accessibility, increased transportation friendliness for disabled people, more accessible sightseeing and museums, leisure activities focused on the disabled people, and stuff training) and the enhancement of destination competitiveness.

Despite the opportunities that accessible tourism can offer to the tourism industry and the vital role that it's going to play in the near future to destination market positioning and competitiveness, accessible tourism remains largely under-researched. This chapter attempted to unpack the complexities inherent in the field of accessible tourism and shed some light onto the implications of its operationalisation (i.e., the role of caregivers). However, this chapter offers an overview of extant literature rather than delving into the particular requirements of different types of disabilities. Further research should, therefore, focus on examining and understanding the requirements of travellers' with different types of disabilities. It would also be interesting to see the differentiation in these requirements based on the extent of disability. Very little attention has also been paid to the role of caregivers and should therefore be investigated further. Finally, it would be worthwhile to evaluate the tourism industry's readiness for the upcoming changes.

References

Agovino, M., Cassacia, M., Garofalo, A., & Marchesano, K. (2017). Tourism and disability in Italy: Limits and opportunities. *Tourism Management Perspectives*, *23*, 58–67.

Bergstad, C. J., Gamble, A., Gärling, T., Hagman, O., Polk, M., Ettema, D., et al. (2011). Subjective well-being related to satisfaction with daily travel. *Transportation*, *38*(1), 1–15.

Black, G. (2005). *The engaging museum: Developing museums for visitor involvement*. London/ New York: Routledge.

Buchalis, D., & Michopoulou, E. (2011). Information-enabled tourism destination marketing: Addressing the accessibility market. *Current Issues in Tourism*, *14*(2), 145–168.

Buhalis, D., & Darcy, S. (2011). *Accessible tourism issues: Inclusion, disability, ageing population and tourism*. Bristol: Channel View Publications.

Buhalis, D., & Michopoulou, E. (2011). Information enabled tourism destination marketing: Addressing the accessibility market. *Current Issues in Tourism*, *14*(2), 145–168.

Burnett, J. J., & Baker, H. B. (2001). Assessing the travel related behaviors of the mobility-disabled consumer. *Journal of Travel Research*, *40*, 4–11.

Carbonneau, H., Caron, C., & Desrosiers, J. (2010). Development of a conceptual framework of positive aspects of caregiving in dementia. *Dementia*, *9*(3), 327–353.

Currie, G., & Delbosc, A. (2010). Modelling the social and psychological impacts of transport disadvantage. *Transportation*, *37*(6), 953–966.

Daniels, M. J., Rodgers, E. D., & Wiggins, B. P. (2005). "Travel Tales": An interpretive analysis of constraints and negotiations to pleasure travel as experienced by persons with physical disabilities. *Tourism Management*, *26*(6), 919–930.

Darcy, S. (2002). Marginalized participation: Physical disability, high support needs and tourism. *Journal of Hospitality and Tourism Management*, *9*(1), 61–72.

Darcy, S., & Buhalis, D. (2011). Introduction: From disabled tourists to accessible tourism. In D. Buhalis & S. Darcy (Eds.), *Accessible tourism: Concepts and issues* (pp. 1–20). Bristol: Channel View Publications.

Darcy, S., & Pegg, S. (2011). Towards strategic intent: Perceptions of disability service provision amongst hotel accommodation managers. *International Journal of Hospitality Management*, *30*, 468–476.

Davis, L. J. (2002). *Bending over backwards: Disability, dismodernism, and other difficult positions*. New York: New York University Press.

Dodd, J., & Sandell, R. (2001). *Including museums, perspectives on museums, galleries and social inclusion*. Leicester: Research Centre for Museums and Galleries, Department of Museum Studies, University of Leicester.

Dominguez Vila, T., Darcy, S., & Gonzalez Alen, E. (2015). Competing for the disability tourism market: A comparative exploration of the factors of accessible tourism competitiveness in Spain and Australia. *Tourism Management*, *47*, 261–272.

Eichhorn, V., Miller, G., Michopoulou, E., & Buhalis, D. (2008). Enabling access to tourism through information schemes? *Annals of Tourism Research*, *35*(1), 189–210.

ENAT (2007). Services and facilities for accessible tourism in Europe: Working together to make tourism in Europe accessible for all. *European Network for Accessible Tourism*. Retrieved November 7, 2020, from www.accessibletourism.org/?i=enat.en.reports

ENAT (2016). Access city award 2016 for accessible-friendly cities to Milan. *European Network for Accesibe Tourism*. Retrieved March 14, 2021, from www.accessibletourism.org/?i=enat.en.news.1900

European Parliament. (2018). *Research for TRAN committee: Transport and tourism for persons with disabilities and persons with reduced mobility*. Strasburg: European Parliament.

European Union. (2010). *European disability strategy 2010–2020: A renewed commitment to a barrier-free Europe*. Retrieved October 18, 2020, from http://eur-lex.europa.eu/LexUriServ/LexUriServ.do?uri=COM%3A2010%3A0636%3AFIN%3A

Farfan-Portet, M. I., Deboosere, P., Van Oyen, H., & Lorant, V., (2007). Informal health care in Belgium. *Cahiers de sociologie et de déMographie médicales*, *47*(2), 187–214.

Figueiredo, E., Eusebio, C., & Kastenholz, E. (2012). How diverse are tourists with disabilities? A pilot study on accessible leisure tourism experiences in Portugal. *International Journal of Tourism Research*, *14*(6), 531–550.

Gladwell, N. J., & Bedini, L. A. (2004). In search of lost leisure: The impact of caregiving on leisure travel. *Tourism Management*, *25*(6), 685–693.

Goldstein, N. E., Concato, J., Fried, T. R., Kasl, S. V., Johnson-Hurzeler, R., & Bradley, E. H. (2004). Factors associated with caregiver burden among caregivers of terminally ill patients with cancer. *Journal of Palliative Care, 20*(1), 38–43.

Grady, J., & Ohlin, J. B., (2009). Equal access to hospitality services for guests with mobility impairments under the Americans with disabilities act: Implications for the hospitality industry. *International Journal of Hospitality Management, 28*(1), 161–169.

Hooper-Greenhill, E., Sandell, R., Moussouri, T., & O'Riain, H. (2000). *Museums and social inclusion: The GLLAM report*. Leicester: Research Centre for Museums and Galleries, Department of Museum Studies, University of Leicester.

Horner, S., & Swarbrooke, J. (2004). Tourism and travellers with disabilities. In *International cases in tourism management* (pp. 324–337). Oxford: Elsevier Butterworth-Heinemann.

Hunter-Jones, P. (2003). The perceived effects of holiday-taking upon the health and well-being of patients treated for cancer. *International Journal of Tourism Research, 5*(3), 183–196.

Hyde, K. F., & Olesen, K. (2011). Packing for touristic performances. *Annals of Tourism Research, 38*(3), 900–919.

Israeli, A. A. (2002). A preliminary investigation of the importance of site accessibility factors for disabled tourists. *Journal of Travel Research, 41*(1), 101–104.

Joling, K., van Hout, H., Scheltens, P., Vernooij-Dassen, M., van den Berg, B., Bosmans, J., Gillissen, F., Mittelman, M., & van Marwijk, H. (2008). (Cost)-effectiveness of family meetings on indicated prevention of anxiety and depressive symptoms and disorders of primary family caregivers of patients with dementia: Design of a randomized controlled trial. *BMC Geriatrics, 8,* 2.

Kastenholz, E., Eusébio, C., Figueiredo, E., & Lima, J. (2012). Accessibility as competitive advantage of a tourism destination: The case of lousã. In K. F. Hyde, C. Ryan, & A. G. Woodside (Eds.), *Field guide to case study research in tourism, hospitality and leisure*. Advances in Culture, Tourism and Hospitality Research, Vol. 6 (pp. 369–385). Emerald Group Publishing Limited.

Kim, S., & Lehto, X. Y. (2012). The voice of tourists with mobility disabilities: Insights from online customer complaint websites. *International Journal of Contemporary Hospitality Management, 24*(3), 451–476.

Landsman, G. H. (2005). Mothers and models of disability. *Journal of Medical Humanities, 26*(2–3), 121–139.

Lee, B. K., Agarwal, S., & Kim, H. J. (2012). Influences of travel constraints on the people with disabilities' intention to travel: An application of Seligman's helplessness theory. *Tourism Management, 33,* 569–579.

Mactavish, J. B., MacKay, K. J., Iwasaki, Y., & Betteridge, D. (2007). Family caregivers of individuals with intellectual disability: Perspectives on life quality and the role of vacations. *Journal of Leisure Research, 39*(1), 127–155.

McCabe, S., & Johnson, S. (2013). The happiness factor in tourism: Subjective well-being and social tourism. *Annals of Tourism Research, 41,* 42–65.

McKercher, B., Packer, T., Yau, M. K., & Lam, P. (2003). Travel agents as facilitators or inhibitors of travel: Perceptions of people with disabilities. *Tourism Management, 24,* 465–474.

Michopoulou, E., & Buhalis, D. (2013). Information provision for challenging markets: The case of the accessibility requiring market in the context of tourism. *Information and Management, 50*(5), 229–239.

Michopoulou, E., Darcy, S., Ambrose, I., & Buhalis, D. (2015). Accessible tourism futures: The world we dream to live in and the opportunities we hope to have. *Journal of Tourism Futures, 1*(3), 179–188.

Minnaert, L., Maitland, R., & Miller, G. (2009). Tourism and social policy. *Annals of Tourism Research*, *36*(2), 316–334.

Morris, J. (2001). Social exclusion and young disabled people with high levels of support needs. *Critical Social Policy*, *21*(2), 161–183.

Newman, A., McLean, F., & Urquhart, G. (2005). Museums and the active citiz tackling the problems of social exclusion. *Citizenship Studies*, *9*(1), 41–57.

O'Grady, A., Pleasence, P., Balmer, N. J., Buck, A., & Genn, H. (2004). Disability, social exclusion and the consequential experience of justiciable problems. *Disability & Society*, *19*(3), 259–272.

Oliver, M. (2013). The social model of disability: Thirty years on. *Disability & Society*, *28*(7), 1024–1026.

Oliver, M., & Barnes, C. (2012). *The new politics of disablement*. Basingstoke: Palgrave.

Páez, A., & Whalen, K. (2010). Enjoyment of commute: A comparison of different transportation modes. *Transportation Research Part A: Policy and Practice*, *44*(7), 537–549.

Pagán, R. (2012). Time allocation in tourism for people with disabilities. *Annals of Tourism Research*, *39*(3), 1514–1537.

Page, S. (2009). *Transport and tourism: Global perspectives*. Harlow: Pearson Prentice Hall.

Palhares, G. L. (2003). The role of transport in tourism development: Nodal functions and management practices. *International Journal of Tourism Research*, *5*(5), 403–407.

Pearlin, L. I., Mullan, J. T., Semple, S. J., & Skaff, M. M. (1990). Caregiving and the stress process: An overview of concepts and their measures. *The Gerontologist*, *30*(5), 583–594.

Pernecky, T. (2012). Constructionism: Critical pointers for tourism studies. *Annals of Tourism Research*, *39*(2), 1116–1137.

Powers, D. V., Gallagher-Thompson, D., & Kraemer, H. C., (2002). Coping and depression in Alzheimer's caregivers: Longitudinal evidence of stability. *The Journals of Gerontology. Series B, Psychological Sciences and Social Sciences*, *57*(3), 205–211.

Pritchard, A., Morgan, N., & Ateljevic, I. (2011). Hopeful tourism: A new transformative perspective. *Annals of Tourism Research*, *38*(3), 941–963.

Ray, N. M., & Ryder, M. E. (2003). "Ebilities" tourism: An exploratory discussion of the travel needs and motivations of the mobility-disabled. *Tourism Management*, *24*(1), 57–72.

Schneider, J., Hallam, A., Murray, J., Foley, B., Atkin, L., Banerjee, S., Islam, M. K., & Mann, A. (2002). Formal and informal care for people with dementia: Factors associated with service receipt. *Ageing & Mental Health*, *6*(3), 255–265.

Schneider, S., Seither, B., Tonges, S., & Schmitt, H. (2006). Sports injuries: Population based representative data on incidence, sequelae, and high-risk groups. *British Journal of Sports Medicine*, *40*(3), 334–339.

Schulz, R., Beach, S. R., Hebert, R. S., Martire, L. M., Monin, J. K., Tompkins, C. A., & Albert, S. (2009). Spousal suffering and partner's depression and cardiovascular disease: The cardiovascular health study. *American Journal of Geriatric Psychiatry*, *17*, 246–254.

Shakespeare, T. (2004). Social models of disability and other life strategies. *Scandinavian Journal of Disability Research*, *6*(1), 8–21.

Shaw, G., & Coles, T. (2004). Disability, holiday making and the tourism industry in the UK: A preliminary survey. *Tourism Management*, *25*, 307–404.

Sherwood, P. R., Given, C. W., Given, B. A., & von Eye, A. (2005). Caregiver burden and depressive symptoms. *Journal of Aging and Health*, *17*, 125–147.

Shi, L., Cole, S., & Chancellor, H. C. (2012). Understanding leisure travel motivations of travelers with acquired mobility impairments. *Tourism Management, 33*, 228–231.

Smith, L., Amorim, M., & Umbelino, J. (2013). Accessible tourism and disability service information provided on leading airline websites: A content analysis. *International Journal for Responsible Tourism, 2*(4), 7–23.

Smith, R. (1987). Leisure of disabled tourists: Barriers to participation. *Annals of Tourism Research, 14*, 376–389.

UNWTO. (2015). *The handbook on accessible tourism for all: Principles, tools and good practices*. Madrid: UNWTO. Retrieved November 2, 2020, from https://webunwto.s3.eu-west-1.amazonaws.com/s3fs-public/2020-04/aamanualturismoaccesibleomt-facseng.pdf

Van Durme, T., Macq, J., Jeanmart, C., & Gobert, M. (2012). Tools for measuring the impact of informal caregiving of the elderly: A literature review. *International Journal of Nursing Studies, 49*(4), 490–504.

Van Exel, N. J., Scholte op Reimer, W. J., Brouwer, W. B., van den, B. B., Koopmanschap, M. A., & van den Bos, G. A., (2004). Instruments for assessing the burden of informal caregiving for stroke patients in clinical practice: A comparison of CSI, CRA, SCQ and self-rated burden. *Clinical Rehabilitation, 18*(2), 203–214.

Visser-Meily, J. M., Post, M., Riphagen, I., & Lindeman, M. (2004). Measures used to assess burden among caregivers of stroke patients: A review. *Clinical Rehabilitation, 18*(6), 601–623.

Wang, W., Wu, Y. C. J., Yuan, C.-H., Xiong, H., & Liu, W.-J. (2017). Use of social media in uncovering information services for people with disabilities in China. *International Review of Research in Open and Distance Learning, 18*(1), 65–83.

Wasfi, R., Steinmetz-Wood, M., & Levinson, D. (2017). Measuring the transportation needs of people with developmental disabilities: A means to social inclusion. *Disability and Health Journal, 10*(2), 356–360.

World Bank. (2016). The World Bank. Retrieved October 12, 2020, from www.worldbank.org/en/ topic/disability/overview#1

WHO (2013). *The European health report 2012: Charting the way to well-being*. Copenhagen: WHO Regional Office for Europe.

World Health Organization (WHO). (2016). Global Health Observatory (GHO) data. *World Health Statistics 2016: Monitoring health for the SDGs*. Retrieved October 15, 2020, from www.who.int/ gho/publications/world_health_statistics/2016/Annex_B/en/

Yau, M., McKercher, B., & Packer, T. (2004). Traveling with a disability: More than an access issue. *Annals of Tourism Research, 31*(4), 946–960.

11 Employee well-being in guest-oriented industries
Evidence from food and beverage sector

Javaneh Mehran, Oscar Escallada and Hossein Olya

Introduction

Interest in employees' well-being is growing – a key driver being the mounting appreciation that mental health is linked to performance and psychologically healthy employees are more productive and less likely to quit their jobs (Wright & Huang, 2012). Employee well-being is particularly significant in the service-driven industry where there is close interaction between guests and hosts such as hospitality services. Employees' well-being seems to be playing an increasingly strategic role in European guest-oriented organisations because the employment and personal income of many Europeans, particularly those who are living in tourism-dependent countries, are dependent on hospitality services (Radic et al., 2020).

In the last two decades, the travel and hospitality industry experienced vicissitudes and alternations that have transformed the nature of the jobs and employment policies in the hospitality industry. On the one hand, the rapid development of transportation, digitalisation, and personalisation in customer experience contributed to the emergence of job demand and increased employment growth in the hospitality industry. On the other hand, political and environmental issues such as terrorism, climate change, and visa bans had a negative effect on employment and availability of part-time jobs. To an extent, the COVID-19 pandemic has intensified the fluctuations experienced in the tourism and hospitality industry, exerting negative impacts on employees. These transforming factors contribute to the instability of job demand and job insecurity, which can be mentally draining for employees and affect their well-being.

The hospitality industry represents nearly 5% of the EU GDP and, together with tourism, is the third largest socio-economic activity in the EU. Based on a report of the 2015 European 'Working Conditions Survey (EWCS)', the food and beverage industry provides employment to 4.4% of the European workforce. The highest rates were found in southern European countries such as Greece (9.4%), Cyprus (8.3%), and Spain (6.6%). One of the most challenging issues that affect the well-being of employees in the hospitality industry is job conditions which are tailored with uncertainties (e.g., instability, seasonality, low wages, part-time job hours, and draining workdays). Food and beverage service industry seeks to alleviate the effects of employee challenges; for instance, some employers are

DOI: 10.4324/9781003105930-12

implementing employer-driven health-and-wellness initiatives directed at creating more attractive workplace environments and increasing retention. According to a recent report of the Chartered Institute of Personnel and Development (CIPD) in 2020, mental health remains the most common focus of well-being initiatives and a gradual increase is being seen in the proportion of organisations including counselling services and employee support strategies among their well-being benefits (Sinclair & Suff, 2020).

Several economic and socio-psychological theories (e.g., exchange theory choice and well-being theory) recommend that employees look for employment in industries that offer fair working conditions (Radic et al., 2020). Therefore, the food and beverage industry may lack motivated and committed workers if it does not offer proper working environments and fails to publicise the psychological well-being of employees. More precisely, lack of subjective well-being has been associated with lost productivity, increased absenteeism, sick leave, burnout, and increased job turnover rates (Warr, 2007). While relevant literature extensively investigates employee well-being, relevant hospitality studies particularly in food and beverage management are almost scarce. To fill this gap, this chapter contributes theoretically to the understanding of employee well-being in the food and beverage industry. To be more precise, complexity theory confirms the complex configuration of rewards system, training, and leadership style on employee well-being, which ascertain the role of a comprehensive reward system in higher performance and the positive impact of continuous training and development on the improvement of the employee's well-being. Therefore, the outcome of well-being including engagement and turnover intention of employees would extend the knowledge in the context of European food and beverage industry, which is suffering from serious uncertainty issues.

This study is trying to address the following questions: What are the most important antecedents of employee well-being in the food and beverage industry? To what extent employee well-being could increase employee engagement and decrease employee turnover intention? The conceptual model for this study was tested, based on responses from 100 employees at seven restaurants in the city of Santander, Spain. This empirical study uses symmetrical and asymmetrical analysis to investigate the effects of rewards system, training, and leadership style on employee well-being and the model outcomes. The rest of this chapter is structured as follows: development of the conceptual background, description of the methodology, report of the complex empirical results, and discussion of the major implications and limitations of this investigation and a suggestion for future studies.

Theoretical background and literature review

Employee well-being and leadership style

Some of the most important antecedents of well-being at work seem to be a comprehensive reward system (monetary and non-monetary), training and development, and a culture of trust based on ethical leadership (Great Place to Work, 2016). Social exchange theory supports a positive relationship between base-line employees and managers when the relationship is based on trust, resulting in benefits for both parties. The role of the leader in the hospitality industry is crucial, not only because the service industry has become very competitive and customers demand consistently high service quality but also because the very nature of hospitality is based on a continuous interrelation between customers and employees. Accordingly, the positive effect of transformational leadership on quality of work life and life satisfaction of employees of the hospitality industry is reported in the literature, which implies that hospitality managers need to be qualified to use a transformational leadership style to improve employee well-being at the workplace (Kara et al., 2013).

Food and beverage service operations are characterised by high turnover rate, low income, and stressful environments. Thus, efficient leadership practices become extremely beneficial. To support that, Tsai (2008) carried out a study with 500 hospitality employees where it showed that manager support and open communication were some of the top characteristics preferred by employees. Generally, the availability and minimum criteria of eligibility have become a challenge in the food and beverage industry since the incompatibility of workers' individual characteristics and interest with the nature of job description can negatively contribute to their well-being. On the other hand, the management strategies of senior managers (e.g., internationalisation) can possibly complicate firm's value performance and social responsibility and also ineffective management strategies are reported to have a negative effect on well-being in restaurants' employees (Jung, Lee, & Dalbor, 2016). In Spain, a study carried out in 42 hotels and 42 restaurants showed that inefficient management increased conflicts at work and decreased well-being (Benitez, Medina, & Munduate, 2018) whilst also created higher scores in bullying. Therefore, leadership style has a strategic role in balancing the relationships between employees, employers, and guests. To gather all the points together, this study analysed the significance of leadership style in combination with other factors to model the employees' well-being and turnover intention in the food and beverage industry.

Employee well-being and reward system

In the hospitality industry, if we exempt the minority examples of high salaries (top executive making six figures), the majority of employees earn basic wages (Casado-Díaz & Simon, 2016). Therefore, the company's reward system is crucial for workers' well-being in such a competitive job market (Boella & Goss-Turner, 2019; Olya et al., 2021). Rewarding aims to improve employees' satisfaction by affording them the opportunity to reap more rewards, but in doing so, it could prompt heightened competitiveness amongst employees. When this situation occurs, the social well-being of employees is sacrificed for psychological well-being outcomes (Grant, Christianson, & Price, 2007). By establishing a reward system, employers encourage their staff to be fully involved with guests to create a unique customer experience and superior service quality. On the other hand, perceived unfair rewards in the hospitality industry as well as several related factors do not make this relationship conclusive, especially when both financial (e.g., fair pay, incentive options, and social benefits) and non-financial aspects (e.g., recognition and empowerment programmes) are not taken into account (Day et al., 2014). As a result, the significance of the reward system ranges from negative to positive impact associated with the definition and application of the reward system in the hospitality industry.

Employee well-being and training and development

The literature on employee training and development seems to be divided as to whether training and development positively influence employee well-being or not. According to the norm of reciprocity, when employers empower their employees by supporting them with training opportunities, as well as rewarding systems, employees feel obligated to pay back, thus making them feel more engaged and embedded to their organisations (Afsar, Shahjehan, & Shah, 2018). Moreover, due to the availability and seasonality nature of the food and beverage industry, workers do not have the necessary skills to carry out their duties. For instance, 'People 1st' reported that 21% of hospitality workers in the UK did not have the necessary skills to perform their jobs in comparison to 15% average of workers for other industries in the UK (People 1st, 2018). Therefore, training and development as an HRM approach can improve employee work capabilities and offer opportunities to prosper psychological need which can lead to employee perceived well-being (He, Morrison, & Zhang, 2019). In addition, training and development influence firm performance by enhancing employees' knowledge, skills, and abilities, providing employees the opportunity to use those attributes for organisational benefit and feeling of security as well as aid development of self-efficacy, which are important antecedents of well-being (Guest, 2017; Ho & Kuvaas, 2020).

On the other hand, in several studies, no significant link between learning and development and increased employee commitment and satisfaction was reported (Rowland, Hall, & Altarawneh, 2017). Particularly, in the hospitality industry, the majority of enterprises are small- to medium-sized enterprises (SMEs) and the literature is not conclusive concerning the quantity and quality of training in SMEs (Jameson, 2000). As an example, an empirical study reported that Spanish workers demonstrated clear differences regarding various aspects of development in white- and blue-collar occupations. Specifically, social skills and motivation appeared to be more relevant for blue-collar workers than for white-collar workers (Urtasun & Núñez, 2012). Therefore, the context of training and development in the food and beverage sector due to the labour-intensive nature of the industry seems to be very complex and needs to be extensively studied both in theory and in practice.

Employee well-being, engagement, and turnover intention

According to the literature, happy workers would perform better, engage more, pursue challenging objectives, stay longer with the company, and build great social networks (Cabanas Díaz & Sánchez González, 2016). Pienaar and Willemse

(2008) described work engagement as the experience of feeling full of energy and mentally resilient at work. Employee engagement as a significant outcome of well-being is more strategic than employee satisfaction as satisfied employees tend to stay in the company but focus on just getting benefit from the company, whereas engaged employees focus on giving back to the company, contribute longer, and have higher productivity (Madan, 2017). Engagement as a source of competitive advantage could positively contribute to the success of businesses in the food and beverage industry. However, the literature indicates that there are more employees who are disengaged than there are engaged employees (Kular et al., 2008). While the hospitality industry created 1.6 million jobs in Europe between 2013 and 2016, it also experienced a turnover increase by 20% from €507 to €607 billion over the same period (Hotrec, 2019). For example, Spain which is the second largest tourist destination in the world with 82 million tourists per year saw 4 million working contracts being signed in the hospitality industry in 2017, with nearly half of these contracts lasting barely one week (Radic et al., 2020).

The hospitality industry has one of the highest employee turnover rates in Europe and the United Kingdom (People 1st, 2018) which creates direct costs like training, development, and replacement and indirect costs (e.g., poor quality service, lost customers, missed sales, product wastage, constant retraining of new staff, and higher demands on other employees). When employees are engaged in their work, a logical conclusion would be that they would not be willing to leave the company. However, evidence does not support this in extant literature as position, generation, work climate, and individual characteristics show a different mediating effect. For example, human resource practices (e.g., reward and training) increase engagement and reduce turnover as employees achieve either a higher position or greater income after they improve their skills in the process of training. Contrary, if managers cannot provide them with the expected rewards, they might leave the workplace and look for a better job position. In conclusion, the literature reports a lack of research about the causes and consequences of well-being in guest-oriented industries. Moreover, the complex predictors of engagement and turnover intention need to be modelled and analysed to see under which conditions the antecedents of well-being (e.g., training, rewarding, and leadership) could contribute to higher engagement or result in a lower turnover intention among employees.

Methodology

Research case, research design, and data collection procedures

Food and beverage industry in Santander, Spain

In its 2017 annual Travel and Tourism Competitiveness Report, the World Economic Forum ranked Spain as first among the top ten countries on the Tourism Competitiveness Index. Cantabria ('The Mountain') is located between the Basque Country and the region of Asturias. Santander which is the capital of Cantabria, with around 582,000 population, boasts six Michelin-starred restaurants (with nine

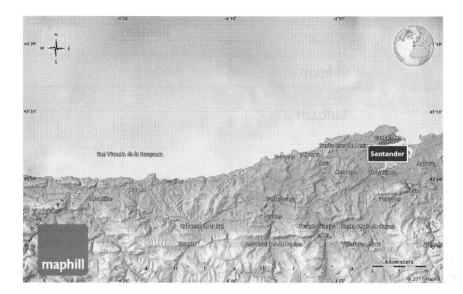

Figure 11.1 Santander map
Source: www.maphill.com/spain/cantabria/3d-maps/physical-map/

stars between them) that fuse tradition and cutting edge to generate consummate modern dishes steeped in local roots, which clearly demonstrates the high level of Cantabrian cuisine. Cantabrian cuisine is varied, offering fish, seafood, game, veal, and beef on local restaurants' menus (Rabanal, 2020, August 20).

Data analysis and measurements

A total of 110 questionnaires were distributed, six of them were not filled out and four were discarded as they were not properly answered. So, the final number of useable questionnaires was 100, indicating a 90% response rate. All male and female respondents belonging to the restaurant departments of kitchen and waiting staff range from 20 to 60 years of age and come from different countries (e.g., Spain, Chile, Ecuador, Colombia, and Venezuela). Among the 100 respondents, 60% ($n = 60$) were female and 40% ($n = 40$) were male. The mean age was 30 (range, 26–35). Among them, 40% ($n = 40$) reported high school diploma, followed by bachelor's degree (35%, $n = 35$), no formal education (20%, $n = 20$), and postgraduate education (5%, $n = 5$); 40% ($n = 40$) reported to be single and the remaining (60%, $n = 60$) married or coupled. Finally, 37% (n=37) had been working for less than one year in the same restaurant, 46% (n=46) between 1 and 5 years, and 17% more than 5 years. The questionnaire was divided into six sections, and seven-point Likert scale questions were applied. All the operationalised variables were measured using valid items taken from other authors. Employee well-being was measured using ten items from the work of Sharma, Kong, and Kingshott (2016). Reward system was assessed with five items from the work of Boshoff and Allen (2000). A five-item scale was used to operationalise training and development (Boshoff & Allen, 2000). Leadership style was analysed with seven items following Gill, Flaschner, & Shachar (2006). Employee engagement was evaluated using nine items from Karatepe (2013). Finally, turnover intention was examined with three items (Karatepe, 2013).

Complexity theory

Recently, many researchers have empirically confirmed that the cause and effect of employee well-being in the guest-oriented industry is complex and application of theoretical frameworks needs to be adopted to explain the behavioural concern in organisations (Ariza-Montes et al., 2019). Complexity theory is used to explain the non-linear, heterogeneous, complex, and dynamic behaviour of employees in the workplace (Schneider & Somers, 2006; Olya & Nia, 2021). The causal asymmetry principle serves as a foundation principle of complexity theory in research on 'highly reliable organizations' (Woodside, 2014). This study uses complexity theory as a core theoretical underpinning of the projected research model to address employees' well-being, engagement, and turnover intention in the food and beverage industry. Using all the six tenets of complexity theory, we evaluate the results of the configurational model based on fsQCA analytical approach (Woodside, 2014).

Analytical approaches

This empirical study used a symmetrical and asymmetrical approach through a systematic process. In the initial stage, the questionnaire was prepared, and hospitality academicians reviewed the questionnaire before finalisation so that content validity was assured. Anonymity was fully guaranteed for all employees, as names were not asked, and it was explained that participation was voluntary. Using convenience sampling, the current study sampled waiting and kitchen staff from seven restaurants in the city of Santander. Using snowball sampling, we started with a reduced number of subjects in one restaurant and through conversations with employees, managers, and owners, more potential restaurants and subjects were contacted, and in the end, the goal of creating a significant pool of respondents was achieved. This study was undertaken in several properties in the city of Santander, belonging to different owners. Therefore, the author explained the purpose of the research to the property managers and then carried out the survey physically in the restaurants, making sure that each participant understood the questionnaire properly and suggesting honesty in answering questions in order to have high-quality results. Furthermore, the general purpose of the study was briefly explained to employees, while the research hypotheses of the study were kept confidential to control potential bias. Besides, questionnaires were undertaken on daily normal conditions, individually or in small groups,

Employee well-being 161

without affecting the operation of the restaurant. Before distribution, the questionnaire was translated into Spanish, as Spanish was the main language used by employees, using the back-translation method to ensure that the content was accurately translated into Spanish. A symmetrical statistical test (i.e., regression analysis) was performed to investigate the causes and consequences of employee well-being (i.e., employee engagement and turnover intention). Finally, configurational modelling using fsQCA was conducted to explore the configurations of employee well-being (i.e., reward system, training and development, and leadership style) antecedents that were sufficient to predict the employee engagement and turnover intention.

In the initial stage, the normality of the data was checked using skewness and kurtosis for all scale items. Harman's single-factor test was applied to evaluate the potential common method variance (Olya, 2020; Podsakoff, 2003). Subsequently, using Cronbach's alpha and composite reliability, the reliability of the constructs was measured. The analytical approach in this study tries to evaluate the objectives of this research as follows. First, the net effect of reward system, training and development, leadership style, and well-being was investigated by performing simple regression analysis. According to Mehran and Olya (2020), simple regression analysis is a compelling approach to explore the sufficient and net effect of variables on the study. Second, using fsQCA, this study explored causal models constructed from an antecedent of well-being in a configuration to predict the engagement and turnover intention of employees in the food and beverage industry (Mehran et al., 2020; Olya & Nia, 2021).

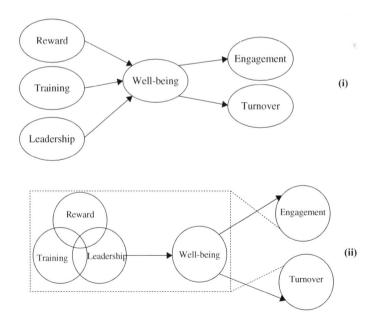

Figure 11.2 Proposed conceptual models: symmetric model (i) and asymmetric model (ii)

Results and discussion

Exploring data with descriptive statistics, the mean and standard deviation are measured. In this case, the mean values are reward system (4.39), training and development (3.93), leadership style (5.06), employee engagement (5.32), employee well-being (4.65), and turnover intention (3.08). The Cronbach's alpha of the measurements ranged from 0.72 to 0.96, exceeding the minimum reliability criteria of 0.70 (Nunnally & Bernstein, 1994). Table 11.1 shows the results of correlation analysis.

Results of regression test

Table 11.2 indicates the net effect of antecedents to predict the two favourable and unfavourable outcomes. According to the regression results, employee well-being was influenced by engagement ($\beta = 0.393$ and $p > 0.05$). As a result, the relation between reward system ($\beta = -0.283$ and $p > 0.05$), leadership ($\beta = -0.327$ and $p > 0.05$), and turnover intention of employees was reported significant. On the other hand, there was no significant relationship found between rewards system and well-being ($\beta = 0.060$ and $p > 0.05$), training and well-being ($\beta = .153$ and $p > 0.05$),

Table 11.1 Means, standard deviations, and correlations

Factor	Mean	STD Deviation	Reward	Training	Leader-ship	Engage-ment	Well-Being	Turnover
Reward	4.393	1.475	(0.886)					
Training	3.936	1.559	0.513**	(0.958)				
Leadership	5.068	1.415	0.513**	0.428**	(0.948)			
Engagement	5.329	0.942	0.244**	0.062	0.621**	(0.898)		
Well-being	4.657	0.607	0.205*	0.182	0.286**	0.393**	(0.716)	
Turnover	3.088	1.749	−0.405**	−0.231*	−0.398**	−0.183	0.001	(0.909)

*: $p < .05$, **: $p < .01$.

Table 11.2 Results of regression

Predictor→Outcomes	B	T
Reward→ well-being	0.060	0.585
Reward→ turnover intention	**−0.283**	**0.009**
Training→ well-being	0.153	0.157
Training→ turnover intention	0.049	0.645
Leadership→ well-being	−0.065	0.629
Leadership→ turnover intention	**−0.327**	**0.014**
Well-being→ engagement	**0.393**	**0.001**
Well-being→ turnover intention	0.019	0.991
Engagement→ well-being	**0.409**	**0.001**
Engagement→ turnover intention	0.086	0.450

Note: Significant factor is highlighted by bold format ($p < 0.05$).

and leadership style and well-being ($\beta = -0.065$ and $p > 0.05$). Accordingly, no significant relationship was reported between well-being and turnover intention ($\beta = 0.393$ and $p > 0.01$) and training and well-being ($\beta = 0.153$ and $p > 0.01$).

The results of the regression analysis show the net effect of well-being on employees' engagement and turnover intention. However, exclusively counting on the results of symmetric modelling may contribute to misrepresented implications about psychological well-being of employees in the service industry (Mehran & Olya, 2019; Mehran & Olya 2020). More precisely, the regression results of the present study were insufficient to explain how combinations of the well-being antecedents form the positive and negative outcomes. This is due to the mere fact that regression analysis does not reveal causal effects of combinations of well-being antecedents to predict employees' turnover intention and engagement. More precisely, explanations of consumer complex behavioural intentions claimed that conventional methods (i.e., regression) are important but insufficient for tackling such complexities (Pappas & Brown, 2020; Olya, 2020). In addition, we need to find a combination of configuration variables to predict sensitivity and complexity in the hospitality industry, specifically in the food and beverage industry. For example, due to the majority of low-paid jobs in the hospitality industry, the rewarding system might be considered to have a positive impact on employee well-being, while it could stimulate the competitiveness amongst employees leading to the elimination of the social well-being of employees over psychological well-being outcomes (Grant, Christianson, & Price, 2007). However, if the rewarding system could be defined along with the proper training system, the negative impact of unfair rewards might be eliminated (Grandey, Rupp, & Brice, 2015). Furthermore, configurational modelling helps to evaluate causal recipes, contributing to low scores of the outcome (e.g., low intention to turnover), which are not simply the opposite mirrors of functions for high scores in an outcome condition (Mehran & Olya, 2019).

Results of configurational model testing

The fsQCA results recommended sufficient causal recipes to predict employee's engagement, well-being and turnover intention in the food and beverage industry (Tables 11.3–11.5). Table 11.3 presents the fsQCA results from the reward system, training, and leadership style for predicting well-being of the employee. According to the results, two causal recipes described the condition of employees' well-being (coverage: 0.725 and consistency: 0.972). Coverage and consistency in asymmetrical modelling are, respectively, equivalent to the coefficient of determination and the correlation in symmetrical modelling. As shown in Table 11.3, the high well-being of employees was obtained when the rewarding system is poor, but training is high in the restaurants in Santander (see M1). The second model indicates that high rewarding and high leadership in restaurants boost the employees' well-being (see M2).

Table 11.4 presents the fsQCA results from reward system, training, leadership, and well-being for modelling engagement intention of employees. According to

164 *Mehran et al.*

Table 11.3 Sufficient causal recipes to predict well-being

Models for Predicting Well-Being WB = f(rew, tra, TLdr)	Raw Coverage	Unique Coverage	Consistency
M1: ~rew*tra	0.595207	0.299374	0.973547
M2: rew*TLdr	0.42616	0.130327	0.986069

Solution coverage: 0.725
Solution consistency: 0.972

Table 11.4 Sufficient causal recipes to predict engagement

Models for Predicting Engagement Intention Eng = f(rew, tra, TLdr, WB)	Raw Coverage	Unique Coverage	Consistency
M1: ~rew*WB	0.714386	0.0174554	0.963501
M2: TLdr*WB	0.828725	0.115394	0.972505
M3: rew*~tra*~TLdr	0.314316	0.0531865	0.927091

Solution coverage: 0.908
Solution consistency: 0.936

the results, three causal recipes described the condition of the employees' engagement (coverage: 0.908 and consistency: 0.936). The results showed that a combination poor rewarding system with high well-being could lead to employee engagement (see M1). The second model illustrates that configuration of high leadership and well-being leads to employee engagement (see M2). The third model shows that a combination of high reward with poor training and poor leadership could contribute to high engagement among employees (see M3).

Table 11.5 presents the fsQCA results from the reward system, training, and leadership for modelling turnover intention of employees. According to the results, two causal recipes described the condition of the employees' turnover intention (coverage: 0.587 and consistency: 0.759). The first model indicates that the combination configuration of high amount of reward with poor training and

Table 11.5 Sufficient causal recipes to predict turnover intention

Models for Predicting Turnover Intention TrnInt = f(rew, tra, TLdr, WB)	Raw Coverage	Unique Coverage	Consistency
M1: rew*~tra*~TLdr	0.554024	0.0179671	0.777816
M2: ~tra*~TLdr*WB	0.56953	0.0334728	0.782814

Solution coverage: 0.587
Solution consistency: 0.759

leadership could lead to turnover intention (see M1). The second model shows that low training and low leadership with high well-being could also be a sufficient predicting model for employees' turnover intention (see M2).

Evaluation of complexity theory and discussion

Using the six tenets of complexity theory, this study discusses the contribution to the extension of knowledge in employee well-being in the hospitality industry. According to the results of the fsQCA, reward is a necessary condition to predict well-being but insufficient to predict the high score in employee well-being (M1; M2, Table 11.3). Thus, tenet 1, which postulates that a combination of factors can explain a causal condition leading to a given outcome, is supported (Woodside, 2014). In other words, the well-being of employees in the food and beverage industry could not be explained merely with the reward system and could not be measured by the net effect of the reward system on well-being of personnel. More precisely, low, and high rewarding in the restaurant industry could contribute to employee well-being only if we could have other variables in a combination configuration with reward systems (M1; M2; M3, Table 11.3). The recipe principle assumes that a complex combination of training, leadership, and well-being is sufficient for consistently high scores of engagements among employees (e.g., Model 3 in Table 11.4). Thus, tenet 2 is supported. Therefore, sustainability of employee well-being in the long run could be achievable, when well-trained employees can benefit from an award system in an organisation with well-designed leadership style.

According to the equifinality principle, a model that is sufficient is unnecessary for achieving an outcome. As an example, reward, training, and leadership are sufficient to predict employee engagement in the food and beverage industry in Santander (e.g., Model 2 in Table 11.4) but is not necessary as the combination configuration of training, leadership, and well-being could also contribute to employee engagement (e.g., Model 3 in Table 11.4). Practically, skilled employees with qualified leaders in the food and beverage industry could contribute to the stability of the business with high engagement intentions.

Concerning tenet 4, the so-called causal asymmetry principle, the fsQCA results showed that recipes that demonstrate a well-being outcome are unique and are not the mirror opposites of recipes of turnover intention in the food and beverage employees. For example, in the regression analysis, if the leadership has positive significance on employee well-being, it could be discussed that the leakage or absence of leadership could result in turnover intention in contrast. The fsQCA results confirm that the solutions contributing to well-being are not mirror opposite of the solutions explaining the turnover intention among employees. Since the role of each antecedent depends on the role of other antecedents, that single antecedent might contribute both positively and negatively to predicting an expected outcome.

In accordance with tenet 5, leadership could contribute to a high score of engagement in a study model, while both positive and negative scores of leadership could contribute to the high score of well-being (see M2 and M3 on

Table 11.4). Therefore, tenet 5 is supported. In other words, quality leadership as an important variable can positively contribute to employee well-being although poor leadership would not necessarily contribute to low levels of well-being. For example, in a restaurant with poor leadership, the establishment of a proper rewarding system would be sufficient for well-trained employees to have quality well-being in their job.

According to the last tenet, for completing high outcome scores, a given recipe is relevant for some but not all cases; coverage should be less than 1.00 for any single solution. The fsQCA results shown in Tables 11.3–11.5 demonstrate that coverage is less than 1 for any recipe, which confirms tenet 6. Therefore, the results of the configurational model testing support the six tenets of complexity theory and complexity theory explains the interactions among the reward, leadership, training, and well-being in predicting engagement and turnover intention of employees in the food and beverage industry in Santander.

Conclusion and implications

The concept of sustainability and the emergence of transformation (e.g., transportation, digitalisation, and pandemic) in the hospitality industry are becoming of significant in theory and practice. This empirical study deepens our knowledge of employees' well-being, engagement, and turnover intention in the food and beverage industry, which has a strategic role in the personal income, social life, and psychology of many Europeans in this critical edge. Nowadays, well-being in the hospitality industry is a key driver of mental health and, thus, of great significance for researchers from two points of views. First, well-being of employees is linked to performance and psychologically healthy employees are more productive and less likely to quit their jobs. Second, the impact of rapid development of transportation and digitalisation caught the attention of the public awareness on labour's mental health and social welfare in service industries. Specifically, the COVID-19 pandemic has confronted the working conditions and well-being of employees in the hospitality industry with an unprecedented challenge. As a result, appropriate application of human resource strategies (e.g., leadership style and training) could alleviate the uncertainty condition of job demand (e.g., instability, seasonality, low wages, part-time job hours, and draining workdays) in the guest-oriented industry.

This study attempted to advance current knowledge of employee well-being in the service context in several ways. Theoretically, this chapter adopts complexity theory to understand how the antecedents of well-being in complex configuration can contribute to employee engagement and turnover intention among employees in the food and beverage industry in Santander, Spain. This study used a symmetrical approach (i.e., regression) to investigate the application of human resource strategies (i.e., training, award, and leadership) on well-being, which influence engagement and turnover intention of employees in the food and beverage industry. Methodologically, this empirical study uses asymmetrical analysis to investigate the effects of rewards system, training, and leadership style on employee well-being and the model outcomes. In addition, it also highlighted the role of a comprehensive reward system in higher performance and the positive impact of continuous training and development on the improvement of the employee's well-being. We suggest that education considers it paramount and a vital element of well-being in the workplace, inviting high-skilled leaders to positively contribute to quality of training and establishing a fair reward system. Educated and knowledgeable business owners could invest in human resource training strategies to boost well-being of their employees and sustainability of their businesses. Governments and service providers' awareness of employees' well-being should be considered as a priority in terms of both employment and the direct contribution to the economy by planning human resource development in the workplace. This study has limitations regarding the application of data obtained in a cross-sectional study that measured a specific region in Spain. However, the leading global tourism market, and the hospitality sector as a subcategory, is one of the key drivers of the European economy, and more research is needed in significant touristic areas in the EU. To generalise the findings, we call for more empirical studies on employee well-being in guest-oriented industries after the COVID-19 pandemic to keep this industry alive and to see how transformations can contribute to the sustainability of these industries in the long run. Future studies should examine the important criteria of employee well-being in the context of new normality and cause and effect of employee well-being on a global scale.

References

Afsar, B., Shahjehan, A., & Shah, S. I. (2018). Frontline employees' high-performance work practices, trust in supervisor, job-embeddedness and turnover intentions in hospitality industry. *International Journal of Contemporary Hospitality Management, 30*(3), 1436–1452.

Ariza-Montes, A., Hernández-Perlines, F., Han, H., & Law, R. (2019). Human dimension of the hospitality industry: Working conditions and psychological well-being among European servers. *Journal of Hospitality and Tourism Management, 41*, 138–147.

Benitez, M., Medina, F. J., & Munduate, L. (2018). Buffering relationship conflict consequences in teams working in real organizations. *International Journal of Conflict Management, 29*(2), 279–297.

Boella, M. J., & Goss-Turner, S. (2019). *Human resource management in the hospitality industry: A guide to best practice*. Abingdon: Routledge.

Boshoff, C., & Allen, J. (2000). The influence of selected antecedents on frontline staff's perceptions of service recovery performance. *International Journal of Service Industry Management, 11*(1), 63–90.

Cabanas Díaz, E., & Sánchez González, J. C. (2016). Inverting the pyramid of needs: Positive psychology's new order for labour success. *Psicothema, 28*(2), 107–113.

Casado-Díaz, J. M., & Simon, H. (2016). Wage differences in the hospitality sector. *Tourism Management, 52*, 96–109.

Day, J. W., Holladay, C. L., Johnson, S. K., & Barron, L. G. (2014). Organizational rewards: Considering employee need in allocation. *Personnel Review, 43*(1), 74–95.

Gill, A. S., Flaschner, A. B., & Shachar, M. (2006). Mitigating stress and burnout by implementing transformational-leadership. *International Journal of Contemporary Hospitality Management, 18*(6), 469–481.

Grandey, A. A., Rupp, D., & Brice, W. N. (2015). Emotional labour threatens decent work: A proposal to eradicate emotional display rules. *Journal of Organizational Behaviour*, *36*(6), 770–785.

Grant, A. M., Christianson, M. K., & Price, R. H. (2007). Happiness, health, or relationships? Managerial practices and employee well-being tradeoffs. *Academy of Management Perspectives*, *21*(3), 51–63.

Great Place to Work. (2016). *3 generations, one great workplace*. Retrieved October 29, 2020, from www.greatplacetowork.com/resources/reports/three-generations-one-great-workplace

Guest, D. E. (2017). Human resource management and employee well-being: Towards a new analytic framework. *Human Resource Management Journal*, *27*(1), 22–38.

He, J., Morrison, A. M., & Zhang, H. (2019). Improving millennial employee well-being and task performance in the hospitality industry: The interactive effects of HRM and responsible leadership. *Sustainability*, *11*(16), 4410–4429.

Ho, H., &Kuvaas, B. (2020). Human resource management systems, employee well-being, and firm performance from the mutual gains and critical perspectives: The well-being paradox. *Human Resource Management*, *59*(3), 235–253.

HOTREC. (2019, December 6). *Facts & figures: Hospitality industry contributions to EU economy society*. Retrieved October 31, 2020, from www.hotrec.eu/facts-figures-2/

Jameson, S. M. (2000). Recruitment and training in small firms. *Journal of European Industrial Training*, *24*(1), 43–49.

Jung, S., Lee, S., & Dalbor, M. (2016). The negative synergistic effect of internationalization and corporate social responsibility on US restaurant firms' value performance. *International Journal of Contemporary Hospitality Management*, *28*(8), 1759–1777.

Kara, D., Uysal, M., Sirgy, M. J., & Lee, G. (2013). The effects of leadership style on employee well-being in hospitality. *International Journal of Hospitality Management*, *34*, 9–18.

Karatepe, O. M. (2013). Perceptions of organizational politics and hotel employee outcomes. *International Journal of Contemporary Hospitality Management*, *25*(1), 82–104.

Kular, S., Gatenby, M., Rees, C., Soane, E., & Truss, K. (2008). Employee engagement: A literature review. ISBN No. 1-872058-39-6/978-1-872058-39-9/9781872058399.

Madan, S. (2017). Moving from employee satisfaction to employee engagement. *CLEAR International Journal of Research in Commerce & Management*, *8*(6), 46–50.

Mehran, J., & Olya, H. G. (2019). Progress on outbound tourism expenditure research: A review. *Current Issues in Tourism*, *22*(20), 2511–2537.

Mehran, J., & Olya, H. G. (2020). Canal boat tourism: Application of complexity theory. *Journal of Retailing and Consumer Services*, *53*, 101954.

Mehran, J., Olya, H. G., Han, H., & Kapuscinski, G. (2020). Determinants of canal boat tour participant behaviours: An explanatory mixed-method approach. *Journal of Travel & Tourism Marketing*, *37*(1), 112–127.

Nunnally, J. C., & Bernstein, I. H. (1994). *Psychological theory*. New York: McGraw-Hill.

Olya, H. G. (2020). Towards advancing theory and methods on tourism development from residents' perspectives: Developing a framework on the pathway to impact. *Journal of Sustainable Tourism*, 1–21. https://doi.org/10.1080/09669582.2020.1843046

Olya, H. G., Altinay, L., Farmaki, A., Kenebayeva, A., & Gursoy, D. (2021). Hotels' sustainability practices and guests' familiarity, attitudes and behaviours. *Journal of Sustainable Tourism*, *29*(7), 1063–1081.

Olya, H., & Nia, T. H. (2021). The medical tourism index and behavioral responses of medical travelers: A mixed-method study. *Journal of Travel Research*, *60*(4), 779–798.

Pappas, N., & Brown, A. E. (2020). Entrepreneurial decisions in tourism and hospitality during crisis. *Management Decision.* https://doi.org/10.1108/MD-10-2019-1412

People 1st. (2018). *"The skills and productivity problem": Hospitality and tourism sector.* Retrieved October 29, 2020, from www.people1st.co.uk

Pienaar, J., & Willemse, S. A. (2008). Burnout, engagement, coping and general health of service employees in the hospitality industry. *Tourism Management, 29*(6), 1053–1063.

Podsakoff, N. P. (2003). Common method biases in behavioural research: A critical review of the literature and recommended remedies. *Journal of Applied Psychology, 885*(879), 10–37.

Rabanal, M. (2020, August 20). *6 Michelin-starred stars of dining in Green Cantabria, Spain.* Retrieved October 29, 2020, from https://love2fly.iberia.com/2020/08/cantabria-spain-michelin-starred-restaurants-dining/

Radic, A., Arjona-Fuentes, J. M., Ariza-Montes, A., Han, H., & Law, R. (2020). Job demands–job resources (JD-R) model, work engagement, and well-being of cruise ship employees. *International Journal of Hospitality Management, 88,* 102518.

Rowland, C. A., Hall, R. D., & Altarawneh, I. (2017). Training and development. *EuroMed Journal of Business, 12*(1), 36–51.

Schneider, M., & Somers, M. (2006). Organizations as complex adaptive systems: Implications of complexity theory for leadership research. *The Leadership Quarterly, 17*(4), 351–365.

Sharma, P., Kong, T. T. C., & Kingshott, R. P. (2016). Internal service quality as a driver of employee satisfaction, commitment and performance. *Journal of Service Management, 27*(5), 773–797.

Sinclair, A., & Suff, R. (2020, March). *Well-being at work: Factsheets.* Retrieved October 18, 2020, from www.cipd.co.uk/knowledge/culture/well-being/factsheet

Tsai, C. W. (2008). Leadership style and employee's job satisfaction in international tourist hotels. *Advances in Culture, Tourism and Hospitality Research, 2*(2), 293–332.

Urtasun, A., & Núñez, I. (2012). Work-based competences and careers prospects: A study of Spanish employees. *Personnel Review, 41*(4), 428–449.

Warr, P., (2007). *Work, happiness and unhappiness.* Institute of Work Psychology, University of Sheffield. Retrieved October 29, 2020, from www.the-iacp.com/assets/CBTBR/cbtbr-vol_55a.pdf

Woodside, A. G. (2014). Embrace perform model: Complexity theory, contrarian case analysis, and multiple realities. *Journal of Business Research, 67,* 2495–2503.

Wright, T. A., & Huang, C. (2012). The many benefits of employee well-being in organizational research. *Journal of Organizational Behavior, 33*(8), 1188–1192.

12 Climbing the virtual mountain
A netnography of the sharing and collecting behaviours of online Munro-bagging

David Brown and Sharon Wilson

Introduction

Munro-bagging is a form of hillwalking. Munro-baggers are hillwalkers who ascend Scottish mountains which are over 3,000 feet (914.4 m) in altitude – the Munros – at least partially for the purpose of increasing their 'collection' of summitted Munros. They are peak-baggers. They may be attracted to their pastime by the promise of exercise, fresh air, exploration, self-sufficiency, beautiful views, companionship, and a host of other factors, but their choice of mountains is influenced by a 'tick-list' mentality. By the 1990s, a thousand walkers had 'compleated' (The Scottish Mountaineering Club and many Munro-baggers adopt the archaic spellings, 'compleat', 'compleated', 'compleation', and 'compleater', which were used by Sir Hugh Munro, originator of the Munro-bagging concept) a 'round' of Munros (McNeish, 1996) – climbed all 282 of them. By 2015, this number surpassed 6,000, with numerous more walkers currently partway through the challenge (Scottish Mountaineering Club, 2018). Most rounds exceed two decades; others are intensive. Although successful ascents cannot strictly 'transfer ownership' to the walker, they contribute towards completion of a prescribed collection. 'Bagged' Munros, unlike tangible collectors' items, cannot be traded or bequeathed but bestow incremental knowledge and experiences to be stored, revisited, and shared.

As the Munros are located in the Highlands and Islands of Scotland, Munro-bagging has been geographical bounded, necessitating repeated visits. However, social media groups enable Munro-baggers to augment the pastime's physical, geographical situatedness with non-physical, temporospatially non-specific elements (e.g., planning and reflection). Part of mountain walking is effectively removed from the mountain, de-territorialised and dematerialised, but intermediated through other community members. Through electronic WOM (eWOM), visitors disperse credible, cost-effective, interactive, and non-timebound communication across geo-cultural boundaries. By reprioritising interpersonal communications against the spatiality of the pastime, a 'telepresence' (Wellman, 2001) challenges the dominance of place and space in defining participation and presenting social implications for members and commercial implications for stakeholders. Moreover, through videos, drone footage, and photographs, participants'

DOI: 10.4324/9781003105930-13

touristic experiences can be shared widely, immediately, and naturalistically to existing and potential Highland tourists.

Munro-bagging, and peak-bagging more generally, has received relatively little focus within leisure and tourism literature. Whilst the deliberate and processual nature of peak-bagging has been acknowledged (e.g., Lorimer & Lund, 2003), this is yet to prompt the introduction of theories on collecting as an analytical lens. This is a curious omission, given the central objective of 'set completion' underpinning much literature on collecting and collectors (e.g., Olmsted, 1987), and is clearly central to the Munro-bagging pastime (McNeish, 1996). Naturally, Munro-bagging has certain characteristics which separate it from, for example, philately (stamp collecting), and either complicate or prevent the applicability of theory into this context. Perhaps the most obvious consideration is that mountains cannot be bought, earned, or acquired as material possessions except by the very wealthy. Instead, the collecting is of experiences, memories, achievements, and perhaps prestige. A second major gap in the research relates to how the advent of the Internet and social media has impacted upon the experiences of Munro-baggers. In the last generation, Munro-baggers have been able to seek information, plan, exchange stories and advice, publish photos and route descriptions, express their explorer identities, and interact with other Munro-baggers, in online spaces. This suggests that the scope and experience of Munro-bagging have expanded beyond its previous temporal, spatial, and social boundaries, demanding fresh research to explore the phenomenon.

The theoretical implication arising from the chapter is that, whilst serious leisure pastimes such as Munro-bagging have been recognised as contributors of tourism in the Scottish Highlands, more research into the role and effects of social media interaction amongst participants is required. The practical implication is that the Scottish Highland brand is socially constructed and transmitted in part by online communities of people drawn together by a common offline pastime and therefore tourism marketers must pursue new ways to engage them and harness their informal marketing potential. Moreover, the 'collecting' approach to Scottish tourism is currently spreading from Munro-bagging to island-bagging (i.e., visiting as many Scottish islands as possible), and anecdotal evidence suggests that visitors are also starting to tick off lists of officially recognised long-distance trails (Walkhighlands, 2021), and even road routes.

In this chapter, we explore how Munro-bagging is quickly evolving as a Scottish hillwalking phenomenon due to the rapid expansion of membership of, and interaction within, social media sites which are specifically for Munro-baggers and hill walkers. Whilst Munro-bagging has collecting as its central focus, the scant previous literature on hill-bagging has largely ignored the rich theory on collecting behaviours which is particularly well developed amongst commentators on consumer culture and social psychology (e.g., Rigby & Rigby, 1944; Johnston & Beddow, 1986; Olmsted, 1987; Belk, Wallendorf, & Sherry, 1988; Belk, 1994, 2014). Likewise, the few previous studies of Munro-bagging (e.g., Lorimer & Lund, 2003, 2008; Bentley & Ormerod, 2009) have largely restricted themselves to traditional interviews and observations – most of them dating from before the popularity of social media and the introduction of social media sites for hillwalkers. Moreover, the intersectionality of social media participation, sharing and collecting behaviours, and hillwalking has not previously been explored. We address this gap in the theory by observing the sharing and collecting of Munro-baggers interacting in online spaces and by analysing how this rapidly evolving phenomenon is not only being transformed but also increasingly transformative to the manner in which potential participants gain knowledge and information about a pastime which, if adopted fully, requires them to indulge in Scottish Highland tourism. As such, this research should be of considerable interest to theorists or practitioners of Highland tourism.

We will appraise the generic academic literature on collecting and collectors, and on online communities, before analysing the theory of sharing and collecting within tourist communities. Using these three fields, we will explore the intersection of them through netnographic observation of Munro-baggers in online spaces. As the lead author is a Munro-bagger who frequents such websites for pleasure, the approach may be deemed interpretative autonetnography. We will then analyse the findings against the extant literature, before identifying emerging insights and proposing how researchers and practitioners may build upon them.

Theoretical background

Hadrup and Larson (2006) argued through the 'cultural turn' in the social sciences that tourism is more closely connected to physical sensations than traditionally assumed. We seek to return to this but to theorise ways in which online sharing might re-constitute the tourism landscape. Munro-baggers undertake experiences which necessitate embodied strain, exposure to the elements, and interaction with specific places. However, as online interactivity becomes ever more pervasive, they also use technology to 'collect' and share specific ascents (Belk, Wallendorf, & Sherry, 1988) as memories, blogs, and digital holograms. We therefore suggest that this work follows the thread that leaves behind the tourist, contemporising a discussion that focuses upon the '*contingent networked performance and production of places that are remade as they are toured*' (Bærenholdt et al., 2004, p. 151).

We argue, in essence, that place is represented as a collage of experience and as a dematerialised gaze. These are manifested as biographies which attempt to constitute the affective experiences of nature and, in doing so, popularise and estrange yet form new socialities. The implications for wider tourism discourse are the potential of the reducibility of connectivities with the 'virtual proximity' (Urry, 2002, p. 265) offered by remote beings and things on the one hand and new ways of seeing and promoting travel into the wild on the other hand.

Collecting

Many people choose, or feel compelled, to collect things for leisure. To frame such behaviours, Belk (1987) saw collections as extensions of self. By imparting ownership and order upon the mundane, objects acquire non-utility status and are sacralised pseudo-religiously (Belk, Wallendorf, & Sherry, 1988). Indeed, mountain exploration by seminal climbers (e.g., Norman Collie's Skye Cuillins) bestows cultural significance. Collecting may be conscious or unconscious, structured or unstructured, or vertical or horizontal (Belk, Wallendorf, & Sherry, 1988). Most Munro-baggers collect vertically, working down lists. A tiny minority climb summits by order of altitude, relinquishing the convenience of combining neighbouring peaks. Munro-bagging by region (e.g., climbing all the Torridon Munros, then all the Glencoe Munros, etc.) constitutes a more horizontal strategy. Some walkers stumble into the pastime unintentionally, thereby blurring the conscious/unconscious distinction, and collecting may begin through serendipitous events such as family summit hikes undertaken without prior awareness of Munro-bagging (Rigby & Rigby, 1944; Johnston & Beddow, 1986).

Collectors enjoy legitimisation through others considering their activities 'worthwhile' (Belk, Wallendorf, & Sherry, 1988), reinforcing their sense of taste and judgement (Stewart, 1984, cited in Belk, 1990). Collecting is sometimes a reaction against anxiety or self-perceived inadequacy and is often considered addictive or compulsive (e.g., Johnston & Beddow, 1986; Belk, Wallendorf, & Sherry, 1988), and this potentially skews the characteristics of those transmitting the Highland brand this way. Participants seek reassurance through ritualised repetition (Peele, 1985) and frequently specialise (Belk, Wallendorf, & Sherry, 1988), explaining the specific forms of mountain-bagging (e.g., of Munros, 'county tops', etc.). They may tangibilise travel experiences with physical artefacts (Belk, Wallendorf, & Sherry, 1988), and the digitisation of photographs and journey logs has not entirely superseded this. Younger users, especially 'digital natives' (Prensky, 2001), are less likely to tangibilise cloud-based assets (Belk, 2013a), whilst older people derive less satisfaction and authenticity from digital possessions, which are therefore more peripheral to their extended selves (Cushing, 2012). This may influence how and what differently aged Munro-baggers collect and share online and suggests that younger walkers' transmission of the Highland brand is often through more ephemeral means.

Items are collectible for their set membership and their role in set completion, rather than for aesthetic or utilitarian value (Duroust, 1932, cited in Belk, 1994). Collectors nearing completion may feel conflicted, desiring fulfilment of an ambition yet dreading its removal (Dannefer, 1980; Olmsted, 1987). Although many collections are bequeathed to heirs (Olmsted, 1987), creating a legacy, Munro-baggers have nothing tangible to bequeath. The Internet facilitates peer-to-peer interactivity and UGC (Carroll & Romano, 2010). Narratives co-create places and touristic experiences (Prebenson, Vitterso, & Dahl, 2013). Kankanhalli, Tan, and Wei (2005) described sharing through social media as motivated by intended usefulness and expected gratification, and Marwick and Boyd (2014) found that users visualise an unknown audience to judge appropriateness, acceptability, and audience reception (Born, 2011). This may be easier where group members are more homogenous and bound by a pastime such as Munro-bagging, demonstrating their values, potentially leading to a largely consistent communication of their touristic experiences.

Online communities

Online leisure communities help members to gain skills, feel accomplished, and express self (Nimrod, 2014). Built upon shared interests, values, and goals, they transcend the geographical boundedness inherent in offline communities (Kraut & Resnick, 2012). Most members never meet offline, so consider their communities 'online' (e.g., Preece, 2000), 'virtual' (Rheingold, 1994), and 'portable' (Chayko, 2008). By sharing mutual interests and perspectives, members establish interpersonal relationships, group cohesion, and identity, despite the turbulence potentially experienced within diverse memberships (MacQueen et al, 2001). Online community members may be categorised by their contributions: posters and creators, lurkers, and trolls (Bishop, 2013).

Some online community members archive and document their activities (Krotoski, 2013). Moreover, digital identity, evolving over time with one's technological, personal, and social contexts, represents users' values and characteristics (Rannenberg, Royer, & Deuker, 2009). The social and psychological benefits of self-expression (Kang, Tang, & Fiore, 2014) are often more attainable online (Chayko, 2008). Self-expressions may change as the user develops competence, an evolving social identity (Schmalz, Colistra, & Evans, 2015) and social integration (Parry, Glover, & Mulcahy, 2013). Therefore, online social identities are unstable, multi-dimensional, and context-driven, and may suggest that users' communications of their pastime and portrayals of Scotland may follow this pattern.

Online communities require a shared purpose, interactions which satisfy a need to perform a role, and common rules and policies to guide such interaction (Preece, 2000). Users overcome social isolation (Chayko, 2008) by maintaining connectivity (Flanagin & Metzger, 2001; Ivan & Hebblethwaite, 2016) and developing friendships (Bishop, 2013; Krotoski, 2013) through support, loyalty, acceptance, and trust (Fehr, 1996; Karbo, 2006). The group identities may be more readily constructed in specialised forums such as Munro-bagging sites, which promote cooperation and reciprocity (Chayko, 2008).

Most tourist Internet usage occurs before trips for planning journeys, and social media underpins that usage (Leung et al., 2013). The difference between Munro-baggers who post content during trips and those who simply access others' content during their trips appears potentially significant to the dissemination of touristic knowledge. Travellers use online communities to collect information, connect with likeminded partners, advise others, and share experiences (Wang, Yu, & Fesenmaier, 2002). Social media can greatly influence tourists' emotions and brand, place or event identification (Hudson et al., 2015). Mkono and Tribe (2017) segmented online tourism community members into trolls, socialites, activists, information seekers, and social critics. Kozinets (2015) categorised online community members, albeit not specifically within travel communities: interestingly, the first category is 'tourists', who post casual questions but feel unbound by community (his tag 'tourists' seemingly conveying negative assumptions); 'minglers' perceive strong social ties but lack motivation towards 'consumption activities' (e.g., climbing mountains); 'devotees' identify strongly with the pastime but not the community; and 'insiders' enthusiastically contribute to intra-community connections, friendships, credibility, and influence. Members' sense of belonging is reinforced by active participation, encouraging the sharing of knowledge and promoting the community externally (Qu & Lee, 2011). Knowledge sharing is stimulated by individual, community, and affiliation factors, producing community identification (Lee, Reid, & Kim, 2014). Therefore, Munro-bagging sites may also enjoy higher levels of knowledge sharing and active participation than those communities focused on easier pastimes. Hedonic outcomes include excitement, enjoyment, happiness, and entertainment (Hoffman & Novak, 1996). Community interaction often derives from 'giving back' (Cothrel & Williams, 1999). Membership may stimulate affiliative feelings (Rheingold, 1993) unattainable to solo Munro-baggers, thereby becoming transformational (Kozinets, 2015) to members' self-concepts.

Although 'tourism as consumption' is a contested notion (Stebbins, 2009), 'community membership as consumption' enjoys wider acceptance (e.g., Denegri-Knott & Molesworth, 2010), including within travel communities (e.g., Hagel & Armstrong, 1997; Preece, 2000). Online community members may contribute for self-gratification (Wang & Fesenmaier, 2004) or to be followed (Ellison, Steinfield, & Lampe, 2007). By posting photographs, members archive materials for future retrieval, contributing to the group's heritage (Quadri-Felitti & Fiore, 2013) and providing the 'bridging capital' of cooperative connections with others (Putnam, 2001). Photographs, by conveying the emotions of a former self to the current self, often underpin autobiographical memory (Belk & Yeh, 2011) but perhaps also the perceptions of those yet to visit the Highlands – a foreshadowing 'folk memory'.

The geographical unboundedness of social media (Boyd, Golder, & Lotan, 2010) may democratise access, but sites are bounded by language, cultural references, and style, which constitute online identity representation (Boyd, 2010) and may bar participation. Whereas most Facebook relationships begin offline (Ellison, Steinfeld, & Lampe, 2007), this is much less true of online travel community friendships (Kunz & Seshadri, 2015), so members are more likely to discuss their pastime with those they have never met. Individuals' prior expectations of participation dictate their interaction levels and loyal consumers harness online community membership to socialise the process of evaluating quality (Kozinets, 2015). This appears applicable to the judging of Munro routes. All communities are subject to spatial and social constraints, socialisation, behavioural norms, and interactivity. Therefore, the following section reviews theories appertaining to sharing, collecting, and consuming more generally, contemplating their applicability to online tourist communities.

Sharing, collecting, and consuming within tourist communities

Through sharing information, tourists interacting through social media can become the 'media' themselves (Li & Wang, 2011), suggesting that tourist organisations which buy media space for promotions should consider the efficacy of these actors. To explore Munro-baggers' online sharing, we adopt Belk's (2010) characteristics of sharing. He states that it is non-reciprocal; it nurtures social links, encouraging social reproduction; it entails shared ownership or rights over something; money is irrelevant to the act; objects are singular; there is networked inclusion; the action is personal, dependent, and inalienable; it occurs within a context conducive to sharing; it demonstrates love of caring; and it is non-ceremonial. He separates 'sharing in', which breaks down materialistic interpersonal barriers and possessiveness from 'sharing out', which is a non-reciprocal, one-off act undertaken with a stranger (e.g., the giving of a cigarette). Moreover, he distinguishes between ownership-based and non-ownership-based sharing (Belk, 2013a), which potentially presents a grey area for community members such as Munro-baggers, who share knowledge freely but may imply some sort of ownership of the Scottish mountain landscape based upon nationality, residency, attachment and identification, or physical engagement and experience.

Lamberton and Rose's (2012) findings on sharing jar slightly against Belk's (2010, 2013a) 'sharing in', as actors are motivated through social utility (e.g., gaining approval). Belk (2013a), illustrating his notion of 'open sharing', describes a host saying 'my house is your house' in a non-specific, undetailed manner, whereas 'demand sharing' services a request for a specific resource, such as a child demanding breakfast (ibid). Intangibles like ideas, values, and time may be shared (Belk, 2010). By contributing online, actors may pursue community or others' generosity, and these actions render resources available to others (Belk, 2014). As users archive and share their personal information and thoughts (Derrida, 1996) and have ever more platforms to do so (Hennig-Thurau, Henning, & Satler, 2007), they retain contact with others, share their opinions, display interest and 'active listening', discuss issues, and express their values. This perhaps suggests that a normative message is likely to form in these groups. Such values have been categorised as social presence, self-presentation, social conversation, easy connection, and self-management (Ham et al., 2018). It is worth noting that tourists' motivational factors on social media differ according to the type of content shared and types of media, although altruistic, community-related motivations most commonly drive tourists' sharing information online (Munar & Jacobsen, 2014).

Sharing may be the primary reason for visiting blogs and social media sites (John, 2013). Recent academic debate considers whether sharing is (Arnould & Rose, 2016) or is not (Price & Belk, 2016) a form of gift-giving, as digital gift-giving is motivated by factors as diverse as altruism and love, the quest for status and reciprocity, and ingratiation (Lampel & Bhalla, 2007). However, its social embeddedness in everyday routines and rituals, values, and norms (Belk, 2010; Price & Belk, 2016) provokes less disagreement. Technology-enabled interaction has encouraged access-based consumption (Bardhi & Eckhardt, 2017) in which users are defined not solely by their production (Ritzer, 2014), consumption, or ownership but through what they access and share (Belk, 2013b). Sharing motivated by reciprocity expectations may be deemed pseudo-sharing (Belk, 2014) and can instigate the phenomenon of prosumption (Ritzer & Jurgenson, 2010), in which actors simultaneously produce and consume a resource. Furthermore, collaborative consumption can occur. Botsman and Rogers (2010) defined it as a marketplace exchange encapsulating both gift-giving and sharing. Therefore, we will explore how online members of Munro-bagging communities share, collaborate, and engage in prosumption, and its effects within the group.

Methodology

Using interpretive autonetnography

Kozinets' (1999, 2002) principles of netnography (and autonetnography) underpin this research methodology and the central ethos of democratising the research through empowerment of participants within a naturalistic setting. More broadly, the research adheres to the central tenets of interpretive auto-ethnography (e.g., Ellis & Bochner, 2000; Denzin, 2014), by exploring the following: the ways in which history, biography, society, and culture intersect and act upon each other; the narratives, meanings, and voice arising from online posts and comments; the emotionality, experience, and reflexivity which underpin how Munro-baggers represent themselves in digital spaces; the myths, performances, rituals, and words which take on special significance and help to bind together diverse members into a coherent and cohesive social unit; any epiphanies or turning points which members experience, such as unexpectedly positive 'unlurking' processes or hostile member reactions to well-intentioned posts, which have brought about changes in perception; and the facts, facticities, fictions, truths, and realities which form the basis by which members understand their communities and their places within them (Denzin, 2014). To ensure methodological robustness, the research has been guided by Bochner's (2000) criteria for interpretive sufficiency and Richardson's (2000) criteria for evaluating ethnography, as per Table 12.1.

Using netnography and autonetnography

Netnography – the study of a social group in an online setting (Kozinets, 2010, 2015) – is well suited to extend knowledge of hillwalkers. Although hillwalking is located outside and embodied (Stevenson & Farrell, 2018), many of the actions, emotions, and interactions associated with the pastime occur at different points in time and place. By studying online communities of Munro-baggers, we aim to uncover otherwise obscured insights. Whilst a netnographic approach to researching Munro-baggers may appear to focus on the 'before' (planning) stage and the 'after' (reflecting) stage, some participants post status updates and photographs to social media mid-activity, sharing the moment, broadcasting their achievement, seeking moral support, or tackling social isolation.

178 *David Brown and Sharon Wilson*

Table 12.1 Criteria for achieving interpretive sufficiency and for evaluating ethnographic research

Bochner's (2000) criteria (adapted):	Richardson's (2000) criteria (adapted):
Narratives' language should convey experience to readers	Substantive contribution to understanding of life in the social unit
Abundance of concrete detail	Aesthetic merit
Structurally complex narrative	Researcher reflexivity, familiarity, and subjectivity
Vulnerability, honesty, and emotional credibility	Emotional, intellectual, and scholarly impact
A sense of transitioning identity	Truth, credibility, and expressive of a reality
High standards of ethical self-consciousness	
Concern for participants and subjects	
Emotionally, not purely intellectually, engaging	
Empowerment and resistance in the narrative of the self	

Netnography can therefore capture a longitudinality which evades other forms of research.

Autonetnography (Kozinets, 2010) is to netnography (Kozinets, 1999, 2002) what autoethnography is to ethnography – the study of an online community to which the researcher belongs. In calling for autonetnographic approach to tourism studies, Mkono, Ruhanen, and Markwell (2015) noted both the pervasiveness of digital communities within modern life and the intersection between researchers' online actions and identities at work and in their private lives. One of the co-authors has been a Munro-bagger since 2001 and a member of associated social media sites long before research commencement. Therefore, this is partially an autonetnography.

Autoethnographic data collection explores and illustrates the following: the involvement which members seek and undertake within the group; forms of engagement between members and the social unit, their frequencies, limitations, importance, and outcomes; the contact and interactions between members at an individual or small group level, and their characteristics; and the ways in which members commune, relate to each other and to those outside the group membership, collaborate and co-create (or co-destruct) value, and forge connections. Analysis of the data is through immersion, reflection, and iterative re-readings.

The main social media sites accessed through Facebook were as follows: Scottish Hillwalking and Wild Camping; Munroaming; Munro Bagging; Scottish Hills; Mountains of Britain; Mountains of the Mind; Scottish Hillwalking, Wild Camping and Mountaineering; I Am Bagging the Munros; Scrambling and Mountaineering UK; and several other sites dedicated to Highland mountain tourism which include Munro-specific content.

Netnographic findings

We used netnography – the study of online groups (Kozinets, 2015) – to examine hillwalkers' collecting and sharing. Whilst this may appear to focus on the 'before' (planning) and 'after' (reflecting) stage, many participants post content mid-activity, sharing the moment, broadcasting their achievement, seeking moral support, or tackling social isolation. Netnography can therefore capture a longitudinality which evades other research. Autonetnography (Kozinets, 2015) is the study of an online community to which the researcher belongs. In calling for autonetnographic approaches to tourism studies, Mkono, Ruhanen, and Markwell (2015) noted the pervasiveness of digital communities within modern life and the intersection between researchers' online actions and identities at work and in their private lives. One of the co-authors has been a Munro-bagger since 2001 and a member of associated social media sites long before research commencement. Therefore, this research is partially autonetnographical and explores those sites.

Sharing content

Photographs and videos typically share the aesthetics and euphoria of hillwalking. Some capture meteorological phenomena, flora, and fauna. Other members routinely add their own photographs or reminiscences – a process of value co-creation (Prahalad & Ramaswamy, 2004). Occasionally, posts are unintentionally controversial, eliciting negative responses. Although Belk (2010) considered the sharing of physical resources inalienable, the sharing of public spaces is negotiated (Griffiths & Gilly, 2012), albeit tacitly. This fits Munro-bagging sites, which are 'third places' where members interact in a publicly accessible area beyond the 'first place' of home and 'second place' of work (Oldenburg, 1999). Where members misunderstood the negotiated, acceptable use of public space, they may subvert it unacceptably, attracting opprobrium.

Selfies – especially summit selfies – proliferate within Munro-bagging sites. Posters share their achievement and elation with peers, perhaps seeking compliments. Sharing summit selfies is not unceremonial (Belk, 2010) but part of a routine and of a rite of passage from Munro-bagger to Munroist – not sharing in its truest sense but partially self-focused.

Munro-baggers' online knowledge sharing

Walk reports, reviews, and route descriptions often carry several photographs or a video, showing summits, views, walkers, wild camps, bothies, flora, or fauna. They are reflexive, first-person accounts posted soon after trips, often incorporating humour and self-critique. (Posts during trips are usually briefer, comprising few photographs.) There may be a blurring of boundaries between landscape, pastime, and walker. As fatigue and blisters are described, the embodied nature of serious leisure (Stebbins, 2009) is conveyed. Posters relate the performativity of hiking (Lorimer & Lund, 2003), even 'breaking the fourth wall' between actors and audience. Some undertake strenuous expeditions which are physically impossible to most and entail specialist skills, resourcefulness, resolve, and independence. For example, two friends 'bagged' the Mullardoch Horseshoe – 12 remote Munros normally split into four tough hikes – within 24 hours. Such descriptions entertain, inspire, and impress others but also perhaps reinforce an unspoken pecking order within the community.

Many posts request advice on gear, routes, destinations, and ground or weather conditions. Most elicit responses not only from well-informed members but also from 'socialites' (Mkono & Tribe, 2017) who lack the skills, knowledge, and experiences to socialise effectively in this environment and are not prepared to wait before becoming 'minglers' (Kozinets, 2015).

Munro-baggers' collecting behaviours

Several websites displayed potted walking biographies beside users' profile pictures, sometimes stating the number of mountains climbed, length of membership, number of posts made, and number of followers. Potentially, this may provide a decision-making heuristic to others when judging a member's social standing, negating scrutiny of other social cues, such as the type of responses to their posts. Someone whose display indicates that many Munro ascents will likely attract respect (although proof is not required), and some seem to display 'classic' experiences (e.g., witnessing Aurora Borealis) as prestige indicators. It is likely that these members accrue credibility and their representations of Scotland and touristic experiences are trusted and impactful.

Many Munro-baggers, especially those early in their bagging careers, prioritise summiting by the easiest self-propelled means, mainly on foot but sometimes as a 'bike-and-hike'. Some summit, take photographs, and then immediately descend – perhaps because of poor weather conditions, time constraints, or public transport schedules. Occasionally, such people are criticised as mercenary or disconnected from the 'mountain ethos', despite the reductionist goal of Munro-bagging. Amongst many participants, who are partially motivated by a quantitative objective, there appears a need to moderate the somewhat arbitrary, prescriptive 'rules' of the pastime and present themselves less as 'collectors', more as 'connoisseurs'. On general hillwalking sites, Munro-baggers have been castigated for reasons such as supposedly prioritising list completion over aesthetic appreciation. For example, detractors note that beautiful mountains like The Cobbler, Suilven, and Stac Pollaidh are below 3,000 feet yet superior to many Munros. The inference that a Munro-bagger would deliberately omit such mountains is only partially accurate – many seem to deprioritise and defer their ascents of them. However, there is clearly a tension between members' pastime and the ethos and characteristics which they wish to transmit to their publics.

Numerous Munro-baggers have expressed regret before completion of the challenge. Having achieved series completion, some move onto the Corbetts (i.e., Scottish mountains between 2,500 and 3,000 feet high), Wainwrights (English

Lake District summits), or other list-oriented challenges like the Great Run events. A few begin fresh Munro rounds. Some vary these, taking different ascent routes or including subsidiary 'tops'. Others introduce relatives and friends to the challenge. This does not bequeath a collection as one might a stamp collection but removes the unsatisfactory closedness of finishing a long challenge. Even those replicating their first rounds as closely as possible cannot achieve identical collections as they could with tangible items, as the weather, encounters, timings, and the walkers' mental and physical states cannot be reproduced. Through communicating their experiences to others, Munro-baggers may pursue continuity and permanence, thereby transmitting highly personalised, subjective portrayals of the Highlands and pinning them once more to a specific temporospatial context which is otherwise blurred online.

Conclusion

Many online Munro-bagging community members share to build identity, social standing, and rapport, to enjoy their pastime whilst away from the hills, and to benefit from full participation online. The work of Witte and Hannam (2017) – who recently looked at the hybrid worlds of five Chinese hillwalking communities in a netnography about the social nature of these spatially and socially stretched networks (Larsen, Axhausen, & Urry, 2006) – analysed online walking identities with only nominal discussion of sharing, focusing instead on identities which developed out of dematerialised space. Therefore, we propose that the literature still currently has minimal engagement with either portals or people who support these socialities of 'mountain love', which this work seeks to consider.

As Munroists check in online as 'proof of life' verification, they share knowledge, emotion, and experiences by posting photographs, videos, status updates, and replies pre-, during, and post-trip. Sharing may be constructive or destructive – for instance, expressing nationalistic sentiment which reinforces the perceptions of some whilst offending others. Members collect information and advice and may display their progress within their Munro-bagging 'career' through conversations and personal summaries. Series completion (i.e., becoming a Munroist) often triggers ambivalence, which online interactions partially address. Elements of serious leisure participation are now extendable into the online domain, elongating its social aspects and enabling actors to derive new value from and within the pre- and post-trip stages, especially through the communitarian sharing of socio-cultural values. By transcending geo-cultural boundaries and dismantling many elements of the pastime's temporospatial situatedness, Munro-bagging is augmented through online technology and its participants interlinked through renegotiations of self which blur the boundary between the communitarian and the hedonic. The power and credibility of eWOM and the extent of knowledge sharing between Munro-baggers suggest that entities such as National Park authorities, local and national governments, and Highland businesses could harness online communications for their benefit. Moreover, the use of social media may be considered transformative both to the pastime of

Munro-bagging and the manner in which it establishes itself as a touristic phenomenon within the Highlands. It has helped to transform the pastime from one of relative social isolation, geographical locatedness, specificity of time, and near-invisibility to one in which adherents can instantly publicise their experiences within an interactive social audience, indulge in remembrances of their own activities and vicarious experiences of others' in unbounded temporospatial situations, and become visible to enthusiasts, novices, and other would-be tourists. This then promotes the Highlands – or at least one facet of them – by eWOM to audiences which would have previously relied on closer social connections and traditional information formats. As tourists hence climb the 'virtual mountain' whilst hiking the real one, we suggest that the industry is yet to fully utilise the personal biographies of these body-nature quests, arguably missing the opportunity to drive more footfall if so desired.

References

Arnould, E. J., & Rose, A. S. (2016). Mutuality: Critique and substitute for Belk's "sharing". *Marketing Theory, 16*(1), 75–99.

Bærenholdt, J., Haldrup, M., Larsen, J., & Urry, J. (2004). *Performing tourist places*. Aldershot, UK: Ashgate.

Bardhi, F., & Eckhardt, G. M. (2017). Liquid consumption. *Journal of Consumer Research, 44*(3), 582–597.

Belk, R. W. (1987). A child's Christmas in America: Santa Claus as deity, consumption as religion. *Journal of American Culture, 10*(1), 87–100.

Belk, R. W. (1990). The role of possessions in constructing and maintaining a sense of past. *Proceedings of the Association for Consumer Research, North American Advances*.

Belk, R. W. (1994). Collectors and collecting. In S. M. Pearce (Ed.), *Interpreting objects and collections* (p. 360). London, UK & New York, NY: Routledge.

Belk, R. W. (2010). *Global consumerism and consumption*. London, UK: Wiley.

Belk, R. W. (2013a). Extended self in a digital world. *Journal of Consumer Research, 40*(3), 477–500.

Belk, R. W. (2013b). *Collecting in a consumer society*. London, UK: Routledge.

Belk, R. W. (2014). Sharing versus pseudo-sharing in Web 2.0. *The Anthropologist, 18*(1), 7–23.

Belk, R. W., & Hsiu-yen Yeh, J. (2011). Tourist photographs: Signs of self. *International Journal of Culture, Tourism and Hospitality Research, 5*(4), 345–353.

Belk, R. W., Wallendorf, M., & Sherry, J. (1988). Collectors and collecting. In M. J. Houston (Ed.), *Advances in consumer research*, Vol. 15 (pp. 548–553). Provo, UT: Association for Consumer Research.

Bentley, A., & Ormerod, P. (2009). Tradition and fashion in consumer choice: Bagging the Scottish Munros. *Scottish Journal of Political Economy, 56*(3), 371–381.

Bishop, J. (Ed.). (2013). *Examining the concepts, issues, and implications of internet trolling*. Hershey, PA: IGI Global.

Born, G. (2011). Music and the materialization of identities. *Journal of Material Culture, 16*(4), 376–388.

Botsman, R., & Rogers, R. (2010). *What's mine is yours: The rise of collaborative consumption*. London, UK: Collins.

Boyd, D. (2010). Social network sites as networked publics: Affordances, dynamics, and implications. In D. Boyd (Ed.), *A networked self* (pp. 47–66). London, UK: Routledge.

Boyd, D., Golder, S., & Lotan, G. (2010). Tweet, tweet, retweet: Conversational aspects of retweeting on twitter. *Proceedings from the 43rd Hawaii International Conference of System Sciences* (pp. 1–10).

Carroll, E., & Romano, J. (2010). *Your digital afterlife: When Facebook, Flickr and Twitter are your estate, what's your legacy?* San Francisco, CA: New Riders.

Chayko, M. (2002). *Connecting: How we form social bonds and communities in the digital age*. Albany, NY: SUNY Press.

Chayko, M. (2008). *Portable communities: The social dynamics of online and mobile connectedness*. Albany, NY: SUNY Press.

Cothrel, J., & Williams, R. L. (1999). On-line communities: Helping them form and grow. *Journal of Knowledge Management, 3*(1), 54–60.

Cushing, A. L. (2012). *Possessions and self extension in digital environments: Implications for maintaining personal information*. (Doctoral dissertation), The University of North Carolina, Chapel Hill.

Daily Record. (2018, July 21). *Scots climber plans to get NAKED at the top of every mountain he climbs after viral starkers summit snap* Retrieved December 2, 2018, from www.dailyrecord.co.uk/scotland-now/scots-climber-sets-trend-getting-12954449

Dannefer, D. (1980). Rationality and passion in private experience: Modern consciousness and the social world of old-car collectors. *Social Problems, 27*(4), 392–412.

Denegri-Knott, J., & Molesworth, M. (2010). Concepts and practices of digital virtual consumption. *Consumption, Markets and Culture, 13*(2), 109–132.

Denzin, N. K. (2014). *Interpretive autoethnography* (2nd ed.). London, UK: Sage.

Derrida, J. (1996). *Archive fever: A Freudian impression*. Chicago, IL: University of Chicago Press.

Ellison, N. B., Steinfield, C., & Lampe, C. (2007). The benefits of Facebook "friends": Social capital and college students' use of online social network sites. *Journal of Computer-Mediated Communication, 12*(4), 1143–1168.

Fehr, B. (1996). *Friendship processes* (Vol. 12). New York, NY: Sage.

Flanagin, A. J., & Metzger, M. J. (2001). Internet use in the contemporary media environment. *Human Communication Research, 27*(1), 153–181.

Griffiths, M. A., & Gilly, M. C. (2012). Dibs! Customer territorial behaviors. *Journal of Service Research, 15*(2), 131–149.

Hagel, J., & Armstrong, A. G. (1997). *Net gain*. Boston, MA: Harvard Business School Press.

Haldrup, M., & Larsen, J. (2006). Material cultures of tourism. *Leisure Studies, 25*(3), 275–289.

Ham, C. D., Lee, J., Hayes, J. L., & Bae, Y. H. (2018). Exploring sharing behaviors across social media platforms. *International Journal of Market Research, 61*(2), 157–177.

Hennig-Thurau, T., Henning, V., & Sattler, H. (2007). Consumer file sharing of motion pictures. *Journal of Marketing, 71*(4), 1–18.

Hoffman, D. L., & Novak, T. P. (1996). Marketing in hypermedia computer-mediated environments: Conceptual foundations. *Journal of Marketing, 60*(3), 50–68.

Hudson, S., Roth, M. S., Madden, T. J., & Hudson, R. (2015). The effects of social media on emotions, brand relationship quality, and word of mouth: An empirical study of music festival attendees. *Tourism Management, 47*, 68–76.

Ivan, L., & Hebblethwaite, S. (2016). Grannies on the net: Grandmothers' experiences of Facebook in family communication. *Romanian Journal of Communication and Public Relations, 18*(1), 11–25.

John, N. A. (2013). The social logics of sharing. *The Communication Review, 16*(3), 113–131.

Johnston, S., & Beddow, T. (1986). *Collecting: The passionate pastime*. New York, NY: HarperCollins.

Kang, J., Tang, L., & Fiore, A. M. (2014). Enhancing consumer: Brand relationships on restaurant Facebook fan pages: Maximizing consumer benefits and increasing active participation. *International Journal of Hospitality Management, 36*, 145–155.

Kankanhalli, A., Tan, B. C., & Wei, K. K. (2005). Contributing knowledge to electronic knowledge repositories: An empirical investigation. *MIS Quarterly*, 113–143.

Karbo, K. (2006). Friendship: The laws of attraction. *Psychology Today, 39*(6), 90–95.

Kozinets, R. V. (2015). *Netnography redefined* (2nd ed.). London, UK: Sage.

Kraut, R. E., & Resnick, P. (2012). *Building successful online communities: Evidence-based social design*. Cambridge, MA: MIT Press.

Krotoski, A. (2013). *Untangling the web*. London, UK: Faber & Faber.

Kunz, W., & Seshadri, S. (2015). From virtual travelers to real friends: Relationship-building insights from an online travel community. *Journal of Business Research, 68*(9), 1822–1828.

Lamberton, C. P., & Rose, R. L. (2012). When is ours better than mine? A framework for understanding and altering participation in commercial sharing systems. *Journal of Marketing, 76*(4), 109–125.

Lampel, J., & Bhalla, A. (2007). The role of status seeking in online communities: Giving the gift of experience. *Journal of Computer-Mediated Communication, 12*(2), 434–455.

Larsen, J., Axhausen, K. W., & Urry, J. (2006). Geographies of social networks: Meetings, travel and communications. *Mobilities, 1*(2), 261, 288.

Lee, H., Reid, E., & Kim, W. G. (2014). Understanding knowledge sharing in online travel communities: Antecedents and the moderating effects of interaction modes. *Journal of Hospitality & Tourism Research, 38*(2), 222–242.

Leung, D., Law, R., Van Hoof, H., & Buhalis, D. (2013). Social media in tourism and hospitality: A literature review. *Journal of Travel & Tourism Marketing, 30*(1–2), 3–22.

Li, X., & Wang, Y. (2011). China in the eyes of western travelers as represented in travel blogs. *Journal of Travel & Tourism Marketing, 28*(7), 689–719.

Lorimer, H., & Lund, K. (2003). Performing facts: Finding a way over Scotland's mountains. *The Sociological Review, 51*(2), 130–144.

Lorimer, H., & Lund, K. (2008). A collectable topography: Walking, remembering and recording mountains. In Ingold, T. & Vergunst, J. L. (Eds.), *Ways of walking: Ethnography and practice on foot* (pp. 185–200). Aldershot, UK: Ashgate.

MacQueen, K. M., McLellan, E., Metzger, D. S., Kegeles, S., Strauss, R. P., Scotti, R., . . . Trotter, R. T. (2001). What is community? An evidence-based definition for participatory public health. *American Journal of Public Health, 91*(12), 1929–1938.

Marwick, A. E., & Boyd, D. (2014). Networked privacy: How teenagers negotiate context in social media. *New Media & Society, 16*(7), 1051–1067.

McNeish, C. (1996). *The Munros: Scotland's highest mountains*. Broxburn, UK: Lomond Books.

Meenagh, J. (2015). Flirting, dating, and breaking up within new media environments. *Sex Education, 15*(5), 458–471.

Mkono, M., & Markwell, K. (2014). The application of netnography in tourism studies. *Research Notes and Reports/Annals of Tourism Research, 48*, 289–291.

Mkono, M., Ruhanen, L., & Markwell, K. (2015). From netnography to autonetnography in tourism studies. *Research Notes and Reports/Annals of Tourism Research, 52*, 167–169.

Mkono, M., & Tribe, J. (2017). Beyond reviewing: Uncovering the multiple roles of tourism social media users. *Journal of Travel Research, 56*(3), 287–298.

Munar, A. M., & Jacobsen, J. K. S. (2014). Motivations for sharing tourism experiences through social media. *Tourism Management, 43*, 46–54.

Nimrod, G. (2014). The benefits of and constraints to participation in seniors' online communities. *Leisure Studies, 33*(3), 247–266.

Oldenburg, R. (1999). *The great good place: Cafes, coffee shops, bookstores, bars, hair salons, and other hangouts at the heart of a community*. Boston, MA: Da Capo Press.

Olmsted, A. D. (1987). Stamp collectors and stamp collecting. In *Proceedings of Popular Culture Association Annual Meeting*. Montreal, Canada.

Parry, D. C., Glover, T. D., & Mulcahy, C. M. (2013). From ƷStroller-StalkerƷ to ƷMomancerƷ: Courting friends through a social networking site for mothers. *Journal of Leisure Research, 45*(1), 23–46.

Peele, S. (1985). *The meaning of addiction: Compulsive experience and its interpretation*. Lanham, MD: Lexington Books/DC Heath and Com.

Prahalad, C. K., & Ramaswamy, V. (2004). Co-creation experiences: The next practice in value creation. *Journal of Interactive Marketing, 18*(3), 5–14.

Prebenson, N. K., Vitterso, J., & Dahl, T. I. (2013). Value co-creation significance of tourist resources. *Annals of Tourism Research, 42*, 240–261.

Preece, J. (2000). *Online communities: Supporting sociability, designing usability*. Hoboken, NJ: Wiley.

Prensky, M. (2001). Digital natives, digital immigrants, part 1. *On the Horizon, 9*(5), 1–6.

Price, L. L., & Belk, R. W. (2016). Consumer ownership and sharing: Introduction to the issue. *Journal of the Association for Consumer Research, 1*(2), 193–197.

Putnam, R. (2001). Social capital: Measurement and consequences. *Canadian Journal of Policy Research, 2*(1), 41–51.

Qu, H., & Lee, H. (2011). Travelers' social identification and membership behaviors in online travel community. *Tourism Management, 32*(6), 1262–1270.

Quadri-Felitti, D. L., & Fiore, A. M. (2013). Destination loyalty: Effects of wine tourists' experiences, memories, and satisfaction on intentions. *Tourism and Hospitality Research, 13*(1), 47–62.

Rannenberg, K., Royer, D., & Deuker, A. (Eds.). (2009). *The future of identity in the information society: Challenges and opportunities*. New York, NY: Springer Science & Business Media.

Rheingold, H. (1993). *The virtual community: Finding commection in a computerized world*. Boston, MA: Addison-Wesley Longman Publishing Co., Inc.

Rheingold, H. (1994). *The virtual community: Surfing the internet*. London, UK: Minerva.

Rigby, D., & Rigby, E. (1944). *Lock, stock and barrel: The story of collecting* (Vol. 692). Philadelphia, PA: JB Lippincott Company.

Ritzer, G. (2014). Prosumption: Evolution, revolution, or eternal return of the same? *Journal of Consumer Culture, 14*(1), 3–24.

Ritzer, G., & Jurgenson, N. (2010). Production, consumption, prosumption: The nature of capitalism in the age of the digital "prosumer". *Journal of Consumer Culture, 10*(1), 13–36.

Schmalz, D. L., Colistra, C. M., & Evans, K. E. (2015). Social media sites as a means of coping with a threatened social identity. *Leisure Sciences, 37*(1), 20–38.

Scottish Mountaineering Club. (2018). *The Scottish Mountaineering Club journal 2018*. Glasgow, UK: SMC Publishing.

Stebbins, R. (2009). Serious leisure and work. *Sociology Compass, 3*(5), 764–774.

Urry, J. (2002). Mobility and proximity. *Sociology, 36*(2), 255–274.
Walkhighlands website. Retrieved March 3, 2021, from www.walkhighlands.co.uk
Wang, Y., & Fesenmaier, D. R. (2004). Towards understanding members' general participation in and active contribution to an online travel community. *Tourism Management, 25*(6), 709–722.
Wang, Y., Yu, Q., & Fesenmaier, D. R. (2002). Defining the virtual tourist community: Implications for tourism marketing. *Tourism Management, 23*(4), 407–417.
Wellman, B. (2001). Physical place and cyber place: The rise of networked individualism. *International Journal of Urban and Regional Research, 25*, 227–252.
Witte, A., & Hannam, K. (2017). A netnography of China's emerging hiking communities. In C. M. Hall, Y. Ram, & N. Shoval (Eds.), *The Routledge international handbook of walking*. London, UK: Routledge.

13 Sustainable Development Goals and tourism organisations

The enabling role of sustainable business models

Pierfelice Rosato, Simone Pizzi, and Andrea Caputo

Introduction

Recent years have been characterised by a range of circumstances that have given rise to a necessity to rethink tourism management (Hall, 2019; Scott, Hall, & Gössling, 2019). In particular, the increasing consciousness about the need to promote the transition towards more sustainable ecosystems and an awareness of the disruptive impacts caused by COVID-19 are two of the main factors that have affected tourism organisations (Higgins-Desbiolles, 2020; Rosato et al., 2021). As a result, such organisations have begun revising their business models in order to ensure that the procedures that they enact in response to the external pressures made by policymakers, citizens, and non-governmental organisations (NGOs) are adequate.

According to the United Nations World Tourism Organization (2017), the road ahead of a sustainable future requires tourism sectors to make significant contributions. In particular, this international organisation highlighted the opportunity for firms to place sustainability at the core of their business models and activities to favour the achievement of the 17 SDGs established by the UN. However, due to the ambiguous relationship between tourism and sustainable development (Manomaivibool, 2015; Scheyvens & Hughes, 2019), the achievement of these ambitious goals cannot be pursued without significant engagement with stakeholders.

Although numerous criticisms have been raised related to the SDGs, an increasing number of organisations have started to integrate practices within their business model inspired by sustainable behaviours. In particular, in recent years, great interest has been demonstrated in the rapid growth of market segments related to the demand of sustainable and sports tourism (Boluk, Cavaliere, & Higgins-Desbiolles, 2017; Pröbstl-Haider et al., 2018). However, due to the need to engage effectively with different types of stakeholders, the development of these practices is a complex activity. In contrast with other sectors, the implementation of sustainable practices in tourism organisations requires the adoption of a multistakeholder approach (Waligo, Clarke, & Hawkins, 2013).

Based on this evidence, the chapter's aims consist of the evaluation of the primary constraints and opportunities related to the implementation of a sustainable business model in tourism organisations. In particular, the analysis examines cycling tourism,

DOI: 10.4324/9781003105930-14

which represents one of the leading emerging practices in tourism and hospitality (Neun & Haubold, 2016; Pröbstl-Haider et al., 2018). Furthermore, the analysis will extend the theoretical debate about emerging transformations in the tourism sector through the identification of new insights related to the need for tourism organisations to integrate sustainable principles within their business models. In particular, the insights offered underline the opportunities related to coopetition and sustainable business models in tourism and hospitality (Pappas, 2014; Rosato et al., 2021).

Literature review

Sustainable business model

The importance of the implementation of sustainable practices by public and private organisations has been widely analysed by academics (Centobelli et al., 2020; Pizzi et al., 2020). The significance of the topic is related to the increasing need of organisations to adopt an environmental, social, and ethical behaviour (Hiller, 2013; Vieira, O'Dwyer, & Schneider, 2017). Furthermore, the evolution from a concept of sustainability limited to environmental impacts towards a more extensive concept based on the integration of environmental, social, and governance topics favoured the development of the field (Hahn et al., 2015; Higgins-Desbiolles & Wijesinghe, 2019). In this sense, management scholars started to analyse the contribution provided by organisations to the sustainable development through alternative lens, in order to consider their different impacts on society (Bartolacci, Caputo, & Soverchia, 2020). In particular, in recent years, there has been a proliferation of studies about the relationship between business models and sustainable practices (Centobelli et al., 2020; Geissdoerfer et al., 2020).

The main contributions on sustainable business models follow the theoretical proposition provided by Osterwalder and Pigneur (2010). In particular, the authors defined a business model as a tool to describe the rationale of how an organisation creates, delivers, and captures value. Following the paradigm proposed by Osterwalder and Pigneur (Bocken et al., 2014), many academics developed research dedicated to integrating the concept of 'the triple-bottom-line' proposed by Elkington (2013). In light of these developments and due to the wide diffusion of studies about the different implications related to the integration of sustainable practices within different types of organisations, the sustainable business model currently represents a standalone field of research within the debate (Tunn et al., 2019; Yip & Bocken, 2018). Furthermore, the different implications related to the implementation of a sustainable business models underline the need to consider inter- and intra-sectorial specificities. Thus, evaluating sustainable business models in tourism and hospitality represents a standalone topic within the scientific field.

Sustainable business models in tourism organisations

Academics and policymakers consider the tourism sector one of the primary enablers for the transition towards a more sustainable planet (Scheyvens & Hughes, 2019; United Nations World Tourism Organization, 2017). However, defining sustainable development in tourism represents a complex task due to the combination of positive and negative externalities caused by organisations on society. In particular, Butler (1999) underlined the need to distinguish between '*sustainable tourism*' and '*sustainable development in the context of tourism*', which represent two independent concepts. In particular, the author stated that contributing to sustainable development through sustainable tourism represents an activity characterised by a high degree of complexity for entrepreneurs. In fact, an organisation inspired by sustainable principles could negatively impact on biodiversity, urban landscape, and natural resources. An example of this phenomenon is represented by the different expectatives regarding the implementation of 'green' infrastructures, which represents an activity that requires a social licence to operate released by local communities (Cole, 2014; Moneva, Bonilla-Priego, & Ortas, 2020).

The theoretical contribution of Butler (1999) can be easily extended to the scientific debate about the SDGs, which represent a novel field of studies with different perspectives regarding the role covered by organisations. On the one hand, tourism can contribute to the SDGs through externalities related to the direct investments made by entrepreneurs and multinational enterprises (MNEs). Prior studies have highlighted the existence of a positive relationship between tourism and human well-being (Musavengane, 2019; Nguyen et al., 2019). On the other hand, many scholars have underlined the critical role of tourism organisations on sustainable development due to the coexistence of positive and negative externalities related to their anthropic activities. Furthermore, this evidence is confirmed by prior studies about the existence of an interlinkage between the 17 SDGs (Nilsson, Griggs, & Visbeck, 2016; Schaltegger, 2018).

Given this evidence, the comprehension of the contribution provided by a tourism organisation requires an in-depth analysis of their business model. Business model's analysis represents one of the main approaches used by academics and practitioners to assess the contribution provided by companies on sustainable development (Yip & Bocken, 2018). In fact, business model's evaluation favours the identification of the main strengths and weakness in terms of financial and non-financial impacts. In this sense, it represents a way to evaluate companies or sectors through an approach based on the integration between financial and non-financial dynamics. The need to evaluate business model is also underlined by the existence of several archetypes within similar sector of activities. This evidence regards tourism sector, which represents a sector of activity characterised by different archetypes (Hunter-Jones, 1997; Rasoolimanesh et al., 2020). An example of this phenomenon is represented by the inclusion within the concept of 'sustainable tourism' of many sub-sectors such as sports and social tourism (Serdane, 2019). Furthermore, the central role covered by the SMEs underlined the need to analyse sustainable business models from alternative perspectives due to their peculiarities.

Cycling tourism: an overview

According to the UNWTO (2018), sport tourism represents a market segment characterised by a high degree of contribution to the SDGs. In particular, the organisation underlined that sport tourism contributes to the SDGs more than other types of tourism due to the coexistence of positive impacts on society and citizens. In fact, one of the main strengths of sport tourism is the high degree of social acceptance shown by local communities, which represents a critical factor for tourism organisations (Shipway et al., 2016). Furthermore, other positive externalities generated by sport tourism for society are represented by the impacts on the environment and tourists' well-being (Jiménez-García et al., 2020; United Nations World Tourism Organization, 2018).

However, evaluating the contribution provided by sport tourism to society is characterised by a high degree of complexity caused by the combination of different externalities (Higham, 1999; Van Rheenen, Cernaianu, & Sobry, 2017). Similar to other types of tourism, it acts as an enabler for the economic development of destinations (Chang, Choong, & Ng, 2020; Hinch, Higham, & Moyle, 2016). In fact, many destinations are characterised by a high degree of dependency from sport tourism (Hinch & Ito, 2018; Mollah, Cuskelly, & Hill, 2021). In addition, it is also an enabler for sustainable development due to its capability to contribute to social and environmental dimensions. In fact, tourism organisations can favour sustainable development adopting more sophisticated managerial control systems (Sriarkarin & Lee, 2018), engaging with stakeholders (Pascual-Fernández et al., 2018), and adopting sustainable practices (Tremblay, Landry-Cuerrier, & Humphries, 2020; Yang et al., 2018).

Recently, many academics have begun to analyse 'cycling tourism', which represents a new segment characterised by the centrality of bicyclings that are the main items that make up the tourists' experience. The relevance of the segment has been confirmed by the latest research, which has revealed an overall economic impact on European countries equal to €513.19 billion (Neun & Haubold, 2016). Yearly, the use of bicyclings by tourists generates an estimated 2 million trips and 20 million overnight stays. The European countries that have achieved the best results in the cycling tourism segment are the countries in which the bicycling is widely used as a means of transport, such as Austria, Denmark, Germany, France, the Netherlands, and Switzerland. These are countries that also, as the result of a consolidated tendency to consider the bicycling as an integral part of their citizens' daily lives, have invested more in specific infrastructure and the marketing and promotion of their destinations. The German cycling tourism market has about 5.5 million practitioners per year with a generated turnover of about 5 billion euro; in France, cycling tourism generates 16,000 employees, 7 million presences, and an estimated turnover of 2 billion of Euros yearly (Unioncamere & ISNART, 2019). Furthermore, some mountain destinations of Central Europe, such as Trentino-Alto Adige and regions of Austria, have based part of their competitive advantage on cycling tourism (Franch, Irimias, & Buffa, 2017; Pröbstl-Haider et al., 2018). Also, cycling tourism represents a 'way of exploring the area' capable of offering some of the responses to the processes of transforming tourist use patterns that seem to emerge in consequence of the current COVID-19 pandemic, which is one of the main challenges to the tourism and hospitality sector (ECF, 2020; Higgins-Desbiolles, 2020).

The chapter aims to extend the scientific knowledge on cycling tourism through the analysis of the Apulia (Italy) case. The analysis was conducted in 2019 on a set of participants that operate in Apulia (Italy), one of the leading tourism destinations in Europe that have tried to develop a tourism ecosystem inspired by smart and sustainable principles (Del Vecchio & Passiante, 2017; Freeman et al., 2018). The choice to analyse the Apulia was driven by the specific attention paid by policy makers, organisations, and local communities to cycling tourism. In particular, one of the main initiatives developed to sustain cycling tourism is represented by the Regional Plan of Cycling Mobility (PRMC), which represents an important and innovative tool of territorial planning (Asset Puglia, 2020). The PRMC consists of 11 routes, and it is part of a set of European and Italian initiatives on cycling tourism.

Methods

The research aims consist of an evaluation of the contribution provided by cycling tourism to SDGs through the triple-layered business model canvas proposed by Joyce and Paquin (2016). The choice to analyse cycling tourism followed as evidenced in prior studies about the lack of scientific knowledge about the interlinkage between the SDGs and tourism (Rosato et al., 2021; Scheyvens & Hughes, 2019). Furthermore, this chapter fills the theoretical gap about the need to identify the interlinkages between economic, social, and environmental dynamics (Schaltegger, 2018).

Building on the theoretical proposition of Osterwalder and Pigneur (2010), the framework proposed by Joyce and Paquin (2016) consists of a multidimensional business model characterised by the combination of economic, environmental, and social dimensions. In particular, the triple-layered business model canvas consists of an economic business model canvas, an environmental life cycle business model canvas, and a social stakeholder business model canvas (Table 13.1).

The analysis was conducted through a qualitative approach based on semi-structured interviews, a focus group, and informal meetings (Longhurst, 2003; Qu & Dumay, 2011). The choice to conduct qualitative research characterised

Table 13.1 Triple-layered business model canvas.[a]

Economic	*Environmental Life Cycling*	*Social Stakeholder*
• Partners	• Supplies and outsourcing	• Local communities
• Activities	• Production	• Governance
• Value proposition	• Functional value	• Employees
• Customer relationship	• End-of-life	• Social value
• Channels	• Distribution	• Societal culture
• Customer segments	• Use phase	• Scale of outreach
• Costs	• Environmental impacts	• End-user
• Revenues	• Environmental benefits	• Social impacts
		• Social benefits

a Our elaboration on the framework of Joyce and Paquin (2016).

by the adoption of research methods with a high degree of flexibility is related to the opportunity to collect unique insights about the observed phenomenon. Contrary to other research methods, such as structured interviews and surveys, semi-structured interviews and a focus group allow researchers to collect data through informal and non-standardised questions (Okumus, 2002).

The data collection was conducted through different stages. The need to adopt different techniques to identify participants was driven by the opportunity to consider a representative sample, which represents one of the main criticisms in qualitative research (Ketchen & Bergh, 2005). In this sense, we involved within the debate the main actors involved within the debate about Apulian cycling tourism. Furthermore, in order to avoid the risks related to the adoption of qualitative research methods (Aguinis & Solarino, 2019), the data were collected through focus groups, workshops, and direct interviews. In particular, the data were collected through:

- Twenty-five semi-structured interviews with cycling tourism's operators
- Three focus groups with cycling tourism tour operators
- One focus group with institutional stakeholders
- Three workshops on cycling tourism

Findings

The following subsections summarise the main insights collected through the qualitative analysis. In particular, Table 13.2 summarises the interlinkage between cycling tourism and the sustainable business model proposed by Joyce and Paquin (2016).

Economic layer

The value proposition is one of the main items that were emphasised by stakeholders during the interviews. In particular, the analysis reveals that participants recognised that cycling tourism played a central role within the process of stakeholder engagement with new consumer segments. In particular, cycling tourism favours interaction with foreign tourists, which make up 80% of the demand. Furthermore, the diffusion of cycling tourism was favoured by the direct investment made by US tour operators on Apulian destinations.

Investments in cycling tourism services supported the seasonal adjustment of Apulian destinations. In particular, participants highlighted that the peaks of bike tourists are in unconventional periods such as October and April. Also, cycling tourism generates positive economic externalities that have impacted partners and channels. The appreciation of bike tourists for the experiential component 'food and wine' has led some operators to build themed tours ('gourmet tours') that have been successful and appreciated even though sold at higher prices.

As regards costs and revenue structures, the development of a cycling tourism destination requires the investment of financial resources on infrastructure and services. In particular, the participants suggested that bike tourists are interested in spending their holidays within destinations characterised by high-quality services. Furthermore, the analysis of the revenues reveals the existence of synergies between tour operators and small and medium enterprises. Also, because of the significant investments of the Apulia region in supporting the birth of start-ups, new companies have been established oriented to the bike offer in Apulia. These companies have the objective of filling supply gaps in the overall bike supply chain using new technologies based on Industry 4.0, which represents enabling factors for the development of a tourism destination (Pappas et al., 2021).

Environmental life cycle layer

In cycling tourism, the environmental dimension is related to the economic. The development of a tourism destination based on cycling tourism represents an activity that requires the implementation of services and products based on sustainable paradigms.

There is a growing interest on the part of Apulian accommodation facilities that want to start specialising in hospitality biking, based on a growing awareness of the opportunities for accommodation to operate with this segment of the market. This is a mostly international clientele, with an average higher propensity to spend, with a seasonality different from the consolidated market targets, and with a propensity towards sustainable lifestyles and significant concern for the environment.

For cyclists, the protection of the environment and care of the landscape are of great importance. Therefore, they demonstrate, in the process of enjoying the territory, virtuous behaviours that make these customers particularly attractive to the destination of Apulia, which represents a region with a high degree of orientation towards sustainable practices. At the same time, it imposes a challenge on the region in terms of the cleanliness, care, and protection of the landscape. In fact, these characteristics are relevant due to the high expectations and the importance that these aspects assume in the choice of a holiday for cyclists.

Social stakeholder layer

The achievement of a social licence to operate is one of the main challenges for tourism organisations (Lyytimäki & Peltonen, 2016). In particular, certain studies emphasised that the achievement of a de facto legitimation by local communities is almost more important than formal de jure regulation (Coles, Fenclova, & Dinan, 2013). Thus, even though the economic and environmental impacts caused by tourism organisations are relevant for destinations, the comprehension of the social dimension represents a central item within the analysis.

The participants highlighted the existence of an adequate degree of social legitimisation expressed by local communities towards cycling tourism operators. Specifically, the participants confirmed the existence of positive externalities related to bike tourists' characteristics. In contrast to other tourist types, bike tourists are typically characterised by the adoption of virtuous behaviours that favour engagement with local communities. Specifically, analysis reveals the existence of a win–win relationship between de jure and de facto legitimisation. The implementation of cycling tourism in Apulia favoured investment by the local governments in public infrastructures, such as roads, parks, and the maintenance of green spaces. Thus, the contribution provided by cycling tourism in local communities is twofold. On the one hand, bike tourists are interested in a region's cultural aspects and food heritage. In this way, they generate positive externalities in terms of economic value. On the other hand, the development of a cycling tourism destination requires extensive investments in destinations. Thus, the direct investments made by governments towards public services represent an item that impacts positively on local communities' well-being.

Discussion and concluding remarks

The scientific debate on sustainable tourism is characterised by an overall scepticism as regards the contribution provided by tourism to sustainable development. Although the leading organisations highlighted the central role covered by tourism on the 2030 Agenda for Sustainable Goals, a large part of the literature emphasised that the development of a tourism destination is an activity that has a direct impact on the environment and local communities (Dauti, 2017; Rosato et al., 2021). Accordingly, the comprehension of its real impacts requires a cautious approach based on the evaluation of the different externalities caused by tourism organisations. However, the comprehension of the different impacts caused by organisations in society is a topic that has been widely analysed by academics (Bocken et al., 2014; Yip & Bocken, 2018).

Building on the theoretical debate about the criticisms of tourism sector, we have tried to conceptualise the contribution provided by cycling tourism to sustainable development through the framework proposed by Joyce and Paquin (2016). The Apulian experience suggests that cycling tourism is a useful strategy for generating economic value through the implementation of activities with low environmental impacts and characterised by a high degree of legitimisation released by local communities. In particular, the social legitimisation expressed by local communities represents the main items within the analysis. In fact, the analysis underlines that social legitimisation contributes positively to economic and environmental dimensions. In this sense, the evidence collected within the paper confirms, as identified by Coles, Fenclova, and Dinan (2013), the relevance of de facto legitimisation. Furthermore, the interlinkage between the three dimensions proposed by Joyce and Paquin extends the scientific debate about the necessity to analyse the 17 SDGs through a holistic approach (Bebbington & Unerman, 2020; Schaltegger, 2018).

The chapter will extend the scientific knowledge on emerging transformation in tourism sector through new insights about the opportunity to rethink tourism destination in order to contribute to the SDGs. In fact, despite sustainable tourism represents a scientific topic widely analysed by academics,

Table 13.2 Proposed triple-layered business model canvas in cycling tourism

Partners	Activities	Value Proposition	Customer Relationship	Customer Segments
• Tour operators	• Trips • Food tastings	**Economic** • Sustainable experiences	• Development of new services	• International tourists
	Resources		Channels	
• SMEs	• Natural and social capital	• Sport experiences	• International communities	
	Costs		Revenues	
• Seasonal adjustments			• Seasonal adjustments	
• Development of new infrastructures			• Increase of the tourist offer	

Environmental Life Cycle

Supplies and Outsourcing	Production	Functional Value	End-of-Life	Use Phase
• Local communities	• Sustainable cycling routes	• Decrease of environmental impacts related to tourism	• Any impacts	• Maintenance of green routes
			Distribution	
• Coopetition with operators			• Bike • e-bike	
	Environmental impacts		Environmental benefits	
• Green routes			• Green routes • Investment in services	

Social Stakeholder

Local Communities	Governance	Social Value	Societal Culture	End-User
• Local communities are involved within the trips	• Cycling tourism contributes to Governments' strategies	• Central role covers by social value	• Bike tourists are interested to food and cultural heritage	• Green routes' quality
	Employees		Scale of outreach	
	• New form of entrepreneurship		• Cycling tourism is suitable for different types of destinations	
	Social impacts		Social benefits	
• Safeguarding of traditions			• Economic development	

contributing to the SDGs represents a relevant transformation for tourism organisations. In fact, as evidenced by the UN WTO (2017), tourism industries will cover a central role within the policies related to the achievement of the 17 SDGs proposed by the 2030 Agenda. In this sense, the contribution of the study is twofold due to the need to consider managerial and political implications. As regards managerial implications, the analysis has shown that tourism organisations could contribute to the SDGs through the development of new strategies based on cycling tourism's paradigm. In fact, cycling tourism favours the achievement of specific advantages in terms of revenue streams, cost structure, and social and environmental dynamics. Thus, it represents an archetype particularly suitable to engage with tourists inspired by sustainable and ethical principles. Regarding the political implications, the case has shown the opportunity for policy makers to rethink tourism destinations in order to contribute both to the SDGs and to the local economies. In fact, it represents a model with many impacts on local communities due to its capability to favour the economic growth of the entire entrepreneurial ecosystem. However, as evidenced by the Apulian case, cycling tourism requires support from policy makers. In this sense, the implementation of policies to sustain the development of new practices represents one of the main drivers to achieve positive financial and non-financial impacts.

References

Aguinis, H., & Solarino, A. M. (2019). Transparency and replicability in qualitative research: The case of interviews with elite informants. *Strategic Management Journal*, *40*(8), 1291–1315. https://doi.org/10.1002/smj.3015

Asset Puglia. (2020). *Piano Regionale delle Ciclovie di Puglia*. Retrieved from http://asset.regione.puglia.it/?mobilita

Bartolacci, F., Caputo, A., & Soverchia, M. (2020). Sustainability and financial performance of small and medium sized enterprises: A bibliometric and systematic literature review. *Business Strategy and the Environment*, *29*(3), 1297–1309. https://doi.org/10.1002/bse.2434

Bebbington, J., & Unerman, J. (2020). Advancing research into accounting and the UN Sustainable Development Goals. *Accounting, Auditing and Accountability Journal*, *33*(7), 1657–1670. https://doi.org/10.1108/AAAJ-05-2020-4556

Bocken, N. M. P., Short, S. W., Rana, P., & Evans, S. (2014, February 15). A literature and practice review to develop sustainable business model archetypes. *Journal of Cleaner Production*, *65*, 42–56. https://doi.org/10.1016/j.jclepro.2013.11.039

Boluk, K., Cavaliere, C. T., & Higgins-Desbiolles, F. (2017, September 2). Critical thinking to realize sustainability in tourism systems: Reflecting on the 2030 sustainable Development Goals. *Journal of Sustainable Tourism*, 25, 1201–1204. https://doi.org/10.1080/09669582.2017.1333263

Butler, R. W. (1999). Le tourisme durable: Un état de la question. *Tourism Geographies*, 1, 7–25. https://doi.org/10.1080/14616689908721291

Centobelli, P., Cerchione, R., Chiaroni, D., Del Vecchio, P., & Urbinati, A. (2020). Designing business models in circular economy: A systematic literature review and research agenda. *Business Strategy and the Environment*, *29*(4), 1734–1749. https://doi.org/10.1002/bse.2466

Chang, M. X., Choong, Y. O., & Ng, L. P. (2020). Local residents' support for sport tourism development: The moderating effect of tourism dependency. *Journal of Sport and Tourism, 24*(3), 215–234. https://doi.org/10.1080/14775085.2020.1833747

Cole, S. (2014). Tourism and water: From stakeholders to rights holders, and what tourism businesses need to do. *Journal of Sustainable Tourism, 22*(1), 89–106. https://doi.org/10.1080/09669582.2013.776062

Coles, T., Fenclova, E., & Dinan, C. (2013). *Reviews in tourism tourism and corporate social responsibility: A critical review and research agenda.* https://doi.org/10.1016/j.tmp.2013.02.001

Dauti, M. B. (2017). Differences in perception of economic, social and environmental impacts for tourism in four groups of interests: Case study Kosovo. *Journal of Environmental Management and Tourism, 8*(2), 344–353. https://doi.org/10.14505/jemt.v8.2(18).07

Del Vecchio, P., & Passiante, G. (2017). Is tourism a driver for smart specialization? Evidence from Apulia, an Italian region with a tourism vocation. *Journal of Destination Marketing and Management, 6*(3), 163–165. https://doi.org/10.1016/j.jdmm.2016.09.005

ECF. (2020). *Cycling against the COVID-19 | ECF.* Retrieved May 12, 2020, from https://ecf.com/news-and-events/news/cycling-against-covid-19

Elkington, J. (2013). Enter the triple bottom line. In *The triple bottom line: Does it all add up* (pp. 1–16). https://doi.org/10.4324/9781849773348

Franch, M., Irimias, A., & Buffa, F. (2017, May 1). Place identity and war heritage: Managerial challenges in tourism development in Trentino and Alto Adige/Südtirol. *Place Branding and Public Diplomacy, 13*, 119–135. https://doi.org/10.1057/s41254-016-0019-5

Freeman, E. R., Civera, C., Cortese, D., & Fiandrino, S. (2018). Strategising stakeholder empowerment for effective co-management within fishery-based commons. *British Food Journal, 120*(11), 2631–2644. https://doi.org/10.1108/BFJ-01-2018-0041

Geissdoerfer, M., Pieroni, M. P. P., Pigosso, D. C. A., & Soufani, K. (2020, August). Circular business models: A review. *Journal of Cleaner Production, 277*, 123741. https://doi.org/10.1016/j.jclepro.2020.123741

Hahn, T., Pinkse, J., Preuss, L., & Figge, F. (2015). Tensions in corporate sustainability: Towards an integrative framework. *Journal of Business Ethics, 127*(2), 297–316. https://doi.org/10.1007/s10551-014-2047-5

Hall, C. M. (2019). Constructing sustainable tourism development: The 2030 agenda and the managerial ecology of sustainable tourism. *Journal of Sustainable Tourism, 27*(7), 1044–1060. https://doi.org/10.1080/09669582.2018.1560456

Higgins-Desbiolles, F. (2020). Socialising tourism for social and ecological justice after COVID-19. *Tourism Geographies, 22*(3), 610–623. https://doi.org/10.1080/14616688.2020.1757748

Higgins-Desbiolles, F., & Wijesinghe, G. (2019). The critical capacities of restaurants as facilitators for transformations to sustainability. *Journal of Sustainable Tourism, 27*(7), 1080–1105. https://doi.org/10.1080/09669582.2018.1510410

Higham, J. (1999). Commentary: Sport as an avenue of tourism development: An analysis of the positive and negative impacts of sport tourism. *Current Issues in Tourism, 2*(1), 82–90. https://doi.org/10.1080/13683509908667845

Hiller, J. S. (2013). The benefit corporation and corporate social responsibility. *Journal of Business Ethics, 118*(2), 287–301. https://doi.org/10.1007/s10551-012-1580-3

Hinch, T. D., Higham, J. E. S., & Moyle, B. D. (2016). Sport tourism and sustainable destinations: Foundations and pathways. *Journal of Sport and Tourism, 20*(3–4), 163–173. https://doi.org/10.1080/14775085.2016.1254139

Hinch, T., & Ito, E. (2018). Sustainable sport tourism in Japan. *Tourism Planning and Development, 15*(1), 96–101. https://doi.org/10.1080/21568316.2017.1313773

Hunter-Jones, P. (1997). Sustainable tourism. In *Annals of Tourism Research* (2nd ed., Vol. 24). https://doi.org/10.1016/s0160-7383(97)80024-2

Jiménez-García, M., Ruiz-Chico, J., Peña-Sánchez, A. R., & López-Sánchez, J. A. (2020). A bibliometric analysis of sports tourism and sustainability (2002–2019). *Sustainability*, *12*(7), 2840. https://doi.org/10.3390/su12072840

Joyce, A., & Paquin, R. L. (2016). The triple layered business model canvas: A tool to design more sustainable business models. *Journal of Cleaner Production*, *135*, 1474–1486. https://doi.org/10.1016/j.jclepro.2016.06.067

Ketchen, D. J., & Bergh, D. D. (2005). *Research methodology in strategy and management*. Oxford: Elsevier Science.

Longhurst, R. (2003). Semi-structured interviews and 8 focus groups. In *Key methods in geography*. London: SAGE Publication.

Lyytimäki, J., & Peltonen, L. (2016). Mining through controversies: Public perceptions and the legitimacy of a planned gold mine near a tourist destination. *Land Use Policy*, *54*, 479–486. https://doi.org/10.1016/j.landusepol.2016.03.004

Manomaivibool, P. (2015). Wasteful tourism in developing economy? A present situation and sustainable scenarios. *Resources, Conservation and Recycling*, *103*, 69–76. https://doi.org/10.1016/j.resconrec.2015.07.020

Mollah, M. R. A., Cuskelly, G., & Hill, B. (2021). Sport tourism collaboration: A systematic quantitative literature review. *Journal of Sport & Tourism*, 1–23. https://doi.org/10.1080/14775085.2021.1877563

Moneva, J. M., Bonilla-Priego, M. J., & Ortas, E. (2020). Corporate social responsibility and organisational performance in the tourism sector. *Journal of Sustainable Tourism*, *28*(6), 853–872. https://doi.org/10.1080/09669582.2019.1707838

Musavengane, R. (2019). Small hotels and responsible tourism practice: Hoteliers' perspectives. *Journal of Cleaner Production*, *220*, 786–799. https://doi.org/10.1016/j.jclepro.2019.02.143

Neun, M., & Haubold, H. (2016). *The EU cycling economy: Arguments for an integrated EU cycling policy*. Retrieved from www.ecf.com

Nguyen, T. Q. T., Young, T., Johnson, P., & Wearing, S. (2019, October 1). Conceptualising networks in sustainable tourism development. *Tourism Management Perspectives*, *32*, 100575. https://doi.org/10.1016/j.tmp.2019.100575

Nilsson, M., Griggs, D., & Visbeck, M. (2016). Policy: Map the interactions between Sustainable Development Goals. *Nature*, *534*, 320–322. https://doi.org/10.1038/534320a

Okumus, F. (2002, June 1). Can hospitality researchers contribute to the strategic management literature? *International Journal of Hospitality Management*, *21*, 105–110. https://doi.org/10.1016/S0278-4319(01)00033-0

Osterwalder, A., & Pigneur, Y. (2010). *Business model generation: A handbook for visionaries*. New Jersey: Wiley.

Pappas, N. (2014). Hosting mega events: Londoners' support of the 2012 Olympics. *Journal of Hospitality and Tourism Management*, *21*, 10–17. https://doi.org/10.1016/j.jhtm.2014.02.001

Pappas, N., Caputo, A., Pellegrini, M. M., Marzi, G., & Michopoulou, E. (2021). The complexity of decision-making processes and IoT adoption in accommodation SMEs. *Journal of Business Research*. https://doi.org/10.1016/j.jbusres.2021.01.010

Pascual-Fernández, J. J., De, R., Modino, C., Chuenpagdee, R., & Jentoft, S. (2018). Synergy as strategy: Learning from La Restinga, Canary Islands. https://doi.org/10.1007/s40152-018-0091-y

Pizzi, S., Caputo, A., Corvino, A., & Venturelli, A. (2020). Management research and the UN Sustainable Development Goals (SDGs): A bibliometric investigation and systematic review. *Journal of Cleaner Production, 276*, 124033. https://doi.org/10.1016/j.jclepro.2020.124033

Pröbstl-Haider, U., Lund-Durlacher, D., Antonschmidt, H., & Hödl, C. (2018). Mountain bike tourism in Austria and the Alpine region: Towards a sustainable model for multistakeholder product development. *Journal of Sustainable Tourism, 26*(4), 567–582. https://doi.org/10.1080/09669582.2017.1361428

Qu, S. Q., & Dumay, J. (2011). The qualitative research interview. *Qualitative Research in Accounting & Management, 8*(3), 238–264. https://doi.org/10.1108/11766091111162070

Rasoolimanesh, S. M., Ramakrishna, S., Hall, C. M., Esfandiar, K., & Seyfi, S. (2020). A systematic scoping review of sustainable tourism indicators in relation to the sustainable development goals. *Journal of Sustainable Tourism*. https://doi.org/10.1080/09669582.2020.1775621

Rosato, P. F., Caputo, A., Valente, D., & Pizzi, S. (2021). 2030 Agenda and sustainable business models in tourism: A bibliometric analysis. *Ecological Indicators, 121*, 106978. https://doi.org/10.1016/j.ecolind.2020.106978

Schaltegger, S. (2018). Linking environmental management accounting: A reflection on (missing) links to sustainability and planetary boundaries. *Social and Environmental Accountability Journal, 38*(1), 19–29. https://doi.org/10.1080/0969160X.2017.1395351

Scheyvens, R., & Hughes, E. (2019). Can tourism help to "end poverty in all its forms everywhere"? The challenge of tourism addressing SDG1. *Journal of Sustainable Tourism, 27*(7), 1061–1079. https://doi.org/10.1080/09669582.2018.1551404

Scott, D., Hall, C. M., & Gössling, S. (2019). Global tourism vulnerability to climate change. *Annals of Tourism Research, 77*, 49–61. https://doi.org/10.1016/j.annals.2019.05.007

Serdane, Z. (2019). Slow philosophy in tourism development in Latvia: The supply side perspective. *Tourism Planning and Development*. https://doi.org/10.1080/21568316.2019.1650103

Shipway, R., King, K., Lee, I. S., & Brown, G. (2016). Understanding cycling tourism experiences at the Tour Down Under. *Journal of Sport and Tourism, 20*(1), 21–39. https://doi.org/10.1080/14775085.2016.1155473

Sriarkarin, S., & Lee, C. H. (2018). Integrating multiple attributes for sustainable development in a national park. *Tourism Management Perspectives, 28*, 113–125. https://doi.org/10.1016/j.tmp.2018.08.007

Tremblay, R., Landry-Cuerrier, M., & Humphries, M. M. (2020). Culture and the socialecology of local food use by Indigenous communities in Northern North America. *Ecology and Society, 25*(2). https://doi.org/10.5751/es-11542-250208

Tunn, V. S. C., Bocken, N. M. P., van den Hende, E. A., & Schoormans, J. P. L. (2019). Business models for sustainable consumption in the circular economy: An expert study. *Journal of Cleaner Production, 212*, 324–333. https://doi.org/10.1016/j.jclepro.2018.11.290

Unioncamere, & ISNART. (2019). *1° Rapporto Isnart-Legambiente Cicloturismo e cicloturisti in Italia 2019*. Roma: Unioncamere.

United Nations World Tourism Organization. (2017). Tourism and the sustainable development goals: Journey to 2030. In *Tourism and the sustainable development goals: Journey to 2030*. https://doi.org/10.18111/9789284419401

United Nations World Tourism Organization. (2018). *Sport tourism and Sustainable Development Goals (SDGs)*. Madrid: UNWTO.

Van Rheenen, D., Cernaianu, S., & Sobry, C. (2017). Defining sport tourism: A content analysis of an evolving epistemology. *Journal of Sport and Tourism, 21*(2), 75–93. https://doi.org/10.1080/14775085.2016.1229212

Vieira, R., O'Dwyer, B., & Schneider, R. (2017). Aligning strategy and performance management systems: The case of the wind-farm industry. *Organization and Environment*, *30*(1), 3–26. https://doi.org/10.1177/1086026615623058

Waligo, V. M., Clarke, J., & Hawkins, R. (2013). Implementing sustainable tourism: A multi-stakeholder involvement management framework. *Tourism Management*, *36*, 342–353. https://doi.org/10.1016/j.tourman.2012.10.008

Yang, X., Wang, Y., Hu, D., & Gao, Y. (2018). How industry peers improve your sustainable development? The role of listed firms in environmental strategies. *Business Strategy and the Environment*, *27*(8), 1313–1333. https://doi.org/10.1002/bse.2181

Yip, A. W. H., & Bocken, N. M. P. (2018). Sustainable business model archetypes for the banking industry. *Journal of Cleaner Production*, *174*, 150–169. https://doi.org/10.1016/j.jclepro.2017.10.190

14 Cannabis tourism

An emerging transformative tourism form

Yulin Liu and Adam Stronczak

Introduction

Transforming tourist needs and preferences along with destination competition generates the emergence of new forms of tourism with cannabis tourism being a recent addition. Cannabis tourism is a particular emerging type of tourism whereby visitors 'purchase with the intent to consume cannabis products while temporarily traveling away from one's normal place of work or residence' (Taylor, 2019, p. 443). Cannabis consumption in tourists is driven by various motivations (Wen et al., 2018) and influenced by the wider process of the normalisation of cannabis use in societies (Belhassen, Santos, & Uriely, 2007). While recreational use of cannabis is traditionally judged as a deviant behaviour in many societies (Uriely & Belhassen, 2005), cannabis tourism has recently been experiencing rapid growth as the legality of cannabis is being promoted in many jurisdictions across the globe.

Cannabis tourism is sensitive to destinations' legal environment. Governments of various states and countries increasingly realise the taxing potential and relative harmlessness of recreational cannabis use (Barclay, 2014), creating an environment potentially in favour of cannabis tourism growth. On the other hand, some governments tighten their laws for many different reasons, such as to prevent cannabis from becoming their tourist attraction. Taylor (2019)'s definition of cannabis tourism does not specify cannabis legality at destinations, thereby extending to grey areas where cannabis use or possession is depenalised. Previous cannabis tourism studies mostly focused on revealing tourists' motivations or reflecting on the regulation at a specific destination (e.g., Kang & McGrady, 2020; Wen et al., 2018). For such an emerging tourism form, there is a need for scanning current business practices in various legal environments across countries. This chapter aims to present an overview of cannabis tourism and legal environments around the world. Such an up-to-date global review can facilitate further research on the business development, policy arrangement, and legal regulation for cannabis tourism.

This chapter first introduces cannabis uses, explaining different applications of the plant, then classifies different legislative approaches, and finally describes cannabis tourism and legal environments in ten countries from five continents and regions before concluding remarks.

DOI: 10.4324/9781003105930-15

Cannabis uses and legality

Various uses and administration methods

Cannabis is commonly known by other names such as marihuana, ganja, hemp, pot, dope, weed, and many more. There are at least 1,200 terms to describe cannabis (Steinmetz, 2017). Cannabis psychoactive properties are the reason that it is mostly known as a recreational drug. As a depressant drug, cannabis slows down messages travelling between brain and body, whereas a large dose may produce hallucinogenic effects (Alcohol and Drug Foundation, 2020). The plant has the potential to cure a number of medical conditions and its potential remedial effects are being researched on the global scale (HealthDirect, 2019). Cannabis Campaigners Guide (n.d.) claims that there are estimated 50,000 commercial uses of cannabis in various industries.

Generally, medicinal cannabis is prescribed to relieve the symptoms of a medical condition, while recreational cannabis is used to get high (Alcohol and Drug Foundation, 2020). A recreational user can take cannabis for any form for pleasure including altered state of mind, happiness, and/or improved social interactions. There can be an overlap between motivations for recreational and medical uses of cannabis such as to aid sleep or manage anxiety (Whitmire et al., 2016). Furler et al. (2004) found that the overlap between medical and recreational cannabis consumption is substantial among patients infected with HIV.

There are countless ways that cannabis can be consumed. The most popular way is smoking, which has different variations (Varlet et al., 2016). Cannabis can also be consumed in the form of edibles like cakes, cookies, and candies. It can be added into commercial cooking oils or butter and used in all types of dishes (Widdicombe, 2017). Cannabis has also been brewed into teas for centuries, while nowadays cannabis-infused sodas, fruit juices, and coffees may be found in the market (Sebastien, 2017). Moreover, there are numerous transdermal solutions of administering cannabis through lotions, patches, and creams (Loflin & Earleywine, 2014). In tourism, cannabis is used for recreational and medical purposes in various forms and in different types of settings.

Legislative approaches to legality

There are different approaches taken by various governments of countries when it comes to the legality of cannabis depending on the distinction between medical and recreational cannabis. Some countries ban cannabis completely; others make medical cannabis legal while banning recreational one; and some countries make cannabis legal but heavily regulated. Different contradictory approaches to the legality of cannabis can be found within one single country, political entity, and/or governmental jurisdiction. This reflects the fact that opinions, law interpretations, and law enforcements, as well as the definition regarding recreational cannabis differ substantially.

Depenalisation is popular among many nations where cannabis use is illegal but no longer punished. Decriminalisation in this case refers to laws that reduce or eliminate penalties for sale, purchase, and possession of cannabis; however, the substance itself remains illegal. Spain was one of the first countries in Europe to decriminalise cannabis possession and cultivation for personal use (Gamella & Rodrigo, 2004). Czech Republic, Portugal, Italy, Argentina, Germany, United Kingdom, and Australia have also followed. The first country that comes to mind when one thinks of cannabis could be Jamaica because of its strong ties to the Rastafari religion. However, cannabis has been illegal in Jamaica since 1913 and it is only recently that it has been decriminalised (National Library of Jamaica, 2015). Coffeeshops in the Netherlands are probably the widest known example of tolerant cannabis legislation. Cannabis is an illicit soft drug for sale in the Netherlands (Korf, 2002). Nevertheless, selling maximum five grams of cannabis per person to adults over 18 in coffeeshops is not punishable; it is legal to smoke cannabis in a coffeeshop, but not tobacco, due to Dutch smoking ban (AmsterdamTourist.info, 2020).

Uruguay is the first country to make cannabis legal regardless of the purposes. In 2018, Canada became the second country worldwide to legalise cannabis. Currently, in the United States of America, 33 states and the District of Columbia allow medical usage and 11 states allow recreational usage; however, cannabis is still a Schedule 1 substance prohibited by federal law, which means that federal agents can seize products and arrest people trafficking in cannabis products even in states where it is legal (Hertzfeld, 2019). Illegalisation is at the other end of the spectrum. In many tourism destinations like Singapore, Turkey, Indonesia, and Japan, possession (regardless of purpose) of even trace amounts of cannabis can result in imprisonment and/or death penalty (Powell, 2018). The following section presents the legal status of cannabis in key destinations.

Cannabis tourism and legalities around the world

The Caribbean

Jamaica has been known as a tourism destination for cannabis enthusiasts for decades (Baloglu, Henthorne, & Sahin, 2014), due to cannabis being a big part of the Jamaican culture and the exotic location of the country. Jamaica was a pioneer in drug policy development. It passed what is known as a Ganja Law in 1913 which penalised possession of any part of cannabis, and the colonial government further increased penalties in 1925. Drug control in Jamaica was never about the population's health; it was always about controlling and policing dangerous population groups, and it often involved excruciated force and violence (Klein, 2016).

Even though it was illegal and heavily punished in the past, cannabis tourism always had a substantial economic impact in Jamaica. In 2015, the government finally decriminalised possession and cultivation of small amounts and legalised medical use of cannabis. Leaders in Jamaica begun to see great opportunities to develop the nation using this previously feared plant. Furthermore, they decided to leverage the Rasta population instead of prosecuting them. The economic opportunity of cannabis could potentially help Jamaica to overcome the problem of having one of the lowest rates of economic growth among developing nations (Koury, 2016).

The new laws allow the use of cannabis for spiritual and therapeutic purposes, and these are the specific terms used to support cannabis tourism (Prayag et al., 2015). It is possible to buy a permit to legally purchase and consume small amounts (Curated Caribbean, 2017). According to Forbes, 'Tourism Minister Edmund Bartlett said, the country hopes its medical marijuana scene will "attract new visitors" and ultimately boost the local economy' (Adams, 2018). For instance, one can visit a Kaya (www.growkaya.com) marijuana complex in Jamaica, which offers a wide variety of cannabis attractions. Kaya is the first medical cannabis brand from the Caribbean, focusing on health tourism.

Neighbours in the Caribbean are closely observing Jamaica's innovative approach to cannabis tourism. Recently, the Caribbean Tourism Organization (CTO) discussed the issue of cannabis tourism and acknowledged that while a lot of governmental authorities deny the existence of cannabis tourism, it is entirely up to destinations within the Caribbean to determine whether to use cannabis as a magnet to draw tourists in the best interest of the Caribbean people (The Caribbean Council, n.d.).

Europe

All EU Member States treat cannabis possession for recreational use as an offence. However, close to one-third of them define it as a minor offence, for which they do not allow imprisonment. In EU countries where imprisonment for such criminal act is allowed, national guidelines advise against it (EMCDDA, n.d.). This creates a lenient environment for recreational cannabis use and cannabis tourism in Europe. One such example is the Netherlands which is widely known as a destination for cannabis tourism.

Cannabis has been tolerated in the Netherlands since 1970s. The country is home to the oldest coffeeshops which is how the Dutch name bars or pubs where one can purchase and consume cannabis products. Even though cannabis is illegal in the Netherlands, it is openly sold in 573 coffeeshops operating in 103 of the 380 municipalities (EMCDDA, 2018). Expansion of coffeeshops started in 1976 when Opium Act was passed. The intention was to prevent cannabis users from being marginalised, stigmatised, and criminalised.

Operations of coffeeshops are tolerated, but owners have to obtain their product from the black-market because cultivation of the plant for sale is illegal and enforced. This is an example of a legal paradox and is known as 'Back Door Policy' (AmsterdamTourist.info, 2020). The Dutch government has recently taken steps to solve it. The first stage is to test how legalisation of cannabis cultivation can help with decreasing drug crime (EMCDDA, 2018).

Coffeeshops play an important role in Dutch tourism. Around 25–30% of tourists in Amsterdam spend time in coffeeshops; similar numbers can be found in Rotterdam (Haines, 2017). This brings about not only economic benefits but also overtourism problems. Coffeeshops operating along the country's border are not allowed to sell cannabis to tourists (Rizo, 2018). Hague bans cannabis use in the city centre, train stations, and major shopping areas (Bach, 2018). This is a result of locals being annoyed by constantly growing number of tourists (Gerritsma & Vork, 2017). A law was proposed in 2013 to allow Dutch residents only to coffeeshops, and this 'weed-pass' system is already in effect throughout Dutch cities except the most famous destination, Amsterdam (AmsterdamTourist.info, 2020).

Likewise, Denmark was considered for decades the liberal exception in Nordic drug policy. Some even called it 'the Netherlands of the north'. This is due to the practice of prescribing methadone by doctors to heroin users since early 1970s and Christiana, an area for open cannabis sale in Copenhagen (Stenius, 2013). Christiana was founded in the 1970s by a group of adventurous squatters and hippies on an old abandoned military base. They set up their own rules, laws, regulations, and abolished taxes. The selling and trading of cannabis are illegal but tolerated within its borders (D'Orazio, 2015).

However, things are changing since Denmark's biggest drug bust in 2015 where 83 were jailed for a total 220 years for taking part in an organised drug trade. According to the Danish police, more than two tons of cannabis were confiscated (Hurst, 2015). Furthermore, residents were forced to take radical action against cannabis trade after a shooting incidence on 31 August 2016 which left the gunman dead and three people injured (two police officers and one foreign tourist). After this incident, stalls where people could purchase cannabis on Pushers Street were torn down (Cathcart-Keays, 2016). Pusher Street is known as a 'green light district', a reference to the 'red light district' in Amsterdam with green representing the colour of cannabis.

Notwithstanding, a closer look at the reviews on TripAdvisor (n.d.) offers the idea that cannabis tourism is still thriving today. Reviews like 'the Christiana cannabis walks' and 'purchasing hash and edibles' can be easily found on the website. It indicates that cannabis is still one of the main pull factors of this popular tourist destination. Rachel Bale (2017), an Australian travel journalist, wrote that 'Free Christiana' is Copenhagen's most unexpected tourist destination.

Another country that legalised cannabis for medical purposes in 2013 is the Czech Republic. Unlike its neighbouring countries that are also associated with the former Eastern bloc, Czech Republic does not inherit a legacy of drug policy aiming at a drug-free society and in consequence harsh repressions of drug users (Csete, 2012). Czech drug policy is considered modern, pragmatic, rational but sometimes too liberal (Mravčík, 2015). Yet, the sale, distribution, possession, and cultivation of large quantities of cannabis are still against the law.

Even though the sale of recreational cannabis is considered to be a serious offence, with imprisonment time of one to five years, it is possible to find shops and bars in Prague that supply small amounts of cannabis under the table to their guests (Kavanagh, 2017). Due to the Million Marijuana March, which takes place every year since 1998 and attracts thousands of visitors, Prague has become known not only by recreational users but also by activists that support full legalisation of the plant (Filipková, 2015).

Retailers all over the country that provide souvenirs targeted for tourists take an advantage of the popular misconception of cannabis legality in Czech Republic. One finds a myriad of items that claim to have cannabis in them, such as cannabis-infused beer and cannabis cosmetics. All of those products use a legal strain which has very little psychoactive content, thus causing no psychoactive effects (Jenison, 2016).

Last, Spain has become associated with cannabis tourism. The cannabis culture in Spain has developed quite remarkably over the last 20 years as the decriminalisation for personal use has taken place. However, distribution, sale, and possession of large quantities remain illegal. In Barcelona, it is legal to possess and cultivate up to two plants per household. Consuming cannabis is considered a private and personal matter, hence to be conducted within the constraints of one's home. This legal loophole allows cannabis clubs to operate under the guise of private associations (Elwes, 2020).

A more commercial type of club which closely resembles coffeeshops in Amsterdam has recently appeared, especially in Barcelona. However, to use any of the clubs' services, one needs to be a registered member (Colson & Bergeron, 2017). One can find guidance and register for such clubs online (e.g., on Facebook, BarcelonaWeedGuide, n.d.) before visiting Spain (Cannabis Barcelona, n.d.). Not all of Barcelona's smoking clubs are equal; some are fancy and themed, while others are dodgy and poorly equipped (Hudson, 2014). The majority of the clubs grow their own cannabis, but some are known for obtaining it from street dealers, which is strictly against the law. All clubs are non-profit organisations and are taxed by the government.

Barcelona's art scene, unique architecture, and vibrant nightlife blend in with cannabis tourism, creating a truly unique experience for visitors. Nevertheless, this popular destination also deals with tourist overcrowding, and a sustainable solution is yet to be found (Nofre et al., 2018).

North America

The United States of America is pioneering the frontier of cannabis legalisation at the state level, which also causes confusion in some states (Governing, 2020). For example, Virginia passed laws a few decades ago allowing for the possession of cannabis if individuals received prescription from doctors. However, federal law does not allow doctors to prescribe cannabis, making those laws invalid. Physicians can only write a recommendation for medical cannabis, which is different from prescription. In other states, such as Louisiana, only non-smokable forms (e.g., oils, creams, etc.) of cannabis are legal.

The first recognisable and measurable sign of recreational cannabis' commercial potential on impacting the tourism industry happened on 20 April 2014, after recreational cannabis use was legalised in Colorado, with a travel booking site noting an almost 75% year-over-year increase in the number of searches for Denver. Oregon and Washington experienced similar search increases after cannabis was legalised there as well (Marijuana Doctors, 2017). Moreover, tourist interest in cities and states where it is legal to purchase and consume cannabis without a medical prescription has increased (Burke, 2016). A survey conducted by Strategic Marketing & Research Group at the request of the Tourism Office (Blevins, 2016) concluded that 23% of people who visited Colorado in 2015 said that the availability of cannabis positively influenced their decision to visit the state. In the age group from 25 to 34, these numbers went up to 33%. One can easily find cannabis-friendly accommodation providers online in those states. The industry is targeting locals as well as tourists with tours, shops, lodging, and advertisements (Brown, 2018; Miller, 2018; My 420 Tours, n.d.).

While it is quite evident that cannabis tourism exists in the United States, there are a variety of considerations when it comes to foreign visitors. There is a big discrepancy between federal and state laws. Therefore, if the foreign visitor engages in cannabis use, they might get deported by the federal authorities. This stands true even if the alleged person consumed cannabis legally according to the state law. If a 'green card' holder is found with a receipt from a dispensary, social media photos at the weed shop, or any other evidence indicating the immigrant used cannabis, the person could be deported (Schipp, 2018). This legal paradox presents an obstacle for international cannabis tourism development in the United States. 'The regulatory situation in USA is very complex with widely divergent state and local regulations, making it difficult or impossible to formulate uniform procedures and business approaches' (Butler, 2019, p. 28).

Likewise, Canada became in 2018 the second country worldwide (after Uruguay) to formally legalise the recreational use, possession, and cultivation of cannabis (Ross, 2018). One can find cannabis dispensaries or so-called compassion clubs in any major Canadian city. In Vancouver, there are more than 70 cannabis shops (Howell, 2018). The quality of these places varies greatly from empty rooms to modern and carefully designed spaces. Some require customers to provide medical documentation, but others are less strict (Keller, 2015). Many Canadians are welcoming cannabis consuming tourists by renting homes through a website budandbreakfast.com which is similar to Airbnb. In Vancouver, the 300 block of West Hastings Street is commonly known as the 'Pot Block'. It is home to The New Amsterdam Café as well as headquarters of Cannabis Culture magazine and Herb Museum where for a small fee one can smoke cannabis using their vaporisers (Odessa, 2018).

In Toronto, there is a HotBox Café (https://hotboxshop.ca/pages/events) which has been operating for more than 20 years. It is not possible to buy cannabis there, but people can use a vaporiser inside or can combust their cannabis on an outdoor patio (Ibrahim, 2017). Their website claims that they serve 500 unique customers daily. The company has an online shop with cannabis-related products like smoking accessories, cosmetics, growing kits, and much more. Canadian Kush Tours (http://kushtours.squarespace.com) is a cannabis tour provider based in Toronto. They offer a wide range of services like airport pick-up, limousine rental, dispensary tours, extract classes, cooking classes, growing class, and grow room tours, and can help with finding cannabis friendly accommodation. Exactly how the tourism and hospitality sector can be transformed by legal cannabis is still very uncertain for most hope to capitalise on the potential of providing cannabis-related services. President of Tourism Association of Canada said that there is a lack of clarity from federal, provincial, and municipal governments on what will and will not be allowed (Szklarski, 2018).

Other destinations

Uruguay is the first country to legalise cannabis entirely, allowing for consumption, possession, and cultivation in 2013. Only citizens and registered residents of the country can purchase the product. Tourists and visitors are not allowed to obtain cannabis legally. There are ways around the system as 'sharing' cannabis is not against the law. Multiple hospitality providers around the country are capitalising on cannabis. For example, in La Barra, the THC Hostel welcomes its patrons with a lobby decorated with cannabis merchandise, smoking devices, and real cannabis plants. Hostel Ejidonia has legal plants growing on their terraced roof, where many guests are attracted to freely consume cannabis (Reiss, 2018). Uruguayan home growers and clubs are getting around the ban by offering cannabis tours, which can be classified as social and educational experiences where sampling of the product on a paid tour is free (Hudak, Ramsey, & Walsh, 2018).

In Australia, medical cannabis became legal in 2016 at the Commonwealth level. In South Australia, Australian Capital Territory, and Northern Territory, possession of small amounts of cannabis for personal use is decriminalised where users face caution or civil penalty. The rest of the country deals with the consequences of cannabis use with diversion schemes and discretion of the police and courts (Bartle, 2018). It is difficult to find any substantial information and/or data regarding the existence of cannabis tourism in Australia as a whole; however, one town in New South Wales is an exemption to the rule. Nimbin makes the list as one of the top tourism destinations for cannabis lovers (Buultjens, Neale, & Lamont, 2013).

Nimbin is known as the country's most famous hippie destination and alternative lifestyle capital. It is also known as home to the annual Mardi Grass Festival and a hub for Australian cannabis culture. The town's main street has a Hemp Embassy which was established in 1992. Their website informs that they are drug reform advocates and do not sell any drugs, but the trade is quite adequately catered for on the street. Streets are usually full of visitors of all ages and places of origin like UK, Canada, and China. A quick look at TripAdvisor gives a transparent understanding that in Nimbin it is fairly easy to obtain potent cannabis (McHardy, 2014). There are varieties of shops that sell cannabis-related products and arts, among them a Hemp Bar where one can purchase cannabis infused smoothies and cookies. The bar was forced to shut its doors few times due to allegations of drugs being sold there (Atkins, 2008). There have been numerous amounts of crackdowns on Nimbin's illicit drug offenders. However, that does not stop Nimbin from being a popular destination for cannabis enthusiasts from all over the world.

Discussion

Cannabis tourism in a transforming world

Cannabis tourism as a non-institutionalised form of tourism (Belhassen, Santos, & Uriely, 2007) or marginal tourism (Uriely & Belhassen, 2005) is often overlooked for various reasons, such as social stigmas associated with recreational cannabis use. As the policies on legalising and regulating cannabis are gaining momentum on the global scale, the general public's view and overall awareness of this subject matter are transforming as well. There is a worldwide rapid shift from demonising cannabis to understanding and accepting it and using this plant for medical, industrial, and recreational purposes. This societal transformation has generated 'numerous business opportunities as well as legal and operational challenges for the hospitality and tourism industry' (Kang, O'Leary, & Miller, 2016, p. 1). Retail businesses, hospitality providers, DMOs, and governments are experiencing an increasing need for effective and sustainable management or regulation strategies for this rapidly emerging niche market.

Now, it is important more than ever to have a good understanding of how this special interest tourism segment operates under different legal circumstances. Kang, O'Leary, and Miller (2016) suggest that cannabis tourism can learn from the gambling tourism development in the 1980s–1990s, since these two leisure activities are often related to social vices and both industries have been legalised in many places to benefit the local economy. As the varieties of cannabis products flourish, people's interest in learning about their production processes may also grow, which could stimulate a market for educational tours similar to grape cultivation, wine making, and beer brewing (Keul & Eisenhauer, 2019).

It should, however, be noted that commercialisation may pose a threat to the healthy development of cannabis tourism. Commercialisation of cannabis in the United States of America, for example, is experiencing a situation where the psychoactive content tends to be overly emphasised in marketing. This mimics the alcohol industry and the 80–20 rule, where a business' 80% of profits are made from 20% of consumers (Cort, 2017). In other words, the profits are made on the addicted users. Jurisdictions developing cannabis tourism should learn from the early adopters in prescribing regulations in response to challenges by employing a 'harm-reduction' approach to minimising potential social, civic, and health harms, particularly to protect 'newborns (i.e., during pregnancy), children, and adolescents where choice is not "informed" and harms are clear' (Calonge, 2018, p. 790).

Cannabis tourism to transform the world

The growth of cannabis tourism around the world can have not only economic but also cultural impacts (Kang & McGrady, 2020). According to worldmaking theory (Hollinshead, 2009), tourism creates cultures and places through the dynamics in broader social contexts. This world transforming process does not 'occur in a "bubble" of tourism independent from an externalised society, but thoroughly shapes, and is shaped by, the lived cultural and political worlds where tourism takes place' (Keul & Eisenhauer, 2019, p. 142). Cannabis tourism provides opportunities for the application and advancement of tourism social science theories in its unfolding geographies. For instance, Belhassen and Jackson (2018) argue that cannabis tourism enclaves can be used as an experimental place to examine the destination's cannabis legalisation, which illustrates the role of tourism as an escalator of cannabis normalisation as observed in many countries. The vibrancy of emerging cannabis tourism presents 'an attractive opportunity for small producers who exercise a direct yet fragmented control over the cultural product' (Keul & Eisenhauer, 2019, p. 157).

Tourists' distance from their home societies allows them to ignore the power of norms and values that govern their daily lives (Turner & Ash, 1975, as cited in Belhassen, Santos, & Uriely (2007). Taylor (2019)'s definition of cannabis tourism stresses tourists' temporary condition of being away from home, which implies the incorporation of tourist home legal environment in cannabis tourism research. Such a holistic approach towards tourism and daily life resonates with Moore, Cushman, and Simmons's (1995) advocacy of studying tourist behaviours in the context of individuals' everyday lives, rather than in fragmented domains. Existing research mostly focusing on destinations has not paid much attention to this point.

From the marketing perspective, the market of cannabis tourists is heterogeneous; business and destination management need a good appreciation of this tourism form to successfully promote existing offerings or develop related products and services. International segmentation can assist in structuring the heterogeneity and identifying segments to target. A two-stage international segmentation (Steenkamp & Hofstede, 2002) can be performed, where markets are first grouped based on home-destination cannabis legal environments and then individuals are classified based on such as cannabis consumption motives.

Conclusion

Tourism promoters capitalise upon cannabis legality changes that reframe the discourses of deviance and economy (Keul & Eisenhauer, 2019). This chapter makes a first attempt to review this emerging tourism form in relation to destination legal environments. Cannabis tourism not only unpacks the rapidly transforming world within tourism sector but also contributes to the societal transformation of destinations. Destinations developing cannabis tourism should learn from the forerunners in seizing opportunities and addressing challenges.

This chapter relies on English-based literature, which poses limitations in the delineation of complex realities and the coverage of destinations in Asia and Africa. Future studies are encouraged to explore under-researched destinations, incorporate tourists' home cannabis legality, establish long-term projects to monitor natural experiments, and employ a multi-disciplinary approach with diverse paradigms and methods to research the political economy, legal geography, socio-cultural impacts, and tourist-host encounters in relation to cannabis tourism.

For such a controversial tourism form, practitioners and researchers must think beyond the box defined by conventional monetary and marketing parameters.

References

Adams, M. (2018, May 3). Toker travels: How to buy marijuana legally in Jamaica. *Forbes*. Retrieved from www.forbes.com/sites/mikeadams/2018/05/03/toker-travels-how-to-buy-marijuana-legally-in-jamaica/#6f9dc97538df

Alcohol and Drug Foundation. (2020, October 6). Cannabis. *Alcohol and Drug Foundation*. Retrieved from https://adf.org.au/drug-facts/cannabis/

AmsterdamTourist.info. (2020, March 19). Coffeeshops in Amsterdam. *AmsterdamTourist.info*. Retrieved from www.amsterdamtourist.info/things-to-do-in-amsterdam/amsterdam-coffeeshops

Atkins, J. (2008, October 22). Hemp bar closure was no drag. *ABC Local*. Retrieved from www.abc.net.au/local/videos/2008/09/02/2397939.htm

Bach, N. (2018, April 17). The Netherlands isn't as weed-friendly as it used to be. *Fortune*. Retrieved from http://fortune.com/2018/04/17/netherlands-weed-the-hague-cannabis-ban

Bale, R. (2017, January 20). 'Free Christiania' is Copenhagen's most unexpected tourist destination. *Nine*. Retrieved from https://travel.nine.com.au/2017/01/20/13/26/christiana-copenhagen-what-to-do-how-to-get-there

Baloglu, S., Henthorne, T. L., & Sahin, S. (2014). Destination image and brand personality of Jamaica: A model of tourist behavior. *Journal of Travel & Tourism Marketing*, *31*(8), 1057–1070. DOI:10.1080/10548408.2014.892468

BarcelonaWeedGuide. (n.d.). Buying weed as a tourist in Barcelona. *BarcelonaWeedGuide*. Retrieved from https://barcelonaweedguide.com/buying-weed-tourist-barcelona

Barclay, C. (2014, April 11). Top 10 marijuana tourist destinations worldwide. *The Richest*. Retrieved from www.therichest.com/rich-list/the-biggest/top-10-marijuana-tourist-destinations-worldwide

Bartle, J. (2018, July 5). Most Australians support decriminalising cannabis, but our laws lag behind. *The Conversation*. Retrieved from https://theconversation.com/most-australians-support-decriminalising-cannabis-but-our-laws-lag-behind-99285

Belhassen, Y., & Jackson, A. (2018). The case for a regulatory cannabis enclave in the resort city of Eilat. *International Journal of Mental Health & Addiction*, *16*(4), 828–831. DOI:10.1007/s11469-018-9910-z

Belhassen, Y., Santos, C. A., & Uriely, N. (2007). Cannabis usage in tourism: A sociological perspective. *Leisure Studies*, *26*(3), 303–319. DOI:10.1080/02614360600834958

Blevins, J. (2016, July 20). Only 4% of Colorado tourists came for the legal weed in 2015, survey says. *The Denver Post*. Retrieved from www.denverpost.com/2016/07/20/colorado-tourism-legal-marijuana-2015

Brown, A. (2018, April 28). Recreational marijuana in Washington state. *TripSavvy*. Retrieved from www.tripsavvy.com/guide-to-recreational-marijuana-in-washington-1609146

Burke, K. (2016, April 23). Marijuana tourism is a budding industry. *MarketWatch*. Retrieved from www.marketwatch.com/story/marijuana-tourism-is-a-budding-industry-2015-08-25

Butler, J. (2019, November 4). Why are so many hoteliers talking about cannabis hotels? *Hotel Management*. Retrieved from www.hotelmanagement.net/legal/why-are-so-many-hoteliers-talking-about-cannabis-hotels

Buultjens, J., Neale, K., & Lamont, M. (2013). Hosts, guests and a drug culture in a destination: A case study of Nimbin, Australia. *Journal of Destination Marketing & Management*, *2*(3), 185–195. DOI:10.1016/j.jdmm.2013.08.003

Calonge, N. (2018). Policy pitfalls and challenges in cannabis regulation: Lessons from Colorado. *International Journal of Mental Health Addiction*, *16*, 783–790. DOI:10.1007/s11469-018-9923-7

Cannabis Barcelona. (n.d.). *The best cannabis clubs*. Retrieved from http://cannabisbarcelona.com

Cannabis Campaigners Guide. (n.d.). *Cannabis used for medicine, food, fuel, paper, rope, maps, bricks, oil, paint, furniture and much more*. Retrieved from www.ccguide.org/uses.php

The Caribbean Council. (n.d.). *Ganja and the tourism industry*. Retrieved from www.caribbean-council.org/ganja-tourism-industry/

Cathcart-Keays, A. (2016, September 23). Paradise lost: Does Copenhagen's Christiania commune still have a future? *The Guardian*. Retrieved from www.theguardian.com/cities/2016/sep/23/copenhagen-christiania-drugs-commune-future

Colson, R., & Bergeron, H. (2017). *European drug policies: The ways of reform*. London, England: Routledge.

Cort, B. (2017, November). *What commercialization is doing to cannabis? [Video file]*. Retrieved from www.ted.com/talks/ben_cort_surprising_truths_about_legalizing_cannabis?language=en

Csete, J. (2012, February). A balancing act: Policymaking on illicit drugs in the Czech Republic. *Open Society Foundations*. Retrieved from www.opensociety foundations.org/reports/balancing-act-policymaking-illicit-drugs-czech-republic

Curated Caribbean. (2017). *Marijuana tourism in Jamaica: A guide for visitors*. Retrieved from http://curatedcaribbean.com/marijuana-tourism-jamaica-guide-visitors

D'Orazio, J. (2015, October 14). "A social experiment": The place where people make their own rules. *News*. Retrieved from www.news.com.au/travel/travel-ideas/adventure/a-social-experiment-the-place-where-people-make-their-own-rules/news-story/d20ba1a50a38884e1c9520b3a1be2989

Elwes, E. (2020, October 23). Is marijuana legal in Barcelona? *ShBarcelona*. Retrieved from www.shbarcelona.com/blog/en/marijuana

EMCDDA. (n.d.). Cannabis policy: Status and recent developments. *European Monitoring Centre for Drugs and Drug Addiction (EMCDDA)*. Retrieved from www.emcdda.europa.eu/publications/topic-overviews/cannabis-policy/html_en

EMCDDA. (2018, March 23). Dutch ministers outline 4-year trial to supply cannabis to coffeeshops. *European Monitoring Centre for Drugs and Drugs Addiction (EMCDDA)*. Retrieved from www.emcdda.europa.eu/news/2018/dutch-ministers-trial-supply-cannabis-coffeeshops_en

Filipková, T. (2015, September 28). Cannabis policy in the Czech Republic. *TNI*. Retrieved from www.tni.org/en/article/cannabis-policy-in-the-czech-republic#sdfootnote2sym

Furler, M. D., Einarson, T. R., Millson, M., & Walmsley, S. (2004). Medicinal and recreational marijuana use by patients infected with HIV. *AIDS Patient Care and STDs*, *18*(4), 215–228. DOI:10.1089/108729104323038892

Gamella, J. F., & Rodrigo, M. J. (2004). A brief history of cannabis policies in Spain (1968–2003). *Journal of Drug Issues*, *34*(3), 623–659. DOI:10.1177/002204260403400308

Gerritsma, R., & Vork, J. (2017). Amsterdam residents and their attitude towards tourists and tourism. *Coactivity: Philosophy, Communication*, *25*, 85–98. DOI:10.3846/cpc.2017.274

Governing. (2020). *State marijuana laws: U.S. map*. Retrieved from www.governing.com/gov-data/state-marijuana-laws-map-medical-recreational.html
Haines, G. (2017, February 21). Everything you need to know about marijuana smoking in the Netherlands. *The Telegraph*. Retrieved from www.telegraph.co.uk/travel/destinations/europe/netherlands/amsterdam/articles/everything-you-need-to-know-about-smoking-marijuana-in-the-netherlands
HealthDirect. (2019, December). Medicinal cannabis. *HealthDirect*. Retrieved from www.healthdirect.gov.au/medicinal-cannabis
Hertzfeld, E. (2019, October 28). Hoteliers high on cannabis-based hospitality possibilities. *Hotel Management*. Retrieved from www.hotelmanagement.net/operate/hoteliers-dip-toes-into-cannabis-based-hospitality
Hollinshead, K. (2009). The "Worldmaking" prodigy of tourism: The reach and power of tourism in the dynamics of change and transformation. *Tourism Analysis*, *14*(1), 139–152. DOI:10.3727/108354209788970162
Howell, M. (2018, February 7). More than 70 marijuana shops in Vancouver continue to blaze without business licences. *Vancouver News*. Retrieved from www.vancourier.com/news/more-than-70-marijuana-shops-in-vancouver-continue-to-blaze-without-business-licences-1.23167686
Hudak, J., Ramsey, G., & Walsh, J. (2018). *Uruguay's cannabis law: Pioneering a new paradigm*. Retrieved from www.brookings.edu/wpcontent/uploads/2018/03/gs_032118_uruguaye28099s-cannabis-law_final.pdf
Hudson, R. (2014, September 18). 10 things you need to know about Barcelona cannabis clubs. *Marijuana Games*. Retrieved from https://marijuanagames.org/10-things-you-need-to-know-about-barcelona-cannabis-clubs
Hurst, L. (2015, March 27). 83 jailed in Denmark's biggest ever drugs bust. *Newsweek*. Retrieved from www.newsweek.com/83-jailed-denmarks-biggest-ever-drugs-bust-317325
Ibrahim, S. (2017, September 17). Toronto cannabis lounges, in operation for 18 years, to ask for the right to exist legally. *CBC*. Retrieved from www.cbc.ca/news/canada/toronto/cannabis-lounges-asks-for-licensing-1.4293733
Jenison, D. (2016). Meet the man making cocaine and cannabis spirits. *PROHBTD*. Retrieved from https://prohbtd.com/meet-man-making-cocaine-and-cannabis-spirits
Kang, S. K., & McGrady, P. (2020). Support for cannabis tourism: A tale of two states. *Tourism Review International*, *24*, 233–250. DOI:10.3727/154427220X15990732245691
Kang, S. K., O'Leary, J., & Miller, J. (2016). From forbidden fruit to the goose that lays golden eggs: Marijuana tourism in Colorado. *SAGE Open*, *6*(4), 1–12. DOI:10.1177/2158244016679213
Kavanagh, R. J. (2017, November 22). At a glimpse: Cannabis in the Czech Republic. *CannabizDaily*. Retrieved from http://cannabizdaily.co/blog/glance-cannabis-czech-republic
Keller, J. (2015, June 10). Pot shops: Everything you need to know about marijuana dispensaries. *The Globe and Mail*. Retrieved from www.theglobeandmail.com/news/british-columbia/vancouvers-pot-shops-everything-you-need-to-know-about-marijuana-dispensaries/article24880914
Keul, A., & Eisenhauer, B. (2019). Making the high country: Cannabis tourism in Colorado USA. *Annals of Leisure Research*, *22*(2), 140–160. DOI:10.1080/11745398.2018.1435291
Klein, A. (2016). *Ganja in the English-speaking Caribbean: From security threat to development opportunity*. Retrieved from www.swansea.ac.uk/media/Ganja-in-the-English-speaking-Caribbean-From-Security-Threat-to-Development-Opportunity.pdf
Korf, D. J. (2002). Dutch coffee shops and trends in cannabis use. *Addictive Behaviors*, *27*(6), 851–866. DOI:10.1016/S0306-4603(02)00291-5

Koury, S. (2016). Jamaica readies for economic benefit from marijuana. *Jamaicans*. Retrieved from https://jamaicans.com/jamaica-readies-economic-benefit-marijuana

Loflin, M., & Earleywine, M. (2014). A new method of cannabis ingestion: The dangers of dabs? *Addictive Behaviors*, *39*(10), 1430–1433. DOI:10.1016/j.addbeh.2014.05.013

Marijuana Doctors. (2017, February 21). *An in-depth look at cannabis tourism*. Retrieved from www.marijuanadoctors.com/blog/cannabis-tourism/

McHardy, M. (2014, October 7). This is Nimbin: Inside the "refugee camp for the war on drugs". *SBS News*. Retrieved from www.sbs.com.au/news/this-is-nimbin-inside-the-refugee-camp-for-the-war-on-drugs

Miller, M. (2018, May 21). Los Angeles for tourists: Hollywood, beaches: And pot? *The Denver Post*. Retrieved from www.denverpost.com/2018/05/21/los-angeles-tourism-marijuana

Moore, K., Cushman, G., & Simmons, D. (1995). Behavioral conceptualization of tourism and leisure. *Annals of Tourism Research*, *22*(1), 67–85. DOI:10.1016/0160-7383(94)00029-R

Mravčík, V. (2015). (De)criminalisation of possession of drugs for personal use: A view from the Czech Republic. *International Journal of Drug Policy*, *26*(7), 705–707. DOI:10.1016/j.drugpo.2015.01.022

My 420 Tours. (n.d.). *North America's original cultivator of cannabis experiences*. Retrieved from https://my420tours.com/about-my-420-tours

National Library of Jamaica. (2015). *Ganja: A select bibliography of resources at the National Library of Jamaica*. Retrieved from http://nlj.gov.jm/wp-content/uploads/2016/11/Ganja20Bibliography.pdf

Nofre, J., Giordano, E., Eldridge, A., Martins, J. C., & Sequera, J. (2018). Tourism, nightlife and planning: Challenges and opportunities for community liveability in La Barceloneta. *Tourism Geographies*, *20*(3), 397–417. DOI:10.1080/14616688.2017.1375972

Odessa. (2018). A Canadian guide to cannabis tourism. *PROHBTD*. Retrieved from https://prohbtd.com/a-canadian-guide-to-cannabis-tourism

Powell, B. (2018, February 24). The 7 countries with the strictest weed laws. *High Times*. Retrieved from https://hightimes.com/guides/countries-strictest-weed-laws/7

Prayag, G., Mura, P., Hall, M., & Fontaine, J. (2015). Drug or spirituality seekers? Consuming ayahuasca. *Annals of Tourism Research*, *52*, 175–177. DOI:10.1016/j.annals.2015.03.008

Reiss, A. (2018, January 8). Uruguay government mulling over cannabis tourism. *Green-Dorphin*. Retrieved from https://greendorphin.com/cannabis-tours-in-uruguay

Rizo, C. (2018, April 20). Cannabis laws are about to change in the Netherlands. *Travel and Leisure*. Retrieved from www.travelandleisure.com/travel-news/netherlands-getting-more-strict-about-smoking-pot-in-public

Ross, S. (2018, June 6). All eyes on Canada as first G7 nation prepares to make marijuana legal. *The Guardian*. Retrieved from www.theguardian.com/world/2018/jun/06/all-eyes-on-canada-as-first-g7-nation-prepares-to-make-marijuana-legal

Schipp, D. (2018, January 18). Cannabis is legal in California but for non-citizens, there's a catch. *News*. Retrieved from www.news.com.au/travel/travel-advice/cannabis-is-legal-in-california-but-for-noncitizens-theres-a-catch/news-story/eeb1e772739d8795d6d71a9768201f42

Sebastien, M. (2017, May 10). Top 15 ways to consume marijuana: Which one have you tried? *Alpha-Cat*. Retrieved from www.alpha-cat.org/top-15-ways-consume-marijuana

Steenkamp, J.-B. E. M., & Hofstede, F. T. (2002). International market segmentation: Issues and perspectives. *International Journal of Research in Marketing*, *19*(3), 185–213. DOI:10.1016/S0167-8116(02)00076-9

Steinmetz, K. (2017). 420 day: Why there are so many different names for weed. *Time*. Retrieved from http://time.com/4747501/420-day-weed-marijuana-pot-slang

Stenius, K. (2013). Commentary on Vibeke Asmussen Frank, Bagga Bjerge, and Esben Houborg: Medicalization can be beneficial, but is no guarantee for user influence. *Substance Use & Misuse, 48*(11), 1069–1070. DOI:10.3109/10826084.2013.808527

Szklarski, C. (2018, August 14). Uncertainty looms over Canada's cannabis tourism. *CTV News*. Retrieved from www.ctvnews.ca/business/uncertainty-looms-over-canadas-cannabis-tourism-1.4052683

Taylor, L. L. (2019). Defining marijuana tourism. *Journal of Hospitality & Tourism Research, 43*(3), 438–446. DOI:10.1177/1096348018804610

TripAdvisor. (n.d.). Christiania. *TripAdvisor*. Retrieved from www.tripadvisor.com.au/ShowUserReviews-g189541-d259687-r612364848-ChristianiaCopenhagen_Zealand.html

Turner, L., & Ash, J. (1975). *The golden hordes: International tourism and the pleasure periphery*. London, UK: Constable.

Uriely, N., & Belhassen, Y. (2005). Drugs and tourists' experiences. *Journal of Travel Research, 43*(3), 238–246. DOI:10.1177/0047287504272024

Varlet, V., Concha-Lozano, N., Berthet, A., Plateel, G., Favart, B., De Cesare, M., . . . Giroud, C. (2016). Drug vaping applied to cannabis: Is "cannavaping" a therapeutic alternative to marijuana? *Scientific Reports, 6*, Article 25599. DOI:10.1038/srep25599

Wen, J., Meng, F., Ying, T., Qi, H., & Lockyer, T. (2018). Drug tourism motivation of Chinese outbound tourists: Scale development and validation. *Tourism Management, 64*, 233–244. DOI:10.1016/j.tourman.2017.08.001

Whitmire, M., Belz, M., Cacioppo, L., Iorio, P., & Peters, T. (2016). *Recreational marijuana insights and opportunities*. Retrieved from www2.deloitte.com/content/dam/Deloitte/ca/Documents/Analytics/ca-en-analytics-DELOITTE%20Recreational%20Marijuana%20POV%20-%20ENGLISH%20FINAL_AODA.pdf

Widdicombe, L. (2017, April 24). The Martha Stewart of marijuana edibles. *The New Yorker*. Retrieved from www.newyorker.com/magazine/2017/04/24/the-martha-stewart-of-marijuana-edibles

15 The Tourism Lab

A place for change, participation, and future destination development

Daniel Zacher, Hannes Thees, and Valentin Herbold

Introduction

Imagine a city in which a robust economic development has taken place in recent decades. Our case study, *Eichstätt, Germany*, can be regarded as such a city, as it is characterised by comparatively low unemployment and high social security. Eichstätt also has a high attraction potential due to its architectural substance and the fact that it is embedded in an attractive natural environment. In cities like that, big portions of the population benefit significantly from the economic situation but feel a certain satisfaction and saturation that prevents them from thinking of alternative development scenarios.

Meanwhile, the public space in Eichstätt has to struggle with vacancies in the retail sector. The baroque squares seem to be abandoned, and the gastronomy is limited to a few established restaurants. These challenges are accompanied by a subjective withdrawal of the citizens into private spaces, which results in limited leisure and tourism dynamics in the city. Such situations reduce the places for encounters, which are necessary for the formulation, testing, and implementation of urban development on a community level (Karaçor, 2016). The urban community have discussed the described apathy of big portions of the population in terms of public engagement for some years. However, it is mainly the local politics that is made responsible for such unfavourable development.

From a meta-perspective, this complicated status quo has been formulated by different stakeholders in Eichstätt. They use the example of tourism and the missing discussion on its future development to call for participation-based development. As a result of these discussions, the City Council and the local university established the Tourism Lab as a joint initiative. The Eichstätt Tourism Lab was a temporary committee in 2019, which aimed to discuss the previously mentioned challenges in a comprehensive development process.

This chapter analyses the processes carried out by the Eichstätt Tourism Lab and asks the following research question:

> With its dynamic and participative approach, how can the Tourism Lab launch an integrative understanding in changing destination environment?

DOI: 10.4324/9781003105930-16

From a theoretical perspective, destination change can be understood as a process of different interactions within a multi-level system, which is often depicted in a simplified way in models (Haugland et al., 2011). Linear development models, such as the Tourism Area Life Cycle by Butler (1980), have received great attention but have also provoked criticism (Hovinen, 2002). Nordin et al. (2019) identified three modes of change when differentiating between prescribed, emergent, non-linear, and constructive approaches. This distinction of change concepts illustrates the multi-layered complexity of destination systems. However, *'the literature on destination evolution has paid little attention to how structure and institutions interact dynamically'* (McLennan et al., 2012, p. 179). Meanwhile, a holistic conceptualisation of the processes, structures, and actors involved in destination change is rare. Peculiarly, overcoming sector-specific thinking is a key to the contemporary development of a city or region, which is often not explicitly defined (De Lucia et al., 2020; Rastegar, 2019). In combination with different sectors' perspectives, it is crucial to structure and process stakeholder management (Calzada, 2019).

This chapter addresses a research gap in the literature on cross-stakeholder participation as an answer to transforming factors and the need for a methodological foundation. Thus, we pay attention to the local population, which is usually not directly involved as a tourism stakeholder. Systemic destination models frequently mention locals but hardly ever in terms of their direct participation in forward-thinking change. The authors of this chapter answer the particular need to professionalise methods for participation, as identified by Dupre (2019). This process analysis is intended to discuss the structural adaptability of a destination system related to transforming factors (e.g., smart technology or overtourism) and normative sustainability goals.

Against the background of the gaps mentioned earlier, we approach the research questions through the interlinking of the city and destination (section 'Framing change in the destination environment'), before describing the respective processes of the Tourism Lab in the case of Eichstätt (section 'Exploring new perspectives at the Eichstätt Tourism Lab').

Framing change in the destination environment

A shift in the understanding of local space drives changes in the destination environment. Various stakeholder demands define a city or place as an economic location, as a living space, and as a destination, in which the boundaries of the reference systems are increasingly blurred. The resulting opportunities and requirements for cross-stakeholder participation can be identified and concretised in the form of innovative social methods, such as the Living Lab.

Towards a contemporary understanding of local space

Futurologist and realists frequently negotiate global changes in the shape of megatrends. The current megatrends are the 'technological breakthrough' towards 'shifting economic power', 'climate change and resource scarcity', 'demographics and social change', and 'rapid urbanization' (PwC, 2020). These trends have caused new requirements for tourism, such as seamless and data-supported experience, diverging target groups, and the anticipation of travel motivations or the mitigation of and adaption to climate change (Boschetto Doorly, 2020). Given these examples, the combination of fluidity and seamlessness meets the importance of the local place, as a space for living, working, and leisure activities. In line with these trends and the current COVID-19 crises, tourism destinations are now at a turning point, requiring a rethinking of places in terms of their functions for various stakeholders, including, but not exclusively, tourists and citizens.

These considerations call for an integrated perspective regarding the living environment and the tourist destination. Different fields of interest might be added, such as the economic location and the local environmental ecosystem. A region entails various stakeholders with specific interests, competencies, and roles, which increasingly blur the frontiers between sectors and traditional living concepts (Erina, Shatrevich, & Gaile-Sarkane, 2017). Considering a local space or a region as a container for various activities leads to the question of how to shape the local space's future according to the various stakeholders' needs and activities.

To answer such a question theoretically requires new perspectives, but on a practical level, it also supports the solving of disputes concerning the transformation of sectors. In the case of tourism, which witnesses a high degree of local interlinking, several established organisational approaches have accompanied past changes. They can now help to find new pathways for destination/ place development: The traditional *DMOs* have evolved from mere network organisations over marketing organisations towards regional competence centres. Similarly, the tasks have changed from providing space for cooperation, support in infrastructure, and marketing towards knowledge-intensive mentoring and sustainability management (Pechlaner, Kozak, & Volgger, 2014; Saarinen & Gill, 2019). Besides, *competitiveness* has long been central to the formulation of strategic plans for gaining competitive advantages (Ritchie & Crouch, 2005). This has often been led by *innovation-* (Hjalager, 2010) or growth-related discussions, which have taken on a qualitative dimension. Tourists' *experience* and locals' well-being are now factors that must be considered in connection to tourism (Rahmani, Gnoth, & Mather, 2018). Thus, the design of living environments and community *participation* have gained importance (Jordan et al., 2013).

Similarly, mere customer-centrism is less relevant than locals' needs, since overtourism has accentuated a socio-cultural carrying capacity (Eckert et al., 2019). With these developments, tourism management is becoming more complex: *Motivations* and target groups have become increasingly heterogeneous (Sun et al., 2020). New requirements are also imposed due to digitalisation, the platform-economy, and environmental degradation (Hossain & Lassen, 2017). *Sustainable tourism* illustrates a normative framework for tackling these challenges, but it is still challenged by the implementation and the attitude–behaviour gap (Juvan & Dolnicar, 2014). In this field of tension, tourism has to account for its global contribution to environmental pollution, but it also has a significant impact on a local scale.

The Tourism Lab 219

The mentioned characteristics and conceptual approaches have influenced destination management greatly but are open to the addition of components that reveal a locally bound understanding of space, such as:

- City and destination development as integrated playgrounds for increasing the quality of life/ experience
- Equality of stakeholders and their active involvement
- Joint responsibility to shape the diverse requirements pertaining to sustainable development
- Cross-sectoral exchange for the efficient use of resources
- Increased value of internal communication and trust in the network
- Questioning and breaking with established processes and frequent change management
- Innovative and creative atmosphere, along with space for entrepreneurial opportunities
- Data and data possessing on digital platforms as a prerequisite for the use of capacities and monitoring of measures and goals

In this vein, here, we implement the understanding of a local space, as a collective and dynamic ecosystem serving the stakeholders' needs and delivering a high adaptability to trends and crises. Therefore, alternative approaches are shown in Figure 15.1 to stress the integrated perspective on a local space and the necessity for flexibility in increasingly dynamic markets.

Unleashing cross-stakeholder participation

A necessary competence in the future might be to adapt to changes from all kinds of environments and proactively shape the future of tourism by raising new questions and concepts. How to break with such patterns? There are three concepts that we would like to focus on here: (1) external shocks; (2) strategic change management; and (3) individuals.

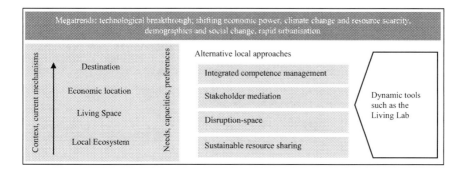

Figure 15.1 Framing the local space in line with alternative development approaches

1   External shocks, such as the COVID-19 crises, entail a transformational element, which forces us to rethink established patterns of running businesses and travelling (Gössling, Scott, D., & Hall, 2020). Beyond the short-term impact of shocks, a long-term transformation may occur as crises expose problematic social practices and catalyse change. In the case of COVID-19, the crises may considerably change the individuals' travel behaviour and aid in catalysing a critical reflection on the role of travel (Galvani, Lew, & Perez, 2020). Changing travel patterns is an important way to achieve a transformation towards sustainability. Taking the supply-side perspective, touristic service providers have previously undergone crises. For example, they have suffered losses due to environmental catastrophes, which have partially forced them to rebuild their infrastructure. When such a destruction occurs, it is the occasion to restart businesses in a modern or adapted way (Laws, 2012).

2   The structured organisation of a change process is often seen as a strategic task of management personnel, whereby barriers inhibiting change should be removed and transition actively managed (Todnem By, 2005). In economics, the term, change management, has been established for this task. It can be described as a '*process of continually renewing an organisation's direction, structure, and capabilities to serve the ever-changing needs of external and internal customers*' (Moran & Brightman, 2001, p. 111). Change management has been discussed in connection with changes in tourism organisations (Beritelli & Reinhold, 2010) or as an effective regional policy element to actively manage changes at the network level (Gretzinger et al., 2019).

3   Individuals have the power to shape local development through creativity, leadership, and engagement. For example, new leaders or innovators frequently provide alternative services and products for recent problems (Gundry et al., 2011). Beyond such outstanding people, individual engagement opens space for collaboration in various activities. The importance of including all local stakeholders in bottom-up processes pertaining to destination management has been highlighted in the past. By recognising the various destination models (Flagestad & Hope, 2001), the number and degree of stakeholders' participation vary. Nevertheless, these participatory initiatives may be limited to the local service providers, rather than the local community, with its great variety. Against this background, a recent local development – in either cities or destinations – requires the openness of the current administrative approaches to change. It is essential to recognise that participation is a two-sided process that requires all stakeholders to be active and take responsibility for joint projects.

Implementing the living lab as a dynamic tool

Dynamic tools in destination development should question established patterns and take on new perspectives. Based on the previously elaborated components of the local space's recent development, a central concern is to overcome the barriers between stakeholders. The scientific study of tourism applies, for example, the ladder of participation, ranging from non-participation, through informative participation, to legitimate participation (Kantsperger, Thees, & Eckert, 2019). There are several well-established tools for collaboration in cities and destinations, for example, public forums, workshops, committees, and round tables (Moscardo, 2011). Lately, digital tools, such as crowd-sourcing of ideas, virtual market places, and online project management, have expanded collaboration tools (Egger, Gula, & Walcher, 2016). Rivalry, free-riding, and creating a dynamic atmosphere are challenges associated with both digital and analogue forms of meetings (Pechlaner & Volgger, 2012).

A dynamic alternative for facing these challenges is the living lab. Practitioners have applied living labs, for example, in local mobility, architecture, and green development, as well as in tourism (Calzada, 2019; Guimont & Lapointe, 2016). Definitions of living labs usually include managing synergies, supporting cooperation and communication, sharing resources between stakeholders, and methodological concerns, like the participatory design, testing, and evaluation of innovation- or user-centrism. A living lab's output can be diverse and ranges from a guided exchange, through prototyping, to innovation. In this line, Thees et al. (2020) derived the following definition:

> *Living Labs are cooperative environments that follow a user-driven and cross-stakeholder approach in order to provide a shared space for experiments and tests of innovative products and services in a real-life environment. Living Labs offer digital infrastructure and can be perceived as a research approach, which includes design elements to support collaborative innovation processes.*
>
> (p. 13)

As the application of living labs in the tourism context remains rare, it is essential to address some central opportunities. First, the flexibility of living labs allows for mixed methods to meet the aims of a respective session or set of specific incentives. Second, the idea of the living lab focuses on the process rather than the final output. Therefore, it offers a space for the creative definition of objectives and ideas or trial and error. Third, it aims to create community participation in very diverse settings. Thus, it is a strength to integrate various regional levels and stakeholders beyond the administrative borders.

Exploring new perspectives at the 'Eichstätt Tourism Lab'

The Eichstätt Tourism Lab aims to explore new perspectives by combining various methods in a living lab approach to implement the previously elaborated requirements for destination development in a concrete project. Given the ongoing exchange between the Chair of Tourism at the Catholic University of Eichstätt-Ingolstadt and local actors in Eichstätt, it became apparent that the city has a high potential for tourism development. A temporary committee, the 'Eichstätter Tourismuskonvent' (Eichstätt Tourism Lab), was established to initiate the

222 *Daniel Zacher et al.*

destination's future through a collaborative approach within a series of workshops from May to July 2019. The participants of the Tourism Lab stated the aims of the Tourism Lab as follows:

- With the Tourism Lab, we can network, bring people together, develop ideas, and think outside the box.
- With the Tourism Lab, we can motivate and awaken stakeholders.
- With the Tourism Lab, we can influence dynamic urban development.

Overall, the objective of the Eichstätt Tourism Lab was to discuss the aforementioned benefits and potentials in a comprehensive process together with various actors of public life in Eichstätt. Table 15.1 provides an overview of the Tourism Lab, including its procedure and agenda. The Tourism Lab has been implemented using scientific standards, with alternating phases of data preparation and collection, documentation, and analysis. The preparation of interim results was used to explicate the previous work of the Tourism Lab and provided the opportunity to interpret the advances made since then. Besides, moderation and participant support took place throughout the process.

The first column of Table 15.1 illustrates the ten steps of action of the Tourism Lab (column S). As the first step of the Tourism Lab, the involved university researchers interviewed selected local personalities in an initial series of talks, which was also the starting point for defining a fixed working group. Attention was paid to the representation of different interest groups that are typical for the city. Thus, the organisers invited representatives of the church, politics, university, businesses, citizens, and students to participate in the Tourism Lab. The limitation of the circle of participants to a fixed defined group enabled the work to be conducted efficiently. Simultaneously, the deliberate opening of the process to the public allowed for awareness and participation. After a systematic analysis of the initial interviews, the results were presented to the City Council, showing the manifold potential for further developing tourism in Eichstätt. Based on these discussions, it became clear that sustainable tourism and local space development rely not only on tourism service providers and officials but also on the citizens.

The workshop dates and the subsequent steps illustrate the intention to provide a space for open and creative cooperation (column I). In this line, the open discourse phases and the adoption of alternative perspectives were alternated with presentations of interim results to concretise what the working group had achieved so far. This also promoted the sharing of information and the inspiration and participation of other stakeholder groups that have not yet been reached.

The guiding questions (column Q) helped to focus on particular aspects of the joint work. Each workshop included retrospective and, with the increasing progress of the lab, more prospective perspectives. In the same way, the questions raised became more specific and thus served the purpose of triggering a focus on action and action-oriented results.

A methodological toolbox (column M) enriched the Tourism Lab. Interactive workshop methods, with a high degree of participation on the part of the

The Tourism Lab 223

Table 15.1 Overview of the Tourism Lab from an organisers' perspective

S – Structure	I – Intention	Q – Leading Questions	T – Topics	M – Methods Used
1. Initial interview series	Stimulation of target-oriented discussion Looking forward and not backward Providing impetus to overcome existing challenges Identifying first possible strategies that could be pursued in the near future	What is typical for the people of Eichstätt? What are the characteristics of Eichstätt? Who forms the community of Eichstätt and what makes them special?	Strengths, opportunities, weaknesses, and threats of the tourism in Eichstätt Destination atmosphere and design The role of institutions (university, church, and tourism office) Cooperation between stakeholders in the context of the local space	15 Qualitative Interviews (approx. 45 minutes) with participants from the economy, society, education, culture, church, and tourism sectors
2. Composition and organisation of the Lab	Setting up a heterogeneous group of actors from relevant areas of public life (church, industry, professionals, students, citizens, and culture) representing Eichstätt	Who are the central actors in the city? What is a constructive mixture of participants?	Definition of participants, formats, and methods and principles	
3. Definition of problems and objectives	Defining the 'rules of the game' Building openness and a common spirit	What challenges does Eichstätt face? What should be the goals for the city? What is the role of the Tourism Lab?	Reflection and determination of the status quo Defining goals for the Tourism Lab Defining desirable and undesirable development scenarios	Impulse lecture/intervention Individual presentation Knowledge Café
4. Identification of key topics and strategies	Putting the implicit statements from the previous session into an explicit scheme for distinguishing strategies	What topics does Eichstätt stand for from the citizens' and visitors' point of view? Which strategies can be pursued?	Distinguishing strategies for quality and service; innovation and product development; cooperation and networking; and participation and engagement Defining and interrelating relevant topics for tourism development	Flow rotation World Café

(Continued)

Table 15.1 (Continued)

S – Structure	I – Intention	Q – Leading Questions	T – Topics	M – Methods Used
5. Exploration of attractions, infrastructure, and development areas	Fostering creativity in touristic experience spaces	Which development corridors are emerging? How can citizens be involved in the process? (suggesting the online survey)	Naming and underlining attraction points Defining development corridors and spaces	Knowledge Café and subjective mapping
6. Generation of ideas, projects, and their implementation	Disclosing controversies and different positions Showing ways to reach consensus	Which projects could be planned and implemented based on the defined goals, topics, and attractions?	'Unheard voices': externally inputting story-line-development; and project-design	Story telling Pro-Action Café Think tank
7. Citizen participation I: online survey	Including citizen opinions on local tourism development Gaining insights into previously disregarded development scenarios and stimulating interest and willingness to participate	What is the perception of the citizens towards their city? How do the citizens evaluate their quality of life? How do the citizens evaluate the tourism supply? What challenges do the citizens perceive with regard to future development?	Dominant characteristics attributed to Eichstätt: provincial, idyllic, sleepy, unused potential, familiar, cosy, charming, and home	Online survey ($N = 145$)
8. Citizen participation II: workshop	Presenting selected preliminary results of the Tourism Lab Creating interactive discussion between permanent Tourism Lab members and the population	What does tourism development in the context of the local space mean for the urban population?	Affirmation and confirmation of previously developed results and gaining important medial awareness for the Tourism Lab	Impulses World Café

9. Closing of the Tourism Lab	Summing up and defining projects for action Clarifying publications and drafts of resolutions	What does the Eichstätt Tourism Lab suggest? Which priorities should be set?	Fostering citizen participation by providing financial support for projects initiated and implemented by the citizens. Development of the five so-called 'experience spaces' within Eichstätt: spirituality and power; architecture; places of wisdom; Altmühl (river); and active and healthy	Open panel discussion
10. Transfer of the results	Focusing on the main results and communicating the results on an emotional level	How can the results be made available to a broad public? To what extent can the local community participate in the future?	Motivating citizens to participate and to engage: Effective publicity communication via a brochure: Launching an online platform to foster citizen engagement	Design and public distribution of a brochure and platform launch: www.eichstaett.de/zukunft/

Source: Own elaboration

participants (e.g., World-Café, Flow Rotation, and Subjective Mapping) created a stable basis of trust among the participants and enabled the involvement of relevant opinions in the strategy development. The data collected by the Tourism Lab were enriched by empirical methods (citizen survey and expert interviews). Important topics of the Tourism Lab included the agreement on defined 'experience spaces' for future development. It was possible to take up impulses from different actors in the process and channel them in one direction (column T). Thus, a holistic picture of the destination's atmosphere was obtained and interpreted in an iterative process. As a final step, the results were published in cooperation with a professional marketing agency to create an aesthetically appealing and comprehensible medium, which allows for the transfer of the results to large parts of the population. With this output, the committee called the citizens again to take the initiative and shape their city. In 2021, an additional project will be launched to build upon the Tourism Lab's results and push its implications further.

In retrospect, the public warmly welcomed the realisation and implementation of the Eichstätt Tourism Lab. The project consolidated not only local partnerships and networks but also achieved transparent communication with the public. The local media strengthened the local perception of the initiative's progress and results.

Discussing participation to transform destinations

Using the city of Eichstätt as an example, special attention was paid to citizens in the tourism participation process. In doing so, a carefully orchestrated variety of methods could be transferred into an effective participation format. The thematic openness beyond purely tourism-related issues was identified as an important success factor. At the same time, this raises new questions of responsibility within the framework of regional stakeholder constellations.

In the case study, the multilevel system of a destination (Haugland et al., 2011) was analysed. Beyond the pure creation of tourism value, it could be shown that latent dissatisfaction with urban development issues requires explicitly dealing with local and dynamic change processes. There is a need to deal productively with diffusely articulated wishes for change, using them constructively for development (Nordin et al., 2019). It could be shown that this requires a certain openness, change management, and cross-sectoral thinking. For cases like Eichstätt, De Lucia et al. (2020) stated that the use of local knowledge in order to increase the attractiveness of tourism is only successful if the development topics relate to both tourism concerns and quality of life. The participation of the local people serves as a source of creativity and diversity. It should be seen as an early investment in the innovativeness of destination development. Defining tourism in a participatory way results from a community negotiation process (Kantsperger, Thees, & Eckert, 2019). To be open-minded and to open tourism processes could foster the implementation of new ideas from outside the mentioned sectors. In this way, citizens are nowadays a source of innovation and also a key stakeholder group.

At the same time, the participatory approach provides new ideas and proposes a new level of commitment that increase the likelihood of implementation. In this way, participation can be seen as a value and serves both as a key for unravelling existing structures and as a directional guide for re-organising these structures (Burnes, 2009). This could promote a transformation of established patterns of thinking and acting in tourism in the long run. In order for both to take place in a coordinated interplay, a sophisticated methodological approach must be chosen, which is provided in this contribution by the Tourism Lab. The Tourism Lab intended to uncover new development perspectives towards a transformation of tourism in Eichstätt by questioning established patterns. The participatory process has shown that a mere tourism-oriented view of the problem definition and objectives is not enough. Nevertheless, the Tourism Lab is only a starting point in satisfying broader urban and regional development needs. The trend towards a more wide-ranging approach is also emerging at the organisational level, and this is reflected in recent literature on destination management (Pechlaner, Kozak, & Volgger, 2014; Saarinen & Gill, 2019). The Tourism Lab process, which is open-ended, goes hand in hand with these expanded perspectives and provides additional dynamics for regional development.

With its participation formats and results, the Eichstätt Tourism Lab can be regarded as the groundwork and as a preliminary stage for concrete strategy development at the interface of tourism and non-tourism areas. On the one hand, tourism is the starting point, because the touristic view of a city helps to identify the beauty and particularities of the city, but it also unveils the necessary changes (Pechlaner et al., 2019a). In a city with a high attraction potential and attractive natural environment, tourism functions as an anchor of identification and as a vehicle for initiating participation, which addresses citizens' identification with their living environment in a unique way (Bernardo, Almeida, & Martins, 2017).

The identification and mobilisation of medium- and long-term responsible persons in the environment of urban administrative structures and civil society engagement can be considered as a crucial step in the aftermath of a change process that has already begun (Pechlaner et al., 2019b). Concerning the steps to be taken following the implementation of the Tourism Lab, one should reflect on the existing organisational structures of tourism and regional development, together with initiatives and the commitment of citizens. Impulses for new approaches should alternate between a narrower tourism industry context and a community initiative. By implementing the Tourism Lab, different methods are tested in a given city. The continuous interaction of different interests requires moderation and the use of different methods, even after the temporary Tourism Lab has been terminated. Participating actors should use their acquired methodological competence in subsequent projects that they launch on their own. These dynamics of the Tourism Lab, as a kind of living lab (see Table 15.1), meet the principles of destination governance. While the Tourism Lab illustrates a kind of self-organisation, it may need organisational support relating to technical issues or steering processes (Thees et al., 2020).

The search for self-governance and creative ideas requires every party to focus on future prospects and to deal with its individual challenges, instead of blaming someone for past events. In our case study, this aspect is reflected in the complaint that talking about problems has not led to concrete action so far. Talking about problems alone inhibits development and does not contribute to overcoming existing structures. Assuming responsibility is characterised by showing the courage to see crises as an opportunity for creative action, consciously trying out new things, and following a planned change in a destination's organisational structures.

This shared responsibility in the interplay between organisational structures and civil society is also a cultural issue and a constant common urban learning experience, which can positively affect future, cross-sectoral planning processes.

Conclusion

A destination system is challenged in its structure and process dynamics by transformative factors. The participatory involvement of the population in this process of change is both a necessity and a methodological challenge. The Eichstätt Tourism Lab was created as a joint initiative of the City Council and the university in Eichstätt and serves as an example of a moderated participation process, which approaches these transforming factors and avoids prohibitions on thinking in the context of structural changes towards an openness to results. Due to its realisation by the university, the process showed a high affinity for different methodological approaches. This directly raises the question of the general role of science in a dynamic participation process. Derived from the experience of the process conducted, science can take responsibility in the professional design of a Tourism Lab. The special situation created by the involvement of scientific expertise in the destination area had a positive effect on this assumption, and an above-average number of resources and a known spatial context were thus available.

In practical terms, the result of the Tourism Lab is an individual picture of the future for the present case study location. The success factors of the Tourism Lab are (1) a neutral problem identification and heterogeneous participants; (2) collaborative work on development goals through new perspectives, including external consultation and methods that enable rethinking; (3) scientific monitoring; and (4) a follow-up and self-sustaining initiatives. Due to the high interest in participation, the case of the Eichstätt Tourism Lab can be regarded as successful. The high public interest was accompanied by high expectations and a controversial debate on the implications of the Tourism Lab.

Indeed, the case study is a methodological guide for similar participation processes in other cities and regions, in which the transfer of scientific expertise is of particular importance. The dissemination of this specific approach requires further research concerning how participation supports change or even transformation of a destination in the long run. Ultimately, there is a need for well-designed monitoring to systematically evaluate different methods in the context of such participation processes. In addition to offline formats, online formats should also be taken into account. We suggest a structural development of multi-level systems with a focus on process innovation beyond a specific industry focus such as tourism, also in order to promote the transformation of these industries. To address these concerns, future research should focus more on inter-local exchange in terms of good practices and toolboxes and hence examine the role of superordinate governance structures to promote synergies.

References

Beritelli, P., & Reinhold, S. (2010). Explaining decisions for change in tourist destinations: The garbage can model in action. In P. Keller & T. Bieger (Eds.). *Managing change in tourism: Creating opportunities: Overcoming obstacles* (pp. 137–152). Berlin: ESV.

Bernardo, F., Almeida, J., & Martins, C. (2017). Urban identity and tourism: Different looks, one single place. *Proceedings of the Institution of Civil Engineers-Urban Design and Planning, 170*(5), 205–216. https://doi.org/10.1680/jurdp.15.00036

Boschetto Doorly, V. (2020). *Megatrends defining the future of tourism*. Cham: Springer.

Burnes, B. (2009). Reflections: Ethics and organizational change: Time for a return to Lewinian values. *Journal of Change Management, 9*(4), 359–381. https://doi.org/10.1080/14697010903360558

Butler, R. W. (1980). The concept of a tourist area cycle of evolution: Implications for management of resources. *Canadian Geographer, 24*(1). https://doi.org/5-12.10.1111/j.1541-0064.1980.tb00970.x

Calzada, I. (2019). Local entrepreneurship through a multistakeholders' tourism living lab in the post-violence/peripheral era in the Basque Country. *Regional Science Policy & Practice, 11*(3), 451–466. https://doi.org/10.1111/rsp3.12130

De Lucia, C., Pazienza, P., Balena, P., & Caporale, D. (2020). Exploring local knowledge and socio-economic factors for touristic attractiveness and sustainability. *International Journal of Tourism Research, 22*(1), 81–99. https://doi.org/10.1002/jtr.2320

Dupre, K. (2019). Trends and gaps in place-making in the context of urban development and tourism: 25 years of literature review. *Journal of Place Management and Development, 12*(1), 102–120. https://doi.org/10.1108/JPMD-07-2017-0072

Eckert, C., Zacher, D., Pechlaner, H., Namberger, P., & Schmude, J. (2019). Strategies and measures directed towards overtourism: A perspective of European DMOs. *International Journal of Tourism Cities, 5*(4), 639–655. https://doi.org/10.1108/IJTC-12-2018-0102

Egger, R., Gula, I., & Walcher, D. (Eds.). (2016). *Tourism on the verge: Open tourism: Open innovation, crowdsourcing and co-creation challenging the tourism industry* (1st ed.). Berlin, Heidelberg: Springer.

Erina, I., Shatrevich, V., & Gaile-Sarkane, E. (2017). Impact of stakeholder groups on development of a regional entrepreneurial ecosystem. *European Planning Studies, 25*(5), 755–771. https://doi.org/10.1080/09654313.2017.1282077

Flagestad, A., & Hope, C. (2001). Strategic success in winter sports destinations: A sustainable valuecreation perspective. *Tourism Management, 22*(5), 445–461. https://doi.org/10.1016/S0261-5177(01)00010-3

Galvani, A., Lew, A. A., & Perez, M. S. (2020). COVID-19 is expanding global consciousness and the sustainability of travel and tourism. *Tourism Geographies, 22*(3), 567–576. https://doi.org/10.1080/14616688.2020.1760924

Gössling, S., Scott, D., & Hall, C. M. (2020). Pandemics, tourism and global change: A rapid assessment of COVID-19. *Journal of Sustainable Tourism, 29*(1), 1–20. https://doi.org/10.1080/09669582.2020.1758708

Gretzinger, S., Royer, S., Matiaske, W., Burgess, J., & Brown, K. (2019). Entrepreneurial ecosystems, smart specialisation, industry clusters and regional development:

Understanding change at the network level. *International Journal of Globalisation and Small Business*, *10*(2), 101–104. Retrieved from www.inderscience.com/info/dl.php?filename=2019/ijgsb-6173.pdf

Guimont, D., & Lapointe, D. (2016). Empowering local tourism providers to innovate through a living lab process: Does scale matter? *Technology Innovation Management Review*, *6*(11), 18–25. https://doi.org/10.22215/timreview/1031

Gundry, L. K., Kickul, J. R., Griffiths, M. D., & Bacq, S. C. (2011). Creating social change out of nothing: The role of entrepreneurial bricolage in social entrepreneurs' catalytic innovations. In G. T. Lumpkin (Ed.), *Advances in entrepreneurship, firm emergence and growth: Vol. 13: Social and sustainable entrepreneurship* (pp. 1–24). Bingley: Emerald.

Haugland, S. A., Ness, H., Grønseth, B. O., & Aarstad, J. (2011). Development of tourism destinations: An integrated multilevel perspective. *Annals of Tourism Research*, *38*(1), 268–290. https://doi.org/10.1016/j.annals.2010.08.008

Hjalager, A.-M. (2010). A review of innovation research in tourism. *Tourism Management*, *31*(1), 1–12. https://doi.org/10.1016/j.tourman.2009.08.012

Hossain, M., & Lassen, A. (2017). How do digital platforms for ideas, technologies, and knowledge transfer act as enablers for digital transformation? *Technology Innovation Management Review*, *7*(9), 55–60. https://doi.org/10.22215/timreview/1106

Hovinen, G. R. (2002). Revisiting the destination lifecycle model. *Annals of Tourism Research*, *29*(1), 209–230. https://doi.org/10.1016/S0160-7383(01)00036-6

Jordan, E. J., Vogt, C. A., Kruger, L. E., & Grewe, N. (2013). The interplay of governance, power and citizen participation in community tourism planning. *Journal of Policy Research in Tourism, Leisure and Events*, *5*(3), 270–288. https://doi.org/10.1080/19407963.2013.789354

Juvan, E., & Dolnicar, S. (2014). The attitude: Behaviour gap in sustainable tourism. *Annals of Tourism Research*, *48*, 76–95. https://doi.org/10.1016/j.annals.2014.05.012

Kantsperger, M., Thees, H., & Eckert, C. (2019). Local participation in tourism development: Roles of non-tourism related residents of the Alpine destination Bad Reichenhall. *Sustainability*, *11*(24), 6947. https://doi.org/10.3390/su11246947

Karaçor, E. K. (2016). Public vs. private: The evaluation of different space types in terms of publicness dimension. *European Journal of Sustainable Development*, *5*(3). https://doi.org/51-51.10.14207/EJSD.2016.V5N3P51

Laws, E. (Ed.). (2012). *Tourism crises: Management responses and theoretical insight.* London: Taylor and Francis.

McLennan, C. L., Ruhanen, L., Ritchie, B., & Pham, T. (2012). Dynamics of destination development: Investigating the application of transformation theory. *Journal of Hospitality & Tourism Research*, *36*(2), 164–190. https://doi.org/10.1177/1096348010390816

Moran, J. W., & Brightman, B. K. (2001). Leading organizational change. *Career Development International*, *6*(2), 111–119. https://doi.org/10.1108/13620430110383438

Moscardo, G. (2011). The role of knowledge in good governance for tourism. In E. Laws, J. F. Agrusa, & H. Richins (Eds.), *Tourist destination governance: Practice, theory and issues* (pp. 67–82). Wallingford: CAB International.

Nordin, S., Volgger, M., Gill, A., & Pechlaner, H. (2019). Destination governance transitions in skiing destinations: A perspective on resortisation. *Tourism Management Perspectives*, *31*, 24–37. https://doi.org/10.1016/j.tmp.2019.03.003

Pechlaner, H., Kozak, M., & Volgger, M. (2014). Destination leadership: A new paradigm for tourist destinations? *Tourism Review*, *69*(1), 1–10. https://doi.org/10.1108/TR-07-2013-0043

Pechlaner, H., & Volgger, M. (2012). How to promote cooperation in the hospitality industry. *International Journal of Contemporary Hospitality Management*, *24*(6), 925–945. https://doi.org/10.1108/09596111211247245

Pechlaner, H., Zacher, D., Eckert, C., & Petersik, L. (2019b). Joint responsibility and understanding of resilience from a DMO perspective-an analysis of different situations in Bavarian tourism destinations. *International Journal of Tourism Cities*, *5*(2), 146–168. https://doi.org/10.1108/IJTC-12-2017-0093

Pechlaner, H., Zacher, D., Gavriljuk, E., & Eckert, C. (2019a). Does the living space prevent destination development? The Bavarian town of Eichstaett as a space of possibilities. In M. Volgger & D. Pfister (Eds.), *Atmospheric turn in culture and tourism: Place, design and process impacts on customer behaviour, marketing and branding* (pp. 209–222). Bingley: Emerald Publishing Limited.

PwC. (2020). *Megatrends*. Retrieved from www.pwc.co.uk/issues/megatrends.html

Rahmani, K., Gnoth, J., & Mather, D. (2018). Hedonic and eudaimonic well-being: A psycholinguistic view. *Tourism Management*, *69*, 155–166. https://doi.org/10.1016/j.tourman.2018.06.008

Rastegar, R. (2019). Tourism development and conservation, do local resident attitudes matter? *International Journal of Tourism Sciences*, *19*(3), 181–191. https://doi.org/10.1080/15980634.2019.1663998

Ritchie, B. J. R., & Crouch, G. I. (2005). *Competitive destination: A sustainable tourism perspective* (2nd ed.). Wallingford: CABI Publishing.

Saarinen, J., & Gill, A. M. (Eds.). (2019). *Routledge studies in contemporary geographies of leisure, tourism and mobility: Resilient destinations and tourism: Governance strategies in the transition towards sustainability in tourism*. London: Routledge.

Sun, X., Xu, H., Köseoglu, M. A., & Okumus, F. (2020). How do lifestyle hospitality and tourism entrepreneurs manage their work-life balance? *International Journal of Hospitality Management*, *85*, 102359. https://doi.org/10.1016/j.ijhm.2019.102359

Thees, H., Pechlaner, H., Olbrich, N., & Schuhbert, A. (2020). The living lab as a tool to promote residents' participation in destination governance. *Sustainability*, *12*(3), 1120. https://doi.org/10.3390/su12031120

Todnem By, R. (2005). Organisational change management: A critical review. *Journal of Change Management*, *5*(4), 369–380. https://doi.org/10.1080/14697010500359250

Conclusion

Anna Farmaki and Nikolaos Pappas

During the writing of this book, the world was experiencing the devastating economic and social disruption caused by the COVID-19 pandemic. Initially detected in the Chinese city of Wuhan in early December, COVID-19 spread rapidly across the globe costing the lives of more than 3.4 million people while over 165.5 million reported cases of infected people were reported worldwide by 2021. Attempts were made to deal with the unforeseen challenges of the pandemic which has taken a toll on people across the world, with governments imposing restrictive measures such as lockdowns in order to contain the spread of the pandemic at the local level. One of the industries that has been heavily impacted by the restrictions imposed was tourism. While the global tourism industry is no stranger to socio-economic, political, and/or health crises, the longevity of the COVID-19 pandemic created an unprecedented situation that the industry never experienced before. As such, the pandemic brought to light the vulnerability of the tourism industry to externalities, highlighting the need to consider the immense changes global tourism is undergoing and will most likely continue to experience in the near future as a result of the continuous dynamics shaping the tourist activity and the tourism system.

This edited book has gone some way towards presenting several of the significant transformations that are currently taking place and which influence how the global tourism industry operates. Many of the chapters included in the book have identified a number of pressing questions and issues that need to be considered in order to better understand the evolutionary perspective of the tourism phenomenon. As noted in the introductory chapter of the book, the continuously increasing demand for tourism despite adversities challenging the industry suggests that attention deserves to be paid by destinations and tourism businesses to the numerous factors transforming the tourism environment. A reading of these transformations carries both practical and theoretical value and, hence, this edited book may prove to be a useful resource to various stakeholders in the tourism industry including practitioners, educators, students, and researchers. First, the rapidly changing tourism environment implies that factors pertinent to externalities will affect how the industry is to be managed in the foreseeable future as a result of technological, socio-economic, and environmental changes. Industry practitioners and managers can thus benefit from the holistic perspective offered

Conclusion 233

by the book and which may better equip them to deal with unexpected changes impacting tourism processes, practices, and structures. Second, as global tourism is experiencing transformations, it becomes apparent that tourism and hospitality programmes need to adapt curricula to meet the needs of the changing tourism industry. This book, therefore, may help educators understand the dynamics shaping the tourism industry and allow them to effectively proceed with informed decisions regarding any potential adaptations and modifications of curricula. Last, the transformative environment shaping the tourism industry also offers a fruitful landscape for researching important emerging themes pertinent to the tourism system and activity that emanate from related challenges and opportunities afflicted by external factors.

More specifically, the contributors to this edited book presented a wide range of transformations impacting the tourism industry. Each chapter discussed a specific topic that represents a transformation in tourism, examining how it may impart significant implications to theory and practice. For instance, in discussing the transformations occurring in the aviation industry in the post-COVID-19 era, Chapter 1 highlighted the need for transport companies to reconsider their business models and operational standards to effectively deal with the emerging needs of consumers and the economic effects of the pandemic. Tourism businesses will indeed need to introduce health and safety measures and undertake the necessary operational changes in order to remain competitive. As the chapter demonstrated, there is a need for further research to capture the changes of the dynamic transport environment by considering supply-side and demand-side perspectives. Chapter 2 examined how tourism contributes to climate change, posing questions relevant to the sustainability of the industry which researchers could further analyse. The chapter also emphasised the responsibility of policymakers and businesses in enacting changes to reduce the adverse effects of the short-term, profit-oriented approach dominating tourism. Further on, Chapter 3 discussed the transformative effects of the sharing economy in relation to inclusive tourism, yielding important insights that enable industry practitioners and destination planners to improve decision-making processes. The inclusive sharing tourism perspective is worth investigating in light of the need for greater sustainability in the sector. Chapter 4 explored the evolution of digital technology and its effects on the tourism industry, suggesting that businesses need to shift their focus on strategies that develop database-oriented services, personalised tourist experiences, and real-time service deliveries. The impact of technological advances on the industry was also foregrounded by the authors in Chapters 5–8. These chapters provided analyses of the technology and tourism interface by discussing attitudes towards robot adoption in tourism and hospitality, smart tourism applications in a destination resilience context, social media influence on destination image, and the digital potential of archaeotourism.

Chapter 9 presented the emerging phenomenon of meme tourism, contributing to the discussion on pop-culture tourism whilst yielding significant managerial and research insights. Chapter 10 touched upon the importance of accessible tourism as a transformational force for tourism and hospitality that contributes to a more inclusive society and a more sustainable future for the leisure sector. Moving on, Chapter 11 examined employee well-being in the food and beverage sector in relation to engagement and turnover intention to provide insights on the management of human resource tools, while Chapter 12 examined the potential of munro-bagging on adventure tourism. Moreover, Chapter 13 evaluates the enabling role of cycling tourism on the achievement of the Sustainable Development Goals. In sum, these chapters thus offer significant perspectives that may further research attempts on sustainability and well-being issues whilst providing a roadmap to improve related management tactics. The emergence of cannabis tourism as a transformative tourism form was presented in Chapter 14, indicating the potential of the industry to capitalise on emerging opportunities. Finally, Chapter 15 discussed the requirements for future destination development by presenting the Tourism Lab as an alternative tool for broad stakeholder participation.

The editors believe that this book reflects the key emerging transformations noticeable in the global tourism industry in the contemporary era. Collectively, the contributors to this edited book have attempted to capture the influence of emerging externalities on tourism and hospitality by presenting important themes that have both research and managerial value. Notwithstanding, this book does not provide a full reference to all the factors shaping the industry. Even so, the depth and breadth of those explored in this book reveal patterns, relationships, and viewpoints that contribute to the ongoing discussion on the evolution of the tourism environment. It is therefore our wish that this book offers inspiration to scholars for exploring new, emerging avenues for further research whilst enhancing industry practitioners' understanding of key issues pertinent to global tourism and hospitality, the environment of which is ever-changing and constantly evolving.

Index

Note: Page numbers in *italics* indicate a figure and page numbers in **bold** indicate a table on the corresponding page.

'Accessible City' competition (2016) 146
accessible tourism 142–153; barriers to be overcome 148, **148**; 'Handbook on Accessible Tourism for All: Principles, Tools and Good Practices, The' (UNWTO) 143; industry 143–144; primary requirements 143; types of obstacles 143–144
active listening 176
Active Travel apps 93
Adobe Connect 120
Aegean Airlines **8**
age factors 38, **45**
Agenda for Sustainable Goals 194
Airbnb 2, 35, 47
Airbus **23**
air carriers: actions taken to address financial difficulties posed by COVID-19 7–9, **8**
Air France – KLM **8**, 10
air transport 5–17, 22; demand forecasting 10–11; emerging transformations expected to take place 12–14, *13*; marketing strategy 11–12; operational reshuffling 10; operational tactics 9–10; recovery from COVID-19 9–12; revenue management 10–11
Air Transport Action Group (ATAG) 6–7
Alien Research Center 131
Alienstock 131–133
Alien-Stock 131, 133
alternative development approaches 219, *219*
American Airlines 8
Amsterdam, the Netherlands: cannabis tourism and legality 205

Angkor Wat 115
Apulia (Italy): cycling tourism 191, 193–194
archaeotourism (AT) 115–126; digital archaeological tourism (DAT) 116–122; digital potential 117–121
Area 51 (Nevada) 130, 132, 134
Argentina: cannabis legality 203
Arnu, Joerg 132
Arrow Towing 135
Australia: actions taken to address financial difficulties posed by COVID-19 **8**; cannabis tourism and legality 203, 208
Austria: cycling tourism 190; ski tourism 26
autonetnography 177–179; criteria for interpretive sufficiency 177, **178**; interpretive 177, **178**
aviation: contribution to climate crisis 19; COVID-19 and 6–9

Bale, Rachel 205
Barcelona, Spain: cannabis tourism and legality 206
BAU (Business-as-Usual) 18–19, 22–24
bicycling *see* cycling tourism
big data analysis of social media sharing 98–111; data collection and analysis 101–103, **102**, *104*; research methodology 101–103; research results 103–107
BlaBlaCar 35
Boeing **23**
Braille code 147
brand community 58–59

British Airways **8**
Bronx, New York (USA): Joker Stairs 134–138
budandbreakfast.com 207
Bud Light 133
Budweiser 132–133
Burger King 131
Business-as-Usual (BAU) 18–19, 22–24

Canada: cannabis tourism and legality 203, 207–208; ski tourism 26
Canadian Kush Tours 207–208
cannabis: commercialisation 209; legality 202–203; medicinal 202; recreational 202; uses and administration methods 202
Cannabis Culture 207
cannabis tourism 201–215
Cantabria (The Mountain) 158–159
Čapek, Karel 66
caregivers 144–145
Caribbean: cannabis tourism and legality 203–204
Caribbean Community (CARICOM) 25
Caribbean Tourism Organization (CTO) 204
Çatalhöyük, Turkey 120
Cathay Pacific **8**
Catholic University of Eichstätt-Ingolstadt 221–222
Central Europe: cycling tourism 190
change: in destination environment 217–221; framing 217–221; strategic management of 220
Chartered Institute of Personnel and Development (CIPD) 155
China 100
Choice hotel chains 57
Christmas tourism 26
Churchill, Winston 15
climate change 18–34; impact on tourism 24–26; responding to 27–28; tourism's contribution to 19–22
Clorox 9
CNN 135
coastal tourism 25
collaborative economy 35
collecting 172–173; Munro-baggers' behaviours 180–181; Munro-bagging 170–173; netnographic findings 180–181; online Munro-bagging 170–186; in tourist communities 175–177
Colorado, USA: cannabis tourism and legality 206–207

ComicBook.com 134
community membership 175
community participation 218
competitiveness 218
complex adaptive systems (CAS) 84, 86–87, **90**
complexity theory 160, 165–166
connectivity 85–86, 89, **90**, 94
consumer-to-consumer (C2C) applications 61
consumption: community membership as 175; tourism as 175; in tourist communities 175–177
contactless travel 10
Convention on the Rights of Persons with Disabilities (2006) 142
cost management *13*, 14
COVID-19 29–30, 220, 232; digital tourism and 60–61; emerging transformations expected to take place 12–14, *13*; financial difficulties posed by 7–9, **8**; impact on aviation and tourism 6–9, 21–23, **23**; recovery from 5–17
cross-stakeholder participation 219–220
cruise ships 19
Cruz, Ted 129
Customer Relationship Management 14
cyber-physical systems age 56–57
cycling tourism 194; data collection 192; overview 189–191; proposed triple-layered business model canvas for 192–194, **195**; research findings 192–194, **195**; research methods **191**, 191–192
Cyprus: food and beverage industry 154
Czech Republic: cannabis tourism and legality 203, 205–206

Daily Mail, The 131
Dancing Joker meme 134
data gathering 119
data processing 119
data representation 119
Dawkins, Richard 128
Delta Airlines **8**, 9, 129
demand forecasting: advanced methods 11; after COVID-19 10–11
demand sharing 176
demographic factors 38–40, 45, **45**
Denmark: cannabis tourism and legality 205; cycling tourism 190; Free Christiana (Copenhagen) 205
destination environments: components that reveal locally bound understanding of

space 219; framing change in 217–221; marketing 138–139; transformation of 146–148, 226–228
development, sustainable 189
Diaz, Ruben, Jr. 135
diffusion of innovation 54
digital age 55–57
digital archaeological tourism (DAT) 116, 121–122; goals 118–119; potential for 117–121
digitalisation 54–61
Digitally Efficient Cost Management (DECM) *13*, 14
Digitally Efficient Revenue Management (DERM) *13*, 14
digital marketing 12
digital skills 42, **44**, 45, **45**
digital tourism: and COVID-19 60–61; transformation of 57–63, 115–126
disabled people *see* persons with disabilities (PwDs)
diversity 85, 89, **90**
dynamic tools 220–221

easyJet 8
economics: collaborative economy 35; sharing economy 35–51; triple-layered business model layer 191, **191**, 192–193
education factors 39, 45, **45**
efficiency 92
Eichstätt, Germany 210, 226–228
Eichstätt Tourism Lab 216–231; aims 222; implementation as dynamic tool 220–221; new perspectives 221–226; overview 222, **223**–**225**; success factors 229
Emirates (UAE) **8**
employees: engagement 157–158, 163–164, **164**; global travel and tourism jobs 21–22; reward systems 156–157; training and development of 157; turnover intention 157–158, **164**, 164–165
employee well-being 154–169, *161*–*162*; analytical approaches 160–161, *161*; causal recipes to predict 163–164, **164**; configurational model 163–165, **164**; data analysis and measurements 159–160; research case 158–159; research results **162**, 162–166, **164**
environmental change 217–221
environmental life cycle 191, **191**, 193
Ephesus 115
ethical leadership 155–156

ethnography: autonetnography 177–178, **178**, 179; criteria for evaluating 177, **178**; netnography 177–181
Europe: 'Accessible City' competition (2016) 146; cannabis tourism and legality 204–206; food and beverage industry 154–155; hospitality industry 158
European Network for Accessible Tourism (ENAT) 144
European Union (EU): cannabis tourism and legality 204; collaborative economy 35–47, **44**–**45**; Emission Trading System 27; European Disability Strategy 2010–2020 142
eWOM 181–182
experience, tourist 218
external shocks 220

Facebook 12, 55, 98, 100, 132–134; Munro-bagging sites 178; 'W Maple Omaha Rock, The' page 135, 137
fame: meme tourism 136–137
FARO Scene 119
feedback **90**
Finland: Christmas tourism 26
Flickr 99
Flow Rotation 226
Fontainebleau Miami 60
food and beverage industry: employee well-being 154–169; workforce 154–155
Four Demonstrators project 92–93
Fox News 133
France: actions taken to address financial difficulties posed by COVID-19 **8**, 10; cycling tourism 190; greenhouse gas emissions 27–28
Free Christiana (Copenhagen, Denmark) 205
Full-Service Network Carriers 8
Funyuns 131
Future City Glasgow 85; case study 89–93; Four Demonstrators 92–93; Glasgow Operations Centre 91; Open Glasgow 91–92
Fyre Festival 132

gender differences 39, 45, **45**
Germany: actions taken to address financial difficulties posed by COVID-19 **8**; cannabis legality 203; cycling tourism 190
Glasgow, Scotland: Four Demonstrators project 92–93; Future City Glasgow 85,

89–93; Glasgow Operations Centre 91; MyGlasgow app 92–93; Open Glasgow project 91–92; Social Transport app 92–93
global travel and tourism jobs 21–22
Google 134
Google Maps 134–135
Google Trends 135
Greece: actions taken to address financial difficulties posed by COVID-19 **8**; food and beverage industry 154
greenhouse gas emissions 19–20, 23–24, 27–28
green infrastructures 189
Guangdong–Hong Kong–Macao Greater Bay Area (GBA) 98–99, 101, *102*, 108; city clusters and distinctive features 106; city TextRank information **111–114**; discussion topics on social media 103, *104*, **105**; regional destinations for photo-taking 106
guest-oriented industries 154–169

'Handbook on Accessible Tourism for All: Principles, Tools and Good Practices, The' (UNWTO) 143
Health and Safety Marketing (HSM) 12–13, *13*
health certification 9–10
Herb Museum 207
Hilton Worldwide 60
Hong Kong SAR: actions taken to address financial difficulties posed by COVID-19 **8**; discussion topics on social media 103, *104*, **105**
hospitality industry: emerging transformations in 1–4; job creation 158; leadership role 156; turnover rates 158; workforce 154–155
Hostel Ejidonia (La Barra, Uruguay) 208
HotBox Café (Toronto, Canada) 207–208
hotels, smart 60
household size factors 40, 45, **45**

iFunny 134
images: destination 98–111, **102**, *104*; online sharing of 179; regional destination for photo-taking 106; selfies 179; social media sharing of 98–111, **102**, *104*
inclusive tourism 233; overview 37–38; sharing economy and 35–51
income factors 39–40, 45, **45**
individuals 220
Indonesia: cannabis legality 203

Industrial Revolution 54–55
Industry 1.0 54–55
Industry 2.0 54–55
Industry 3.0 54–56
Industry 4.0 55–57, 193
information technology (IT) 53–54
Innovate UK 89
innovation 54, 218
innovativeness 41, **44**, 45, **45**
Instagram 12, 98, 134, 136
instrumentation 88
Integrated Environmental Solutions 92
integrated social transport: Four Demonstrators project 92–93
intelligent street lighting 93
Intergovernmental Panel on Climate Change (IPCC) 19–20
International Air Transport Association (IATA) 5–6, 8, 20
International Civil Aviation Organization (ICAO) 5, 7
International Energy Agency (IEA) 22–23, **23**
International Labour Organization (ILO) 7
Internationally Harmonised Measures and Protocols (IHMP) 12, *13*
International Maritime Organizations **23**
international tourism: arrivals and forecasts 20–21, **21**; *see also* tourism
Internet memes 128–129; *see also* memes
Internet of Things (IoT) 56, 88–89
Internet usage 174–175
interpretive autonetnography 177, **178**
IPCC (Intergovernmental Panel on Climate Change) 19–20
Italy: cannabis legality 203; COVID-19 6; cycling tourism 191, 193–194

Jamaica: cannabis tourism and legality 203–204
Japan: cannabis legality 203
JetBlue 8
Joker Stairs 134–136, 138

KLM **8**, 10
Knapp, George 131–132
knowledge sharing 175, 179–180
Kofi Outlaw 134
Kool-Aid 131

leadership 155–156; ethical 155–156; transformational 156
learning: encouraging 86–87, **90**
Lee, Kerry 132

legislative approaches 202–203
Lemus, Jose 136
lighting, intelligent 93
Little A'Le'Inn, The (Rachel, Nevada) 131–133
living labs 220–221
local space: alternative development approaches 219, *219*; contemporary understanding of 217–219
Los Angeles, California (USA): Pink Wall 136–138
Lufthansa 8, **8**
Lyft 35
Lysol 9

Machu Pichu 115
marginal tourism 209
marihuana *see* cannabis
marketing: cannabis tourism 210; after COVID-19 11–12; digital 12; Health and Safety Marketing (HSM) 12–13; memes as 138–139
Mars Bar and Grill 135, 137
materialism 41, **44**, 45, **45**
McAndrews, Laura 131
medicinal cannabis 202
Mediterranean 26
memes 128–129, 138–139
meme tourism 127–141; case studies 130–136; evolution of 137–138
Milan, Italy 146
Million Marijuana March 205
mobile applications 57–58
motivations 218
multinational enterprises (MNEs) 189
Munro, Sir Hugh 170
Munro-baggers: collecting behaviours 180–181; online knowledge sharing 179–180
Munro-bagging 170–172; Facebook sites 178; online 170–186
Munroists 181–182
Munros (Scotland) 170–171
MyGlasgow app 92–93
Mysterious Universe 131

Naruto 131
Naruto running 131, 133–134, 137–138
NBC 135
Nepal 100
Netherlands, the: actions taken to address financial difficulties posed by COVID-19 **8**; cannabis tourism and legality 203–205; cycling tourism 190

netnography 177–181
Nike 129
Nimbin, New South Wales: cannabis tourism and legality 208
North America: cannabis tourism and legality 206–208
Norway: ski tourism 26

Omaha, Nebraska (USA): West Maple Omaha Rock 135, 137, 139
Omar the Troll 135
online communities 174
online events 61
online knowledge sharing 179–180
online Munro-bagging: Facebook sites 178; sharing and collective behaviours of 170–186
online search frequency 42, **44**, 45, **45**
Open Glasgow project 91–92
operational tactics 9–10

participatory approach 226–228
Paul Smith (Los Angeles, CA): Pink Wall 136–138
peak-bagging 170–171
People 1st 157
persons with disabilities (PwDs) 144–145; Convention on the Rights of Persons with Disabilities (2006) 142; European Disability Strategy 2010–2020 142; *see also* accessible tourism
Petra 115
Philippines 139
Phillips, Gordon 59
Phillips, Kevin 132
Phoenix, Joaquin 134
photos: regional destinations for photo-taking 106; sharing destination images on social media 98–111, **102**, *104*
Pink Wall 136–138
Pointools software 119
polycentric governance: promoting 87, **90**
Pompeii 115
pop-culture tourism 129–130, 137–138
Portugal: cannabis legality 203
psychological factors 40–41, 45, **45**
public opinion: attitudes towards robots 66–80, **70–71**, **73–76**, **77–78**, 79–80; perceived appropriateness of service robots 72, **73–76**; preferred human–robot ratio 72, **77**; willingness to pay for fully robot-delivered services 72, **78**
public transport networks 146

Index

Qantas **8**
QR (Quick Response) codes 58

Rachel, Nevada: Storm Area 51 130–134, 136–138
RED 98, 100; data collection and analysis 101–103, **102**, *104*; destination image building on 107–108; discussion topics 103, *104*, **105**; regional destinations for photo-taking on 106
redundancy, system 85
reference groups 59
regional destinations for photo-taking 106
Regional Plan of Cycling Mobility (PRMC) 191
resilience: pillars of 89, **90**; in smart tourism destinations 83–97
revenue management: after COVID-19 10–11; Digitally Efficient Revenue Management (DERM) *13*, 14
reward systems 156–157
RFID smart tag applications 60
Roberts, Matty 130–134, 137
robophiles 66, 68–72, **70–71**, 79–80
robophobes 66, 68–72, **70–71**, 79–80
robots: attitudes towards 66–80, **70–71**, **73–76**, **77–78**; perceived appropriateness of 72, **73–76**; preferred human–robot ratio 72, **77**; research findings 69–72, **70–71**, **73–76**, **77–78**; service robots 72, **73–76**, **78**; study methodology 68–69; in tourism 68–82, **70–71**, **73–76**, **77–78**; willingness to pay for fully robot-delivered services 72, **78**
Rocko (boulder) 135
Ryanair 8

Santander, Spain *159*; food and beverage industry 158–160
Scotland: Munro-bagging 170–173
sea level rise (SLR) 25
search, online 42, **44**, 45, **45**
seasonal tourism resources 26
selfies 179
service robots: perceived appropriateness of 72, **73–76**; preferred human–robot ratio 72, **77**; willingness to pay for fully robot-delivered services 72, **78**
sharing: of content 179; demand sharing 176; of destination images on social media 98–111, **102**, *104*; Munro-baggers' 179–180; netnographic findings 179; online knowledge sharing 179–180; online Munro-bagging 170–186; in tourist communities 175–177
sharing economy 35–51; data analysis 44; logistic regression analysis 45, **45**; participant demographics 38–40, 45, **45**; participant psychological factors 40–41, 45, **45**; participation factors 38–42, 45, **45**; principal component analysis (PCA) 44, **44**; research data and sample 43, **52**; research results **44**, 44–45, **45**; study measures 43
Sina.com 100
Sina Weibo 100, 108
Singapore: cannabis legality 203
ski tourism 26
small- to medium-sized enterprises (SMEs) 157, 189
smart applications 59–60
smart hotels 60
smart tourism 59, 93–94
smart tourism destinations 87–89; case study 89–93; main characteristics 83–84; pillars of resilience 89, **90**; ultimate goals 83–84
social-ecological systems (SES) 83, 85–87
social exchange theory 156
social media 174–175; big data analysis of 98–111, **102**, *104*; digital marketing strategy 12; discussion topics 103–106, *104*, **105**; research methodology 101–103; sharing destination images on 98–111, **102**, *104*; in tourism 99–101; and tourism transformation 107–108; user-generated content (UGC) 98
social media applications 58–59; *see also specific apps*
social stakeholders 191, **191**, 193–194
social tourism 144
social transport, integrated: Four Demonstrators project 92–93
Social Transport app 92–93
Southwest Airlines 8
Spain: cannabis tourism and legality 203, 206; COVID-19 6; food and beverage industry 154, 156; hospitality industry 158
sport tourism 189–190
Storm Area 51 130–134, 136–138
Storm Area 51 Basecamp 131, 133
strategic change management 220
street lighting, intelligent 93
Subjective Mapping 226
sustainability 131–133, 166

sustainable business models 187–200; in tourism organisations 188–189; triple-layered proposal **191**, 191–194, **195**
sustainable development 189
Sustainable Development Goals (SDGs) 107, 187–200
sustainable tourism 189, 194, 218
Sustainable Travel Renaissance *13*, 14
Switzerland: cycling tourism 190
systems connectivity 85–86

technology acceptance model (TAM) 54
telepresence 170
THC Hostel (La Barra, Uruguay) 208
theory of reasoned action 54
3D Studio Max 119
TikTok 100
Toronto, Canada: cannabis tourism 207–208
tourism: accessible 142–153; archaeotourism 115–126; barriers to participation 143–144; Business-as-Usual (BAU) 18–19, 22–24; cannabis 201–215; climate change and 18–34; coastal 25; as consumption 175; contribution to climate crisis 19–22; COVID-19 and 6–9; cross-stakeholder participation 219–220; crucial interactive aspects of destinations 84; cycling 189–194, **195**; destination for photo-taking 106; destination resilience 85–87, 93–94; digital 60–61; digitalisation 54–61; digital transformation in 57–63, 115–126; emerging transformations in 1–4, 24–26, 29–30; global jobs 21–22; inclusive 35–51, 233; industry development 54–61; international arrivals and forecasts 20–21, **21**; Internet usage 174–175; long-term forecast growth rates 22–23, *23*; marginal 209; meme 127–141; mobile applications 57–58; as participatory 226–228; pop-culture 129–130, 137–138; responding to climate change 27–28; robots in 68–82, **70–71**, **73–76**, **77–78**; seasonal resources 26; ski 26; smart 59; smart applications 59–60; smart destinations 83–97; smart transformations 93–94; social 144; social media applications 58–59; social media sharing of destination images 98–111, **102**, *104*; sport 189–190; sustainable 189, 194, 218; sustainable development in context of 189; system diversity and redundancy 85; system panarchy 28, *29*; system resilience 83–97; transformation and change in 28, *29*; *see also specific destinations*
Tourism Area Life Cycle 217
Tourism Competitiveness Index 158
Tourism Lab (Eichstätt) 216–231; implementation as dynamic tool 220–221; new perspectives 221–226; overview 222, **223–225**; success factors 229
tourism organisations: sustainable business models 188–189; triple-layered business model **191**, 191–194, **195**
tourist communities 175–177
training and development 157
transformational leadership 156
transportation: air transport 5–17, **8**, *13*, 22; Four Demonstrators project 92–93; social 92–93; travel 145–146
travel: air transport 5–17, **8**, *13*; contactless 10; global jobs 21–22; Sustainable Travel Renaissance *13*, 14
Travel Nevada 130
travel transportation 145–146; air transport 5–17, **8**, *13*, 22
Trentino-Alto Adige 190
TripAdvisor 58–59, 205, 208
triple-layered business model: economic layer 191, **191**, 192–193; environmental life cycle layer 191, **191**, 193; proposed canvas for cycling tourism 192–194, **195**; social stakeholder layer 191, **191**, 193–194
trust: and participation in sharing economy 40, 45, **45**; principal component analysis (PCA) **44**
Turkey: cannabis legality 203
twitter 12
Twitter 55, 98

Uber 2, 35
UberX 36
Unimate 66
United Airlines 9
United Arab Emirates (UAE) **8**
United Kingdom (UK): actions taken to address financial difficulties posed by COVID-19 **8**; cannabis legality 203; Future City Glasgow 85, 89–93; hospitality workers 157
United Nations (UN): Convention on the Rights of Persons with Disabilities

(2006) 142; Sustainable Development Goals (SDGs) 107, 187–200
United Nations Environment Program (UNEP) 22–23, **23**, 24
United Nations World Tourism Organization (UNWTO) 6–7, 20–21, 29–30, 115, 187; expected growth rates **23**; 'Handbook on Accessible Tourism for All: Principles, Tools and Good Practices, The' 143
United States of America (USA): 2016 presidential election 129; actions taken to address financial difficulties posed by COVID-19 **8**; cannabis tourism and legality 203, 206–207, 209; carbon footprints 27; ski tourism 26
Uruguay: cannabis tourism and legality 203, 208
USA Air Carriers **8**
user-generated content (UGC) 98
Ustream 120

Vice 133
Vienna, Austria: public transport network 146
Virgin Atlantic **8**
virtual/online visits 61
Visit Omaha 135
volunteering: and participation in sharing economy 41–42, 45, **45**; principal component analysis (PCA) **44**

Warhol, Andy 138
Washington Post, The 131

Washington state (USA): cannabis tourism and legality 206–207
Web 0.5 55
Web 1.0 55
Web 1.5 55
Web 2.0 55
Web 2.5 55
Web 3.0 55
Web 3.5 55
Web 4.0 55
Web 5.0 55
WeChat 108
well-being, employee 154–169, *161*, **162**, *162*, **164**
West, Connie 132–133
West Maple Omaha Rock 135, 137, 139
WHO (World Health Organization) 6
World-Café 226
World Economic Forum **23**
World Health Organization (WHO) 6, 60
World Meteorological Organization (WMO) 22–23, **23**
World Tourism Organization (WTO) *see* United Nations World Tourism Organization (UNWTO)
World Travel and Tourism Council (WTTC) 20
World Wide Web 55–56

YouTube Live 120

#ZodiacTed 129
Zoom 120

Printed in the United States
by Baker & Taylor Publisher Services